The
FOXFIRE BOOK
of
SIMPLE LIVING

The
FOXFIRE BOOK
of
SIMPLE LIVING

Celebrating Fifty Years of Listenin', Laughin', and Learnin'

Edited by

Kaye Carver Collins, Jonathan Blackstock,

and Foxfire Students

ANCHOR BOOKS

A Division of Penguin Random House LLC

New York

AN ANCHOR BOOKS ORIGINAL, AUGUST 2016

Copyright © 2016 by The Foxfire Fund, Inc.

Some of the material in this work was originally published in slightly different form in *The Foxfire Magazine*.

The Foxfire Fund, Inc.
PO Box 541
Mountain City, GA 30562-0541
706-746-5828
www.foxfire.org

Library of Congress Cataloging-in-Publication Data
Names: Collins, Kaye Carver, editor of compilation. | Blackstock, Jonathan, editor of compilation.
Title: The Foxfire book of simple living : celebrating fifty years of listenin', laughin', and learnin' / edited by Kaye Carver Collins, Jonathan Blackstock, and Foxfire Students.
Other titles: Foxfire book of simple living
Description: New York : Anchor Books, a division of Random House, Inc., [2016]
Identifiers: LCCN 2015046304
Subjects: LCSH: Rabun County (Ga.)—Social life and customs. | Appalachian Region, Southern—Social life and customs. | Country life—Georgia—Rabun County. | Country life—Appalachian Region, Southern. | Folklore—Georgia—Rabun County. | Folklore—Appalachian Region, Southern. | Handicraft—Georgia—Rabun County. | Handicraft—Appalachian Region, Southern. | Rabun County (Ga.)—Biography.
Classification: LCC F292.R3 F716 2016 | DDC 975.8/123—dc23
LC record available at http://lccn.loc.gov/2015046304

Anchor Books Trade Paperback ISBN: 978-0-8041-7310-0
eBook ISBN: 978-0-8041-7311-7

www.anchorbooks.com

Printed in the United States of America
10   9   8   7   6   5   4   3   2   1

The Foxfire Book of Simple Living is dedicated to all the people—contacts, students, staff, parents, community members, board members, and donors—who have made it possible for Foxfire to preserve Appalachian heritage for fifty years. Without their steadfast commitment, Foxfire would not have reached this amazing milestone in its mission of documenting our heritage and culture.

CONTENTS

ACKNOWLEDGMENTS

Compiling a volume like *The Foxfire Book of Simple Living* would be an insurmountable task without the remarkable support of numerous individuals. If each page bore the fingerprints of those who played a part in producing it, this document would be almost unreadable.

Foxfire president Ann Moore encouraged, advised, and supported our work—and us—throughout the process. Barry Stiles, Paulette Carpenter, and Jessica Sheriff assisted with digging out photos, loaning thumb drives, collecting permission slips, and everything else we requested. Earline Benefield, Lisa Gibson, and Holly Williamson, who were digitizing tapes in the Foxfire Archives one floor above, were interrupted frequently by our inevitable cries for an immediate, unbiased sounding board. Lee Carpenter ensured that we had working computers, cameras, and Internet, as well as providing other much-needed expertise.

Our contacts graciously allowed us to invade their homes, disrupt their schedules, and create more work for them. Janie P. Taylor, a lady we all loved dearly, and her wonderful family allowed us to interview her in her final days on this earth. T. J., Jenny, Briar, and Moses Stevens allowed us to spend most of the day asking a zillion questions, and they answered each with smiles and graciousness. They even fed us watermelon and gave us each a bar of their homemade soap as we left. Beth Kelley Zorbanos drove up to Mountain City, Georgia—all the way from Danielsville, Georgia—to share the art of cornshuck doll making and philosophies about life. We are forever indebted to all the contacts, both in this volume and throughout the years, for their kindness, their shared knowledge, and their continued friendships.

Jeff Carver, a former Foxfire student, introduced us to Eric Legge and John Roper, for which we can't adequately thank him. Both Eric and

John are incredible artists, but more important, just like Jeff, they are amazing human beings. Joyce Green, a former Foxfire facilitator, not only introduced Foxfire to her aunt and uncle, Lois and Clarence Martin, but also dropped everything to bring us family photographs when we needed them. Don Brooks drove up from Lawrenceville to sign a permission slip for his dad, Lawton. While here, he had us all doubled over with laughter at his youthful shenanigans and quick wit—a burst of much-needed therapy during our last frantic days of compiling.

Foxfire's board of directors provides guidance and continues to see the intrinsic value in funding the magazine class and its documentation of the community. The Foxfire Community Board pitches in whenever needed, providing potential contacts, advice, and hard work when necessary. Both boards' commitment to our heritage, our students, and the Foxfire Museum and Heritage Center helps to keep us motivated.

The Rabun County Board of Education and Rabun County High School continue to assist us by allowing the Foxfire Magazine program to be a part of the school's curriculum. Former principal Mark Earnest's unfailing support of the class and facilitators has encouraged the program's growth in a time when many programs across the country are being cut. This volume could not have been completed without countless hours of work done over the past six years by Justin Spillers, a former *Foxfire Magazine* facilitator. His guidance was missed as he assumed new administrative responsibilities in our school system. Numerous students have helped with chronicling the culture since 1966. With cameras, tape recorders, and notepads, they have single-handedly preserved a disappearing way of life and recorded contemporary daily life for future generations to enjoy. For the first few weeks of work on this book, students Breanna Finley, Heather Giovino, Stephanie Jones, and Corey Lovell helped us by interviewing several new contacts, taking pictures, and transcribing during their time in the Summer Leadership Program. We want to give a special thanks to Heather for her ceaseless efforts when it came to researching and assisting us for an additional week.

Andrea Robinson, our editor at Random House, was always available to answer questions. She gave us insightful feedback and encouragement throughout the process. She had a vision of what this book could become and helped us remain true to that concept throughout our work.

Our families need also to be thanked. Many times we were so driven to get something just right that we were oblivious to our responsibilities at home. Our families probably suffered, but if they did, they did so silently, enduring our absentmindedness toward daily tasks and family obligations.

Finally, we thank you. The dedication and support of readers world-wide allows us to invest our time and energy into something we value and love: our community. Your patronage of our books, the magazine, and our heritage center doesn't go unnoticed and is deeply appreciated.

FIFTY YEARS AND COUNTING

*A Note from Ann Moore, Foxfire President
and Executive Director Emeritus*

As I sit on the porch of the Moore House cabin with Max Woody, one of our oldest and dearest Foxfire contacts, during Living History Days at The Foxfire Museum and Heritage Center—our "mountain"—memories flood my mind: memories of all our elders who lived the life that we continue to portray each year as we share our Appalachian history with others.

I hear the ping of the hammer as it hits the anvil in the blacksmith shop as the smithy teaches others to make items that were necessities for farm life in the early 1800s. I hear the church bell tolling as the teacher calls the children to class in the one-room schoolhouse or as the preacher calls the congregation to church services in the chapel—the same building that also served as the school. I hear the laughter of the children as they play traditional games on the lawn of the Shooting Creek Cabin while musicians perform old-timey music for our hundreds of visitors. While talking with Max, I am also watching Joe Williams demonstrate the art of making a berry bucket from the bark of native trees (something you will read about in this book). I think of the early years when what is now a beautiful creation that I admire at home was a utilitarian piece for our ancestors to collect fruit for feeding their family or to carry water from the creek for the family's use.

When Max is busy talking with our guests about chair making, I listen to the mallets and froes in the distance as the men hew replacement logs for the historic Beck Barn while they reconstruct it for preservation in the Bungalow area of our beautiful village. I meander down to watch the logs lifted in place by the four men, and on my way, I stop at the Village Weaver's cabin to admire Sharon Grist's skill as she demonstrates the art of weaving. Then I pause outside her door at the Gott Cabin to watch as the broom maker, Carole Morse, shares her art with others. The warmth of a woven shawl or a handwoven bedspread was welcomed in the cold, cold winters in the Appalachians, and the handmade brooms were necessities for sweeping out the cabin floors or sweeping down the cobwebs in the corners of the logs. There were no vacuum cleaners with which to suction up the dust in those days!

As I make my way over from the barn to cross the well-worn dirt road to the Museum Cabin, I stop to greet T. J. and Jenny Stevens and boys, watching as T. J. throws pottery on the potter's wheel, and Miss Jenny makes soap in a black iron pot over an open fire. Pottery and soap, again, were necessities that couldn't be bought back in the 1800s, but were essential for cooking and cleaning. I then arrive at the Museum Cabin, our woodworking shop, to visit with Jerry and Isabel King on the porch, watching as they use the shaving horse to make beautiful, one-of-a-kind yet useful hiking and walking sticks that were and are necessary for trekking through our mountain terrain. As I talk with them, I am listening to the amazing music of the dulcimer as John Huron performs for guests, or stops to demonstrate the making of the dulcimer or a banjo, the family entertainment on long winter evenings by the fire or for barn dances at the end of a long day's or weekend's work of raising a barn or home—another wonderful custom in our mountains where your friends and family and neighbors came together to help their fellow man.

While lingering on the porch to admire the work of my friends, I hear the children across the way beating the laundry as they learn to do "the wash" the old-fashioned way, with handmade bucket and battling boards, and I smell the aroma of fresh-baked cobbler being cooked over the open hearth in the Savannah House. I, of course, must ramble on over to sample the delicious food of Mary Bohlen. Samples in hand (and mouth!), I head back up the trail to watch a bit as Foxfire student Katie Lunsford interviews Beth Kelley Zorbanos on the gristmill porch while she makes beautiful cornshuck dolls, a treasured toy of young girls in the 1800s, and still today—another article that you will read about in this 50th anniversary edition.

Fifty years—wow, what a milestone! I am so proud to have been a part of the history of Foxfire for forty of those years, for as I told you all in Foxfire's 45th anniversary book, "I was reared in these Appalachian Mountains that I love so much—the customs and traditions and expressions preserved throughout the pages of The Foxfire Magazine and Foxfire Book series were a part of my everyday life here in Rabun County and influenced the person that I am today."

While making that trek up the trail that leads thousands of visitors through the Heritage Center each year, I thought not only of the beauty of our mountain or the contacts who share a bit of history with us during Living History Days each year, I also thought of those students who cared enough about their heritage and culture that they chose to preserve a part of it for others—students who learned so much from their elders while helping to develop the educational process that is now known as the Foxfire Approach to Teaching and Learning—an approach that allows students to have an active hand in their own learning.

I thought of the students with whom I shared summers on our mountain while they studied the environment, learned to blacksmith, conducted interviews, learned photography, or documented the music of our hills, during which they also wrote magazine or book articles, and I thought of the memorable times we shared at lunch, either playing volleyball or conducting a square dance for documentation, or watching as one of our contacts made handmade shingles or apple cider on the old cider press. I long for those days again, all while realizing that times have changed, and we can't return to the past. However, here at Foxfire we can and do continue to share the work product of some of those students—the museum—built by their hands with adult supervision, a collection of twenty-two historic and replication log structures that continues to provide educational programs on traditional skills and crafts that are steeped in the Appalachian culture, like Children's Heritage Days, a summer program that introduces ages seven through eighteen to traditional skills and crafts from an era long before the modern technological world brought them iPods and iPads.

Foxfire Magazine students are still on-site each June in leadership-training courses, or writing books such as this one over the course of a summer; the magazine is in continuous publication at Rabun County High School, under the leadership of teacher Jon Blackstock and with the full support of Principal Joi Woods; an archive of historical significance for the region now exists as a result of that oral history collected by our students; guided and self-guided educational tours are provided to thousands of visitors each year; and teacher-training courses in the educational approach are held on-site each summer, conducted by our Partners in Education at Piedmont College. Other events we conduct, the Foxfire Mountaineer Festival (www.foxfiremountaineer.org), our fund-raising event for local programs, and "Folk on the Mountain" folk art show, also continue to share a bit of the rich culture and heritage of our Appalachian region with thousands of visitors each year.

And, our scholarship program, one of the programs that I helped to establish with our community board in 1976, continues to provide annual scholarships of more than $40,000 to our students in the Foxfire program, with more than $1,003,000 having been awarded through 2016. Underwritten since 1987 by philanthropist Julia Fleet, our community board continues to administer the awards process, revising the guidelines, if needed, for the changing times.

Due to the leadership of our caring board of directors, the advice and assistance of our community board members, multiple former students, and other volunteers who assist us each and every year, as well as our generous financial contributors, Foxfire continues to flourish, and like its namesake, *foxfire*, the luminous fungus that glows on decaying wood in these beautiful Appalachian Mountains, so does the glow of our Foxfire organization continue to shine!

With sincere love and gratitude, I dedicate this 50th anniversary book to our wonderful "contacts" who invited our students into their homes and shared their stories, for had they not, this amazing educational organization called Foxfire would not exist today. I also dedicate this book to our students who began this preservation work fifty years ago and our current students who continue the great work of their peers; to my staff, who work so very hard to help me accomplish all that we do; and especially to my precious, loving mentor Margie Bennett, the Foxfire staff member who taught me so very much when I began here in May 1976 as an eighteen-year-old and who was "Mama" to so many young folks. She and her husband, our Daddy Bob, are so loved and so special to those of us whom they took under their wing.

All of our contacts are special to us and have provided us with a never-ending education. We've learned so much from their wisdom and will be forever grateful to them for sharing their sometimes hard but happy lives with us. So, in closing, I share with you just a few more quotes from some of our many beloved contacts over the past fifty years, others of whom you will meet in the pages of this book:

> *"I think your heritage is as much a part of ya as anythin' else. It's somethin' that should be carried on and preserved in some way for the next generation." —Connie Carlton*

> *"I'll tell ya, be a neighbor and you'll have neighbors. Now, I've tried that by experience. I do try t' be good t' ever'body, an' I try t' treat ever'body just as I'd have them treat me. I don't care th' goodness you do, you'll always get repaid for it, double or four-*

fold . . . Th' more you do for people, th' more they'll do for you. Always remember, t' have a friend, be one." —Aunt Arie Carpenter

"I have found that sometimes just talkin' to people doesn't do as much good as how you act in front of them." —Matt Arthur, Sr.

"I sit here an' study by myself when I have a lot of time, an' I think about things. I've got so I can't read my Bible much 'cause I can't see to read for long at a time. I think how thankful people ought to be that they're living in this beautiful world, an' I wonder how they can ever think that there is not a higher power. Who makes all these pretty flowers? We can make artificial flowers, but they don't smell an' are not as pretty as the flowers that we pick out there. We can't make flowers like the Almighty." —Aunt Addie Norton

Please listen and learn from *your* elders, for as Jake Waldrop once told us years ago, "If people today would take an interest, they could learn a lot from the way things used t' be."

And, finally, here's to the next fifty years, and a whole new generation of contacts, students, teachers, and leadership to carry on the Foxfire tradition!

MAKING REAL HUMAN CONNECTIONS

A Note from Our Editors

I am often asked how Foxfire has affected my life, and I don't have an easy, or short, answer. The truth is that, over the years, being associated with Foxfire has influenced me in so many positive ways that I often have a hard time distinguishing between Foxfire's impact and my own free will.

I first discovered Foxfire as a ten-year-old in 1968, when a group of high school students interviewed my father about making moonshine. My mother, twin sister, and I came home from a pee-wee football game to discover three teenagers sitting on the floor at my dad's feet, asking him how a liquor still worked and capturing every detail with a tape recorder as they took notes and made diagrams. I was a little taken aback; my dad was a moonshiner, and I knew that the revenuers had raided our home many times, and could raid it again. Why was my dad telling these kids about something that could get him arrested?

After the students were gone, he told us he had agreed to talk as long as his name wasn't mentioned in the article. He was pleased that some-one was taking an interest in his lifetime profession and that they were interested in doing it right. At that time, newcomers to the art were using radiators as condensers, and he was ashamed that they called themselves moonshiners. He was proud of the fact that he made some of the finest "shine" to come out of Rabun County.

Despite that stressful introduction to Foxfire, I was thrilled to see my father's words in print, even if his name was never attached. Afterward, Foxfire students came to interview my parents and my neighbors numer-ous times on a variety of subjects, but I didn't pay it much attention. They were recording what I considered everyday life; planting a garden by the signs was standard practice in my family, and canning and preserving that food was essential to our survival. If we had asthma, there was a guy who would take a sapling only a little taller than we were, cut a notch in it, and throw it in the rafters, and when you outgrew the notch you were cured. He couldn't divulge how he did it, but it worked.

I became a Foxfire student when I was fifteen, not because of any great passion for my community or heritage, but because it was a way to get out of school. Not to mention, if you worked hard, you could take some really cool trips to places like New York or Chicago. We interviewed our elders, transcribed the interviews, and edited them into articles, which eventually wound up in *The Foxfire Magazine* and, sometimes, in the *Foxfire* book series. Looking back now, I suppose I came into Foxfire at a turning point in its history. In its earliest days, kids borrowed equipment, begged for donations to get issues published, and ran all aspects of the magazine production business. When I joined the class, money had just started to pour in from royalties earned by the earliest *Foxfire* books. *The Foxfire Book* had been on the *New York Times* bestseller list, and students had made television appearances on *Today* and *What's My Line?* It seemed that people from all over the world were curious about both the students and the old-time way of life. As a result, Foxfire had hired three additional staff members and was beginning to put money away in an endowment fund to ensure that what we were creating would endure. The kids still ran most aspects of the magazine production, but we didn't have to worry about whether there would be money to print the next issue. We still did everything by hand—no computers, or Internet, or digital cameras and recorders—but we had it much easier than the original students. We had our own darkroom. We had electric typewriters and single-reflex cameras, as well as small, portable tape recorders. We went on trips to places like Puerto Rico, Maine, New Mexico, and Colorado to show other classrooms how to do cultural journalism. We thought we had it made!

My class decided to take some of the money from those royalties and purchase 150 acres of land on the side of Black Rock Mountain. Our contacts had been giving us irreplaceable stories and artifacts, and we needed a place to preserve and share them. Over the next few years, nineteen log cabins were donated or purchased from the surrounding communities, disassembled, moved to the mountain, and reassembled by students. At the time, we never foresaw that this would eventually become the Foxfire Museum and Heritage Center.

Still, although we had money and additional staff, some things did not change. As I grew up, Rabun County, Georgia, remained an extremely isolated place. Only two roads were busy enough to require two lanes; one ran east to west, the other north to south. If you were lucky enough to have a television, you had to rely on an antenna and favorable weather for reception. Saturday was the only day you went to town, and then only to buy what you didn't grow yourself. Most people didn't have a telephone, and those who did were on a party line, multiple families on one phone line, so there was very little privacy. The majority of people could trace their families back several generations and find them all living in Rabun County or Macon County, North Carolina. We were a micro-society, holding on to our past and unaware of how things would change in the future.

Just like all teenagers, I thought I knew it all! I couldn't wait to grow up, get out, and start living. Boy, did I have a lot to learn, and I am forever grateful to Foxfire and my community elders for giving me the opportunity to learn so many valuable life lessons. Through my association with Foxfire, I was able to see people I had known all my life through a different lens. My first interview was with Aunt Arie Carpenter. She was featured in *The Foxfire Book* and was a lady who, in many ways, came to symbolize Foxfire. Small and stooped, she had no phone and no television and had never traveled more than thirty miles from where she was born. To me, however, she was the wisest, kindest, most giving human being I had ever met. Most of the people I interviewed had no high school education and had lived their lives in anonymity with few material things. They grew up in a time where automobiles were scarce, radio was the only form of entertainment, and survival was based on the determination and knowledge to use what they had available. Among the many things they taught me, I learned that your word is your bond, that you should always do your very best, and that being "book smart" doesn't necessarily make you educated.

Ultimately, I learned that I could be proud to call these people friends and this place home. Some of my deepest and most lasting friendships were with "old folks" whom I had only barely noticed before. They helped me see the value in myself and in my community. Because they helped me discover a sense of belonging, I chose to never leave this community. Years later, when my husband asked me to marry him, I said, "Yes," then added, "but I won't move any farther north than Dillard, Georgia, or any farther south than Tallulah Falls." This place and these people are my touchstone, my calm in the storm, and my anchor in an ever-shifting world.

Years later, I became a Foxfire staff member. In 1990, they had a part-time position available for a "community liaison." At the time, my husband and I worked together in a local factory. As much as I loved him, he was an early-morning person, and I definitely was not. Hearing him whistle and sing at five a.m. every morning was wearing thin, and I thought changing jobs might help us survive those early years of marriage! I also still had a deep appreciation of Foxfire and all it had given me, and I wanted to give back.

The job allowed me to start working with other agencies in our community, like Ninth District Opportunity and the Clayton Housing Authority, to help our residents in whatever ways I could. I also got to visit our contacts, which I loved, and work with the high school classes and *The Foxfire Magazine* kids in our summer program, too. The Foxfire Approach to Teaching and Learning had been officially "defined" in the 1980s, although it had been used for more than fifteen years in the magazine class. By then, of course, the kids worked on computers to transcribe and lay out their articles, and their photos were processed at the brand-new Walmart. All of them had their own transportation and cell phones, something that was unheard of when I was growing up. Once again, my involvement in Foxfire profoundly affected me. My delight in working with those students led me to make another life-changing decision: to go back to college and get a degree in teaching.

Through it all I have continued my connection with Foxfire. How could I not? Foxfire and all it embodies is a part of me. I love the past—my parents', my grandparents', and mine. As a teacher, I have discovered that making real-world connections with my kids has an intense impact on their learning. I want the kids at Rabun County High School to also love and appreciate the past, but, most important, I want them to feel the same connection to this place and these people. They have more distractions than I did as a teenager. While we dragged Main Street on Saturday nights, they can find endless activities for the weekend. However, I know that if they make at least one human connection with an older person in the community, it will have a major impact on them and their lives.

It was a hard pill to swallow when I finally came to realize that their past was my present. A good friend of mine commented to me that he and I were "the last of the dinosaurs." We are a dying breed—those of us who remember gardens plowed by mule, suppers cooked on woodstoves, and houses with no insulation and cracks in the walls large enough to let in snow. I remember staying up most of the night, listening to some of the finest musicians in the world playing winsome ballads and hearing the lonesome whine of a fiddle echo off the nearby mountains. I remember Saturday nights spent with family, stringing and breaking green beans till I thought I never wanted to see another one. I remember lazy summer days spent in the woods where our only worry was that we might run up on a snake. Those days are gone, and while I miss them, I do not mourn them: I have my memories, and I have *The Foxfire Magazine*, books, and archives to remind me of that simpler time.

There are still students preserving all those memories, skills, and stories for current and future generations. A way of life is still being preserved, and while it is perhaps not Aunt Arie Carpenter's way of life, it's a way of life that deserves to be preserved even as it changes yet again. I have no time for mourning, only celebrating what is and what is yet to come.

As we compiled this anniversary volume, we wanted to commemorate fifty years of our archived interviews, all of which document a culture that has disappeared or is quickly disappearing. We wanted to honor the connections made between older folks, teenagers, and the world beyond these mountains. We wanted to celebrate the continued connections being made by current students and their contacts. We particularly wanted to explore how things used to be when we began fifty years ago and compare them to how they are now. Do people here still have the same values, ideals, and cultural beliefs? Was what was once done for necessity still a valued part of our community? We knew that we were no longer an isolated little spot in the Appalachian foothills, but how had our global, mobile, society affected the lives of a newer, more modern generation?

What we discovered was that there are still people, both old-timers and new-timers, who believe in close-knit families, in kindness to their neighbors, and who take tremendous satisfaction in how they construct meaning from their corner of the world. They still believe in the nobility of mankind, in the dignity of everyone. This place, while changing, is still our touchstone in this often senseless world—a tie that cannot, and will not, be broken. It has taught us to cherish things that others would leave behind. What others find odd we still see as valuable. We place immense worth on individual style and preference, principles and practices, self-determination and selflessness. I am certain that rather than the newcomers influencing us, we are transforming most of them. Just like our much-loved mountains, our people always rise back up with pride that is steeped in tradition, but open to change. Instead of surviving, we are reviving; much of what was good remains.

As we celebrate fifty years, we also look ahead. There are still stories to be told, lessons to be learned, and connections to be made. As long as there are students interested and older people willing to share, there is more to be saved and shared. Fifty years from now, I will, in all likelihood, be pushing up daisies. But, I hope my descendants will be as beholden for the chance to read the memories I shared, to see the ties that bind, to nod in agreement over the values that unite us, or to learn a skill that I saw done, as I have been to read about my mom's and dad's lives, values, and hardships. My life, in another fifty years, will also be a recollection of a time that once was. My hope is that future generations can learn as much from my contemporaries' stories, those shared by both "native" and "naturalized" citizens, as we have learned from those who came before us. As the old gospel song so impeccably says, the circle will continue and will be unbroken.

My favorite poem is "Heritage," by James Still, whom you will meet in this volume. The line that strikes me most deeply is: "Being of these hills I cannot pass beyond." You will see some familiar voices in this manuscript, but others are new to *Foxfire* books, and some even to this region. All are of these hills, both then and now.

—*Kaye Carver Collins*

The first time I picked up a *Foxfire* book, I was trying very hard not to learn anything.

I was attending fourth grade at a school just on the South Carolina side of the Savannah River, near Augusta, Georgia. Every Tuesday, I was pulled out of regular classes to engage in "gifted" activities. I was never really sure what the purpose of these classes was or why we were gifted only on Tuesdays, but they soon became, as Juliet says of marriage, "an honor that I dreamed not of."

Our teacher dressed as if someone might soon whisk her off to a European paradise, and she taught from the comfort of a high-backed wicker chair. The class was based on a free-learning model, in which students would spend an hour or so at one of several learning centers before moving on to the next. One center included an early French-language computer program where the words came at random, and the acquisition strategy was so passive that I soon gave up and retreated. At another, we had the opportunity to learn a computer programming language that would be obsolete by the time any of us made it to high school. And at yet another, students were free to sit in front of an aquarium and write fictional stories about whatever we wanted, except, as I found out, fishing. Only one of the centers—the one in the far back corner of the classroom—had learning materials that were *sans* technology, *sans* graphic organizers, *sans* modernity. That corner had books.

One was titled *The Foxfire Book,* and next to it were other *Foxfire* books with numbers on the spine. The books caught my attention because there was nothing about them that should catch anyone's attention. It was the early eighties. Everything was flashy and glittery, but the *Foxfire* books didn't look advanced, modern, or gifted; they looked mysterious. They looked like something a wizard might have, books that Merlin would pull out to find all of the wisdom mankind had forgotten. As it turns out, I was right—except for the thing about Merlin, of course.

Inside this understated cover, the book had what all great books should have: pictures. Granted, it had a whole lot of words that explained a proud cultural heritage, but the pictures drew me in, showing happy people in "The Mountains," a place where Grandma, Granddaddy, Uncle Ricky, and Aunt Darlene lived. These people in the book lived in log cabins and used hand tools on felled trees. Most important, "The Mountains" surrounded these people in the pictures, surrounded them like Grandma's hug when we would visit her.

I did end up reading some of the articles in the books. I had to when I ran out of pictures. I learned to cheat the learning-center system. The teacher didn't pay me much attention, so I was able to sit with the *Foxfire* books longer than I was supposed to, and thus they became the first happy place that I can remember. I remember an article about lumber that described different types of wood and what each type looked like. I would try to memorize these wood types. I don't remember why.

Years later, the *Foxfire* books almost inspired me to avoid college. My best friend's family had promised that if he graduated, they would give him their vacation home, a single-wide trailer in Sylva, North Carolina. That became our postsecondary plan: we would live in that mountain "cabin," grow a garden, and make just enough money to survive. He had the cabin, and I had the *Foxfire* books. There were several articles about planting, as well as an article about a certain illegal fine art that could earn us some extra spending money. Unfortunately, my friend didn't graduate, so I had to go to college and major in another fine art.

Many years later my desire to live in the mountains was realized, after accepting a job at Rabun County High School. A teacher in the Foxfire program asked if I would help edit an article for the magazine. I didn't try to explain what an honor that was. As you can see, it's a rather long story with very few pictures.

I have been working with the program as a magazine co-facilitator now for a few years and have worked with some of the best students in the world, some of whom are now my coworkers on *The Foxfire Book of*

Simple Living. Still, when Kaye Collins asked me to work with her on this book, I couldn't possibly explain to her what an honor this would be.

I feel grateful to be a part of this process because, ironically, working with these students in the Foxfire educational program has taught me what it means to be gifted. People are gifted and/or talented when they find something they enjoy and take the initiative to excel at what makes them happy. Foxfire students are able to explore subjects they find interesting, becoming knowledgeable by interviewing experts in their community. Those students whose interests require manual skills have the opportunity to practice that talent. Not many teachers get to work with gifted and talented students like Ethan Phillips, who is not only incredibly knowledgeable about birds of prey but who can also trap a hawk and raise it to hunt. David Campbell has taken classes to learn blacksmithing, and he has proven to be such a talented artist that I have gone from being one of his teachers to one of his customers. Katie Lunsford is majoring in athletic training as an undergraduate, but she is a better writer than many of my fellow literature and philosophy students in graduate school. She has an amazing gift for setting up an article so that readers get to share the experience as if they were there. As it turns out, the pictures aren't the only wonderful part of the *Foxfire* books and magazines; gifted and talented students wrote the words.

A former student from the 1980s told me about how an English professor asked if he was from Rabun County, Georgia, after reading one of his essays. When he said he was, the professor then asked if he had been a part of the Foxfire program. When he asked how the professor knew, the answer was simple: nothing else teaches a student to make a scene come to life, to make it so that readers feel as if they were there, more than Foxfire.

Laurie Brunson Altieri expounded on this sentiment when she visited the classroom. Foxfire is not about churning out articles that portray personalities or teaching mountaineering skills. If articles do either of these, that is a side benefit. Instead, Foxfire is about making real human connections. Those interviewed over the last fifty years are not called "subjects"; they are "contacts." They are not resources to be tapped in order to prove an agenda; the contacts are experts—gifted and talented people—who are asked for their advice and appreciated for their help. Foxfire is an inclusive community of writers, contacts, and readers.

The writers of this edition want to make the readers feel as if they are there on the interviews with the contacts. I would like to take all of you with me to visit Eric Legge's folk art studio in real life, but we wouldn't all fit, so you'll have to visit that happy place on your own. Until then, we submit this *Foxfire Book of Simple Living* in honor of our contacts, our readers, and our student writers, who continue to create a happy place for learning, sharing, remembering, and celebrating.

—*Jonathan Blackstock*

The

FOXFIRE BOOK

of

SIMPLE LIVING

WISDOM
of
OUR ELDERS

Livin' High on the Hog

There is a lot of education around us. There's a lot of elderly people that we can learn from, but sometimes we don't have time to sit down and talk to them.

—*Willie Fortson*

Life in Appalachia is a pleasure. Time moves slower. Experiences become sweeter. Tradition grows stronger. However, one of the most outstanding qualities of these hills I call home is the people who occupy them. Even the smallest facets of their lives are influenced by the culture that teems within the Southern Appalachian Mountains, the culture that envelops residents from birth until death. Old-timers raised in one of the harshest environments imaginable have extraordinary words of wisdom to share with those who are keen enough to lend an ear.

When considering Appalachia, many assume that none of the culture remains, and it's true that not everyone today owns a sow hog or a milking cow and chickens. While many folks here in the hills do maintain livestock and grow crops, the customs have changed since the days of Foxfire's beginnings. However, this is not to say that the culture of past times is no longer present or observable. In fact, what you will see throughout all the mini-sections, entitled "Wisdom of Our Elders," is evidence that the past way of life lingers still. The words of Appalachian residents are recorded here, some from contacts interviewed decades ago, some from contacts in the post-2000 era.

The Southern Appalachians have given me a refuge in which to be reared. The people and traditions I was blessed enough to grow up with impact my daily life and what I see as my future. It took entering college to understand the effect my home has had on me. I see countless differences between other students and myself. I attribute all my tendencies, all my ways, to my Appalachian forefathers and mothers. Thanks to Foxfire, I am continually learning more about my heritage and my culture. Each section of "Wisdom of Our Elders" conveys sentiments on life from previous Appalachian generations and current Appalachians. What's most surprising are the effects the former appear to have had on the latter.

—*Katie Lunsford*

HOW TO ENJOY A SIMPLE LIFE

If I can just feed my chickens and cook my breakfast and keep warm, I'll just be happy. —Harriet Echols

One of the Appalachian culture's defining characteristics is a plainness of life. Beauty lies within simplicity. The snippets included here provide a representation of Southern Appalachia's take on what enjoying life means and, in some cases, how it can be done. It is apparent when reading these quotes the emphasis that, even today, the Appalachian culture places on the intangible. The appreciation for nonmaterial goods is dynamic in the Appalachian culture.

When thinking on a name for this section, I recalled the old saying "living high on the hog." This phrase originates from the fact that when a hog is slaughtered, the most desired meat comes from the upper half of the body. Elsewhere, the idiom may be used to describe the lifestyle of those with surplus means. In Appalachia, however, Foxfire has discovered that "livin' high on the hog" has a different connotation. Smaller things are appreciated, and these small things are essential to the Appalachian people.

—*Katie Lunsford*

"Somebody called me the other day and asked me if I was happy. I said, 'Yeah.' They asked me if I'd been happy all my life, or if I'd been sad, and I told them, I said, 'Well, I've been happy. When I was seventeen years old, I give my heart to The Lord, and I've been trying to live fer Him ever since, and He's blessed me and give me strength fer almost eighty-three years. . . . He keeps me happy.'" —**Annie Chastain (1999)**

"Whatever you do, be happy and enjoy it, an' always try to do the right thing." —**Mary Story (2006)**

"It's through God we have all our enjoyments, all of our good things. It's through Him that we get it—we know that's for sure. We see some of His handiwork every time we look out and see something because He made everything on the earth, and He is the Creator of all the beauties everywhere.

"The first thing when I get up of a morning that I want to do is get to a door or a window to look out, and I stand there and look and thank the Lord for being able to see that beauty one more time. It's a wonderful thing to try to live a Christian life and to love the Lord. We have so much to be thankful for." —**Beulah Perry (1974)**

"Don't lose the time worryin' about things that you don't have that you might want. Don't dwell on your losses. You can make do. I've not suffered. I don't maybe get everything that I could use, but I've managed to be once in a while where I could help somebody that had losses.

"It's [laughter is] ninety-eight percent [of coping]. I don't mean to leave the Lord's blessings out of it, but being cheerful is [important]. Mother was good at that. Like I say, she enjoyed the young folks comin' in with the instruments and things like that. In a way, they liked that because not too many people living in the community liked that type of thing. But Mama was always putting on a happy face; not dwell on it, but be aware of it." —**Vernice Lovell (2014)**

"My health isn't very good, and I have to take it easy, but here I am now over eighty years old and still making my own way. If I can just feed my chickens and cook my breakfast and keep warm, I'll just be happy."
—**Harriet Echols (1979)**

"My mama always said, 'If you're gonna dig a ditch, you be the best ditch digger you can be.'" —**Carlene Lovell (2006)**

"Don't waste time, but take the time to enjoy it." —Oscar Martin (1979)

"We were really pioneers. We lived in a log house, and we had no running water and no bathrooms. We grew our own food. If we got out of sugar, we used sorghum or molasses to sweeten things. We made sorghum—grew cane and made sorghum. The only thing we bought was sugar, coffee, and lamp oil, kerosene. We had to use lamps. And we didn't owe anybody. We didn't pay any taxes. We swam and fished in the creek. We enjoyed life. It was a good life. At the time, we thought it was hard, but it really wasn't because I think we enjoyed life more than people do now. They don't take time now to enjoy life." —Lois Duncan (2000)

"And ever'body's in a hurry. Where they goin'? Back then you could meet an ol' feller with an ol' ox wagon, and he'd stand there half a day if you wanted t' talk. Stand as long as you'd talk. You meet a feller now, he'd run over ya. Where's he goin'? Just ain't got no patience."

—Kenny Runion (1973)

PLATE 1 Kenny Runion

"Give yourself to the Lord and follow Him and do what's right. Don't lie or cheat; be honest with yourself and with all your companions. . . . Have a lot of fun. The Lord made tickle boxes, and he expects you to use them. My advice for young people is to have a lot of fun, decently, decent fun; laugh a lot, have a good time, but let it be decent. I think they'll do just fine." —Ernest Vinson (2005)

"If [you] go to church, love God, and keep good morals, the world will be easier to get through. I like the country more than I think I would like the city because it is in a much slower pace and not as on the go as much. Country people have more time to stop and chat; they are friendly and show more respect than city people, I think." —Roberta Hicks (1994)

"Set ye some goals. If you're married and got kids and whatnot, that housework is just life. Make ye some goals. Get that housework done. Just set ye some goals and getche [get your] housework done, and lay back. Work hard, and then you can rest. Keep workin' till you get it done, but slow down. Don't fill up your schedule too much. I've tried to do two things in one day so many times. I said, 'I ain't doin' this no more,' you know, like two events in one day. You can't do it. Clear your schedule. That's what you need to do, maybe one thing at a time. When you get that done, you can start on somethin' else 'cause you'll stress yourself out tryin' to do it all. I don't know. I just, I guess I've just learned to slow down and not try to do it all, especially in one day. You can't.

"When the kids were small, we would camp. That's a laid-back situation. Of course, the woman always has to do the cookin' and stuff, but it's a whole lot more laid-back. You don't have to be so clean, not that I had any dirt in my cookin'! I mean you're outside. You can throw stuff, you know, and not have to be so neat and clean. Just campin'. We enjoyed stuff like that: fishin'. I told somebody, 'I raised mine in the woods.'"

—Sue Patton (2014)

"Then, time didn't mean anything. Time was something you just didn't worry about. But now, I don't have no time. My time is missing. But, old people don't get in a hurry. They take all day to do anything, and they get it done." —Coyle Justice (1973)

"You got to love people to get stuff done. If you don't love people, you're just out in the cold. That's all you got. But today, I don't know a soul that I don't like, not a soul. I couldn't name you one to save my life. I just like everybody. It just come natural to me. Now, my grandfather Nix Brown was like that. Oh, he loved everybody. He helped everybody he could help. He just loved everybody, and I take it from 'im. We was pretty close.

"I guess I look at him to learn to enjoy life. He was always happy. He didn't care what the world done. He enjoyed life. I'll tell you what he'd do. I remember growing up, Daddy and 'im would be workin' in the fields. He'd come in when it was time for lunch. He had a porch up against his house. After lunch, he would go get him one of those straight-back chairs. You know what I'm talkin' about? Old-timey. He'd lay that thing like 'at [propped up against the wall]. He'd get him a pilla', and he'd take him a nap. He didn't care if it was gonna rain. He didn't care what it was gonna do. He did; he took him a nap. He had an old pipe, a great, ol' big pipe. He raised his own tobacca. He'd have this big, ol' pipe. He'd fix them leaves and twist 'em and put 'em in the bowl. Then what he'd do, he'd take a sharp knife, and he'd shave that twist off a' that bowl, and he'd light it. You could smell him from the church to the end of Highway 76 over there. Oh man, they was stout. He'd puff that ol' pipe and then lay there and go to sleep. Daddy'd say, 'You gotta get up? It's gonna rain.' He said, 'Let it rain.' He didn't worry about nothin'. I think I get a lot from him on that account. I've tried not to worry myself to death about every little ol' thing, especially somethin' I can't do nothin' about.

PLATE 2 James Paul Wooten

"Live a clean life. Just live a clean life, and you'll enjoy it. Help somebody down the road as you go. Laughter is important. It is. It is. It is. I believe in having a little fun. If you can't have any fun, you're just an ol' sour head. I believe in havin' fun, but like I said, I don't know a soul in this world that I don't like. Love people. They may do you dirty or wrong, but love 'em anyway." —**James Paul Wooten (2014)**

THE VANISHING ARTS

Some of my favorite people in the world, I came to know up here at Foxfire, and they were doing the same thing as I'm doing. They're doing something with a natural material, and it's become their work. They're getting to be creative every single day, and they're getting to be close to nature every single day. Because of that, they have a more peaceful life and a more loving life, and everything in their life is just a little more harmonious to their beliefs and so on. I've met a lot of people like that.

—*Beth Kelley Zorbanos*

Basically, I've found a way to make a living doing what I love. It doesn't get any better than that.

—*Cleve Phillips*

Life in the Appalachian Mountains has been hard, and while the fight for survival helped shape this culture, the art inspired by the region's sublime beauty has defined and celebrated the region and its people. The struggle to survive often absorbed mountaineers' time and energy, but when people found time to create something that represented their values, showed the pride in their craftsmanship, and expressed gratitude for neighbors and beliefs, the region's art became a priority, especially when that art established a connection between the artists and members of their community.

The arts in this section have different purposes. Some help us sustain life, and some help us enjoy life. Regardless, all of these arts have been created by artists and artisans who are full of life and are willing to share their vitality with us and with the art itself. If the purpose of art includes legitimizing one's culture, practicing what many people would consider "lost arts" exhibits the artist's culture twofold by maintaining both the cultural values and the art itself.

At the celebration of life for Rabun County's greatest storyteller, we continually heard the word "grateful." Storyteller, educator, and Foxfire contact Janie P. Taylor lived a life of gratitude, appreciative of her community, of her family, and of the connections she made as a teacher and writer. Like Janie P., many of the artists in this section discuss their own gratitude for how their craft connects them with people and with the traditional life. The recurring theme of gratefulness, in fact, becomes so prevalent that we have to wonder if that is the purpose for art in general. These artists work with repurposed and natural materials, hoping to share with their communities a lifestyle that they are thankful to have.

Foxfire is grateful to have met these wonderful artists over the years who have found the most enjoyable ways to share our culture and our traditional values. To these grateful artists, we say, "Right back at ya!" Thank you for preserving, and at times even rescuing, our cultural traditions through what we hope will be reemerging, rather than vanishing, arts.

—*Jonathan Blackstock*

COMMUNITY AND GRATITUDE

The artists in this section freely give credit to their ancestors and influences, many of whom have been Foxfire contacts over the last fifty years. Still, while they may have learned various methods from their predecessors, they have changed the creative methods for reasons that range from ingenuity to necessity, making the arts in this section more evolving than vanishing. After all, King Kudzu (Cleve Phillips) tells us ". . . basket making is all in our genes because it doesn't really matter what color you are; your ancestors made baskets." They may not have made them out of kudzu, as he and Mother Vine (Joleen Oh) do, but people have always made baskets out of what was available.

Regardless of the changes and evolutions, the creative process still requires imagination, creativity, and a heightened awareness. Knowing what's available requires a connection to the environment, just as knowing what the community will find useful or beautiful requires a connection to the members of that community. These are the connections that open, as Eric Legge says, "a can of infinite possibilities."

—*Jonathan Blackstock*

THE ART OF MAKING CORNSHUCK DOLLS AND REAL CONNECTIONS

An interview with Beth Kelley Zorbanos

Mama Lottie taught me to make pine needle baskets and shared with me the idea of going outside, picking something up off the ground, bringing it in, working with it, and ending up with something really beautiful. —Beth Kelley Zorbanos

Cornshuck dolls may have always been appreciated more as works of art than as toys. In *Foxfire 3*, students interviewed several cornshuck doll makers, including Daisy Justice and Lassie Bradshaw, but even then, the dolls were made more for the enjoyment of collecting than for playing with them. "Not many of our contacts remember making or playing with cornshuck dolls as children," Daisy said. "They remember more about homemade rag dolls, although they did make little horses and dogs from the shucks. The cornshuck dolls now are usually made for doll collectors more than for toys."

For this reason, the dolls inspire nostalgia more because they represent a time when art was made by hand and by our neighbors' hands, at that. In fact, the doll shape itself may not be as important as the creative process and the collection of works made by natural materials.

PLATE 3 This photo, used in *Foxfire 3*, shows Mrs. Ada Kelly cutting shucks into half-inch squares to make a cornshuck flower.

PLATE 4 This photo, from *Foxfire 3*, shows the finished cornshuck flower.

Still, Daisy Justice's method for creating these dolls has become legendary. Many cornshuck doll makers vary their methods from Mrs. Justice's, but even in doing so, they show an appreciation for the meticulous skill Daisy Justice showed in making the dolls many years ago. Beth Kelley Zorbanos, who was once a student of Daisy's, refers to it as a "purer version," one that remains the benchmark by which the craft is measured today.

Inspired by Daisy Justice and by her grandmother Mama Lottie, Beth Kelley Zorbanos continues to practice the art of making cornshuck dolls almost entirely from materials many people might overlook or even discard. Each cornshuck doll is handmade with attention to the details of traditional life. Ms. Zorbanos has personalized the "purer version" with different tying methods and dyes, but the art lives on through the artist's passion for her work and her desire to share that art at various local festivals, including Foxfire's annual Folk on the Mountain festival.

During the interview, Ms. Zorbanos creates a doll that represents a humble, yet fun-loving Appalachian girl carrying a basket, and while the doll is not meant in any way to be a self-portrait, the expression reminds us of the artist who says throughout the interview how grateful she is.

PLATE 5 Daisy Justice holding one of her cornshuck dolls.

She is grateful to her grandmother and to Daisy Justice for teaching her how to create pine straw baskets and cornshuck dolls. She is grateful to her art for allowing her to live a peaceful and meaningful life. She also says she is grateful for the real connections she has made with people all over the southeastern United States.

Ms. Zorbanos says that really connecting "is this right here," referring to people sharing their time and their art with others. We divided the doll-making process into fourteen steps that appear throughout the article, but the process of bringing one's self present and making real connections may be at least as important.

—Jonathan Blackstock

Mama Lottie, my grandmother, instilled in me the joy of crafting beautiful objects from natural materials. Years later, inspired by the work of Daisy Justice of Rabun County, Georgia, I began to make cornshuck dolls. Over time, I developed my own styles of cornshuck dolls to continue to share this art and keep this craft alive.

My big dolls are like the ones that I studied in the book with Daisy Justice . . . you know, the *Foxfire* book [*Foxfire 3*, 451–64]. These are made with similar steps to what were in the early *Foxfire* book.

These were some of my very first dolls, and when my mother-in-law passed away, she had them in a box with my name on it. You're going to see that these look a lot like Daisy's did in that early *Foxfire* book. Then,

PLATE 6 Dolls in a line

PLATE 7 Storyboard

what I've done is made changes: different proportions, new techniques, different styles, and I've added color. I make all of the dyes. You can see the evolution here on just using the same steps but changing them around a little bit by adding some and deleting some. You can see the transition between Daisy's method and this method.

I started doing Native American–style ones and African American–style dolls with the dyes. This is another style that I started doing from the Native American journal.

[Ms. Zorbanos holds up two dolls made with braided arms and legs.]

These are the ones that I put on the table for children to play with. That design, I saw in a Native American journal. And then, this simpler style right here I developed just because I used to do a program where they would have little four- and five-year-olds, and they would come to me for ten or fifteen minutes, and then they would go to somebody else—another artist. I developed these in order to come up with something I could do in about fifteen minutes. I also make angel ornaments.

The storyboard here has a picture of Daisy Justice and me together, and I tell how she really inspired me and encouraged me to make the dolls. But I think I need to go back even farther because my grandmother Mama Lottie was such a big influence on me. She was born in 1894, and when I was a little girl, I lived with her in the summers. She taught me to make pine needle baskets and shared with me the idea of going outside, picking something up off the ground, bringing it in, work-

PLATE 8 Pine straw basket

ing with it, and ending up with something really beautiful—something that will last. This basket will last for more than one hundred years.

Having a grandmother who embraced crafts from natural materials influenced me as a child. Then, years later, in my twenties, I was actually living up here in Tallulah Falls, and I learned about Foxfire and just started reading the books. Then, over time, I started coming up and visiting some of the people in the books. I have these pictures of Kenny Runion. I used to drive him all over the place because he didn't drive.

I just became really interested. I learned a lot of things out of those books. I was drawn to the cornshuck dolls because it's a similar idea to the pine straw basket—something that would normally be thrown away can be turned into something beautiful. I first started working from the directions in the book—Daisy's directions. Then I met her. When I met her, I was just so inspired to continue the idea of cornshuck dolls because, at the time, I wasn't sure if that was going to happen or not. I know other people were learning from the books, but she just really inspired me and encouraged me to do it, so I just began working on it. As a mother, I would work at home and make some dolls just to make a little extra income, but all the while feeling like it was preserving something really important that wasn't done that much. Daisy was the only cornshuck doll maker I knew. So going from this to that was just a natural evolution because I really believed that you could make beautiful things from natural materials.

I have shared my art for years. There was a junior high school in Rockingham, North Carolina. The principal, Dr. Langley, was so ahead of his time. He would basically shut down regular school for a week every year and invite about forty traditional artists to come. The children could sign up for two classes, a morning class and an afternoon class, so each of the instructors had two classes, three hours in the morning and three in the afternoon. The children would come for three days, so it's really quite a lot of instruction. By the time the students graduated junior high, they had six traditional crafts under their belts. I did that program for years and years. They would house us in the community, they fed us three meals a day from the home economics department, and the kids were invited to sign up for two different classes every year. It was just an incredible program. Just in that program alone, I taught twenty-four young people a year for probably fifteen years.

Dr. Langley was someone who put so much value on the simple hand-made items and the people who made them. You know, he was valuing that and feeling like it was as important to the education of young people as their reading and writing and arithmetic.

It was everything from wood carvers to potters and blacksmiths to a chair maker, who would teach how to make a stool and weave the seat. Classes also included watercolor painting and tinsmithing, even the ladies from Charleston that do the sea grass baskets. Some of the people that came were quite well known, and they would just teach what they knew best.

Then, I've also gone to Girl Scout groups and homeschool groups, and over the years I have been just teaching as many people as would be interested. I'm not doing that quite as much anymore because I'm so busy now with so many other things, but I've taught many people.

You know, I think it's around thirty years now that I've been mak-ing cornshuck dolls. I can't remember how old I was when I started. I remember everything according to how old my children were, and my youngest son is going to be thirty his next birthday. He was just a baby when I started really working on the cornshuck dolls on a regular basis.

These angel ornaments have become really important to me, and it's sort of like it's a healing kind of thing for me. I feel like I infuse that in them. I don't know how else to describe that, but it's healing when

PLATE 9 Angel ornament

I make them, and then, I feel like they have that healing in them. If I know someone who's not feeling well, this is what I give them. That's sort of like a special thing for me to pass over, almost like meditative qualities. As I have said before, I still do them so much because of that aspect. It's really important to me.

Step 1: Soak the corn shucks.

I will go ahead and start putting some of the shucks in the water.

When I was first doing this about thirty years ago, I had a neighbor who would let me come and get shucks from his field corn. Field corn, of course, is the best because when it dries on the stalks, the shucks stay bigger. With sweet corn, you take the shucks off green and then they shrivel up, but if they dry on the stalk, they're bigger.

This dark rosy pink color right here is from Brazil wood shavings. And this is what's so cool; I love this part of the story. So I make the dye bath, and you have this dark pink from the original dye bath. Then, I take those shucks out and divide the pot out into two pots. In one pot, I put just a tiny bit of powdered tin. I use only like a quarter of a teaspoon.

When I do that, then it gives me this very light pink color from the same dye material.

Then, the other pot, I put a little quarter teaspoon of iron, and it gives this lavender color. So all three of these come from one material for natural dyes. And they match each other. You know, the colors harmonize. It's just an amazing thing about natural dyes, and it's fun.

Once a year, usually, I try to make enough dyed corn shucks for a whole year. I get out in my front yard with my Coleman double-eye cookstove, and I just get out whatever materials I'm going to use, and I start. First, I boil the corn shucks in alum for about an hour, and that makes them take the dye. Then, I have to rinse them very well and hang them to dry. That's step number one.

Then, after that, I started making different dyes from different materials, and I'll work, usually, like the whole week or maybe even ten days of just dying corn shucks and hanging them out on my clothesline to dry. I do that, like I said, until I have enough for the whole year so I'm not having to do that often. Sometimes, it's the time of year as well that determines when I make the dye. Pokeberries are available just at certain times. The fall tends to be a really good time; walnut hulls are available then. I don't wait until deep in the fall, because I use mimosa leaves to make green dye. Then, I put a little tin in the pot and get this golden color. Both of those come from that one material, which is really amazing.

PLATE 10 Soaking the corn shucks

PLATE 11 Measuring a yard

I try to keep my palette to about ten colors because it's just—you know, you could go on and on with it. There's a few colors that I would like to find a source for that I haven't really found yet.

Step 2: Measure and cut string.

I do use string to hold the dolls together. I use waxed linen to tie the dolls. I usually cut about a one-yard-long piece.

Do you know this trick? This is usually a yard.

[Ms. Zorbanos stretches the waxed linen thread from her nose to the tip of her finger to show how a person can easily measure a yard. She pinches the string near the reel, cuts it there, then laughs.]

Maybe not on everybody, but you can almost guarantee that this is a yard.

Step 2: . . . if we were using Daisy Justice's method.

I have to tell you that this is what Daisy Justice would do. If she wanted to tie something, she would take a piece of corn shuck and twist it to make a piece of string out of it. Then, she would use that to tie the parts together. She would make a part, like the head. Then, to tie it around the neck, she would twist it and tie it. Then, she would make an arm, and then she'd tie it and make another one of these extensions and twist it.

One of my adaptations is to take a piece of string, and I'll put the

PLATE 12 Little baskets crocheted for the dolls

whole doll together with this without ever taking it off. It's just ease that caused me to make this adaptation. I mean, [Justice's method] is what I would call the purer version because then the whole entire doll is corn shucks, where with mine, I've chosen to tie it with a yard of linen thread. To make a part of the doll and hold it, hold it to another part, and then twist a piece and then tie it—that is a lot to do with two hands.

I crochet little baskets to use with the dolls. That one goes with the big dolls. Then, I make these little teeny-tiny ones to go with the littler dolls. It doesn't take very long to make them—you know, five minutes to crochet this little basket. The baskets are made of raffia. I used to put the dolls together with raffia, and then I switched over to this waxed linen because the raffia sometimes would break when I would pull hard.

PLATE 13 Heather Giovino passes the husks to Beth.

Step 3: Remove husks from the liquid.

It doesn't take the husks very long to soak; they absorb the water pretty quick. [Ms. Zorbanos passes the husks around so we could feel the difference between the wet and dry husks.]

Feel this. When a corn shuck is dry, notice how stiff it is. And here, after it's been in the water, notice how different it is. This dry one is more like paper, and when it's wet, it's more like fabric, so just think of the shift of what you can do with paper. Like, if you tried to twist paper, it would crack or tear, where fabric, you start twisting it and turning it. You can tie these in a knot, now, because they're so flexible. Look at that; that whole piece, I just tied up in a knot without breaking it, where, when they're dry like that, there's no doing that.

Step 4: Roll the head.

The head is a piece that I just roll down, and I roll it up like a sleeping bag. That's all corn shuck just rolled up inside. Take another piece and cover it.

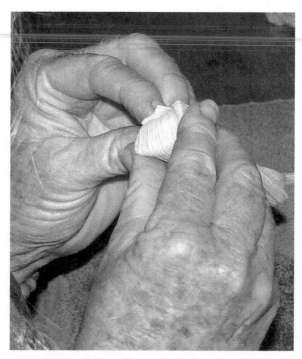

PLATE 14 Roll the head

PLATE 15 Tying on the arms

Step 5: Add the arms.

This is an arm I'm working on. Then, I tie it, so you can imagine if I was doing the "Daisy style" with making a piece of string from corn shuck. I've got two parts. I'm holding this in place, and then I've got to make the string. More power to her for tying the doll together with pieces of corn shuck, because I don't know how she did it. I already have the string, so I'm using the table. See how I was letting the table hold it, and it requires a lot of square knots. So that's one arm tied on to the doll.

I'm going to get to do the Foxfire Mountaineer Festival this year because it's not in conflict with the North Georgia Folk Festival in Athens, Georgia, that I've done all of these years. Even before I started making dolls, my family did that festival. I danced with a performance dance group; it was a traditional-style clogging group. My family also made apple cider there every year, and I made ginger cookies every year, and so we were real involved with that festival. So when I started making dolls, it was just a natural addition to what I do there. This year, though, it's the second weekend of October, and it doesn't conflict with the Foxfire one, so I'm going to get to do both of those. I'm also doing one over at Blairsville, Georgia, this year that I've never done, and I'm going over there with Jerry and Isabel King.

I'm a member of the Southern Highland Craft Guild and have been a member for twenty-one years. I've just come back from a demo up there—a four-day demonstration, where I sit at the Parkway Craft Center [Milepost 294] on the front porch there, and visitors on the Parkway come in, and I just show them what I'm doing and sell if they want to buy. That's not really so much like a festival because they feature one artist at a time on that porch. I just did one in June, and I'll go back and do one in October 2014.

The guild is based at the Folk Arts Center on the Blue Ridge Parkway in Asheville, North Carolina. It's been around for many, many, many years, and you jury into it. It's not just traditional crafts; it's contemporary, as well, but it started out as a guild to make a way for mountain artists to have a place to sell their work. They hold the Craft Fair of the Southern Highlands twice a year at the Civic Center in Asheville.

Step 6: Connect the arms and head.

I made the head first and then the arms. I tied them both on, and now I've just wrapped both of the arms.

After all these years, I've only met and know about five other cornshuck doll makers. For years, I used to go to the Florida Folk Festival, and then, on down in central Florida, there's a place called Barberville, which is a pioneer village. It's in the Ocala Forest, and it's an old farm,

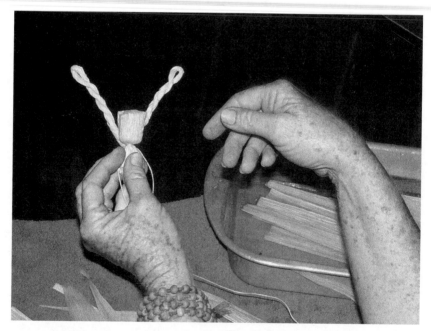

PLATE 16 Arms and head together

similar to the Tullie Smith Farm at the Atlanta History Center, where they've moved an entire 1840s farmyard into Atlanta. For years and years, they had a folklife festival that school groups would come to. It was like seven or eight hundred schoolchildren every day for two weeks, Monday through Friday. I was hired to go over there, so a lot of my work has been that, where I dressed the part like I'm from the 1840s or the 1850s, and it's like you're there as part of the farmyard, kind of like your folklife festival is here—you know, your Living History Days. I've done that numerous places in the Southeast. I've hardly gone out of the Southeast, though, but definitely North Carolina, South Carolina, Tennessee, Florida, and Georgia have been my area.

I think it's because of organizations like Foxfire that the traditions continue. I mean, you all have continued this holding on to and valuing these traditions better than anybody else because you continue to offer these Living History Days, and you continue to open your gate for people to come and visit. I think it's vital to life that you remember the way people used to do things, and if for no other reason, it should give you a huge amount of gratitude that you don't have to make your fabric by spinning it. I've thought many times how it must feel to have to raise a sheep, shear a sheep, clean the wool, turn it into roving [a slightly twisted roll of strand fibers] by carding [cleaning and disentangling] it, spinning it, and then weaving it so you can have a shirt. I mean, we don't come close to that anymore, and if that doesn't make you feel grateful for what you have . . . I mean, I think that's a huge part of it: We don't have to depend on our gardens like people used to have to.

I still have a big garden because I value organic, fresh food. That's big on my list of important, wonderful things, so I grow as much as I can possibly grow of my own food because I value the quality and the low impact. You know, it hasn't gone on a truck for hours and used gasoline to get there. I've touched it, I've cared for it, and now that food will nurture and nourish me. You know, it's like a relationship, and I really think that way. I really value that, so I think it's like that with so many things that are traditional ways of doing things. I really value that, and in turn, my whole attitude about life is that I'm just so in awe of being here, and I am grateful for it. And I think it comes from being really connected to the natural world and to a more natural way of being in the world. You know, humans are not necessarily made to be in buildings. I mean, we were born to be connected to our environment, so it's all that. It's almost like a lifestyle sort of connection.

If you want to know my real philosophy, I like to look at the big pic-

ture. I mean, we really are out in space on a planet—and I like to think
of it every day—that we are out in space in a cosmos that is impossible
to imagine. I've been thinking about it for a long time, and I still can't
grasp so many aspects of it. Because of that, I feel like we're connected
to everything on the earth in ways that, unless you spend time thinking
about it, you might miss. Trees are a great example; they give us our oxy-
gen. How can we not have gratitude for every tree and the importance of
it? I mean, it's like a really deep connection. We couldn't breathe without
them; we couldn't exist without them—without everything: water, the
earth, the universe. We're just connected, so to live with an awareness
of the connection is just the way I've chosen to live. I don't like to forget
that connection in my daily life. It's an important part.

It's like what I told you about this particular doll—the angel doll:
There's this healing, compassion, gratitude, and all of these things. It's
like taking a big concept and putting it into little, tiny representations.
It's like loving nature, and then focusing on a butterfly and thinking
about how it came to be and how it transforms. It's taking a big concept
and plugging it into a small concept. It's very much my link. This artwork
has been my work, so instead of having to go work somewhere else and
do something else that I'm not connected to in every way, this has let me
have a job that I feel very connected to in every way. It's very fulfilling,
and I really am grateful for it and appreciative to have found it. This
pine straw basket was the gateway to it, being taught this idea very early.
You just pick something up outside that would otherwise deteriorate and
transform it into something beautiful that's lasting and that you could
give somebody. It's all of those things.

Step 7: Make the shoulders and waist.

See these cross pieces? I did these two cross pieces that made the shoulders and the waist of the doll.

Step 8: Add the skirt.

I am now going to put the skirt on it. I've been cutting pieces. Sometimes, I use four or five pieces of the corn husks. I'm putting one part of
the skirt on from the front and one on from the back and just gathering
it. I always choose the nicest ones for the outside of the skirt.

I am grateful to Foxfire because Foxfire has been a part of my life for
a long time, and I'm just so appreciative that you all are still doing what

PLATE 17 Making the waist

PLATE 18 Putting the skirt on the doll

you did from the start, just keeping this connection alive. I think it's just so valuable, and it does take people back to that time when there was a deeper connection to the natural world. There had to be, but I just think it's good to still have it. Foxfire has been one of the mainstays of that for all these years. I'm just really glad that you still are doing what you do.

People in the past had to be connected to the natural world because they couldn't go down to a store and buy what they needed or wanted. Also, people were really connected to the seasons because, you know, you can't eat cantaloupe in December because it won't grow in Georgia in December, so people adapted and would dry things, drying and preserving in order to extend the season of what you ate, but it was still based on what you had.

Step 9: Form the base.

Here, let me get my hand in there. I open it up and kind of trim the bottom.

When I'm making this style of doll, I place a plastic grocery bag into the skirt because it helps to hold the shape here. The circumference of the skirt is what makes her stand up, and whatever shape I put her in right now, she's gonna stay in. I've seen a couple of doll makers put the

PLATE 19 Forming the base

dolls on an upside-down paper cup, but this plastic bag is what I use. I use these to just go inside, and then, that holds the shape that I want the skirt to be. That's really vital for the doll standing up. That round shape at the bottom helps her stand up. That's one of my techniques of how I'm going to make that shape hold while she dries.

Sometimes, the kind of doll I make is based on orders. You know, the gift shop here at the Foxfire Museum carries my dolls, and if they need twenty of these little people, I'm, of course, going to sit and work on those until I get those. If I'm just working and getting ready for a festival, one day I'll make a style of doll, and another day, I'll make another style. I'll just keep going until I have a variety of everything I make. Sometimes, people call me, and they want a specific doll; they want a specific hair color; they want her to have a certain apron color; they want her to have a broom or a baby, so I'll do special orders sometimes. But in general, if I'm just getting ready for a festival or something, I'll just make a variety, and I just decide as I go what the next one is going to be.

Sometimes, the doll informs me. This one that I'm making—I might look at her and go, "She looks like she might need a broom," and then, I'll just make a broom for her.

There's Foxfire, there's a shop called Homeplace in Athens, and those are really the only two that I keep dolls in all the time. Mostly, I'm just working from home; people still just call me at home and might want to give dolls for Christmas to people, and we'll just talk over the phone about what they want the dolls to look like.

I like that idea of the Native American people that didn't put faces on their cornshuck dolls, and I think there's other traditions that feel that way about it. For me, mainly, it's just this idea that these dolls were actually toys in the past, and the absence of facial features required that children use their imagination. Talk about another thing that's being lost is that idea of teaching and sharing and informing children that their imaginations are such a wonderful part of life.

I always tell children when they ask why don't they have facial features—like eyes and noses and mouths—I just say, "It's so that you can use your imagination, so you can decide what color her eyes are. You can decide if she's crying or if she's laughing." That's a really fun thing to get to do, and so often a child will say, "I think she's happy," and the children will use their imagination right then and there in front of me. I love when that happens. You can tell the kind of children that play that way and already know that it's a fun way.

Once again, the imagination was sort of a necessary feature a hundred and fifty years ago. I happen to believe it is necessary today, but it's not valued in the same way. It's not seen as natural. I really have a lot of concerns about how much we're changing and how much technology . . . I know it has great value in certain aspects, but I also think it steals away a lot of time—"life" time. And it's not what we think. If we think it's a real connection, it's not. There's this idea that things like Facebook are really connecting, but really connecting is this right here, looking into somebody's eyes and being able to connect in a one-to-one way. That's real; to me, that's what's real. I don't ever want to lose that. So all those things—the part about imagination, the part about connection—you just have to think deeply about it and decide for yourself what you value.

And it's okay to be different, y'all. It really is. That's what we're supposed to be: We're supposed to be this unique creation. We're not supposed to look and act like anybody else, and we get to choose, after all, who we want to be and create a way of being in the world that is harmonious with what we feel inside. If you feel connected to the natural world and you feel like you want to share love and compassion, then you get to choose and you can do it. If you don't, you don't. It's just a choice. I, for one, really am grateful to have the connections I have with my food, with my family, with nature, with my work—all these things that really are the same thing.

Some of my favorite people in the world, I came to know up here at Foxfire, and they were doing the same thing as I'm doing. They're doing something with a natural material, and it's become their work, and they're getting to be creative every single day, and they're getting to be close to nature every single day. Because of that, they have a more peaceful life and a more loving life, and everything in their life is just a little more harmonious to their beliefs and so on. I've met a lot of people like that. I'm not saying that everybody goes that way with it; that's been my experience, and I've met people who are like kindred spirits—we have that in common.

It's like a little part of me in my creativity. I like to think of it this way: If you're a writer or if you're a painter, you've taken a space that was empty, and you've put something that's brand-new in the world—a creation— and so that really is a part of you. You've put that into the world, and now you're sharing it. Whether you're giving it or selling it, you're giving some sort of inner aspect out into the world. I think it's a way of being able to give back to this world that supports us. I like to think, like, how many generations can you go back and connect to just in your mind? I can't go very far because I never knew my great-great-grandmother, but I do have a picture of her. I love to think that this connection is not just with the natural world, but it's also with our ancestors. Try to go back one generation to your parents and then to your grandparents. Now, you've got two sets. Then four. Then eight sets. Then it multiplies like that, so when you get to your great-great-great-great-great-grandparents, you've got something like 128 of them. It's huge; it multiplies so fast. To me, it's just a thing I have really enjoyed pondering. I can't wrap my head around it, but I have a lot of people to feel appreciative towards because, without one of them, I wouldn't be here. And it goes all the way back to the beginning of time, y'all. I think all it does is create this huge amount of gratitude.

Again, going from that point of reference where you're trying to think back and imagine, Foxfire is taking us back just a little bit of that, but look how important it is because it was the people before them and the people before them and the people before them. We needed every one of them to get here. It's, again, taking a big concept and putting it in a small one. That's how I see Foxfire. Foxfire has done that and is still doing it, and the program has successfully brought things forward that would have been left behind. It's a good thing to remember and also to continue.

I do believe love is the most powerful force in the world, in the universe, and I believe it's important to be present in this very moment. That takes being—in your head—being here right now and not being way off somewhere else. Even though this is saving traditional things and you've got to think about other things, do it with mindfulness, now, in the present moment because it's really the only thing we have is right this moment. Even if you're bringing history to the present, always have that ability to come into the present and feel what that is. I would say that is my most valuable possession, and that's not a material thing.

I really like to practice that. I'll spend a lot of time out in nature and in the garden and in the woods. I always make sure I bring myself present. I kind of take a breath and not have anything else in mind except where I am, what I'm seeing in front of me, and just realizing that this is true time, and anything else that is just in my mind is just in my mind so I can focus and be present. I think that's where all creativity is. I think that's where a lot of the idea of creating something new is—there in that present time and, if you go there, you have that as a helper. In a way, I think of it as the only time there is—right now, and it's just good to focus on it, you know, throughout the day, to claim it as a true idea that this is it right now, and you can do that with a loving heart. You just get to experience a kind of newness and peace.

It goes both ways. One informs the other, but at the same time, it sounds like it's a way of thinking and a way of being, but it's also a way of remembering that connection.

I really appreciate having work that allows me to put all of these things we've been talking about into it. I think that's true for anybody who does creative work as their work. Whether it's a hobby or it's whatever it is, you get to put into it whatever you choose. It's back to that idea that you really get to choose. I keep saying gratitude, but I'm just very grateful that I've gotten to work at home. I get to be close to home. I started doing this because I wanted to preserve this particular traditional craft, inspired by Daisy Justice, but it still also let me be at home. It let me have a garden; it let me raise my boys without having to send them to somebody else. It lets me do all these other things because I work at home. I go out and do fairs and folk festivals and so on, but I mostly get to work at home. I really like that, and I appreciate getting to go through life doing that.

For anybody that works at home, it's just bringing this whole big creative process to the forefront. I know you can be creative working for somebody else, but working at home is a gift. It has been for me, and I think it is for a lot of people that use their creativity for their work. So it's like those virtues get to be a part of it naturally.

Step 10: Tie on the apron and cut the string.

I've finally cut the string I was using after I put this part of the apron on the doll. I cut the string, and then I took a final piece of corn shuck to tie around her waist, and that covers that string. I've finished with my one-yard-long piece of string and have covered it with that last piece of corn shuck.

Step 11: Add hair.

What I have to do now is to put hair on her head and add a bonnet. I've already cut pieces for the bonnet. I have, for hair, sheep's wool, about three different colors, and these are two colors that are dyed. I purchased these as roving, so they're ready for a spinner to spin into yarn.

PLATE 20 Sheep's wool hair for the doll

This is like a brown and a red, and then these are dyed. This is from a black sheep, so this is the natural color. This has got a little gray in it, as well. Then, I have raw silk that I use for hair and raw flax. These are all raw natural materials that are all spun, so the silk would make silk thread, and the flax would be for linen. I also use the corn silks if I can get a big enough piece of it that's inside the corn. It turns red when it dries, so it looks like a real redhead. I use this little piece of string to tie the hair together, and it makes a part right in the middle.

I've had different sources for wool over time. Sometimes, I even get it from friends that have had sheep, but what I've been doing in the last ten years is I buy materials from a place called Earth Guild in Asheville, North Carolina. I'm able to get all of these items, except the corn silk, just by calling them. I usually get enough to last a few years.

PLATE 21 Attaching the bonnet

Step 12: Tie on the bonnet.

[Ms. Zorbanos begins to attach the bonnet.]

Again, Daisy and those little pieces of corn shuck—can you imagine doing this and making a string, too? That's when you need another hand.

The bonnet changes her a lot.

Step 13: Strike a pose.

While they're wet, this is when I can decide.

[Ms. Zorbanos begins to shift and twist the doll into various poses and add different items that express different feelings.]

Step 14: Add props.

I could add a broom. I could do like this [wrap the arms together] and make a baby to put in her arms. I could let her hold a basket. I could put her arms behind her and turn her head. This is when I can decide on a final posture, if I wasn't already planning on a specific one. Now I'm tying the bow on the back of her bonnet.

[Ms. Zorbanos decides to have the new doll hold one of the raffia baskets behind her back and hold her head in a way that makes the doll appear shy. Zorbanos also explains how the basket was made.]

I just crocheted a piece of raffia to make the little baskets. The raffia is a natural fiber. Actually, when my grandmother taught me how to make the pine needle basket, she taught me to sew the baskets together with raffia. That's when I was first exposed to raffia, so when I first started making the dolls, that is what I used to tie them together. Then, I got a batch that was kind of brittle, and I'd be tying the skirt and pulling really hard, and it would come apart. That's when I started using waxed linen because you can pull really, really hard, and it doesn't break, and the wax kind of keeps it from sticking to your hands. I've known two cornshuck doll makers that used dental floss to tie their dolls together, but that for me doesn't work because I pull, and then I get a little cut. The larger waxed linen keeps that from happening.

It takes just about the rest of the day for this doll to dry, so I could still keep moving things around.

[She shows different positions and gives the doll a small basket.]

She's sort of shy. She's kind of diverting her eyes. I try to think of some of the things somebody would have done a hundred to a hundred and fifty years ago—carrying baskets, picking up kindling, holding babies, using brooms—those are the choices.

Beth Kelley Zorbanos says she doesn't give the dolls names or titles, but all of them are meant to honor her ancestors, especially her maternal

PLATE 22 Doll with basket   PLATE 23 Finished doll

grandparents, Mama Lottie and Pa Jim. Her art honors not only their memories but also the inspiration and talent of her mentor, Daisy Justice. By bringing herself present through the art of making cornshuck dolls, Ms. Zorbanos honors the past and saves what would otherwise be a vanishing art so that it can be enjoyed by future generations.

MOUNTAIN FOLK ART AT ITS PEAK

An interview with local folk artist Eric Legge

You learn a certain part, and then it's all of a sudden, "Wow! I just opened a can of infinite possibilities." Yeah, and I don't need the money, but the landlord does, so . . . I've always said that I never make art to make money, but I make money so I can make art.

—Eric Legge

Art demands sacrifice. A serious artist trades safety, security, comfort, and convenience for freedom. Making art requires time, a dogged faith in an often abstract vision, and a fearless determination to innovate. In the same sense that mediocrity becomes the enemy of excellence, ease becomes the enemy of true art.

While different artistic genres require different sacrifices, folk art often requires the artist to sacrifice the kind of isolation that often enables many artists to thrive. Folk art, by definition, is a community art, and can often become a communal art. In *Foxfire 4*, for example, folk artist C. P. Ligon explains that he likes to keep his art rough and natural looking, but when his grandson and some of his friends want to change Mr. Ligon's art, the artist welcomes the assistance. Mr. Ligon says, "I think kids ought to get involved with things like this early. I was working on that totem pole I put up at the Campfire Girls' Camp in Toccoa, [Georgia,] and one of my grandsons said, 'That just don't look right to me.'

"And I said, 'Well, just go ahead and finish it like you want it.' . . . So he just finished it off. Then the others came—Mark and Perry and Bryan—and they all worked on it some too. I told them, 'Go to it, boys. You can't make it any rougher.'" (*Foxfire 4*, 82)

Folk art often becomes an outlet for community expression as much as self-expression, and it has always been an important part of Foxfire's heritage. *Foxfire 8*, for example, features folk pottery from some of America's most recognized names in this craft. Like many Appalachian

PLATE 24 C. P. Ligon (*Foxfire 4*, plate 69)

traditions, folk art is often learned from a mentor who passes knowledge on to a family member or inspired student instead of in a large and
impersonal academic setting. Folk artists do not so much study artistic
theory as carry on a creative legacy.

For example, our interviews with the Meaders family directly illus-
trates this intimate relationship among folk artists. When a jar was purchased for the Foxfire folk art collection, Lanier Meaders was asked if
his father, Cheever, had created the jar. Lanier explains how he could
recognize that this piece had been shaped by his father's hands:

> *This is one of his earlier ones. You see how it's kind of heavy here at*
> *the bottom? Well, he quit that after he got a little more experience,*

but there was a reason that he would do that. You know, his elbow
was broken on his left arm, and it was stationary . . . And a lot of
times he couldn't reach down in there. It probably bothered him a
lot of times, but he didn't say nothing about it. And he just couldn't
pull the clay out. (Foxfire 8, 123)

To be able to recognize someone's art this way, the collector has to
really know the artist. To recognize his father's work, Lanier had to know
his father's life. In some ways, his struggles and the way he overcame
them made Cheever Meaders's art recognizable.

This relationship among artists remains vital to the creative process
and to the appreciation of modern folk art. The interview that follows
was made possible when former Foxfire student Jeff Carver, who is an art
collector and craftsman himself, accompanied Ross Lunsford, Heather
Giovino, and myself on an interview with folk artist Eric Legge. These
longtime friends discussed not only the folk art that has made Legge
famous, but also what they and Eric's father, Joe, gave up for their respec-
tive arts.

Eric Legge describes Rabun County as a "lost Eden," but his studio
in Dillard, Georgia, may be a rediscovered paradise. Although the building that houses Legge's vast collection of art is small, the colorful, dramatic, positive images displayed both on and inside the studio generate
an inspiring explosion of tranquility.

Legge's success as a serious artist does not keep him from having
a sense of humor. While his words on his art, mentors, and muses are
inspiring, other comments are simply funny. More than anything, we
were amused by his total lack of pretension. For that reason, we have
maintained the dialogue between him and Jeff Carver to the best of our
ability. During this interview, Jeff and Eric discuss a piece of artwork
that was started by Howard Finster, an artist that Eric Legge considers
one of his heroes. Like C. P. Ligon's art, Howard Finster's piece becomes
a collaboration that Eric Legge finishes for his friend Jeff Carver. Foxfire
students and staff were fortunate to be included in the unveiling that
we've shared here.

—*Jonathan Blackstock*

Early Work and Inspirations

Jeff: Why don't you explain everything in here? It's kind of a collection
of family work, would you say?

Eric: Yeah, yeah. Mostly me and my dad [Joe Legge]. I painted the pictures and he made most of the sculptures, and then I collect a little from some people I know.

Jeff: His dad's stuff is beautiful. He did some amazing woodcarvings.

Lunsford: What percentage of the art in this studio would you say that you made?

Eric: Uh . . . 79.4.

Giovino: What inspired you to start making folk art?

Eric: My grandma gave me a box of crayons as a kid and a coloring book, and I left the coloring book on the table and went to my room and started [drawing and coloring] on the walls. I was probably, like, a toddler. I think I got in trouble.

Giovino: What was your first piece, and what year was it made?

Eric: Well, the year was 1894. Just kidding. I ain't that old. My hair might look it, but I ain't. I have a picture of me working on an early

PLATE 25 Portrait of the artist as a young man

piece. I probably did a bunch of stuff before then, but here's a picture of me working on a piece.

Lunsford: Wow, that's young. How old would you say that you are here?

Eric: Maybe, like, first grade. I can't remember; maybe I was five.

Jeff: Was your dad doing art at that time already?

Eric: Yeah.

Jeff: He'd already given up and—

Eric: Yeah, yeah.

Jeff: Not given up. That's the wrong word. He'd already given in. There you go.

Eric: Yeah, yeah, exactly.

Giovino: Why did you move to Dillard?

Eric: It's just that this space is so nice. I lived in Wolffork Valley for a long time, and I lived in Persimmon.

Jeff: I know that your dad is one of your heroes. He inspired you the most. Who else in the folk art community inspired you?

Eric: Howard Finster, definitely. He was a famous folk artist that got a vision from God to make art. I always thought a hero is someone that inspires you to be yourself rather than to be like them. That's the only person you're ever going to get to be is yourself, so that's a beautiful thing.

Then there's a handful of old-timer folk artists that I had the privilege to hang out with. R. A. Miller was one, and he was featured in one of the *Foxfire* books [*Foxfire 10*, pages 457–68]. Howard Finster. And there's a fellow—Clyde Jones. A lot of old-timers.

Jeff: Any strong women folk artists in your background?

Eric: Oh, yeah. Missionary Mary Proctor. Ruby Williams is like God. She's like one of my beloved. She's an elderly African American lady who lives in Plant City, Florida, who's just beyond wise and beyond beautiful.

Jeff: Kind of like a second mom, I would say.

Eric: I've always liked messing with her. I said, "If you weren't so young and I weren't so old, we'd be married." She's like, "No, Eric, I'm too old to get married again."

Jeff: Yeah, Miss Ruby is a strong woman. I love Miss Ruby.

Eric: Yeah, likewise.

In the Shadows of the Mountains

Eric: Have you guys been through Wolffork Valley? I used to have a view of that church, actually.

Jeff: Most of my favorite pieces by Eric are of the Wolffork Valley. He had a great view of the church, and that gets incorporated into quite a bit of his art.

PLATE 26 Photograph and painting of a church in Wolffolk Valley

Eric: Yeah, I used to paint that picture a lot of the church. Yeah, there's one right there. This was my view, and a lot of times, the rainbow would land right on top of the church.

Jeff: Seriously, that was his view.

Eric: That was an inspiring place to live. I mean, it's all inspiring up here, but that was like living in a postcard.

Jeff: A bunch of your pieces are kind of a view of the church. That is kind of looking from the church toward the house.

Eric: I have never sat outside and painted, but I always wanted to. Most of it is from memory and seeing it and stuff.

Jeff: I really wonder how you do it. Just from knowing your work, I think your memory serves you really well.

Eric: Yeah, it does. I think I painted these mountains before I even got here. I just didn't know I wanted to paint pictures of mountains, and I did it as a kid. Lo and behold, I look at them thirty years later and say, "Whoa. The next time, I will start painting pots of gold! [Eric laughs.] Buried in my backyard!"

Jeff: Both of my grandparents are dead now, but they raised me, and it's corny, but I can seriously look at that painting anytime, day or night, and every thought, pleasure, and fear all comes back to me. Just that little square world of the painting! The first time I saw it—you saw me—I lost it. I teared up on you. It was what I saw whenever I woke up. You captured it better than my memory could ever remember it. When I am old and senile, maybe a couple of weeks from now, maybe that painting will draw me out of a dark place.

I just love how he brings the mountains to life. I grew up here. I get a lot of strength from the mountains, so my office at home is filled with his work. Anytime I'm depressed or down or need strength, I go and just sit in my office, and I'm back in Rabun County. He's got views looking from here at the studio, which is the view of our house, my grandma's house. If you look straight out the door, Granny Carver's house is right around the curve. It's the view that I saw as a child every day of my life. It's very inspiring to be able to look up on my wall and see home.

PLATE 27 Strength from the mountains

Eric: That was heart touching when you first told me that. It was like, "This is the view I grew up looking at."

Jeff: Yeah, I got tears in my eyes the first time that I saw it.

Eric: I got chills when you told me that.

Jeff: Eric was working in Asheville when I first started hanging out here. His dad was running the shop, and Eric had a shop over in Asheville at the time. I was buying art from Eric and not knowing Eric. Finally, I got to know his dad really well, and then, I got to know Eric, and I'm very honored.

Eric: From 2007 to 2010, I had a shop in Asheville. I tried to escape Rabun County, but I just can't.

Jeff: It keeps pulling you back.

Eric: Yeah, it does.

Lunsford: What do you think draws you back to Rabun County?

Eric: The beauty and the mountains, and there are some places where you just feel like it's home. Then every day here—the way the seasons change is really beautiful, and the wildlife and the flora and the fauna. It's like a lost Eden to me. I walk through the woods, and I feel like I'm in Disneyland, but I don't gotta pay nothing. And all the leaves are waving at me, and the trees and the birds are singing.

Folk Art Appreciation

Jeff: Now, folk art gets a bad rap, I think, as a huge collector of it. What's your take on the bad rap, and how do you overcome critics of it—when people say it's not art because you haven't been trained or you haven't had classes? Seriously, how do you feel when you hear that, for one, and then, how do you respond to it, secondly?

Eric: I think it's true with everything. There's good and bad, no matter if it's punk rock or rock 'n' roll. There's going to be bands that people say, "Oh, I don't like that," and bands where people say, "Oh, I can't get enough." It's like country music—you either like it or you don't. Or you kind of like it, but you don't. Or you really like it, but you don't.

Giovino: What type of paint do you use? Do you use acrylic?

Eric: Mostly acrylic, and I think the thing about folk art—the essence of it—is that it's made of materials that are unconventional and recycled, so 98.4 percent of what I do is recycled or found objects. I even use mix-match paint from the hardware store.

It's like salvation, finding something that otherwise would be thrown away and turning it into something else. Like, an old cabinet door winding up in a landfill—put a picture on it, and somebody will enjoy it for fifty years. Your kids will get it.

Jeff: We have a mutual friend named Kelli Ramey, who is a former Foxfire student, as well, and she is very blessed to have her house built out of the trees from the tornado that went through the lake. She rescued some of those trees, and her house is built entirely from them. She's very ecology-conscious, but it's very cool that all of her scrap work pieces came to Eric and were turned into art, so those trees were saved twice.

And the greatest gift I gave her as a housewarming present was that I had Eric do a piece for her from the wood scrapped from her house and electric wiring from her house, and that's her pride and joy. That's the first thing that you see in her home is Eric's art, front and center.

Giovino: Why are you so passionate?

Eric: I guess I was born that way. Yeah, I think passion and love are intertwined. If you love something, you're pretty passionate about it.

I could get inspired by many things. I'm good at taming wild animals, and the other day, a butterfly attacked my face. It felt so sweet, but I had never had that happen, a butterfly wanting to party on my nose.

It is like that moth that landed on that angel painting right behind you. It looks real beautiful there.

Jeff: Yeah, a moth landed on an angel.

Eric: Yeah, it had been there all morning.

Jeff: It actually looks like you painted it on there.

Eric: I know, exactly, yeah. That is my greatest painting. [Laughter.] Look at the detail in that one!

PLATE 28 A moth admiring an angel painting up close

Giovino: What motivates you to keep making art?

Eric: It's an ever-evolving process: It's like learning; it's like a long math equation. You learn a certain part and then, it's all of a sudden, "Wow! I just opened a can of infinite possibilities." Yeah, and I don't need the money, but the landlord does, so . . . I've always said that I never make art to make money, but I make money so I can make art.

Giovino: What do you think that the bright colors in your art represent or try to express?

Eric: A lot of different things. I'm, like, really fond of experimenting with color, but when I was a kid, I was a voracious reader, and I just discovered an esoteric book that explained color and frequency as language. It's a different language, like, now we're talking with our voices and that's sound vibration that your brain is picking up, and you know what I'm talking about. Color can work the same way, but when we're little, we're taught to use oral language as our main form of communication. So, I think that, underneath it all, color can communicate things.

I discovered this book when I was a kid by this lady that made all these prayers out of colors that she felt, so I think that sunk in the back of my subconscious.

Giovino: What is your favorite type of art to make? I see some paintings, and then, there's some other things.

Eric: Yeah, I love it all. I build sculptures, too, and do some ethereal things and semi–performance art, but I think that the act of creativity is where it's at for me. It's the joy of making something.

This is a little bull I made. His legs move and everything. I used to make these life-sized. I used to make them yay [about four feet] tall with deer antlers.

That's a friend of mine, Peter Loose's art. That's one of his pieces; you can see the cutout.

Jeff: For somebody who's been collecting your stuff from the mid-nineties, it's very refreshing to see your collaborative works.

Eric: Yeah, thank you.

PLATE 29 A small bull sculpture

Jeff: It brings a whole new depth to it. At your gallery opening in Florida, there was one, and everybody was just drawn to it, so, to me, that's part of you evolving. It's good to see. I come in every three or four months probably, and I always find something new immediately, and it's always good. When I come in and I don't see something new, I'm going to get worried. First time that happens, I'm going to be, "Wait a minute, now! What's going on here?"

Eric: Peter Loose painted a picture on the front of my building, too. He's out of Hull, Georgia, which is outside of Athens.

Jeff: His art name is "Bongo"—Bongo Loose.

Eric: Yeah, he once had a magical dog that played piano.

Lunsford: Did you make the angel?

Eric: My dad made that one.

PLATE 30 Peter "Bongo" Loose's work on the studio's outside wall

PLATE 31 An angel by Joe Legge looks over the studio.

Lunsford: Do you know exactly how he did that?

Eric: He did it with chisels, like *dchu-dchu-dchu-dchu-dchu*.

Lunsford: How long do you think that took him?

Eric: He was pretty proficient, maybe a week or two, to the best of my recollection.

I think it's all from the same tree. It was recycled from a piece from what was a log cabin. They would toss out big boards and blocks and stuff.

Jeff: And also, if you've noticed, Eric has been carving actually in-depth in the paintings. See the Christ there. There's actually detail past the paint. You don't even notice it a lot. It's so subtle, and then you get up close, and suddenly, you see it's incredibly detailed.

Giovino: What is your customer base like?

Eric: Yeah, it's all over the board, from like five-year-olds to like ninety-five-year-olds, from truck drivers to ex-presidents. Amy Carter, Jimmy Carter's daughter, used to collect my work, and Sandra Bullock has a few pieces. John Travolta's wife, I can't remember her name. She's an actress, too. I think she has some.

Jeff: Kelly Preston. She does. She has them in the Gainesville, Florida, home, actually. I attended a fund-raiser at their house a couple of years ago and felt right at home.

Eric: That's all I can remember. There's probably some more.

Jeff: Well, it's interesting because Kelly had a question on that. I don't think you're ignored by any stretch of the word. You're internationally known as a folk artist, but most people in Rabun County don't know you're here.

Eric: Yeah, I keep a low profile. Actually, these people from *Duck Dynasty* who were going to do a reality show, and they came by the other night, but then I said no, I kind of like my anonymity and being able to walk down and people say, "Who's that funny-lookin' guy? I don't know what he does, but I always see him walkin' the streets of Dillard."

Jeff: So, you did turn them down?

Eric: Not really. I just kind of shied off of it, but they got Kip Ramey [a local folk artist] good. He stole the show.

Jeff: Now, the newest thing to me is that you do a lot of hidden stuff. You include a lot of hidden features that people don't normally see, like in this one.

Eric: Yeah, there's some little faces and people in there. There's one right there.

Jeff: And these are a little more obvious.

PLATE 32 Painting with "invisibly visible" faces

Eric: Yeah, a lot of times, it's a happy accident, like hearts'll show up and stuff.

Jeff: Hearts are a recurring theme that always brings me happiness when I see your work.

Eric: And this is one, like, I don't know if you can see it, but I scribbled the word "Love" into that bowl.

It's kind of invisibly visible. You can see it if you look, but if you're not paying attention, you don't even know it's there.

Giovino: What pieces sell the most here, do you think?

Eric: Eventually, everything sells. Yeah, I don't have a standard thing that sells one way or the other. Eventually, everything finds the right place.

Giovino: What is your biggest piece?

Eric: I did a mural in this lady's house. It was maybe fourteen foot high and twenty foot long. And I used to, for a year, I painted on cardboard. I painted on cardboard because it was very liberating because you're not

PLATE 33 The word "Love" written in the bowl

caught up in the cost of the material, and I did some big ol' refrigerator boxes and stuff.

Giovino: What is your smallest piece?

Eric: That would be about—[laughs as he pinches his fingers together]—probably the size of a postage stamp.

Giovino: What are you most proud of out of all of your works?

Eric: Oh, gosh! I don't know. There's been a bunch through the years, and I was like, "Oh, did I make that?" Then, there's others I made, and I was like, "Ugh! Did I make that?" [Laughing.]

Jeff: That's what's nice about knowing you and your pieces since 1995. It is fun to watch your progression, but it's interesting to me, with your new stuff, you are almost back to '95 . . .

Eric: Yeah.

Jeff: . . . in a more passionate way, though, because in '95, you didn't have anything hidden. It was all just very straight out and appeared as it was. Now your style has evolved back to that, with the hidden, so to me, it is kind of full circle.

Lunsford: Do you date your work?

Eric: Ninety percent of the time. I used to be real religious about it because it was like, every day is a day. Then, when you mark it down and look, you can go back and say, "Oh!" Because, you know, time flies so fast. I quit dating my work regularly in 2012, but I still date on occasion.

Jeff: Eric is the only artist that I know that not only signs the front of his paintings, but when you buy the paintings, he signs the back.

Eric: Yeah, I usually love to do art on the back. And that way, it is 360 degrees of art.

Jeff: It is usually a beautiful, hand-drawn, quick piece on the back with another signature. I have got a couple of pieces from the nineties where

PLATE 34 Dated and signed bear painting on a bear-shaped cutout

he signed on the back in like 2010. I can almost flip it over on the wall at any time.

Eric: Yeah! Sometimes the back sides are just as good as the front side.

Jeff: That is rare. The front is usually pretty amazing to me. I think you are your own worst critic.

Eric: Uh-huh, yeah.

Jeff: As are most artists.

Lunsford: Do you ever think about what your piece will be before you begin, or do you just basically do it?

Eric: I basically just do it. I've got an idea, like I may say, "I'm gonna paint a flower, but I don't know how it is going to turn out." It is like in the process of my working, I'll just kind of see it.

Lunsford: So, you are willing to change it in the middle?

Eric: Yeah, yeah.

Giovino: Has the technology age influenced any of your works?

Eric: No, but I wish it would catch up with me! [Lots of laughter.] Or vice versa.

Giovino: You said you use scraps, and I was wondering if you used any of those in any of your art.

Jeff: You did a little electrical wiring.

Eric: Yeah, yeah, I use junk out of the computer.

Jeff: He used a modem, and his robot is quite good.

Lunsford: Do you finish a piece, look at it, and change it into something else?

Eric: Yeah, most of it, I could work on forever. I just keep adding layers. Like that one there, I added the bird like a week or two later. That is a cutout of my friend Peter Loose's bird that he paints a lot.

Jeff: There is also an amazing wolf over here. I think it is a commentary on New York City.

Eric: Yeah, there is a radio show on East Village Radio called *Chances with Wolves*. That is why I did it. It is a howling wolf at the Statue of Liberty.

That one, I did in the nineties. It has got two license plates for texture; I used coffee and mud to give it that texture. There is a David Bowie song called "The Man Who Sold the World," and that is what that reminded me of. The guy has got the world in his belly, but it is in a paint can.

I did those—there was a time when I ran out of money, so I would make stuff out of the stuff laying around. Necessity is the mother of invention. People, human beings in general, are very resourceful like that, and even animals.

Most of my art is unnamed unless it is something really specific and has references to the piece. Most of the time, it is untitled. People will see things in it that I didn't see and teach me more about what I am doing than I, myself, know about what I am doing. So, they might say, "Ahh! Look at that!" And I think, "Dang, I never saw that."

PLATE 35 A howling wolf at the Statue of Liberty

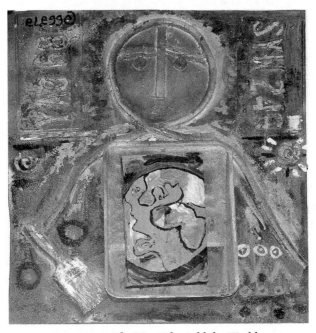

PLATE 36 *The Man Who Sold the World*

Jeff: Out of all of the artists I know, Eric is one of the few that stays open to other people's interpretations. Artists are usually very dug in, and it's "my way or the highway."

Giovino: You said a lot of these pieces are your father's and your father obviously influenced you a lot. Has anyone come up to you and said, "Wow! Your art really inspired me"?

Eric: Yeah, there have been several people who have quit their jobs and become artists because they said, "Oh! That funny-looking kid can do it, maybe I can do it, too!" [Laughter.] It ain't all lollipops and unicorns.

Jeff: There was a really cool art show that Eric did two years ago. Two of his customers were like five and nine.

Eric: Yeah, I do it every year, but two years ago was when it came out. There was like these four little girls. They were spending their parents' money, but their parents told them to pick out something they liked, and they all came to me.

Jeff: The newspaper had them all walking away with their art.

Eric: And they were like that tall and the art was that tall.

Jeff: One was literally, like, all you could see was a painting and feet going down the sidewalk.

Eric: They were my biggest customers of the day, a five-, seven-, nine-, and ten-year-old. Made my show!

Jeff: I came in two weeks after and they were like, "Eric made the cover of the paper." I am like, "Were you staging that?" It was really cool. These little kids just came in and started picking out art.

Eric: They invite me back every year. It is like an art show, so I take a bunch of art. Then people come and buy it.

Lunsford: [Pointing to a winged man sculpture] Do you know what the red eye is symbolic of?

PLATE 37 Joe Legge's winged sculpture with red eyes

Eric: No. I should have asked him. I never did ask my dad about what his art was about. I really wished I would have. I never could figure out how he got those eyes in there—some sort of trade secret. But, the eyes glow when the sunlight hits them.

Jeff: Actually, if you step over here, you can see them glow. I never really thought of it, but it is kinda a self-portrait.

Eric: Yeah, it is.

Jeff: Him taking flight. How late in his life did he do that?

Eric: I want to say he did it in 1999. He always said he could see it in the wood, whatever it was.

Jeff: He talked to me. He would start with a piece of wood and never know what it was going to look like before it was done.

Lunsford: When you are working on a piece, do you just turn and look and see something totally different, or do you see something in it that you didn't see before?

Eric: A little bit of both. I'm a scavenger. I look, and if I see stuff lying on the ground, I'll pick it up, you know, just when I walk the road.

The more time you spend with the materials, the more you see, and it changes. That piece behind you is a tribute to a friend of mine that passed away. Somebody said they saw an owl, like that head in the middle looks just like an owl. I never saw it like that. Art is funny like that. I was just looking at this, and that reminds me of a little cloud. You know, how, like after it rains here, the clouds will sometimes float down below the mountain. But, I just noticed that a minute ago—either a cloud or a UFO. [Laughter.]

Jeff: It could be either up here. I have seen plenty of both.

Eric: Yeah, I have seen UFOs up here. We got bored looking at them! [Laughter.]

Collaboration and "Tribu-lation"

Jeff: Now, is that a Howard Finster in the corner or a tribute of yours to Howard?

Eric: A little bit of both.

Jeff: Ah, that is a collaboration.

Eric: Yeah, a tribu-lation. My friend made the frame on it. [Howard Finster] passed away in 2001. That is a tribute to him. That was the day he died that I painted that picture. That was a rendition of a picture that he painted on the front of his house of George Washington.

Jeff: My favorite painting that I own of Eric's is of Howard Finster on his eighteenth birthday when Christ spoke to him. God actually came to him and told him to be a prophet. That is one that never comes down from my wall.

Eric: Yeah, certain pieces are like that. You can look at them forever.

PLATE 38 Tribute to Howard Finster

PLATE 39 American Indian cutout and painting

Jeff: I see something new in it every time I look at it.

Eric: That is a thing where it is a thing inside a thing, painted on a cutout Indian. It never ends. I mean that in a positive way.

Jeff: The stories tell themselves. It is so creative, the way you do it is just ingenious, and when I compliment you, you go, "Uh-huh, yeah. Anybody could do that." But not that! Not everyone is going to think of that.

Lunsford: What is this piece?

Eric: Yeah, that is art by the Bucket Man, Danny Hoskinson. He made all of his art out of five-gallon plastic buckets. That is about fifty buckets melted down.

Jeff: I have never noticed a house in that painting.

Eric: There is a bunch of hidden stuff in there. What is auspicious about that is [that it's] what they call a basilica; it is a type of church. I did that piece in 2003. In 2007, I moved to Asheville, and about three blocks

PLATE 40 The Bucket Man's elephant

PLATE 41 Basilica in the bottom right

away from where I lived was St. Lawrence's Basilica, which looks almost identical to the picture in the painting of the little church. I would go there a lot and sit and enjoy it because it is a beautiful, beautiful church. A famous architect designed it, Gustav something [Rafael Guastavino Moreno].

Jeff: I think everything you paint, whoever gets the painting has a very personal meaning to them. Everybody who has a piece of yours, it means something to them.

Eric: The right person, sometimes, gets the right thing.

Jeff: They do. With your work, I think it is more often than not.

Eric: Yeah, I had a couple do that the other day. They live on a farm and don't like to leave because it is so nice. They came to visit me and I had a picture of a couple behind a farmhouse, and it was them. They were like,

PLATE 42 Clyde Jones's alligator

"Wow!" It was something I had done years ago and had in my personal collection, but then I released it and hung it on the wall.

Lunsford: Is that an alligator?

Eric: It is. That is my friend Clyde Jones's alligator. He built these animals and put them in his yard. He doesn't sell them, but if he likes you, he will give you one. There is the story of Mikhail Baryshnikov, a famous ballet dancer that came to visit him, you know, and wanted one, but he told him, "No, it is not for sale."

The Angel and the Mask: Folk Art Comes to Life

Eric: The angel, yeah. My dad did that one. I want to say 1999. There is an old house in Wolffork Valley. These sticks are from the front porch. I forget what you call it, like the picket fence that goes along across the front porch. That is part of that. The crown is made from a brake pad that come out of his car.

The wood was cast-off from a timber-frame house. He made that when we lived in Wolffork. He kept it on the back porch when he was working on it, and late at night, I would go to visit him, and I was young. It was like, "Who was standing there?" Some old guy came in, I think it was last summer, and was like, "That piece winked at me!" and I was like, "Whoa!" He even brought his family back. Yeah, "This is the one! This is the one that winked at me!" And I swear, I was standing over there, and I thought I saw her turn her head. It was probably just hot, or that dude tricked me into thinking it.

PLATE 43 The winking angel

I have got a mask that I swear winked at me when I first saw it. It is a Mexican mask. It is hanging up in the center over there. It has got glass eyes. It has got eyelashes and everything.

Jeff: I don't make eye contact with it! Weird that you brought that up. You and I have never discussed that in all these years, but I will not make

PLATE 44 A Mexican mask

eye contact with that. I kind of glance at it, kind of like a dog looking at somebody that might kick it: "I'm just gonna lie here and let them walk on by."

Following the Artist's Bliss

Eric: There are certain old-timers that did everything, but they have slowly passed away. Folk art is something that I don't think will ever go away. I think it will always be. I think it has its ebbs and flows. I think it does seem to be popular now, but then again, it always seems to be, in a weird way.

Jeff: It is frustrating sometimes because everyone thinks they can be a folk artist. I was at AthFest this weekend, and there are some really cool artists at AthFest—some amazing ones, but every college student that can pick up a piece of wood and a paintbrush is suddenly a folk artist now, but time weeds that out. It was interesting this weekend to walk up and down the street and think, "Okay, you started out last week. You won't be doing this your whole life."

How many shows a year do you do now?

Eric: Just the two big ones: the Kentuck is in Tuscaloosa, Alabama, and there is one called Fearrington Village, which is in North Carolina, right up there in the Chapel Hill area. Those are the ones I get invited to.

Jeff: So, Eric, you are saying if I can get you invited to more, you will do more? I am going to start paying his entry fee, and say, "Eric, you are invited to so-and-so."

Eric: Yeah.

Jeff: I would love for you to do more shows. They are hard, but one day I am going to sneak in and kidnap him. He will wake up in the Holiday Inn in Athens and wonder, "How did I get here?"

It is hard taking artwork to shows. It is hard enough doing it with smaller pieces when you are traveling with stuff like this, and it becomes almost impossible with larger pieces like these. It's not an easy gig at all. I have respect for anyone who can travel with larger pieces like these. It is hard work. I do silverware jewelry. I recycle as well, but nothing on this scale.

Eric is blessed to have a home base. I am blessed; I am not going to complain. I am able to travel fifty weeks a year and do what I love for a living. So you know, this is a day at the office. I got no complaints. You spend too much time complaining, the Lord will show you differently. I got up yesterday morning, and I said, "I would love to go a whole month and just not wear any jewelry." I am a walking advertisement. I immediately went, "Lord, I did not mean that! I want a month of not wearing jewelry by choice." You have got to be specific. As soon as you say that, the Lord will say, "Okay, I will give you a month off, bud." He will strike you down, and you will be in the hospital for six months. I got real quick in clarifying that, and you have taught me that.

Eric: That is sweet.

Jeff: You have taught me that being specific is very important in life.

Eric: Dang, I am the vaguest person I know. [Laughter.]

Jeff: But you are not, and that is the funny part. You think you are. Kelli can be having the worst day of her life, and she can swing back by Eric's studio for five minutes and see you. She will call me, and all her sorrows are gone. You are not vague. I think you are much more of a prophet than you know. I don't think I have ever heard you say the word "no" out loud. Look on the front of his building, on the back of his paintings, and everywhere is the word "yes." It is incorporated into his whole life. I think if we all spent time saying yes more than no, our whole lives would open up.

Now, this is one of your early pieces. What year would you say that was?

Eric: Maybe a couple of years old.

Jeff: I have got one similar to this that is in the nineties. Is this a nineties piece?

Eric: Yeah, it is probably '95.

Jeff: I have been wanting to do a photo of a current painting side by side: I know a lot of times there will be like a transition—what current painting would you like to compare this to?

Eric: Probably this one.

Giovino: Do you have any advice for young artists that are just starting out?

Eric: "Follow your bliss." That's a famous Joseph Campbell quote. Follow what makes you happy and what you enjoy and what you love.

The Dillard Studio

Jeff: So, you have got a number of artists that have created your wall out front.

Eric: Yeah, this fellow named Ralph Frank did the one on the far left.

Jeff: Do you ever see yourself leaving this studio space? I know we have talked about that.

Eric: On occasion, maybe go for greener pastures.

Jeff: I don't think there are any greener pastures.

PLATE 45 Eric Legge's studio: "The Museum of Wunder"

Eric: No, but sometimes I think it would be nice to have a double-wide and big studio out back and a monster truck in front. [Laughter.]

Jeff: When I came up here the first time, I had not been home in a long time. I grew up in Rabun County. I was driving through and saw this great sign in my hometown. I thought, they have got something really cool in Dillard now other than McDonald's! There is something cool in Rabun County now! So, I pull in, and it is hard to say, but I felt more at home walking through this door than I had ever felt in all my life in my own hometown. This became my safe place. Every time I came home, before I went to visit my mom before she died, before I went to visit any family member, I would come see Eric first. It put me in the right frame of mind. It was like, "Okay, I've got my Zen on, and I can handle them now." You have actually encouraged me to come home and not have any issues anymore. Even Kelli noticed that a couple of years ago.

I can walk in here anytime, day or night, and my whole body just goes to ease because I know that whatever is going to happen in here is always beautiful, never a place of negativity, for me.

Giovino: Is that something that you pride yourself in, as an artist, having this as a safe place for someone to come?

Eric: Yeah. I mean like some people will come in and, a handful of people come in, and it is like their vitamin D.

Jeff: I know many artists who—you have helped more local artists than anybody else I know. Eric does a lot of pro bono work, advice, and help. What is great is that every Memorial Day, Eric says if you want to come, come. If you don't, don't, but they just all set up here on the weekend and have a sale. Y'all are crazy if you don't come shop, because it is bargain city. I am always doing a show, but next year, I am coming. I don't care if I make a penny. Next year, I am taking Memorial Day off and sitting out here in a lawn chair and listening to good talk all weekend long.

Eric: I encourage other artists to be themselves. Everybody goes their own way; it is just a matter of doing it.

Jeff: I was working a corporate job that I hated, absolutely hated. Eric didn't directly tell me to leave my career, but I was always complaining that I was mad and tired and miserable. He said, "You need to find something that makes you happy." I quit my job eight years ago. I think that was Eric's way of saying, "Boy, just shut up! Come on! What is wrong with you! You are always just pitiful, Jeff." I am a happy person now.

Blackstock: I want to ask both of you: It takes a lot of kind of faith in something—in yourself, your own abilities, something to leave the corporate world. How do you muster up the faith to decide that is what you are going to do? Did you go through that period when you were worried about leaving your career?

Eric: Yeah, I did. It is like jumping off a cliff and not knowing what is waiting down there.

Jeff: I make one-tenth the money that I used to make, and I work at least ten times harder, maybe more. I tell people it is basic math. Do the math: Ten times ten is one hundred percent happier. It is true. You have in your mind what is best now. [Jeff asks Eric] If you had to work behind a desk now, wouldn't it be like emotional suicide?

Eric: I would be like escaping out the door. Gotta go on a cigarette break and be out the door!

Jeff: People ask me in my business, "Oh, you have got something new you came up with? What inspires you?" My favorite answer is, "My fear of ever having to sit behind a desk again." As soon as I think, "I am going to have to get a desk job," I think of something new. Okay, let's see if I can make an elephant out of this fork! What else can I make out of a fork? It is a labor of love. Once again, in a roundabout way, a very polite way, you taught me that!

Eric: I've got a degree in anthropology and philosophy from Valdosta State. I studied a lot about native cultures. I paid my way through college working with special people over at the developmental center. I think I learned just as much working with them as I did going to college.

Jeff: Do you think working with people with special needs made you the person you are today?

Eric: Yeah. It was major because, at that time, I got a job offer from a country club, and I had that job, and it was like, "Do I want to leave that job to go make more money or do I want to help these special people?" It was hard work, but it was okay.

Jeff: I didn't know you before it, but I can't imagine that it wouldn't help make you the person that you are. I have a niece with autism, and she is really awkward around people, and she comes in with Eric, and she really gets along with Eric. I think that comes out in Eric's essence.

My aunt Hilda lives right up there, and sometimes at night when I am there and can't sleep, I come down here and sit in your parking lot and just relax and daydream—get some positive enjoyment. I have never asked you: Who painted the "Legge" on your sign?

Eric: That was Ralph Frank's. He is actually a sign painter.

Blackstock: You were talking about this being an oasis here in Dillard. What makes this a good location for artists?

Eric: Ancient Indian legends.

Jeff: There is a huge Indian spirit presence here. There is a mound right behind that Rabun County Bank. Cross over the Little Tennessee River, and go up the hill. There is a huge Indian burial mound there. I used to go to it as a kid. There is a giant boulder; if you look under it, you can see where they laid it on top of another rock, and there are bodies in that rock. When I was a little kid I used to go lay on top of that rock all the time. We used to hunt arrowheads. My friends would find them and

PLATE 46 Legge's sign at the studio in Dillard, Georgia

I would get mad, and I would sneak in their bedrooms and take them and put them back; I thought they should stay with the Indians. It is still there. It is private property. There is a lot I feel—there is really a lot of strong spirituality in this area.

The Unveiling

We returned a week later to witness the unveiling of Eric Legge's latest artwork, which Jeff Carver will add to his folk art collection. With this piece, Eric has collaborated with Howard Finster, adding a mountain scene and positive messages. The shoe is one of Finster's staple icons, while the mountain scene shows Legge's inspiration from the area he describes as a "lost Eden."

Ultimately, art demands a refusal to sacrifice. A true artist refuses to trade a strong spirituality for the benefits of a fleeting materialism, recovering an Edenic Covenant that shuns the fruits of mediocrity and ease in order to preserve a sanctuary of freedom, creativity, and inspira-

PLATE 47 Jeff Carver adds Eric Legge's latest work to his collection.

PLATE 48 A tribute by Eric Legge to his hero, Howard Finster,
and to his friends Jeff Carver and Bill Gridley

tion. Eric Legge said of his hero, Howard Finster, "A . . . hero is someone
that inspires you to be yourself rather than to be like them. That's the
only person you're ever going to get to be is yourself, so that's a beautiful thing." Although we won't all work in the arts, true artists like Eric
Legge inspire us all to be brave enough to be ourselves, to say, "Yes!" to
our callings, and to enjoy the paradise around us.

The interview with Eric Legge inspired the Foxfire staff and students
so much that we asked Rabun County High School art teacher Amy Jarrard to share any materials she might have on folk art so that we could
learn more about this. She brought over a few books, including Foxfire
8. She had other books, but she recommended the articles about the Meaders family above all other resources. As it turns out, her appreciation
for the Foxfire books is natural, since she is a former Foxfire student herself. She also helped create a perspective for folk art that became clearer
than any of the resources she shared. Ms. Jarrard said that folk art is
often criticized for being simple and even elementary-looking. People will
even say, "That's simple; I could have thought of that." As Ms. Jarrard
explained, when someone first invented the wheel, there were probably a
host of caveman art critics who said, "That's simple; I could have thought
of that." The thing is, though, they didn't think of it. It takes an innovator
to think of these things first. Her explanation reminded me of a famous
quote by jazz musician Charley Mingus: "Anyone can make the simple
complicated. Creativity is making the complicated simple."

MOTHER VINE AND KING KUDZU

An interview with Kudzu artists Joleen Oh and Cleve Phillips

The baskets make themselves; they just use my hands. —Joleen Oh

I'm a modern-day artist, so having to eat really inspires me.

—Cleve Phillips

Many craftsmen take as much pride in the way they practice their art as they do in the finished products. However, for Appalachian artisans, creative process often starts before the method even begins. Creativity begins with a harvesting. Before a basket can be made or before a chair bottom can be woven, the artist has to go out and find the materials to create these household necessities.

Foxfire books have always featured their artists' creative processes, and many times, the methods for gathering materials is an integral part of the art. In *The Foxfire Book*, the contacts explain that white oak splits had to be worked on the day they were cut so that they wouldn't dry out. If they had no time to work with the newly cut oak, they set the timber in nearby creeks to keep them moist and malleable. Before Beulah Perry and Aunt Arie Carpenter could make the baskets, some of which would be added to the Foxfire Museum collection, the timber itself had to be collected and worked to make the pliable materials (115–22).

Just as methods might change over time, so might the harvests. In some cases, artists use traditional methods to work different materials. One of the most interesting variations we have found in recent years came when we interviewed King Kudzu and Mother Vine at the Kudzu Factory. Like many of Foxfire's original contacts, the artists at the Kudzu Factory show an immense gratitude for their art, and they prioritize the spiritual benefits of doing what they enjoy over any greater monetary gain that might come from producing more impersonal goods.

—*Jonathan Blackstock*

Joleen

I have been working with kudzu since I was seven years old, and I have been a teacher since I was eight years old. My mom figured out how to make the kudzu paper in 1989, so she taught me how to do it when I was in the second grade. My mother didn't learn from my grandma; it's not passed down that way. My grandmother was Margaret Basket, and that's as far back as we can trace. We don't know if she took her name from the work that she did, but I'm assuming so. It's a tradition when you're Cherokee that you find your red road that you're supposed to be on in life. Until then, you take one of the last names of your ancestors. That's what my mother did, so her name is legally Nancy Basket.

I'm not there yet; I'm still working on finding my red road. I don't know if I want to follow the tradition and take a last name. It's kind of up in the air still. I was married once and took his last name and didn't like it, so I've been Joleen Oh for quite a while now; it suits me. I got the "Oh" from my father. He is actually Korean. He was born in Seoul, Korea.

When I was little, it was harder for me to learn because when I was about eight years old, I had a go-kart accident. I was in the hospital for ten weeks with a brain injury. I was in a coma for about a month. I used making baskets as therapy. My mom had just figured out how to make the kudzu paper when it happened. My mom became interested in making the kudzu paper and read about it.

It isn't as easy as it looks; my first basket actually turned into a boat. I worked hard to get where I am today. I learned how because of my willingness to practice every day.

Art hasn't always been an interest of mine; I was a math and science kid when I was in school. I took nine years to develop my art. I was an insurance agent at the time, and I had a child. I have a twelve-year-old little boy, and I lived in South Carolina. I moved up here three years ago and said, "What now?" The mountains called me home. That is when I opened my art studio.

My husband and I met five years ago, and from then on, we have made kudzu art. I had the business up here for about three years and in South Carolina for about two years. Location is everything, especially in a business like mine. In South Carolina, I didn't have the foot traffic or the road traffic of people coming to see it, so when I moved here, it just kind of took off in its own little way.

Since we moved here three years ago, I have been given access to a lot of kudzu, acres full of kudzu. Ever since we put that "Kudzu Wanted" sign out there two years ago, we have been blessed with at least forty to sixty acres of kudzu that we have free access to all around the state. Georgia Power gave us access to their right-of-way, so we've got all that kudzu that we can have when we are anywhere in the state, plus several different private locations where we go and get it from. My company

PLATE 49 Mother Vine splitting kudzu

only likes to harvest off the trees, so if it's growing into a pine thicket, we like that stuff. We like to help to give back to the trees a little bit because it's choking them out. We need our trees.

My husband can harvest kudzu faster than anyone I know. He's just really good at what he does. He can go to a big kudzu patch and harvest a ton of it in about an hour.

Everyone thinks that it's growing all through the trees and the bushes. It goes about two feet inside a perimeter, and it does not like to go [deep] into the forest. It goes on top of the trees to get the sunlight. The way kudzu kills a tree is it actually covers [the tree] to where it can't get sunlight to photosynthesize and create its own food.

Kudzu thrives off of moisture. We put our dry pieces out on a rainy day, so they will still be thin, flexible, and wet. It absorbs the moisture in the air. We actually had a friend put one of our baskets in her most humid room as a dehumidifier, and it worked. It took a little bit longer than a dehumidifier would have, but it still did its job.

You can tell kudzu is fresh if it's bendable and flexible. You see this same quality in the trees and forest and everything. It has a white dot in the middle of it, and it's called the pith. [**Editors' note:** The pith is the soft, sponge-like central cylinder of the stem of most flowering plants.] The pith can be split. Just cut it right along the pith area.

I know I make it look easy, but there is a technique to splitting it. I split it into two pieces, and I keep splitting it, depending on how big a piece I want or what I'm doing. You have to have the pith to split a vine. Wisteria is the only other vine I've worked with that has a pith and can be split. You cannot split grape vines; they are solid. I use wisteria when I'm able to get it. I like it because it dries a little bit yellower and woodsier. I also use the pine needles, and my husband uses bamboo.

Working with kudzu uses different muscles to make different things and styles. I don't want to get carpal tunnel syndrome, so I try to do different things. Even when I'm stripping kudzu, I try to do it in different motions. The larger pieces are for my husband because he likes to work with the bigger vines, and I'm not that strong anymore.

You know, kudzu is part of the bean family. It's also edible and has more protein than alfalfa. It helps to liven and boost the immune system, so I make candy out of the small, tender, young leaves, the very small ones that are no bigger than the palm of your hand. I put it in white chocolate, so if you like white chocolate, that's all you taste because kudzu has no flavor on its own. It's kind of like working with tofu. It takes on the strongest flavor of whatever you put with it, so it kind of melts together. [**Editors' note:** Our magazine class was able to try some of the white chocolate with kudzu, and it tasted just as she said it would.]

My husband and I make completely different styles of baskets. One is woven, and one is coiled. Woven is harder for me because I have been coiling my entire life. It uses a different part of your brain. In making

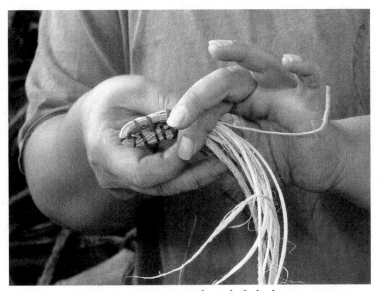

PLATE 50 Beginning the coil of a basket

woven baskets, you don't have to go by any rule, which throws me for a loop. I have to have some kind of structure to start with, or I'm kind of lost. Like I said, I'm more math- and science-minded, where you have to follow specific steps. The coiling style, on the other hand, starts from the middle and you build your way up. My husband has been weaving with cotton since he was sixteen years old, so he has taken the kudzu vine and started weaving with that. He is smart; the woven is more his style.

The method of coiling I use is all basically the same, but this method has been passed down to me. Some basket makers use nuts or shells and weave them in.

My son has been making baskets like my style and my husband's style since he was about seven, but it's his choice to take over the business or not. My responsibility was to teach him how. He knows how to make a basket, and he has sold many of his baskets already to different people. I've done my job. I have taken care of it. I passed it down. It just depends on what he wants to do. Right now, he wants to grow up and be a lawyer.

I like to create my own Indian designs, so they are all individual and unique. My baskets kind of have a way of talking to me. You know how you're working on a project, and it nags at you until you get it done? These will do that to me. I'll get up in the middle of the night because I was dreaming about them. It tells me what it's going to look like. The baskets make themselves; they just use my hands. We are modern-day artists; we see things differently.

I have been making baskets for about twenty years, but it still takes me sixteen to seventeen hours. We actually made the banisters for Tangerine Dream Salon spa in Tiger, Georgia. That was all on-site work. It was difficult work, but I enjoyed it.

I'm starting to do a new design with my handles on the baskets. You can see the natural indention in there now; it's not just wadded up. I tried to go for the smallest basket in *The Guinness Book of World Records*, but the one I made didn't use a microscope, so I was disqualified. I've made a basket that was four millimeters by five millimeters. It didn't take me a long time to split material at all. It just took me a long time to make it because it was so small. It doesn't really matter to me if I do big art or little art; I like the challenge of both.

I get the colors in my kudzu by hand-dyeing my own raffia. The raffia is what I sew it together with, but it has to be hand-dyed. You don't want to buy the stuff that has already been dyed. It is fireproofed, and it will break and tear. It is not good for baskets; it's just for decoration.

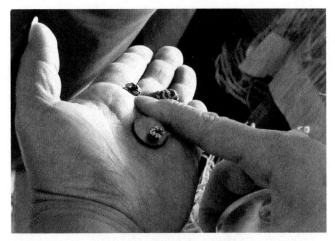

PLATE 51 The smallest basket

I use fabric dye on the raffia. It shows more color, it lasts longer, and it doesn't fade as fast. I just dyed some like two days ago, and it took me fifteen minutes. You have to let it absorb the color for a while before you can take it out and do anything with it.

I also dye my pine needles. I like the ones that are still green and sappy from the tree because I can dry those. If I dry them out in the sun, they dry this beautiful mint green. Then, they turn that chocolate-brown color. If I dry them myself, I cover parts of them so the sun hits certain parts and colors some more than others. When you're dyeing, you take what you get. It doesn't always turn out the exact color you wanted.

Too much moisture can eventually hurt your kudzu art. You can see that my older ones—[the art pieces] that are sitting outside—are slowly decomposing. If you treat it, it does a lot better. You can use something like Australian Timber Oil or anything that is going to preserve it after the kudzu is completely dry. My baskets are a part of me; they are my soul. I don't like to treat my baskets because I want my soul to be free.

The most unique thing I've ever made is probably my duck or the elephant that is in my house. These have been the most fun. It took me about three weeks. I didn't exactly know what I was doing. I had a lot of fun making [the duck], though. It's always fun to do something new and different.

The big vine in the front of the factory was actually taken from Kingwood Country Club, in Clayton, Georgia. I also have earrings, bracelets, and necklaces.

Every season brings new challenges. Sometimes, I do wholesale/retail, but other times, I do consignment. We don't go after location; we

PLATE 52 A kudzu elephant

go after the people who own the store. If we like you, we will let you sell our stuff there.

I also make pine needle baskets. I am very fortunate that friends of mine, who lived in South Georgia, Alabama, and Mississippi, have homes here. They will bring me long leaf pine needles and drop them at the door. I've had people bring me huge limbs of long leaf pine, and they just drop them at the door.

My husband also uses bamboo. Bamboo is just as invasive as kudzu, if not more so. Bamboo grows three feet a day, while kudzu only grows one. You can use just about anything, but we like to use the pests— plants that are absolute nuisances. We decided to make it out of the kudzu because it was just everywhere. In South Carolina, all the festivals I went to never used kudzu to make their baskets; they just had a lot of it around. I know there are many kudzu festivals in Atlanta where they actually use the plant. I would love to get into one of those.

I teach classes for papermaking and sell the paper, but I will probably never be as good as my mom. Kudzu paper takes two weeks of fermentation in its own juices. The fermented kudzu vines start to smell like a more pungent sauerkraut. If you let them sit out in the hot summer sun, they start to cook. Two weeks later, you take them out, and they look decomposed. Then, you cut them into one-inch pieces, and you put them in a blender. I also put in a little bit of recycled paper; it's about a four-to-one ratio. I put the lid back on after I fill it up with water. Then, I blend it for thirty seconds to a minute. I put it back into a vat with a little water and dye if you want to dye.

Next, I take needlepoint canvas, dip it down into the vat, and pull it up. I put felt on the vat, and then put one hand on the top one and one on the bottom. I squeeze all the water out, flip it screen side up, take a paper towel, and soak up as much water as I can, squeezing it back over the vat. Then, I take the screen (felt) off of the vat, and I have one sheet of paper.

I also offer pine needle classes. The pine needle classes are more for adults, and they are forty-five dollars a person. That includes teaching time and lunch. It will take about three to four hours. You have a lot of fun in my class, and if you don't, you get thrown out.

Joleen Oh is an inspirational woman who is passionate about her art. She is also passionate about her environment and turns something other people believe useless into a resource. At the Kudzu Factory, Joleen's husband, Cleve Phillips—"King Kudzu"—transforms the invasive vines and bamboo stalks into positive works of art that decorate the storefront. They have even brought the community together during Christmas.

Cleve

My daddy was from Long Creek, and my mother was from Mountain Rest. [**Editors' note:** Both Long Creek and Mountain Rest are located in Oconee County, South Carolina.] I was born in Morgan City, Louisiana, in Saint Mary Parish. I have an older sister, Tammie Bennett, that's an RN at Oconee Hospital [in Seneca, South Carolina], and I have a brother, Stacy, that's a Fortune 500 builder and lives in Mountain Rest. I have another sister, Chrystal, that's a nurse, too. I've got plenty of brothers and sisters.

We were poor children; Daddy was a farmer and a logger from Long Creek. Mother was a cotton mill worker, and my step-daddy was a cotton mill worker.

I was lucky enough to go to work in a satellite mill on Duck Pond Road in Walhalla—it was a Chicopee mill—when I was eight years old. The doctor pulled my arm out of place when I was born, and no one ever put it back in place. I slipped and fell, and they had to put my arm in a cast. I couldn't go to school, so I went to work with my step-daddy. Later on, I lied about my age and went to work when I was sixteen; I was supposed to be seventeen. I started sweeping the floors at Chicopee Ste-

PLATE 53 King Kudzu talking about his art

phens and cleaning up around the facility. I eventually worked my way up to weaving. We would run several looms, around seventy or eighty looms per floor.

I was good at art in high school, but in the area where we lived, art wasn't pushed that much. I went to West-Oak and Walhalla High School. In most of the areas now, they push only painting in high school art classes. You don't have access to a lot of other mediums.

We've been here at the Kudzu Factory for about three years now. We've been doing kudzu art together for about five years. I had no experience with kudzu or basket making before I met Joleen. I only had experience with cotton mill weaving. Joleen and I started this whole home-based business that was a pyramid scheme, and it failed miserably. So, she had quit making baskets because her previous husband didn't want her to make baskets; the baskets made a lot of mess. So, we set out on the front porch one night, and instead of giving up, we decided to do something. We started making baskets. I made one, and she kept it. The second, third, and fourth basket that I made, I sold. I was hooked then. I was selling kudzu, and I was just as happy as I could be!

I first learned how to work with kudzu by sitting down and doing it. Joleen showed me a little, and I learned the rest by doing it. Every now and then, when I get burnt out, I have to go back and start from the beginning. I start making a few like my first baskets, and it helps me get back on track.

We work pretty well together. She's got her own way of doing it [her art], and my way is different. It works out good as a business. Joleen does the coiling-style baskets, and I do the bigger stuff, like the building panels, lamps, and Christmas trees.

My agricultural background came in handy with making kudzu art. Daddy made me handle pulpwood when I was little. It comes in handy working with kudzu now. I grew up on a farm tractor, so it all helps out, working in the woods and gathering and harvesting.

I use kudzu because of availability; it's free. Plus, it really educates people about the sustainability of kudzu. We've got a lot of kudzu, and people are now trying to poison it. I really don't like to see it poisoned because we can't even go up to a stream now and drink out of it. The poison we use to kill kudzu is getting into the water supply. If we can

PLATE 54 Kudzu Christmas tree

use the product and control it, I think it will be a lot better. We won't be putting as much poison into the environment.

Kudzu was first introduced into the United States in Florida. We actually had the descendants of the family that owned the land where the first kudzu was introduced come by and visit our shop a few years back. They have a cabin up here in Rabun County. They don't have it growing there now, but that's where they first brought it in and shipped it out to the rest of the country.

I do any kind of kudzu art that you can imagine. I make seats for chairs and building panels. I made Mountain City's twenty-foot bamboo/kudzu Christmas tree the past two years. It was at the courthouse, but they move it back and forth. I also made a big globe. It was about an eight-foot ball that I wove. I'm a modern-day artist, so having to eat really inspires me. Sometimes, I can make something, and I really don't know what it's going to be. I lay it to the side, and I make something else that seems to go with it. I will put them together and get a really neat finished product. I've also been able to develop a lot of

PLATE 55 Kudzu lamp

big sellers like handbaskets, wall pieces, little angels, and the kudzu Christmas trees.

The lifespan of a piece of kudzu art differs based on where you keep it. Inside, it can last forever. It will stay the same color and maintain its shape. If you put them outdoors in the weather, they will only last three to five years. You can also treat it. I only do that if the customer special requests it. I use Thompson's WaterSeal or something like that. You can keep up the treatment so that it lasts a little longer. It's like anything, really. If you take care of it and keep it out of the elements, it will last much longer.

Sometimes, I use the whole kudzu vine. Some people want me to use the whole vine. Sometimes, I split the vine and use the split pieces in my designs. I like to do a lot of different stuff. I don't really like staying stuck on one thing. I can have four or five different projects going at one time. A lot of people will say that they want the whole vine, or they want it split. We tailor each piece to meet the customers' needs or their likes.

The inner bark of kudzu is white, so you get the white coloring from working with that side, and the outer bark is kind of black. I can mix it up and create stripes, or I can color the kudzu. You can dye it whatever color that you want. I've made an American flag by dyeing the fibers red, white, and blue. I usually take Rit Dye and mix it up. I spray it on the kudzu, and most of the time, it dries just right. You can also spray-paint it. If I clear coat it, it will last from three to five years. Once again, if you put it inside where it's not exposed to the elements, it will last a lot longer.

We just pick the kudzu and use it; we don't have any special treatments that we put it through. You can let the vines shrink a little bit and use it for wreaths and stuff. You have a little less shrinkage, and you can make a better circle, but some things you have to do fresh. You can't let it dry out.

I go all over Rabun County to get my kudzu. All kudzu is not the same. Some of it looks really good, but when you get in there, it's dead or poisoned. You can tell if it's been poisoned or going bad if it's brown. You can tell when they've been out and poisoned it, especially around the power poles.

We use every part of the kudzu, from the root to the tip of the vine. The root can be used to make root starch, and we use it just like corn-starch. Harvard University did a study on it and found that it cut down alcoholics' cravings for alcohol. We have another friend that makes cloth out of the vine, as well. Kudzu retains its moisture very well, especially depending on the weather. In the wintertime, it dries out a lot quicker.

PLATE 56 Sign that greets customers

You can tie knots with kudzu when it is fresh and green. You can tie it or twist it or braid it. I can also soak a finished basket, untwist it, and make something new out of it. All of the kudzu that I have is reusable. It's biodegradable, reusable, and one hundred percent green.

You can actually eat kudzu. They make wine out of the blossoms, and you can eat the kudzu bean. It's like a green bean. They say that the kudzu green beans have a type of natural estrogen in them. Kudzu has big, flat beans that grow on them. It is actually a part of the legume family. I've read about scientists trying to create hybrid beans by mixing kudzu beans with regular green beans in an attempt to get them to grow a foot a day. They are pretty good; I eat them all the time when I'm in the patch.

I like to go harvest my kudzu early in the morning and get it over with. I can have a van full of harvested kudzu in about two hours. I really like to harvest during the winter. There are no snakes or bees, and the briars are gone a little bit. In the wintertime, I'll cut my trails in for when I come back in the summertime.

When I go out and harvest kudzu, the main thing I look for is if it's easy to get to. I really like picking out vines that are a little twisted and have grown up the trees a little bit. I like the bigger vines, personally. I usually bring it back and separate it. I use a pole saw that has a sixteen-inch blade on the end of it to harvest the vines. That's why they call me King Kudzu—when I go out in the woods, all kudzu bows down before me.

I have made peace with the kudzu bug. At first, when I would go out in the kudzu patch, the bugs always seemed to attack the giant by flying in my eye. It was like they had intelligence. I was a giant invading their territory, and they would attack my most vulnerable part. Well, I picked a lot of blossoms, and in those blossoms were a lot of kudzu bugs. When I brought them back, I just laid the bag out so they could escape and be free. They've been pretty good since then. I know it's strange, but it seems to have worked.

The most unique piece that I have ever made is a tough choice. I kind of like the bamboo/kudzu Christmas tree. A whole town kind of came together around the one we made for Mountain City. It was our first Christmas tree. The whole town came together, and kudzu brought them there. I think that would be my favorite. Besides, I really like Christmas. You wouldn't believe this, but I got the idea while I was on my front porch. In my mind, I thought, "I wonder what Old Man Winter likes most about winter?" I decided it must be Christmas trees, so I started making one. That's the best thing about winter, isn't it? A Christmas tree will cost about a dollar per inch, so a ten-foot tree would sell for about $120.

I also use kudzu to make chairs or chair bottoms. I have made a whole chair out of kudzu, but most of the time, I just get the chair frames and weave the bottoms out of kudzu.

We offer a class for people interested in learning how to make kudzu art. I have taught a lot of teachers and other people how to create art using kudzu. I seem to end up with a lot of special education teachers. I am happy to teach people whenever they come by. There are so many different ways to make a basket, I always just let them go when I teach and let them figure out which way works best for them. Me and Rabun Martin had a "Vino and Vine" class, where about twenty ladies came in and made whole-vine baskets. One of the students left her basket here, and I sold it for her. It was her first basket, and somebody came in and bought it. Sometimes, people don't have time to do a full class. They just want to come in here and do little quick, simple classes. We'll start by teaching them to make something small like a kudzu flower and move

PLATE 57 Cleve Phillips weaving a chair bottom

PLATE 58 King Kudzu's art display

up to bigger things like a basket. Actually, we can make whatever they want to make.

I believe that people in the old days used kudzu. They didn't have a store to buy the things that they needed, so they made it out of the things they had available to them. I don't think that I'm doing anything new; I'm just doing it in a location where a lot of people can see me doing it. People have never seen it, so they think it's new. I've talked to people who were doing chair bottoms from kudzu and using it around the house twenty or thirty years ago. That's just the way the area was back then. You didn't have stores. You had to go out and get what you had.

Any art that you create using nature is a spiritual experience. You are doing something that you are supposed to. I do think that you are supposed to go out in the woods and pick stuff and make it. I've noticed that when we teach little kids. We went down to DeKalb County Technological Center and taught a group of kids how to create art from kudzu. This one little kid made a kudzu basket, and he said, "I've finally made something worth something for my momma." He was just so happy; he was like a totally different little kid. I think there is definitely a connection between art and your spirit or your soul.

There are aspects of my personal beliefs exhibited through my artwork. I compete, and I try to please God. I'm not really worried about anyone else. I really think that He laughs at me a lot. It's good if you can make God laugh. I haven't been bitten by a snake, and I've been pretty safe in the kudzu patch, so I guess He likes my work!

I think that basket making is all in our genes because it doesn't really matter what color you are; your ancestors made baskets. Black, white, pink, or green—they all made baskets. They are probably my biggest seller. My smaller baskets go for about $5–$10 because I can turn them out pretty fast. When we first started this business, some of the nicer baskets sold for $150, but in this economy, we're getting around $30–50 for them. If you want to do what you enjoy, you roll with the changing environment. This day and time, people are working harder. There are no more "riding around" jobs.

I'm kind of flexible with my prices because if the customer loves it, likes it, and will give it a good home, I'll let it go pretty cheap. She [Joleen] says I'm cheap, but if they love it, I want them to walk away with it. Plus, that's better than advertising anywhere. Our happy customers go out and advertise for us and say good things about us. Customer service is our best form of marketing. A lot of people want us to be a bigger business than what we are, but in this day and time, I think we want to stay a mom-and-pop kind of business until things with the economy get settled down and people get back to working. You don't want to grow too fast in this day and time.

I can make a basket in six minutes. I can make a flower in about three or four minutes. I weaved in a cotton mill running all of the looms, and we had to tie weaving knots. It was a production job, so you have to develop your talent with the speed of the hands. That helps me with creating my kudzu art because I have developed that talent and speed with my hands.

A lot of stuff I just started doing because it was fun. I thought it was neat to take kudzu and make all this different stuff. When I first started, it was like, "Let me make as many different things as I can or see how many different things that I can make out of kudzu." It just went from there.

The good thing about making a basket is that there are so many different ways to do it. There's no right way or wrong way. You can't mess up. You can start by making the bottom, the handle, and then the sides; or you can start with the sides and add the bottom and the handle. You can't mess up with a basket.

I think the longest project that I've ever had was a twenty-foot tree. It took me about two or three weeks to build it. I had some help with that one. We built it right here in the Promenade building. We laid it down on its side and rolled it out the door. I don't think it would fit back in here since we put the angel on it. That tree is now sitting outside of our shop. I think that I'm going to have to build another one. I think the current one is going to go out in front of the Mad Hatter Salon. I'm going to see if I can help her do some advertising with it.

It's hard to stay on one project for very long because your hands start to cramp up. You have to take breaks in between your weaving. I weave really hard for like an hour or two, and I have to take a thirty- to forty-minute break. I mix it up and do a lot of different things.

I have a kudzu man sitting out in front of the shop. They had a creative Georgia economy thing a while back at the Dillard House, and they wanted me to put some pieces up there. I made a kudzu man, a kudzu woman, and a kudzu little girl. The woman and the little girl ran off to Atlanta, and all I've got left is the man. He stays around and hangs out with us. The sign maker next door wants him, so I may trade with him for some signs.

Those were the first people that I had made from kudzu. It's really difficult. You have to fight gravity with kudzu art. If you weave the lines just right, they will hold it up. Some of my pieces are made to stand up because they have longer pieces woven into them. If you set it on its side, it wouldn't be as strong. When you weave pieces, you have to weave them with a purpose. You have to balance out your products. You just keep trying until you get it right.

Basically, what I do when I build something like a tree or basket is build the frame first. I build my frame any way that I want it, and I then fill in the spaces with kudzu. For a Christmas tree, I build a circle, and I stand my bamboo frame up. I build the basic frame, and I start going around it weaving in vine to fill in the spaces. Sometimes, I use a jig with screws and use that to help build my outline. You create your slats for weaving and then start filling in the spaces. It all sounds pretty simple. It's like anything else: the more you do it, the better you get.

I also do some bamboo art. I like to make different stuff out of bamboo. I made a bamboo carrying case that you flip open, and I've made bamboo planters that you can put your flowers in. We make bamboo cups and piggy banks. You can take and cut the bamboo off at each end, cut a little hole in it, and have a piggy bank.

I get my bamboo from a couple of places. I get some from up past Osage Farms and some from around the nursing home. I also get some off of Betty's Creek Road at Brooke Franklin's farm. He has some black bamboo that he lets me harvest. You don't find that a lot around here. It's lucky bamboo, the kind that panda bears eat.

Basically, I've found a way to make a living doing what I love. It doesn't get any better than that. If you can draw it, dream it, or think it, we can probably build it. The imagination is the limit with kudzu.

MAKING WHAT WE
NEED BY HAND

An industrial plant can make enough tables to fill an IKEA store in the same time it takes John Roper to make one table. In the time it takes T. J. Stevens to cut the lard that will be rendered for making soap, a family could have driven to Target, bought a table and a carton of soap, and returned home before any member of that family missed a favorite television show. Making what we need by hand does not increase our efficiency and, in many cases, does not simplify our daily routines. When almost everything that can be made by hand is made faster and cheaper by a factory, why do some people continue to make these items one at a time?

It's the "hand" that counts. Individual craftsmen like Roper and Stevens impact our lives because their priorities focus on the quality of their living. The clocks my grandfather made will hang on my wall even after the little motors stop working because, honestly, the time just isn't as important as the clock maker. These interviews aren't about processes and productions; these people are members of our community making usable items for their families and other members of the community. When Jenny Stevens ships a bar of soap, she sends a personal message that reads more like one sent from friend to friend than company to customer. As with the artists who are reclaiming vanishing arts, the artisans who make what they need by hand are rescuing arts that make and strengthen real connections to the resources and people around them.

Modern traditional artists still maintain strong connections with their predecessors. While their methods and even their reasons for practicing the arts may change, so many of the new outlooks resemble those of the past. In *The Foxfire Book*, Andrea Burrell and several fellow Foxfire students interview her grandmother Pearl Martin. Burrell says, "When we asked about putting perfume in the soap, I thought she would never stop laughing." Later, when the students and Mrs. Martin are making soap, she offers to add perfume for the students even though that is against her nature. "Youn's want me t' put perfume in there? I can perfume it up for youn's if you want. But I'll tell you; if for me, I like th' smell a' that [the lye soap]. It smells like old times."

—*Jonathan Blackstock*

MAKING SOAP, LIVING CLEAN, AND GIVING THANKS

A day of crafting with Jenny, T. J., Briar, and Moses Stevens

We want . . . a process you can understand and ingredients you can pronounce, and that's what we are about. —Jenny Stevens

The dark green leaves of a large, stout tree keep the June sun at bay. Under the tree's welcoming canopy, nine stumps stand as if part of a pastoral amphitheater looking toward two worktables and a fire pit. Two children split wood for the fire and carry jars to the table. A lazy haze of

PLATE 59 Classic Foxfire photograph of Pearl Martin making soap and enjoying life. [Foxfire Archive 01778]

gray smoke rises and then rushes off with the wind as cows moo deeply and move leisurely in the surrounding pasture. A father sets up a large iron cauldron to boil hog fat, and a mother gathers jars to mix lye and water. Many tools, containers, and ingredients are assembled as Jenny Stevens prepares to teach the art of making soap, but one staple item of modern culture is conspicuously missing—a garbage can. People who are thankful for what they have seem to have nothing to throw away. Nothing is wasted.

In Southern Appalachia, found items are used to make sculptures, rescued wood is made to create furniture, and the fat of a hog is used to make soap. Nothing is thrown away. In many cases, this resourceful-ness is born of necessity, but the finished product is often better than store-bought items. Jenny Stevens started making soap because she was allergic to the harmful chemicals that factories used to make cleaning supplies. T. J. Stevens says that while he and his wife, Jenny, use natural ingredients to add scents, some soap makers add ingredients that may not be as wholesome as the old-timey methods. "When people adver-tised that the soap was homemade, just because it is homemade doesn't mean that there are not things in it that you shouldn't be bathing with," T. J. warns. "So that was [Jenny's] thing."

Along with her husband, T. J., Jenny experimented and worked to perfect the art of soap making to create a product that is simply better—a product that is simple, and therefore, better. Jenny says of her ingredi-ents and process, "We want . . . a process you can understand and ingre-dients you can pronounce, and that's what we are about." That simplicity and resourcefulness, which the Stevens family uses to make soap and cracklin's, is what the traditional arts are about. Nothing is wasted, not even the time, since it is spent as a family. This interview includes their two younger sons, Briar and Moses.

—*Jonathan Blackstock*

Jenny: In 1995, T. J. and I went to college. I couldn't find a soap that didn't irritate my skin, so he bought me some books, and I started mak-ing the soap. Then, it got a little more expensive. He was like, "Honey, you are making all this soap and giving it away. We need to start selling it." I wasn't very business-minded; I was pretty much a hermit. I didn't want to talk to people, but T. J. got me out of my comfort zone and took

PLATE 60 Learning soap making in the outdoor classroom

me out of my little shell. We started selling the soaps, and I guess it was probably in 1999 that we started selling it. The business started growing.

This is our outdoor classroom. This is where we do a lot of our teaching with the homeschoolers. We are very fancy here! Pull you up a stump. T. J. is going to bring the lard that we will be renderin'. We can

PLATE 61 Getting the ingredients together

do the soap, the cracklin's, and y'all can see the whole process from start to finish. Y'all can help cut up the fat. Y'all can help render the lard. You can help stir the soap, and we also have some fresh green soap to cut up. Then, I'll take you in the house and show you the soap room—where we do it and how we do it a more modern way.

This is how we do it when we make the old-fashion lye soap. Basically, when I teach lye soap makin', I want everybody to know that there are three basic things it takes to make soap: lard, lye, and water. That's it.

The lye, if you get it on your hands, will burn you. If you do happen to get the green soap on you or the lye, use this vinegar in this bottle. Put it on there as soon as possible, and the vinegar will neutralize any of the green soap or the lye. This is what lye looks like when it's store-bought.

T. J.: We have to go to Cleveland, Tennessee, and buy our lye at a chemical supply house. We have to sign for it, and we buy about four or five hundred pounds, two or three times a year. Since they jacked the gas prices up so much, a lot of times, there will be a fifty- to eighty-dollar fuel surcharge, whether you get a sack, ten sacks, or a truckload, so we try to hold off until we can buy a lot at one time. I think it is about sixty-five dollars a sack now. When we first started buying it over there, it was like a quarter a pound. You could buy one hundred pounds for twenty-five bucks—two sacks for twenty-five bucks. Now you can only get one sack for like sixty-five. That has just been in fifteen years. People tell me there is no such thing as inflation, that we don't have that much inflation! It wasn't that long ago that we were paying a buck and a quarter for gasoline, too.

The bad thing about it now is that people use that lye to make methamphetamines, so they took it out of the stores. I don't think it is illegal to sell lye. It was just like people were saying the only thing we sell it for nowadays is unstopping drains, and if you are gonna unstop a drain, then use Drano. They just didn't want to sell the lye to contribute to [making methamphetamines]. It is sad that a few people that are doing something stupid can mess it up for other people.

Jenny: I'll show y'all how to make lye like they would've back in the old days with the wood ashes. We have a recipe where you can learn how to do it from start to finish with the wood ash lye, too, but for time's sake today, we are going to do it with the more modern method. That way, it's easier for everybody to see it from start to finish. Now, this soap here is one that we made and put it down in the cooler. It goes in the cooler to

PLATE 62 Mixing water and lye

allow it to stay insulated. The insulation factor is very important to the chemical reactions of saponification. When the lard and the lye interact, you get saponification. The lard and the lye changes to soap and glycerin, so until that reaction is complete, you have lard and lye, but once it is complete, you have a whole new product.

To mix our lye up, we are going to do it in a plastic container. We'll do it in this one right here. All right, are y'all ready for a recipe? We use

PLATE 63 Sharing the recipe

four pounds of lard. For our lye, we're gonna use fifty-two hundredths of a pound. Then, we're gonna use a pound and a half of water. All right, here's our water, and if we take and fill this jar up two times, it's exactly a pound and a half. So, we can go ahead and do that. It needs to be twenty-four ounces of water.

I'm gonna add the lye to it. So, there's our water. Now, this is our handy-dandy lye-stirrin' stick. If you stir it with a wooden spoon or anything like that, it will eat it up, so it's just a regular ol' piece of trim. Your lye is going to be a little more than eight ounces. Now, when you mix your lye and your water together, you got to be real careful not to stand in the fumes because the fumes are caustic. They'll burn your lungs and your nose, so you got to be very careful, and you need to know the wind is blowing this way.

We'll carry them back over here before we mix them up. That way, the fumes are gonna go that way and dissipate. Basically, pour our lye in here, and we'll stir it. As we stir it, it instantly comes to the boiling point, so you need to make sure that you don't mix them in glass containers. When we are finished dealing with our lye container, either rinse it out or put a lid back on it to where it is safe until you can take care of it properly.

I broke a lot of jars when we first started makin' soap. I did them in the sink. In the rental house we were livin' in, the lye ate all the pipe out of the house, so Mr. T. J. had to go back under the house and replace all the pipes.

The book on safety says it's good to have gloves and goggles and all of your safety equipment. If you're doin' it inside, make sure that you have great ventilation. Even though we make soap in the house, we mix up all the lye outside because there is not enough ventilation in the house for it. You'll see the steam come off of it. It was made from ash in the old days. How we make it is with oak ashes or hickory, any of your hardwood ashes. We'll take and add our ashes to a bucket.

The lye we are using today comes from salt. They take table salt and chemically shock it with electrolysis. It makes the chloride evaporate off of it, and you're left with sodium hydroxide. And I'm not a chemist, so I don't quite understand that whole process of how this particular lye is made. Now, when you have your fire and you burn all your wood down, you're left with that real white powdery ash. I've got some in a jar I'll show you.

T. J.: Miss Jenny wanted to make soap with wood ash lye instead of just the old Red Devil method, the commercial lye. She looked and looked

PLATE 64 A bag of lye

and looked, but she couldn't find anybody that did it. She asked her grandma, who was ninety-something years old and comes from down in Cleveland, Georgia. She said, "How did y'all make your soap?" She said, "We didn't make our soap; we traded for it." They owned a store, a little country store. Miss Jenny couldn't find anybody that did it. That little community, little museum place, down in South Georgia, called Westville . . . She had read an article about a lady who demonstrated soap down there, Miss Vinnie Miller. I think she was on up in her eighties. Jenny called her and couldn't hardly communicate with her on the phone 'cause Jenny had a mountain accent, and she had a South Georgia accent. So, the lady actually wrote her a letter and gave her the recipe.

When you use the wood ash, a lot of folks say, "Ugh! Lye soap is harsh on your skin." If the lye and oil are mixed properly, it turns to soap and glycerin. You add too much lye, and it will be alkaline and burn your skin. You add too much oil, and your soap starts getting greasier. When you make your wood ashes, you get these things called black salt. This is some lye that we leached. You see those white crystals on the bottom? You see that kind a' grayish stuff? That is what they call black salt. That is what is harsh on your skin because it is kind a' like the impurities that you get out with the lye.

Jenny: If you take ten cups of those ashes, put 'em in a pillowcase, put 'em down in a bucket, and pour two gallons of boilin' water over it, that boilin' water pulls all of the salt that occurs naturally in a hardwood tree. Then, we let it steep in there overnight, and we'll pull it up like a big tea bag—let it drip back in there and settle. We'll take that two gallons of water and cook it back down till we're left with about a cup and a half of lye. We'll take about a cup of grease, and we'll start mixin' 'em together just like a tablespoon at a time over a real low fire. You'll stir it and keep cookin' it. You'll see the change chemically start happening as it changes from grease and lye water into soap and glycerin. You can be too heavy on the lye or too heavy on the grease, and you have to kind of play with it. It takes a little bit of practice and a little bit of skill, but you can really make some nice soap out of just ashes and recycled grease. That's actually quite fun.

We are gonna let these cool off. The lye has got to be roughly room temperature, and the lard needs to be about 120 degrees before we start making the soap with it. It is very hot! If it's cold outside, it will shock your jars. Today, we've got the weather workin' with us. It's not cold; it didn't shock the jar, but I always like to be extra cautious. Let's get our lard ready.

All right, we need to go ahead and make the mold. [**Editors' note:** The mold is a wooden box lined with wax paper.] The one thing you need to do when you are making soap is to make sure you have your mold prepared before you start stirring unless you have lots and lots of help, because once it's ready to pour up, it's too late to make your mold. The way I line my mold—the old way was to grease it with lard or grease or something—but what we do is we take a freezer paper, and I take the waxy part and put that to the inside.

PLATE 65 Wax paper in the mold

A lot of people will just pour it in the mold and let it sit, just cool off. If you pour it in the mold, it has the opportunity to just set up, but if you pour it into a mold that is insulated, it will stay warmer for a lot longer. As it stays warm, it will heat back up to about 180 degrees. It will cause it to re-gel. It will cook itself in the mold. That is what is important with our soap; that is what makes our soap different from other people's soaps. We put it in the molds and let it set for forty-eight to seventy-two hours.

When we have the opportunity, we go by the moon's phases when making our soap. In July, we make most of our soap for August 'cause we are gone. The first week of August, we have to have it made and on the racks curing, so it is ready for September and October. No matter what the moon phase might be, you are just kind of stuck with a time when you have to make it. Cinnamon and clove we always make on the new moon because if it traces out [congeals] and gets hard too fast, you lose your whole batch of soap. On a full moon is the best time for all the other soaps. When you are making soap near a full moon, it will come out harder and will trace quicker. On a new moon, it don't trace near as quick and it always seems like it is a little softer.

We pour it into that mold, and as it goes through that second heat, it causes the glycerin factor to be a lot better and the soap is more gentle. It is a more translucent soap. It gets a little bit more translucent. The chemical reaction is different. The chemical reaction, the saponification, actually takes seven days to complete. That is what we are doing right here with our stirring; we are agitating it, forcing it, the lye and the lard, to come together and change it chemically into soap and glycerin. That reaction is not complete for seven days, but we still don't use the soap or sell it until it is about thirty days old. At two weeks, it is fine to use, but we let it sit that extra time on the shelf with the fans on it so that it gets harder and lasts our customers longer. When we made the soap recipe, we wanted a soap that bubbled really good. We wanted it to last a long time. We wanted it to be real gentle. We didn't want a soap that would wash away really fast. We are ready to start stirring the lye and lard. The best part of making soap is the stirring part if you like to sit still. It is fun if you don't have anything else to do. Let's go over here and let Mr. T. J. tell you about the grease first.

T. J.: There's a slaughterhouse over on Highway 129. It's called Chambers. I think they've been slaughtering for seventy years in that place. They usually give us the beef scraps, but what they typically made soap with in Appalachia was the lard because you could raise a hog up really

PLATE 66 T. J. explains how to prepare the grease.

big, really quick. You could start with a pig, and at the end of the year, you could slaughter it. You could put your meat up.

A lot of people think that old-timers rendered their fat just to make soap. They rendered it because that was your cooking oil. Basically, they would have big crocks, and they would salt cure their meat or put it up,

PLATE 67 Cutting the lard into small chunks

and they'd pack it in these crocks. Then, they would render their lard and pour it over their meat, and it saved. It preserved their food. It was their cookin' oil, and it was a preservative. Whatever they had left over at the end of the year is what they would use to make their soap. It would be all right for soap, but not as good for eatin'. Then, they would start all over again with the new lard.

A little lady that lives down here in Owltown, Georgia, says that they were so poor that they never had enough—even back in the sixties. Every bit of the lard that they used they had to eat. They would actually take the innards and let the lye break the innards down and make the soap out of it. You know beef fat makes a harder soap, but it is not as good on your skin as the lard is. It's just the lard is real moisturizin'.

Miss Jenny started makin' soap almost twenty years ago because she couldn't use a commercial product. That's how we kind of got started into the soap makin' business. We can't even use commercial laundry soap because it breaks her skin out, and it just so happens that there's a couple of my boys that are the same way. But out of all the soaps we make, the soap that she likes the best is the lye soap that's made with the lard. I mean, we make fancy soaps out of olive oil and coconut oil. We

PLATE 68 Jon Blackstock prepares the lard for rendering.

PLATE 69 Briar chops poplar for the fire.

put the palm oil in it that makes it last long. It's a good recipe. I like the soap. A lot of people like the soap, and a lot of people look at this and go, "Ew, that's fat. I'm not going to bathe with fat on my skin." But it's just real moisturizin'.

The way to make it a more cleaning soap is you add more lye to it. Miss Jenny can give you all the chemical analysis; I'm not that smart, but

PLATE 70 Chunks of fat in the big black pot

when you add more lye to it, it cuts the super fat down. Where lard has got a lot of super fat in it that makes it more moisturizin' for your skin. That's the difference in our cleanin' and laundry soaps and our bathin' soaps. You want it to have a little more oil in it to where it moisturizes your skin. You have to add more lye to it just to make it soap, so they tend to be more drying to your skin. I guess the best soap that we ever made was made out of bear fat.

If y'all notice, I'm cutting this hog fat up in just small chunks. We'll put them in that pot, and basically, you're cooking the oil out of it. You'll notice when we start that it's kind of like frying bacon, but the more oil that gets in the pot, the quicker it fries out and the quicker the process goes. I brought that commercial lard down. Normally, if we got some rendered in a bucket, I'll add some grease to the pot to get started, and it makes the process go quicker. I don't want to mix that because it has other chemicals in it. This will be a better product, and typically, people in their right mind would never make soap or render fat on a day like today or in this time of the year. It would be done in October or November when it's cooler and you didn't have to contend with the flies.

Basically, they would keep the solid pieces. Once these fry out, you will have little crunchy things we call cracklin's. They would put it in cornbread. They would save them, and it gave your food flavor. We'll keep them in the freezer and put them in with beans. You didn't really want to waste good stuff like this.

I don't know if we told y'all, but they put like BHT or BHA, which is

PLATE 71 Cracklin's in the pot

like preservatives, in that store-bought lard, and them chemicals being extra in the lard, it takes longer to trace. When you use lard that you render yourself, it is just a better product. What she is doing over there is the old method of making soap. When you put it all in, it is liquid. Once it starts to react, the lye and the oil together, it starts to thicken up. I like to get it close to a cake batter [consistency]. You know, hold the spatula up and you can see as it lands where you have stirred. It traces the thicker it gets, and the better the trace, the harder the soap is once you pull it out.

Making soap is kind a' like when you are making a pound cake. It is not that the eggs turn to cake, or the sugar turns to cake. It is like all those ingredients together turn to cake—your flour, and your milk, and your sugar. That is the same way it is with soap. When you are stirring it, when it starts to get thicker, like a pudding or like cake batter, and you can see where you have stirred, it is no longer grease and lye. It has turned to soap and glycerin. Soap making is a recipe.

Jenny: We save the old bedsheets, and that's what we run our fat through to catch any of the little cracklin' pieces. Because we don't want any kind of trash in the soap and we want it to be just as clean as it can be, we line the catch bucket with an old pillowcase, and then we throw the

PLATE 72 A sheet used as a strainer

old colander on top of it. The colander catches the big fat, and then the pillowcase will catch any of the smaller trash, and we will come out with a prettier lard.

T. J.: Yeah, that's one thing: If you don't strain all of the cracklin's off the fat, in about a week, the fat will go rancid—it will ruin. If you pour it through there and you get all of the scraps out, it'll last all year. When we do the Miss Jenny's Old Fashion Lye Soap, we make it with the freshly rendered fat. Freshly rendered fat—when you get that freshly rendered lard—it makes a much better soap than it does with store-bought stuff because the store-bought stuff has different preservatives in it. Your homemade rendered stuff makes a far superior soap. It's a lot whiter, and it's a lot prettier. I'm a little picky.

When you're renderin', you want something like pine or that poplar that puts off a lot of heat real quick when you build that fire. If it gets too hot on the pot, you can pull it out, so you don't burn up your grease. Usually, wood like oak takes a long time, and it will hold a coal once it gets going. It's hard to get the temperature up there to frying real good, but you know, the truth is that we use whatever's in the woodpile at the time. We hewed our logs out for our cabin up here, and this was just pieces that was just left over. Normally, I don't get poplar up for burning in the wintertime, and I won't go to the trouble of splitting pine. A lot of times, if I got maple or something in, I'll use it rather than grabbin' oak, but it just so happens that we have a lot of poplar right now.

Y'all can see now that we got that oil in [the pot]. She'll start cookin' down quick now. You put a plate on there, and it has a handle. To get all of the lard out you could, they would press that out. That is what we use as a press.

You take those two paddles and put them together and squeeze those to get all of the grease you could out of it because it was a one-shot deal. It wasn't like you could just kill a pig anytime. It wasn't like goin' to the grocery store and buyin' more lard. You tried to get everything you could out of it. We went and talked to a fellow the other day. Well, Miss Jenny called him and asked him if he had any lard and he said, "Sure." He wanted to sell it for like $1.40 a pound.

Jenny: It was $1.99 at first. I said, "Are you kidding?"

T. J.: I said, "At that price, I can buy Boston butts for that a pound."

PLATE 73 A paddle for squeezing, to use every little bit

Jenny: Yeah, I can buy rendered-out fat.

T. J.: That is what Miss Jenny told him, said, "We give a dollar a pound for stuff that is already rendered out." I went down there and talked to him, and he actually come down to about thirty-five cents a pound.

Y'all can see the difference between the first batch we put in and how long it took to get it going, to the second batch, and now that third batch of cracklin's is coming off. The more oil you get in there and the hotter it gets going, the faster the process is.

Jenny: For my regular soap, we made 24,850 bars a year of just the regular soap. Now, the lye soap, just the lard-based lye soap last year, we made eleven batches. Each batch, we get about 180 bars.

T. J.: A lot of people like the lavender soap. In our scented soaps, we use all essential oils that have been distilled from the plant, whereas a lot of people who make homemade soaps will still use fragrant oils, which are chemically made. Miss Jenny can't use those. We actually put about twice the amount of essential oils as a lot of people put in their soaps, so the lavender is really good. People are just real big into lavender. We sell a lot of the peppermint rosemary shampoo bar and the pet soap.

Jenny's Castile blend that she puts the essential oils in is her own recipe. She made it because you can look around here and tell that we are not financially wealthy—we really could not afford five dollars for a bar of soap. When people advertised that it was homemade, just because it is homemade doesn't mean that there are not things in it that you shouldn't be bathing with, so that was her thing. She wanted a bar of soap, if she was gonna sell it, that would last a long time. Most of our bars of soap will last about a month, bathing on a regular basis. If you are going to charge that much, you want it to last, and she wanted it to be where she could bathe with it. It don't always work out like that. The different characteristics in oils make different consistencies—like if you use soybean oil, it makes a real hard, brittle soap that don't bubble really well. Coconut oil and palm oil make the great big bubbles. There for a long time, your commercial soaps were about eighty percent beef fat or tallow and about twenty percent palm or coconut oil. With your tallow, you get a lot of little bitty bubbles, but with the coconut and palm oil, you get the bigger bubbles. Each oil and any kind of animal fat or vegetable oil you use, you can mix with lye and make soap. You just have to experiment.

As long as you have the measurements right and you go by that recipe, it works good. If you get too much lye, too much lye is what is really gonna mess you up. Now, if you get too much oil, you know, it is just not going to trace hard. A lot of times, if you have too much lye, it will trace out really hard, but you've got that lye in there, and it will burn your skin.

Jenny: If you label the bug repellant and the pet soap on the exact same bar, people will not buy it, so we have to do a bug label and a pet soap label. Miss Paulette [Carpenter] asked us to do a special label for Foxfire that has them put together on one label. It is the same soap, but people are paranoid to use a pet soap. Actually, the pet soap we make is more gentle for your skin than soap you buy at the stores.

T. J.: It has lavender, peppermint, lemongrass, and citronella. All four of those herbs repel bugs, fleas, and ticks. That is why it makes such a great bug repellant bar. What I do if I use it as a bug repellant—you know, if I am sweaty, I'll just take the bar and rub it on my arms and legs. If I am not sweaty, I will wet it just enough. Now, I don't find that it works

PLATE 74 The mold is prepared as more fat is cut to be rendered.

so much as a bug repellant if you bathe with it because you are washing most of those essential oils off. It works better if you put it on there and leave it.

At this point, the Stevens family and our crew have been cutting lard into chunks, stirring the lye and lard for soap, and separating the cracklin's for about two hours. Suddenly a thunderhead comes up, and we all help move the ingredients and the utensils into the house. T. J. covers the hot oil in the pot as he recalls a day that Jenny brought an oil fire under control.

T. J.: One time, we were rendering out there up at our other fire pit, and I got the pot too hot. It was full; the whole pot was all full up. It caught fire, and the only thing I knew to do was to throw a piece of plywood over it to kind a' try to smother it. The flames was just shooting out from under the plywood and burning the plywood. My wife disappears! I say, "Where did she go? I got twenty-five gallons of hot oil here." Here she comes running, and she had two blocks of frozen fat. I think, "What are you doing, woman?" She had got them two blocks out of the freezer and throwed them in there. I am like, "You are crazy!" She threwed them blocks in there, and that fire cut off just like that! It brought the temperature down. I don't know how she knew to do it, but it was the smartest thing I saw that day!

From inside the house, we hear a gentle rainfall. Drops tap on a tin bucket just outside the door, and an occasional roll of thunder echoes along the surrounding mountain range. The house smells like "home"; it smells like the Foxfire Museum Gift Shop, where Jenny's Soaps are sold. In the Stevens home, the natural ingredients in the soap come together as if every fresh scent from the fields had come in out of the rain with us. The scent is not overwhelming; it's fresh, natural, and restful like the rain.

Jenny: I hope he got the lid on that. I am sorry that we got washed out. When that rain hits a full pot of oil like that, it can be very dangerous, so we were very fortunate. Would you all like to see how we make modern soap?

PLATE 75 The fat is placed carefully in the pot to avoid splatter.

We make soap on a rotation schedule. We set up for soap making in January, and we make a run of twenty-four batches, which is about . . . I want to say is about . . . six thousand bars of soap. We will go to Florida and sell. Then, we come back home and set up to do it again. We do it about five times a year. Last year, we made 124 batches of scented bar soaps and 11 batches of lye soap. It is a different market. It is hard because most people prefer, you know, the philosophy, "no smell, no sell." It is a little bit harder to sell soap that does not have a strong smell, but since we started telling people what it is good for and all the different things that people use it for, I can sell it like crazy now, just basically standing there talking to people about it. Then, we have people call back and order quite a few. Lye soap has been our biggest seller this spring, so I think a lot has changed, the mentality of people. People are looking backwards for more natural alternatives, as opposed to the modern world.

Jenny Stevens takes us into the soap room, where the molds of soap are cut into bars. Once they are cut, the bars are stored on several racks, which stand just to the left of the door when we enter the room. The counter directly opposite the door serves as a table for filling and pro-cessing customers' orders. The room is small considering all the work that is done there, but it is organized so that no space is wasted.

PLATE 76 "Welcome to my soap room."

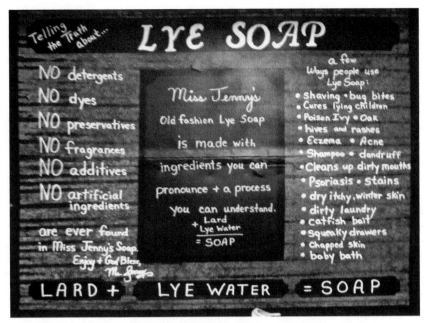

PLATE 77 The sign in the soap room

Welcome to my soap room. This is where all the soap is made, cured, and shipped from. This rack holds about three thousand bars, and then this rack here holds about two thousand bars. We put a dehumidifier in here, and that is why it is warm in here. We run the fans and the dehumidifier so that the soap dries out. One of my biggest concerns is that the soap is dry and cured when a customer gets it so that it lasts longer. A lot of people say that my method is bad for business, but I am all about repeat business and good business, instead of a product that is just going to wash down the drain.

We wrap our soap with a band around it like this. We will put a band around it, and that way the soap is breathable at all times. It can always get air.

This table here is where we do all the wrapping. All of these are soap orders that we need to fill today, but we had something important to do today, so . . . We do the soap orders as they come in. About eight times a year, we make soap. These are the pots that we actually stir the soap out in. This pot makes all of our soap. We weigh out everything in it and get it ready, and we put it down here. We drop the drill down right here, and the piece of plywood holds it as it stirs. It stirs it all in about two hours. Once it stirs it out, these are our molds. We will take and paper-line it, then we will slide them back in here.

PLATE 78 The table where orders are processed

PLATE 79 Soap cures in the drying racks.

We have eight molds, and that is what we do every time. We will do that three different days, so in about ten days, we can make all the soap we need to fill up the racks, until I can get more racks and more square footage. I have outgrown my space.

Once the soap is cut up like this, we will flip this upside down, and it comes out in a great big old block of soap. It weighs about ninety-five pounds. We will set it up in there and put the base on it. Then, you put your block of soap on there and just slide it down. Then, it slices it into big logs for you. This is the one cutter that cuts every bar of soap we make. Now, if you were high-tech and not hillbilly, you would have another cutter head that would cut like twelve at a time. There is never that extra two hundred dollars to invest in that. It is needs versus wants. It is never a big enough need.

So, there is my soap mold. When everything is not in use, it just is stored for a different purpose. This room back here is where we store all the dry soap. The soap has to sit for thirty days, and once the thirty days is up, we will start wrapping it. Here are our labels. We do the cutting,

PLATE 80 Explaining the soap cutter

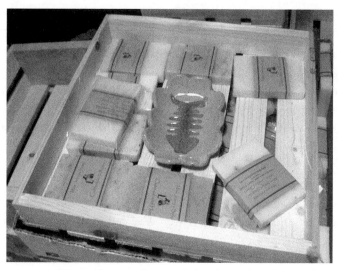

PLATE 81 Wrapped soap and a soap dish to be packaged as a gift set

the wrapping, and the packaging—all of the soap that we send out, for all these orders that you see. We will take the kraft paper and some twine like this and create a little package so that, for everyone getting soap, it looks like a gift. It is the coolest thing. You send them a gift and tell them, "Thank you!" I always write a handwritten note with every order.

I take the order and find the soap I need. We just wrap the soap. All of our shipping boxes are right here. When you write your customer a note, what I always like to do is write, "Dear Shannon, Thank you so much for your order. Enjoy and God bless. Miss Jenny." Then, I am going to take this and fold it like a little package.

PLATE 82 A handwritten note to a customer

Now, behind you on the shelf there, I have some little brochures that are on kraft paper. I fold it and check that "Miss Jenny" is showing with the little flower. I will stick it right there. Then, I write "Thank you" on the package. That is how all of my soap goes out. We put it in the shipping box. We have the shipping label, and I can do all of this from home. This is the beautiful part that is such a blessing. I can print the orders, I can do the website, and I do all the shipping and never have to leave the house. It is really wonderful for an introvert to be able to do that. Sometimes, God doesn't think I need to be a hermit, though, so I get pushed out of my comfort zone.

Then, once I get all my orders filled, and I put the tracking information together, I have a box right up here on top of a shelf that has gift paper and a bow on it. That is my thank-you to God: thank you for letting me have this soap order. And I always put them right there. I keep them for the year, and then, that way, because they are in a little gift package, it is like my gift. My gift box has a word written on it. It is a Greek word, *Eucharisteo*, and it basically means grace, thanksgiving, and joy, kind of all wrapped together. Basically, it means give thanks. Thanksgiving always precedes the miracle, so if you give thanks, thank God ahead of time for what is going to happen. That was my purpose of making the box.

We then apply our postage. There is a tape dispenser behind you. All-righty, Miss Shannon's order is ready to go. She will have her soap in two

PLATE 83 Every item is shipped personally.

days. That is it. I go down to the mailbox, which is one-half mile away, and put it in there. We put a real big mailbox down there.

Now, the soap you see sitting right here with the little burlap bags are for a wedding that we are doing for a lady. I sent her one hundred of them, and she promptly e-mailed me back and said, "I need some more." These are what we have to finish up today, too. These are for the wedding. We label the soap and put the label on it. Then, we put it in the sack and put the little burlap bag on it.

All of our soaps go out with a Bible verse on them. We always put our slogan on each order: "Wash . . . and be clean." We also put "Create in me a clean heart: O God," which comes from Psalms 51:10. That is the Bible verse that goes with all our soap. That is always on our website. Miss Jenny's soap can clean your body, but only God can clean your heart. I do my labels on the computer. All that is done through Word, and when you're financially challenged—we will put it that way—you get very creative in how to make the business profitable. We never have any waste with our soap now. When we cut it up, we get exactly 180 bars. There is enough scrap that we roll the rest of the soap, and that is what you see in the soap room, all those balls.

Off of every batch, we get about seven to eight balls of soap. They are exactly one-half a pound. We sell them for the same price as we do our regular soap. That strategy pays for all of our marketing, any kind of paper printing, or anything like that, so it keeps it from going in the trash. Of course, we didn't put it in the trash. We would use it for laundry soap or different things like that. Anything you can do to keep your busi-

PLATE 84 Balls of soap

ness more financially savvy would be much better. I learn the hard way. I do everything backwards.

I would say God's role in my business is probably one hundred percent. I think, basically, my purpose with the soap is to always put the Bible verse on there. You know, "Wash . . . and be clean" is something I struggled with most of my life. Until I realized that it was actually God who cleans your heart, all the detoxing and herbs in the world was not going to fix my inner problems. Now, the soap that we give away, and even the soap that we sell, always has that message on it. It is not just about us paying our bills; it is just spreading the message that God is love, and God does love us. I really think that plays a huge part in our business.

I think that the first prayer we prayed was for lard, and God answered that one hundredfold. I prayed for a five-gallon bucket, and the next day, a lady called and said, "I have two fifty-five-gallon drums of lard. Would you like it? I need to get it out of here right now." She brought it over that very day. We made all that soap, and we sent it to Zimbabwe with our mission group. I feel like God answered that prayer. God has answered prayer after prayer through our soap business. It is really humbling to me. It is like, why would God choose to use a bar of soap to pay our bills? I mean, it is really humbling.

Ten percent of all the soap we make, we take and make a special soap. It is called the soap of beauty, and that is this one sitting right here. It is my special soap. I label it a little bit different. We cut it just a little bit different, but it is a combination of our two best sellers: one is oatmeal and honey, and the other one is lavender. I send it out to missions all over the place. That is our soap that we give. My favorite part of making soap is to be able to give soap. T. J., he scratches his head sometimes, but that is my favorite part of our business, to be able to give it away.

It is basically my gift back to God. What gave me the idea is a verse in the Bible from Malachi 3:10: "Bring ye all the tithes into the storehouse, that there may be meat in mine house, and prove me now herewith, saith the Lord of hosts, if I will not open you the windows of Heaven, and pour you out a blessing, that there shall not be room enough to receive it." God will bless the rest of your effort. I got to thinking about that, and I thought, you know, "I would really like for my business to be blessed. I'd really like the soap to be blessed." So, when we dedicated that part of our giving back to God, it seems like our business has grown in leaps and bounds. We have to give God the credit for that. He works in spite of us.

When I was diagnosed with a brain tumor, Andrew and Jon Tom, my oldest two boys, knew how to run the business—every part of the business. They knew how to do everything. Because we didn't know what my tumor diagnosis would be, we didn't know how affected I would be by it. They can tell you that I am very affected! [Laughs.] So, they knew how to run all of it. Now, all the boys will help if, like, I am in a pickle. They can help me cut it. Jon Tom is my back! He will come in and pick my really heavy stuff up. He will cut the big bars for me. Moses, Briar, and I do all of the little-bar cutting now. All the day-to-day stuff, I can do. The rendering, we all do that. The boys, even the older two, will help when we get in a pickle.

After my brain tumor, or when I was diagnosed with a tumor, we thought we would quit. Somebody come forward and said, "No! We don't want you to quit! We are gonna give you all the money you need to where you can make the rest of the soap for this year." I said, "Okay!" So, we didn't quit. It was kind a' just real slow the two years afterwards. The boys kept it going, and T. J. kept it going. It was kind of funny. God just keeps opening doors, and the business just keeps growing.

T. J.: When Jenny had her brain tumor, we wasn't doin' as many shows and that position came open at Rainey Mountain Boy Scout Camp, and I was gonna to go to it just for the summer to have something to do. Well, she said, "You're not leaving me at home," so the whole family went over and worked on it for those two years. Rainey Mountain, the camp over in Clayton, they had a camp full of log cabins, and we run programs a couple of summers where the kids would come do blacksmithing and woodworkin', or tanning a hide to make a pair of moccasins, or make like a basket backpack. It was everything I could do to get the hides— from Monday to Friday—to get them moccasins done for the boys. I had another big boy that I'd taught how to scrape and do it all. I guess we did most of the scrapin' for 'em. By the time they left our area on Friday, they all had 'em a pair of moccasins.

Once our business started coming back real good—I mean we started picking our shows back up—the camp was taking away from the business here in the summer. We'd start up and have a lot of shows from August through the fall, and we just wouldn't have enough soap made to be able to sell.

In August, we will go out to Wilson County, Tennessee, about thirty miles east of Nashville. There is a nine-day fair there. They have like a little old-timey area there, like the mountain fair. Have you ever been to the Hiawassee Mountain Fair? We like to do historical, museum-type things. That is how we got started: by going and demonstrating. We do work craft shows. I will be at the North Georgia Folk Pottery Museum in Sautee-Nacoochee, Georgia, Labor Day weekend on the Saturday. Then, we go down to Stone Mountain and do the Yellow Daisy craft show. We just do our soap there. It is a four-day show. It starts the first Thursday after Labor Day. It is always that first week in September. We do Foxfire's Mountaineer Festival in October, and we also do their Living History Days in April or May.

We do another big fair in February. Down in Florida, they have a big state fair, down in Tampa, Florida. It is twelve days. They have an area, kind of like Foxfire, where they have moved in buildings and all from all around Florida, and I think they have twenty-four or twenty-five different buildings. They call it Cracker Country because that is what they called all the old-timers from South Georgia and Florida. They were cow hunters; they didn't call them cowboys. They were cow hunters 'cause of the cows that the Spanish had let go wild down there. They'd go in, and they'd have cow whips. They would crack them whips and get them moving out of them live oak hamlets.

Jenny Stevens explains that we had to stop supplying one vendor because the salesman actually wanted soap that would waste away quicker.

Jenny: We lost a really big wholesale contact in Tarpon Springs, Florida. This gentleman come to the fair, and he wanted me to teach him how to make soap. I was like, "Sure, I will teach you how to make soap." So, I taught him everything I knew. He came back and he said, "My soap just isn't like your soap. I just can't make good soap." I said, "You just can't rush it. Take your time." He said, "How about when the fair is over, I buy all of your soap?" I said, "Great! That works for me!" So, he bought everything we had, and he stocked his store over in Tarpon Springs. Well, he called me back a couple of months later and he said, "I need you to do something for me—change your recipe. I need you to make the soap wash away faster." He said, "The people buy the soap and love it, but they are not coming back to buy soap, so we need it to wash away quicker." I told him, "I can't do that!" He said, "I really want you to do that!" So, we quit selling to him. Then, I had a lady call me, and she said, "Your soap down at Tarpon Springs is just not the same anymore. Your lemongrass, it just washes away. What is the deal with your soap?" I said, "We don't sell our soap there anymore." She said, "What do you mean? Your labels are still there." So, we had to go to Tarpon Springs and pull our labels. The soap recipe does make a difference.

Now, when we go to shows and stuff, all the guys will go with us; Andrew does not go so much anymore because he has got a full-time job now. Jon will go and help us. Briar and Moses are always right there. Now, Moses got tired of talking about soap; all the boys did. They would each get tired of the whole process sometimes, so each one of them developed their own interests, which became a love for something else. Andrew's was woodworking.

All these wooden bowls up here, he made them from different trees that had fallen down. He made all the wooden spoons we have in the house. That is his passion. He had rather do that because he didn't have to talk about soap making. He enjoys making wooden bowls and spoons. He had rather not have to sell them. He had rather it just be a hobby and a passion, something he enjoys.

It is one hundred percent hand tools. He will take and cut the dead tree down, and he will split it out. He will take adze and chisels and all his saws and stuff and do it. He started carving when he was seven. He is twenty now. He made those probably three or four years ago. They smell like my soap room now. He gave one to this lady, and she said, "I love the bowl. It smells just like you!" He does some really pretty work.

Now, Jon Tom, he could sell God air! That is what a lot of people have said! He is a salesman, and that was always what Jon does when he goes to a show; that is his job. Briar would always find a fishing pole, and he will be at the nearest creek or pond. He doesn't care so much for people or demonstrations, but he is very helpful. Moses wanted to do the soap dishes. He started making the soap dishes. He wanted to be a potter like his daddy, so that is where the soap dishes came in.

This is our office. That is where all our business is handled. Around the corner is my cubicle. It is a blessing that I get to stay home and tend

PLATE 85 Wooden bowls on the shelf

PLATE 86 Soap dishes

PLATE 87 *Eucharisteo*: give thanks

to my own. That is a blessing. My website is www.missjennyssoap.com. We have been very blessed, you know. They asked me earlier, is it cost-effective to run a soap business? I can't complain. All of our needs have been met. We don't live in a fancy house, but all of our needs are met. All of our wants are not met, but you choose to invest in what you feel is important. My kids are homeschooled. God gave me a way to stay home with my kids. I don't know how it works all the time, but it works!

The Greek word Eucharisteo *appears written above the window near the Stevenses' table, and the definition—"give thanks"—appears beside the window. Jenny and T. J. Stevens appreciate time with their children, the strength they gain from working together, and the natural gifts from God. Resourceful artists who see everything around them as a gift will likely waste none of that gift.*

MISS JENNY'S METHOD FOR MAKING SOAP

Compiled by Daniel Jackson

INGREDIENTS
0.52 pounds of lye (8.32 ounces)
1.5 pounds (24 ounces) of water
2 quarts of oil
4 pounds of lard, sliced into small, 1-inch-square chunks

Render the lard by dropping the sliced lard into a cauldron over an open flame. (A hotter-burning wood such as pine or poplar is preferable to speed up the rendering process, but any logs will do.) Separate the solid pieces (i.e., the cracklin's) from the oil. These can be mixed into recipes such as cornbread or beans and eaten.

Alternative Lye

The lye that was used during the interview was purchased at a chemical supply store—NaOH solution shocked from salt using modern electrolysis—but Miss Jenny explained how to make lye from wood ashes. This more traditional method pulls the natural hardwood salts from the ashes.

Burn hardwood logs (oak, hickory, etc.) until all coals have turned to ash. Place 10 cups of ashes into a clean straining cloth. (Miss Jenny prefers an old pillowcase.) Tie the cloth so that it resembles a large tea bag, and place into a three-gallon or larger bucket. Pour 2 gallons of boiling water over the bag and allow to steep overnight. When removing the bag, allow the liquid to drip back into the bucket and settle. Cook down the two gallons of strained lye solution until 1.5 cups of lye remain.

Mixing the Ingredients

Pour the lye into the water and stir. Do not let the lye touch your skin, and do not inhale the fumes. Assure that any container/utensil that lye comes in contact with is properly cleaned or set safely aside to avoid accidents. Miss Jenny uses a piece of trim as a stirring stick, since lye will eat away at any wooden utensil.

Prepare a low fire, being careful not to overheat the reaction that takes place as you combine the ingredients.

From the 1.5 cups of rendered lye, mix 1 tablespoon at a time with 1 cup of grease.

Important note for both methods: Too much lye will produce a more cleansing soap, but will not be as gentle on the skin as a soap mixture containing more grease. Similarly, too much grease will make the skin oily and not provide as much of a cleaning effect.

The alternative lye rendered from wood ashes mixes in a slightly different ratio. Indication that the ratio of lye to grease is correct will come from the consistency and trace of the mixture as it is stirred.

Setting the Mold and Finishing the Soap

After the proper consistency is achieved, the soap is ready to be poured into a mold. A wooden box lined with wax paper makes an easy and affordable mold.

The mold, ideally, should form a large enough block so the blocks can be cut. Miss Jenny has a frame to cut several bars at a time, but a cheese cutter will also work.

Miss Jenny recommends letting your soap sit for at least two weeks before use.

HOW TO MAKE ROPE THE OLD-TIMEY WAY

Kermit Rood teaches students to make old-fashioned rope

Rope does come in handy! —Kermit Rood

If you want to "sleep tight" in the Appalachian Mountains, you're going to need a rope. In the late 1800s, rope served several purposes around the Appalachian homeplace, and one of those purposes was to raise straw mattresses off the ground. This improvement made sleeping more comfortable and helped keep the sleeping mountaineer from some crawling bedbugs. The rope would run through holes in a wooden frame, and since the rope would stretch over time, a wooden key was used to tighten the ropes, allowing the mountaineer to sleep tight, aka to sleep well on a tightened bed (see *The Foxfire Book*, pages 139–41).

For many reasons, early mountaineers couldn't go down to the hardware store and buy rope. Rope had to be made, and it had to be altered to fit whatever household purpose it would serve. In this interview, Foxfire contact Kermit Rood shares his knowledge of making rope using a rope maker. This small wooden machine, along with Aunt Arie Carpenter's rope bed, can still be seen at the Foxfire Museum. As Kermit Rood tells us in the interview, "Rope does come in handy!" Rope certainly did come in handy enough to make it an important part of the Foxfire heritage.

—*Jonathan Blackstock*

PLATE 88 A smiling Kermit Rood, showing his humorous personality

'm Kermit Rood. I was about eight or nine years old when I first learned how to make rope. I helped my dad make a rope that was almost fifty feet long. For me, it took forever because I was hanging on for dear life.

I moved up here to Georgia from Florida. . . . When I started volunteering for Foxfire, they had this rope machine and didn't know what it was, so I explained it to them. I named the things that went with the machine: the stand, the twirler, and the separator. I showed them how to work it.

Rope was made mostly from hemp. It must have been in the early 1900s, making rope with hemp. That was a long time ago for you guys.

Making rope doesn't take very long at all. We make just little pieces of rope here for just about everybody. One time, we had a little girl here about your size, just inchin' up her britches, and she said, "Can you make one about this long?" [Mr. Rood holds out his hands to show how long the rope was.] She had forgot her belt, so she strung it on, and she had a belt for the rest of the day. Rope does come in handy!

Steps in the Rope-Making Process

Like most people, I never thought about where rope came from or how it was made. It is string—basically just these short pieces, but rope is twisted the opposite direction, so it stays together and doesn't unwind.

The rope-making machine up here at Foxfire requires three people: one to hold the single-hooked looper and the second to work the separator towards the crank as the rope is twisted. This ensures a tight twist,

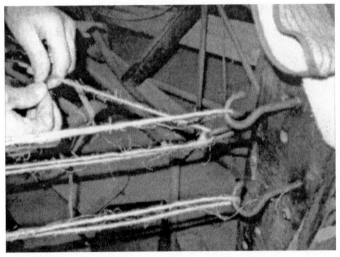

PLATE 89 Looping the rope strand on the second hook of the crank mechanism

PLATE 90 The separator is used as someone on the other side turns the crank.

PLATE 91 The finished rope takes shape.

and the third person cranks the handle that turns the gears on the three whirl hooks.

As the hand on the crank turns, it makes the separated pieces of marline [twisted strands] entwine together. The person holding the single-hooked looper pulls the strands tight while the rope is twisting. The person using the separator then follows the rope as it twists together, making sure it twists uniformly and tight.

THE POINT OF LIFE!

Joe Williams tells of his experience making bark berry buckets

There are a lot of talented people out there that know how to do a lot of things, but if they don't teach someone else, what good is it? There is so much that we can do for other people. —Joe Williams

In *Foxfire 4*, Jason Townsend tells us how his parents used bark berry buckets to pick berries on the side of Grandfather Mountain. When Jason gathered bark, he went by the phases of the moon. He did it when the sap was up, usually about the first of June through the new moon in August, and used hickory bark for the laces. If the bark became too hard to peel, he waited till the new moon when the bark again loosened. Jason said there was a big tourist demand for the buckets and he even used hickory bark for the bail, or strap, because tourists liked the look of it. He told us that mountain people used to use cloth so it wouldn't cut into their shoulders.

Mr. Joe Williams often exhibits at Foxfire events and has taught a new generation how to make the buckets. His method is somewhat different from Jason Townsend's. Mr. Townsend used only the bark of the tree, while Mr. Williams uses every part of the tree—not just to make the bucket, but also to make carvings and for firewood. Mr. Townsend used a sharp stick to peel the bark off, while Mr. Williams created a tool in his blacksmith shop to make the bark peeling easier. Joe explains to us how to make a bark berry bucket, talks about the key points in completing the bucket, and shares the tradition of bucket making and how it is passed down from generation to generation.

—*Brittany Houck*

I grew up on a farm out in the country, doing a lot of the same stuff that goes on here at Foxfire. This is like coming home to me; I feel at home here. From the first day I came here way back in the 1980s, it felt like home. It really did, and it has never changed. The people here are wonderful. Paulette Carpenter is just super. Ann Moore and Barry Stiles, I mean, I love them all to death. I have met a lot of students. Everybody associated with this program are just wonderful people. The place is just super, and I love it here.

My maternal grandfather, Harvey Moore, lived to be ninety years old. He lived just out the road from where I grew up. My paternal grandmother was Bertha Williams. She grew up and lived most of her life in Old Fort, North Carolina, as did my grandfather. My families have been in Old Fort forever. They both taught me how to make these buckets, and I guess that is why it kind a' stuck. Learning how to do different skills is one thing that both my grandparents took time to explain and work with me. My grandfather taught me a lot of stuff and my grandmother did also. Learning how to make bark berry buckets is the one thing that I got from both sides of the family. Both of my grandparents talked about those things and showed me how to do them and whatnot.

When my grandparents would make bark berry buckets years ago, they would leave the tree standing, take some bark off to make a bucket, and go on about their business. Today, I cut down the tree, and I use all the bark. I use everything I can to make small carvings and different kinds of crafts. I carve some animals, and I call them God's Critters. It is my own type of carving developed from an early American style that I do, and it is a lot of fun. The rest of the wood we use for firewood. I really don't waste anything, but again, trees are a renewable resource. It isn't something that people are putting on the endangered species list by any means. Poplar trees are very plentiful. Poplar trees are probably the fastest-growing, most disease-resistant tree we have in the Eastern US anymore, so poplar trees are a great resource to use. They can be replaced quickly.

The hardest part about making a bucket is scoring the bottom. You can't cut too deeply, or it will cut all the way through. You can cut about one-third of the thickness, and then you fold it up, lace it up, and put a handle on it. When you lace it, you can lace it any way you want to.

The buckets are made from one piece of bark. You determine how big you want your bucket to be. If you want a bucket that is a foot tall, you have to have a piece of bark that is two feet long because you fold it in half. So, you cut around the tree's top and bottom, split it down one side, and take the bark off the tree in one big sheet. Then, you flatten it

PLATE 92 Joe Williams teaches the art of making bark berry buckets.

PLATE 93 Demonstrating how to lace a bark berry bucket

out and measure to the center point on each edge of the bark. After that, you score it with a knife by cutting down one-third of the thickness on the bark. The best way to score it is in a cat's eye or in an oval shape. As I mentioned earlier, the hardest thing about making a bucket is scoring the bottom because if you cut all the way through it, you have two pieces of bark rather than a bucket. Once you get it scored correctly, you can kind a' hold it with your fingers, take your thumbs, and push the bark away. When you do that and kind a' flip it back and forth—both sides at the same time—your bottom will cup up. To help fold it, you can actually push up on the bottom a little bit, and it folds pretty easy. The thicker the bark, the harder it is to work with. It is not as difficult to use thin bark as it is to use an older tree. As the tree gets older, the bark gets thicker. It gets more of the striations throughout, and it is just more difficult to work with.

After the bucket is folded up, I drill holes with a keen-pointed knife. The holes are evenly spaced up both edges. I make six holes on each edge of the bark across from each other. Both sides of the bucket are done this way. Holes are then drilled around the top of the bucket, about one inch apart. The bucket is now ready to be laced up and the handle attached. I lace up my big buckets with strips of hickory bark. Hickory bark is very strong and works up easy; it's the best lacing you can use. I make my handle from hickory wood. The wood is split and thinned on the shaving horse. For a working bucket, hickory is not the most comfortable handle, but people seem to like them.

When I first started making buckets, I used my hands to pull the bark off. Your fingers get really sore after a while, so I looked around for something to help me get the bark off. I never could find anything that worked, so I actually made one in my blacksmith shop. It's just a piece of metal that is bent around at a sloping thirty-degree angle, with a wooden handle on it. I cut the bark down one side, take that tool and slip it down under the bark, and it helps peel it off. It keeps my fingers from getting so sore. It works really well. I like using it, especially if I am going to be making a lot of them. It's easier than trying to work with sore fingers the whole time.

The thing about the buckets is that you can lace them just about any way you want to. You are going from the outside to the inside and from the inside back to the outside, all the way up both sides of the bucket.

PLATE 94 Stitching on the side of the bucket

You can crisscross or you can go straight across. It is really up to you how you want to do it. You can make it look any way you want on the outside, which is the good thing about these. Any way you want it to look is the way it should look.

I made my first bucket when I was ten years old with my grandfather. He and my grandmother both taught me how to make buckets, so it comes from both sides of my family. My grandfather on my mother's side and my grandmother on my father's side of the family both used to make them. They didn't make them near as fancy as I do, but they made them to actually go out and pick berries, mostly huckleberries. Back then, they were the big thing that they used. My grandfather Williams came from Yancey County, back in the mountains of North Carolina, and they used them quite a bit up there. Every summer, when the huckleberries would get ripe, they would make them all the time. They were really useful containers back then; they wasn't just for show. They made them to carry things in.

I have been making bark berry buckets for about forty years. I am fifty-five now, so a little over forty years I have been making them. I used to try to keep up with how many I made over the years, but I lost track too many years ago to worry about it now. I stopped for a little while and started back, but overall, I have been making them that long. I have developed my own style of lacing. I kind a' do it the way I want. I put hickory handles on most of my buckets. Something unusual is that my grandfather never did that. He used a piece of bark for the handle, a piece of cloth, or a piece of string. Whatever they had handy, they would use. I just like to say I developed my own style of making them over the years. Of course, now they are mainly for decorating purposes. I sell a lot of them at craft shows and other things. I buy my leather strips at a craft supply store called Crazy Crow Trading Post, and they are precut. I have been buying them for years. It's a little bit expensive, but it's not too bad. It works perfect for making buckets for children. It's exactly the right size. I don't have to do anything to it, and it saves a lot of time.

Primarily, I use yellow poplar or tulip poplar. Those are the most plentiful around my home. You can use others like box elder, white walnut, also known as butternut. Or hickory. Hickory works pretty well. I like poplar because it is easy to get. I can plant a tree this year, and I will have a tree that I can harvest to make buckets out of in three or four years. They grow that quickly, in the right location at least.

I have been criticized for killing trees by making the things, but you know, it's our renewable resource. I plant trees every year to replace the ones that I have cut down. I would rather use a new tree that I planted rather than just finding one in the woods because I know how easy that bark is to work with. You can go out in the woods and find a tree, and you can tell by looking at them how old they are. In a really low-lying area where there is a lot of water, the bark comes off a lot easier. Up on top of a dry ridge where there isn't much water, it doesn't come off really well. I am particular about where I get my bark. I like it to come off really easy because it's easier to work with if there is a lot of moisture in it.

When I was old enough to use a knife, I would start whittling on things and making things out of sticks I would find in the yard. That is how I got started whittling and carving. I do blacksmith work. I have a blacksmith forge, and I make a lot of things. My son is really getting into the blacksmithing with me. He is a fifth-generation blacksmith. He enjoys doing it, so we work together on that quite a bit. I do woodworking and I make furniture and different things. I do the berry buckets, a lot of those. I like doing those because they are a lot of fun.

According to my grandmother, I am the sixth generation in my family that we can prove has made these buckets. If Samuel follows along, or my daughter, they will be the seventh generation. It would be a great tradition to pass on to the next family member, and I hope one of them picks it up.

You know, I just love the old ways of my life. My wife tells me that I was born in the wrong century. I think that I would agree with her; I really do. I would've been happy one hundred years ago. I really like the old ways of life. I feel more comfortable doing things that they did in the 1700s and the 1800s than I do in the twenty-first century. I have nothing against manual labor, and I have done it most of my life; I worked on a farm, worked in a sawmill, worked in the furniture industry and different things. Now I am a registered nurse by profession, and I was a paramedic for ten years. I have been a little bit of everything. I am not the biggest computer geek in the world by any means. If I have a problem with my computer, I get my daughter or son to come fix it. They are fourteen and seventeen years old, so they know a lot more about them than I do.

I just really love preserving the old ways of life and the old ways of doing things. It is something that I enjoy. It is something that I really feel I need to do. There are too many of the old ways that are just dying out. Nobody is carrying on a lot of these traditions and skills and whatnot anymore. It is just a shame not to continue those things.

I am not a big pessimist, but what is going to happen if the computer systems crash and we have to go back to doing some of the old things? A lot of people are not going to know how to do anything. A lot of people couldn't survive nowadays if they had to. If something happened to our economy and the world, they could not survive the way our ancestors did. I know I could, and I know my family could. Imagine how many families couldn't? That is one of the reasons that I like being able to carry on the old ways and some of the old skills is because I know I could make it if I had to. I wouldn't be standing there totally helpless. I could survive in any situation. I have no doubt about that. A lot of families and a lot of people don't have the ability to do that. If something drastic happened, they couldn't make it.

Like I say, I am not a doom-and-gloom-type person. I believe that we are here for a purpose. Things are going to progress, and the world is going to keep changing, hopefully for the better.

I like being able to know that I can do what I have to in order to make it. It is rewarding to me to be able to do these things and to make something with my own hands that is useful, and I can actually use to better my way of life. There is a big satisfaction in being able to do something on your own and not having to depend on other people to supply everything for you. I think that is the biggest reason that I do a lot of things that I do, like blacksmithing work and the woodcarving and making bark berry buckets. It is a personal satisfaction in knowing that I did it with my own two hands and knowing that I can continue if I had to. I don't know that I would want to totally go back to living like they did two hundred years ago; it was hard work. Those people worked eighteen to twenty hours a day, hard labor all their life. Some of the old ways are good and worth carrying on; they really are. It saddens me to see that people don't care about those things anymore, but I guess that is just my personality. There is so much history being lost when the generations grow up now. They are growing up with video games and Xboxes. Seeing these kids up here today at Foxfire at Children's Heritage Day was just wonderful. I love it! They are so happy and enjoy what they are doing. I love teaching these kids. I told some of the parents earlier, "It's not enough for me to know how to do something. If I don't teach it to the next generation, we are going to lose it." I am not saying that I am the end-all-be-all to anything, but what few skills I have are God given, certainly nothing I came up with on my own. If I don't teach the next generation how to do some of these things, then it stops with me, and that is a shame. Other people need to feel the same way. There are a lot of talented people out there that know how to do a lot of things, but if they don't teach someone else, what good is it? There is so much that we can do for other people.

I teach a Sunday school class at my church, and that is one of the primary things that we talk about in most of our Sunday school lessons—helping other people. What can we do to better serve God and better serve others? That is part of it. We have to do a lot to help others around us, especially our families. We are driven to that. That is the thing: you have to be willing to really want to help; that is the way it is supposed to be. God didn't put us out here to serve our own self-interest. He really didn't. He put us here to help other people and spread His word. That is why we are here. At least that is my point on life! Life is what you make of it. It really is! We can sit around and do nothing or we can get out and do something. I have never been one to sit around. I can't sit still. I go in the house, and I am up moving around. I can't sit and watch a TV program without getting up and moving around. I am just not the type to sit still. It can't be done, and I don't like it.

It is nice to come up here on Foxfire's mountain; it's peaceful. I sat down on the porch last night drinking a cup of coffee, and I just listened to the birds, the bugs, the wind, and the trees. It is just wonderful here. It really is.

THE "GOURD" LIFE

An interview with gourd artist Priscilla Wilson

People think, "Aren't you worried about running out of ideas?" Well, it's not like that. In fact, the longer I work with the gourds, the more ideas I get. It is almost like you can teach yourself to be more creative by doing it. The more you stretch your creativity, the better it is.
—Priscilla Wilson

For many students, gourds have a singular purpose: they are cured and hollowed out to make birdhouses for purple martins. The martins are welcome guests because they help control the insect population. The birdhouses certainly serve a practical purpose on farms where thick swarms of insects can ruin crops and infuriate people trying to work the fields. Native Americans have used this natural form of insecticide for centuries, and racks of hollowed gourds can still be seen on family farms.

In *Foxfire 3*, students interviewed Bryant McClure, who found another reason to invite the purple martins. His mother liked attract-

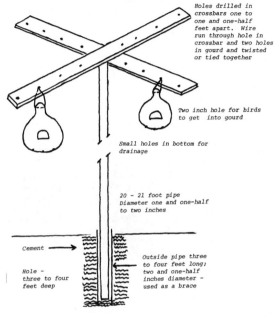

Articles needed:
One galvanized pipe - 20-21 feet long; one and one-half to
two inch diameter
One galvanized pipe - 3-4 feet long; two to two and one-half
inch diameter
Two crossarms - 2x4; seven to eight feet long.
Ten to twenty gourds
Bag of cement

Holes drilled in
crossbars one to
one and one-half
feet apart. Wire
run through hole in
crossbar and two holes
in gourd and twisted
or tied together

Two inch hole for birds
to get into gourd

Small holes in bottom for
drainage

20 - 21 foot pipe
Diameter one and one-half
to two inches

Cement

Hole -
three to four
feet deep

Outside pipe three
to four feet long;
two and one-half
inches diameter -
used as a brace

PLATE 95 Diagram from *Foxfire 3* showing how to make a gourd birdhouse

ing the purple martins because the martins would actually keep hawks
away from the chickens. McClure said, "They'll fight them. They'll fight
a crow. If a hawk comes around, these purple martins will gang up on
him. They'll chase him out of the country." The gourds provided another
way for people to utilize their natural surroundings, especially when the
gourds are grown from seed, as many contacts have done.

Still, while the practical uses for hard-shell gourds show creativity
on its own, they also provide a canvas on which people can stretch their
imagination, and students are often surprised by the uses that artists can
find for gourds. In *Foxfire 12*, for example, John Huron shares his love
for instrument making. Inspired in part by Stanley Hicks and his fretless
banjos in *Foxfire 3* (see pages 139–85), Mr. Huron makes "gourd ban-
jars," which become both the product of his creativity as a craftsman and
the source for his creativity as a musician. Handmade instruments are
an integral part of the Appalachian tradition, and gourds have remained
a large part.

Of course, birdhouses and instruments aren't the only uses for gourds.

PLATE 96 John Huron's gourd banjo

When Foxfire student Stephanie Jobbitt interviewed gourd artist Priscilla Wilson, she discovered a contact whose creativity grows as she finds innovative uses for this natural material. Stephanie said that Mrs. Wilson's gourds were unique and beautiful, a true Appalachian legacy. Her personal memories, advice, and "gourd" life make this artist special.

—*Jonathan Blackstock*

My name is Priscilla Wilson, and I am fifty years old. I graduated from Auburn University in 1972, but I did not get my degree in art or crafts or anything like that. I got it in English. I was a high school English teacher for ten years, and I quickly realized that it wasn't for me. During that time, when I was in my mid-twenties, I just was really looking for the right thing to do, and I was intrigued by the idea of having my own business when my partner, Janice Lymburner, and I had this idea—we were both friends and teachers. We were riding around the country, and she was the one that said, "You know, if we see a roadside stand, I want to stop and get a gourd." She wanted to make a planter for her mother because her whole family loves plants. So, you know, it was no big deal. She really talked me into getting a gourd and doing it, too. However, I was the one that liked it when we took them home and started cleaning them. For me, wheels started turning, and I said, "This is a whole craft that nobody has ever done." Now you see a lot of gourd art, but this was in 1974, and then it was unheard-of. We knew that people in this area traditionally had made them into birdhouses and things, but that was it. That was all that you basically saw. So, what excited me was the fact that, in my mind, this was a new craft that nobody had ever done.

I started making things the year before I quit teaching, and during that year I kept talking about gourds, told my family and friends that I was going to quit my teaching job and start a gourd business. Most people just laughed it off. They didn't think that I would really do it, but I did. It was actually 1976 when I started. I know a lot of people would not have done it, but it was what I wanted. I was young and didn't have

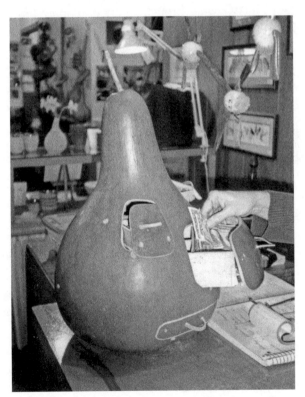

PLATE 97 Cash register made entirely from gourds

any responsibilities. It was different then. I did not start with the painting like you might imagine. Painting gourds is not something that I have ever done. When you look in the shop, you will see that even the artwork done on the gourds is not painted. It is carved.

In the beginning, I was just making really simple things, like planters. I did actually make a few lamps in the beginning, and there were problems; I wasn't happy with the way they worked out. So, I have just recently "re-perfected" them and started making more. I made little vases. They were just very simple, just things that you could put dry stuff in. There was no artwork in the beginning. It was just making simple, useful things with gourds.

In the very beginning, I bought my gourds. I looked in *The Farmers Market Bulletin* and found some ads for gourds. I also just went here and there and found some gourds at roadside stands, et cetera. I knew from the start I felt like growing the gourds should be part of the art. It was, to me, just like part of the process. I was basically a city girl. I grew up in Valdosta, Georgia. It is not a big city, but I did not grow up on a farm or anything, so I didn't know how to grow gourds. So, growing was an adventure in itself. We went through a period of about ten years where we really did a lot of gourd growing. We had our own tractor. We don't grow like we used to. We only grow a few here now, and that's just so that when people visit our shop in the summertime, they can see them. Growing was fun. Now, we've reached a point where I am more into the art than growing. If I ever had some more leisure time, I would enjoy growing the gourds again.

When I started the gourd making, I didn't have a shop. I just went to craft shows. I just did it out of my house. It was done like that for several years. I didn't open a regular retail shop until 1983, so the craft shows were fun, and you didn't have all of the overhead. I didn't have to be there from nine to five or anything like that. Two years after I started the business, Janice Lymburner also quit her teaching job and started as my partner.

I started out just doing basic things, and then I would get an idea and just go with it. It wasn't very long after I started that I wanted to decorate the gourds, even though I had not taken any art courses or anything. My mother was artistic, and I guess it came kind of naturally. I started doing wildflower designs on the gourds with a wood burner. That was fairly simple. Wildflowers are still an interest; then it just grew from there. Of course, through the years, I have done a lot of different designs, but the different concepts are kind of interesting.

PLATE 98 Gourd globe made by Priscilla Wilson

At first, they were containers that the lids came off, and I liked the idea that people could actually use them. Then I started to accumulate these weird, different-shaped gourds that didn't fit what I was doing. I would look at them and think, "What can I do with these?" So, that is how the toys came to be. There would be a gourd that was shaped like an elephant; you know, it had kind of a long body and a neck that would curve around like a trunk. So, I would make it an elephant. Now I have turtles, snails, ladybugs, whatever my gourds look like.

The designs on the gourds were wood burning in the beginning. Somewhere along the lines, I started experimenting with other ways of decorating the gourds. What I do now I call "carving." It is a high-speed drill that is similar to a dental drill. It is really a jeweler's tool. The shells of the gourds are harder than wood, so it takes forever to wood-burn a design with any detail at all. It just was not practical. What I do that really distinguishes my work from a lot of other gourd artists is that my gourds are useful. I believe that I am utilizing the artistic material in a much better way with more integrity. If you're going to paint, you might as well just get a piece of paper or a canvas. The carving actually uses the gourd to its full potential; it gives it a purpose. The gourd can be burned or carved, unlike canvas paper. Using that is something that is more important to me.

The gourd's preparation really starts as soon as the vine dies. The gourd has to go through a drying process; that takes, on the average, about four months. Some people bring them in out of their garden and hang them up to dry. This is okay if they know that the vine is dead. You don't want to pick any gourd before the vine dies because they will rot. The gourds have to mature on the vine; if they are picked early, the vine will rot. People need to know that. When we were growing big fields of gourds, it wasn't practical to bring them in, so we didn't. We would leave them right in the field and let them begin to dry there where they lay. There are always going to be some that rot. They are the ones that come on the vine late in the season. We would wait until about the end of January, and then we would have a big harvest party. About one hundred of our closest friends would help us pick them all up. We would call it a "Gourd Gathering." It was really a fun, old-fashioned thing to do.

The gourds have to be dry before you could do anything else to them,

PLATE 99 A gourd that has been cleaned

so you have to build into your work plan months of drying time. A dry gourd that is not cleaned looks to some people like it could be rotten, but if the shell is still hard, it is not rotten.

Once they are finally dry, you have to clean the gourds. This job is really just hard and tedious; it takes a lot of elbow grease. The way we do it is we get the gourds wet. It's hard to soak gourds because they float, but you can put them outside on a rainy day. That is the thing that we would suggest because the rain just soaks them all over. You just put them out there to get them wet. Now, that does not really get the mold and such off. The soaking softens the skin. Then you have to go back with a knife and heavy-duty scrubber, like you would on pots and pans— not a Brillo pad, but one made of metal—and just scrub. You can scrape a lot of the skin off with a dull knife. You do not want to use something really sharp that will scratch the gourd and mess up the surface because the gourds can scratch very easily when they're wet.

The rest of the process depends on what the gourd is going to be. If it's going to be something simple (a kitchen utensil, a bowl, a colander, a dipper, or something like that), then the next step is to open the gourd. The gourd will be left totally natural. Go ahead and draw the cut lines and just cut it open. You can use a household saw, or we use a jigsaw. Then cleaning out the inside is another fairly tedious process. Sometimes, the gourd will have the pulp all just balled up in a nice neat ball, and you do not have to do much. Other times, the pulp just lines the inside walls of the gourd, and it takes painstaking work to get it out. We have developed a special tool to get the pulp out. It is a wire brush on a flexible shaft. It's attached to a motor, which is attached to a dust collector. With it you can just sit and clean out the inside. It is just a type of wire brush, and it is a fairly common thing for gourd workers to have. They are even made to go on a regular electric drill.

If I am going to make a container that the lid comes off, then I will have a carved design and the gourd will be dyed before it is opened. We use leather dye. After that dries, it has to be varnished, and you can put a finish on the gourds. You can use pretty much anything that you can use on wood, like polyurethane. Some people who just want to do one or two for fun will spray the varnish, but we use it in a liquid form. We kind of dip and pour so we get a nice finish on the gourd.

Well, the carving is done next. The carving is also done before a gourd is opened. It doesn't have to be done that way, but it just makes sense. It is convenient because then you can make the lid fit the carving, and also, it is easier to handle all in one piece. After it is carved and I am

Inside of gourd
(each gourd also contains
hundreds of useable seed)

PLATE 100 A view of the gourd's insides

happy with the design, I will open the gourd. In this case, cleaning out the inside is the last step.

There are also different species of gourds that change the size of the gourds. You can even grow the different species of gourds in the same fields. The little ones most people call "ornamental gourds." They are the ones you see in the grocery stores in the fall. They are different colors: the greens and yellows. Most people don't know that if you grow them right and don't pick them too early, they will dry out. The ones you have to be careful about are growing dipper gourds [the gourds with long handles] with the martin gourds because they will crossbreed. The martin gourds are the ones that people use to make birdhouses.

Nobody taught me my trade. What inspired me was the fact that I was inventing something, and that, in fact, has been my encouragement in everything I have done. I am just fascinated by the idea of doing something that nobody has ever done before. Here I was, in my mid-twenties with no life experience, doing something that I had never done. I just had to figure it out. I would just go to the hardware store and sort of wander around. Back then, in the mid-seventies, it was like women were not really very welcome in hardware stores. It was not that we were shunned. It was just a strange feeling to see a woman in a hardware store. I had to be really determined to get things done because there really was not anyone there helping me along the way. My dad did help me some. I mean, he is not a woodworker by trade, but he was a typical guy when it came to power tools. He let me try his electric jigsaw at one point and just little things to help me.

I use at least two different kinds of saws when I open gourds. I use a little hobby saw or a miniature saw that is electric. These are used on the really intricate parts of the design, like wildflowers use a little saw but a bigger saw for the regular cuts. The one I use is like a regular Black and Decker jigsaw like people use in their homes. I also use this saw for cutting the holes for planters and things of that nature. I have drills also. I use regular household electric drills. I use all sorts of things that you would never imagine. There is a kind of "hole" saw that you can use to make the birdhouses that you see made out of gourds. There are things that you make that need a perfect hole to look right, like match holders or some kind of kitchen utensils. I also use files to make the edges of gourds not sharp.

You would be amazed at the number of people who work with gourds. I bet that one-third to half of the people who come in our store are gourd artists, and if they're not, they know someone who is. People always want to tell us about the people they know who work with gourds. Actually, in the museum there is a wall that has the work of other gourd artists from all over the country. Most of the things on the wall came to us; we didn't go looking for them. People would bring them or send them and ask us if we wanted to display them in our museum. Everyone who comes in thinks it is cool. It has been weird to us to see the number of people who have started to work with gourds since we started twenty-five years ago. We can't help wanting people to know that we were the ones starting this. We encourage people to do gourd work. There is actually a do-it-yourself part to our business. We actually sell the raw gourds with literature that tells how to make just about anything a beginner can imagine. There is a lot of interest in the do-it-yourself portion of the gourd business. I work every available hour either on making the gourds or on the pottery, and I never really get the opportunity to teach what I do to others.

After working with gourds for twenty-five years, I had a completely new idea that came to me out of the blue. It is a completely different way of using gourds. One thing that is also really important in my mind is the tie-in with the origin of pottery and gourds. I have always thought that

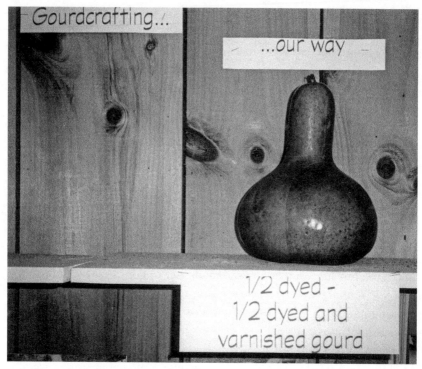

Gourdcrafting...

...our way

1/2 dyed -
1/2 dyed and
varnished gourd

PLATE 101 A half-dyed, half-varnished gourd

the way humans first figured out how to make pottery may have been related to gourds because gourds grow in dirt, and you can picture somebody a long time ago finding a gourd in a field. The gourd could have dirt in it that has hardened like we have seen clay do in the past. That really may have been the first potter's inspiration. The clay could have formed either on the inside or the outside. Conventional wisdom says that it was the basket that had been discarded, and then the same thing had happened. I think that it also could have been gourds. The pottery I make is very unique because I use the gourd as a mold for the pottery. To make the pottery, I use liquid clay to get the shape and keep the texture. As far as I know, I am the only person ever to make gourd pottery. I think that the creative process is absolutely amazing.

The whole thing is based on the fact that gourds are porous, so if you use liquid clay, what happens is the water goes through the pores. Well, I pour the gourd mold full with this liquid clay and let it sit there for a while. What happens is that some of the water soaks into the pores of the gourd. It actually helps the clay wall form in the gourd. After the clay has been sitting in the gourd, you can see the clay forming on the inside of the gourd. Then, I pour back some of the clay from the inside. What you are left with is a little clay piece, and that is wet and stuck to the gourd, so then you have to leave it for several days and let it dry completely. If you're lucky, it will dry without cracking, and you will be left with a beautiful clay piece. If it doesn't crack, the next step would be to remove the clay. If the clay is really nice and covers the whole inside of the gourd, then you will have to cut the gourd off of the clay. The gourds cannot be used after the potter is done, so instead of wasting many gourds, I actually make a plaster mold. It is the only reason that I am able to produce the numbers of dishes and things I produce. The whole concept is so awesome that I wish I could make a new mold for every piece of pottery, but it would not be practical.

I have done some very strange things with gourds. I have actually made drums before. The drums are one of the things that I do not actually consider an original idea because I think that people had made drums out of just about everything. I had never seen the drums before I made them, but after the fact, I have had some drums shipped to me from Africa. I thought it was just a neat thing to do. I like to hear the different sounds the gourds can make. The sounds are different depending on the size and shape of the gourd.

I have so many ideas. It is kind of an accepted fact that the best ideas

PLATE 102 Gourds make great drums.

come to artists and inventors when they're not trying to think of it. I don't just sit and try to think of an idea. The pottery idea come to me while I was just driving down the road, and this big picture came into my mind of how to do it. It just blows you away sometimes. I am sure there were some good ideas that I didn't even do because they seemed so weird to me. I do think that the creative process always gives you ideas. People think, "Aren't you worried about running out of ideas?" Well, it's not like that. In fact, the longer I work with the gourds, the more ideas I get. It is almost like you can teach yourself to be more creative by doing it. The more you stretch your creativity, the better it is.

There was an old man that was retired; he had a green thumb, and he would actually train gourds to do what he wanted. He made them do curls and go into knots. It sounds strange at first, but it sounds stranger when you hear how he did it. He loved to garden. He grew everything, not only gourds. He probably grew tomatoes in little square boxes. The most important thing he needed was the seed for a super-long dipper.

PLATE 103 Some "trained" gourds at the gourd museum

PLATE 104 Gourd lamps

He said he would actually start to train the gourd when the gourds are as thick as a pencil—after it has just come on the vine. He said that you had to bend it just a little every day, and in the heat of the day. Sometimes, if you grow those long-handled dippers on the ground, they actually curl up and form some great shapes. In his case, he would actually go around and put stakes in the ground so that whatever progress they made, he would not lose. The next day, he would do it again until he had the shape that he wanted.

There is an American Gourd Society, which helps to keep track of the gourd's history because many different civilizations used gourds. One really interesting thing is the cricket cage from China. The designs on the cages are actually scar tissue. These gourd cricket cages are really rare. In China, the cricket is a symbol of luck, so people would actually have a cricket in their homes like a pet. Some amazing things have been done all over the world with gourds.

The Native Americans around here used gourds for things both practical and ceremonial. The Cherokee Indians would use gourds in their ceremonies as masks. They also used them for practical uses like white settlers did. They used them as dippers, water carriers, and anything else that needed to be carried. The pioneers used to have a salt gourd and a soda gourd hanging by their stove. They used to use the gourds

PLATE 105 Chinese cricket cages made from gourds

to learn to swim. If you had a gourd that was kind of hourglass shaped or had a way you could tie it and not come loose, they used to tie them around children, and they called them water wings. I have personally had several older people tell me that they learned to swim with gourds. Gourds have an odd quality of insulation, and people have been said to keep their eggs in them. Somebody told us once that their family had a deed gourd, where their family would keep the deed to the property. Civil War soldiers would have a gourd for their gunpowder. There are a few documented cases of gourd powder holders and canteens.

Things like my story give you reason to delve into things that you would never do otherwise. I would not necessarily encourage everybody to work with gourds because, to tell you the truth, as a craft and as a livelihood, it's so labor-intensive. It has a lot of problems and a lot of frustrations, and I'm not sorry I did it. It just would not be for everybody. We have this phrase that we use: "the gourd life." Gourds have all of these really cute puns that just work perfectly. We used to have a little car that said, "Have you driven a gourd lately?" When we talk about "the gourd life," it is just a takeoff on "the good life." What it means to us is to invent it and just go along, and I would encourage people to do this. People should be open to the unlikely things that they never thought that they would do. You have to do what you want to do. You cannot go through life doing things because they are what you are supposed to do. The real "gourd life" is not about how much money you make or what kind of car you drive. It is what your life is really like every day. Artists and craftspeople seem to get a lot of attention for our creativity, but that can happen in any field or walk of life. You just have to do what is right for you. You just have to make sure you are happy about who you are and what you are doing with your life. Live your life for yourself.

THE ART OF MAKING FURNITURE BY HAND

John Roper shares his love for wood, tools, and a vanishing art

I try to rescue something that would burn or rot. I do take pride in that. I'm not a tree hugger, but I believe in preservation.

—John Roper

When Foxfire student Corey Lovell asked John Roper if he had made the rocking chair that was sitting in his shop, Mr. Roper said that he actually found the rocking chair in a brush pile. "I can't stand to see old things destroyed like that," he explained. Although his talent for working with wood is amazing, his penchant for rescuing items and materials from brush piles and decay is at least as inspiring as his creative talent. Most of the wood he turns into furniture is rescued wood, having found it either lying on the ground or waiting to be burned in a brush pile. Along with interestingly shaped pieces, he also found enough American chestnut to build cabinets for his house. He even rescued his trusty shop helper—his dog Jake—from a pound.

And those are just the tangible things. Intangibly, John Roper is saving the art of uniquely and passionately crafting furniture by hand. Roper's method for building furniture is slow—almost meditatively slow—a speed that is necessary to accommodate his incredible attention to detail.

The quiet and self-reliant peacefulness of Mr. Roper's shop resembled the family homeplace of Lon Reid, a chair maker who was interviewed for *The Foxfire Book* almost fifty years ago. The students who interviewed Mr. Reid developed an immediate nostalgia for the experience:

"It's hard to leave at the end of an interview like this one. One is tempted to stay a moment longer, wondering at the fact that here, in December of 1969, men still live as this one does, oblivious to the fact that others are bouncing about the moon."

In many ways, Mr. Roper, nestled in the "quieter coves" of Southern Appalachia, has lived his life like Mr. Reid—by his own standards, and without the modern conveniences of Internet and smartphones.

While touring John Roper's wood shop, we could hear the babbling Burningtown Creek harmonize with the rustle of leaves and the crunch of rocks as he showed us around his home. Like many of the other artists interviewed by *The Foxfire Magazine*, Roper's inspiration comes, at least in part, from a connection with the environment and with the natural world of the Southern Appalachian Mountains. In maintaining this connection, he is rescuing not only the vanishing art of made-by-hand furniture but also the art of living mindfully.

—*Jonathan Blackstock*

At this time of year, I don't have a lot of finished product, but I have a lot in progress. My shop isn't heated, so I don't get to do a lot of work during the winter.

I had a lot of my finished stuff—I took it to Florida, and it's fairly gone. I had items in the Folk Art Gallery down in Sanford. They had some stuff down there for over a year. Of course, it didn't sell. They had it priced so high, but they lowered the prices, and it all went.

These are just pieces in progress, and like I said, I have a bunch in progress. I've got a couple pieces in the house that are some of the first ones I built. They're not as good as some of the latter ones, but I've just been experimenting with different stuff—different types of wood. I try to use a lot of the old tools, like for instance, my drawing knives. I do use modern stuff like sanders, but I do a lot of shaping with the drawing knives. I use these hand tools a lot because there is nothing that does a better job than these things. And I use the rasp. I use electric sanders for my finished work because it's really hard to get a good finish with old-fashioned tools.

This is a desk I'm working on, and those are actually the legs for it. I guess we could set it up on there, so you can kind of get an idea of it. That will be a nice desk or sofa table, but I've gotten mainly into making tables because that's what people seem to want. People come up here

PLATE 106 Two tabletops in progress

and build these multimillion-dollar homes, and they want something made in the mountains instead of something they order out of a catalog. I've been trying different types of media, like this one where I've done some inlay of stone. I've been playing with that some. And that's a couple of the tables I've sold that have really been a hit. I've got to get more into doing that, but like I said, that was kind of an experiment just

PLATE 107 Placing a desktop on wooden legs

PLATE 108 Turquoise mixed-media inlay

to see because I never had done anything with stone, but I try to mix up media.

You put a lot more time into [the mixed-media inlay], and that's very time-consuming. If nothing else, you are working with two different hardnesses of media. That stone is a lot harder than any wood, so if you're not careful, you'll end up with a big dip in your wood and a raised area where your stonework is. [The tabletop with the stonework took] maybe six or seven hours. A lot of the time is just spent sanding because I got this wood slab from the sawmill, and even though it's done with a nice band saw, it's still rough. I spend the biggest part of my time on one of these things sanding because I just like to get that glass finish.

I'll show you my wood storage area. I joined an organization about six years ago called the International Wood Collectors Society, and they have shows all over the United States, and people bring wood from all over. I love working with this. This is camphor wood from down in Florida. This is another table I'm working on: It's a two-piece. I'm book-matching [cutting so it will open and reveal symmetrical wood-grain patterns] it. But that's out of Florida. This is mahogany, and this actually came from a hurricane in south Florida, at, I want to say Fairchild Garden, maybe.

The hurricane came through a few years ago and blew down a bunch of trees. I mean, you can see how big the tree was. This is like the crotch, where it forked out, and I like working with that because you get a lot of

PLATE 109 Dark mahogany slab

flame [wood-grain pattern] in there, and when that has a finish on it, it will just jump right out at you. A plain piece of wood has character to it.

Here is another one I was playing with. It's like I said: I have several pieces in the works. This is eastern red cedar. You see how I'm starting to inlay the stone into it. Like I say, I've just been experimenting with all different kinds of wood, and there is just some I prefer not to use. I try to find stuff with unique grain in it. For instance, this is a piece of sycamore that came out of Alabama, and you can see this is called spalting, where it's been out in the weather. A lot of people call it rotten wood, but I have made some nice pieces out of that, and it is absolutely beautiful when you put the finish on it. It looks like you have drawn it in with a fine-tipped marker. I've had people ask me, "Now, how did you draw that?" It's just the natural pattern, so I like working with that. The only problem is that it's a form of mold, so you have to be really careful sanding. The mold is what gives it the color.

I wear a mask when I sand. I make sure I'm in a ventilated room when I'm sanding because of the dust. I have a big suck fan over there.

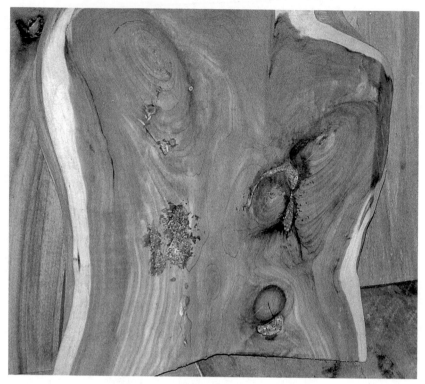

PLATE 110 Stone inlay in red cedar

PLATE 111 Wood slab with spalting marks

That's one of the most important things is that you don't breathe that dust because some people are highly allergic to this camphor. That's actually what they make that Campho-Phenique out of. When it is fresh sanded, you can smell it throughout the entire barn.

There are certain types of cedars that I don't use, something about the dust, and I wish I could think of the others. Some of them will actually break you out. I mean, it's just like anything: some people are allergic to plants or whatever. I've heard of people having really bad experiences just from the dust or from the sap.

I've not had any bad effects from it, but there again, I use a mask and ventilation. When I can, I will go outside and put boards on sawhorses and sand them. If it's raining, I'll come in here and turn that thing [the fan] on, and I'll still wear a mask.

All my wood, I don't work it green [wet, still alive, and growing]. I put it up and let it dry, but the average drying time is kind of a rule of thumb: it's one inch per year. My average slab is an inch and a half to two inches thick, so it has to dry for a year and a half to two years before you can do anything with it. A lot of these slabs and boards, I worked a long time ago. Once you work a piece of wood, I'll let it sit because it will move. When I say move, I mean checking. *Checking* is the term for cracking. Cracks don't matter; wood naturally cracks. People don't really care about the cracks unless the wood has just a huge crack, but that one I sanded last summer, I believe, and I let it stay in the house all winter. So, this one is ready to go; I'm confident it's not going to move too much more.

It started out as a hobby. I've always been into woodworking. I did cabinetry for years, and this is not as complicated as cabinetry, but I've always loved working with wood. When I joined that club and started traveling all over the place, collecting it almost became an obsession, and you'll see when you go in there. They call me the wood hoarder [laughs], and I did have this place so full at one time that you couldn't walk in here, but I've organized it. Well, it was like, I've got lots of wood; I just can't work on it. So, I've added on, and added on, and added on to the barn or the shed here.

My favorite wood to work with is camphor. I spend a lot of time in the woods. See, I found that piece right there about four miles back up on the mountain. I carried that thing out, but I like how nature grew things. So, I'll take that stump, and I will use that as my supports, but that will be a centerpiece on a table right there in between the legs or some-

PLATE 112 Camphor slab inside the workshop

thing like that. It's a rhododendron. That will end up on a choice piece. Like I said, I carried that thing four miles—way back on the mountain. [**Editors' note:** Similarly, in *Foxfire 10*, Clyde Runion explains how he searches the mountain woods to find mountain ivy and laurel.]

And another thing is that I don't kill trees for my lumber, and I can tell you this: ninety or ninety-five percent of the pieces of wood I've got have been saved from a brush pile or have been reclaimed after a tornado. I don't cut down trees to make slabs, so everything is reclaimed or more or less saved from a brush pile. So, that's one good thing about my tables: they would have been in a brush pile.

That's true for a lot of my accent pieces. For instance, that tree was dead when I cut it. Now, if I would have found that green, I would have left it, but you can see it was dead and almost in its decaying stages. You know, if I was to leave that any longer, the next time I get that far back in the woods, it would be rotten. I don't cut green trees. I try to rescue something that would burn or rot. I do take pride in that. I'm not a tree hugger, but I believe in preservation.

PLATE 113 Rhododendron that may be used for table support

I've been doing this about ten years. I moved here and built the place in 2002, and I've been adding onto the barn ever since.

We'll go on to my drying room. All of that right there is in the process of drying. I think that's sycamore and maple, probably.

[Mr. Roper enters the room and has to knock down some spider webs. An impressive display of wood dries in a dark room, lit by only a single window in the back.]

This is the drying room. It is out of the sunlight, and you can take a look in here. Well, you can see, I got enough wood to make . . . Well, I got ten years' worth of work there—or more.

I date everything, and usually before I stack it in here, if I don't know the wood, I'll label it and date it the day that it is put in here. Everything in that barn has been in there long enough to where it's ready for work.

I've been all over the Southeast. Some of it came out of Ohio, Alabama, a large part came out of Florida and then, of course, around here because people got to know what I was doing and said, "Hey, I got a log. You want it?" A lot of times, I just have to say, "No, I don't have room." I can't build another room.

I built the house; I built the barn. I do remodeling for a living. I don't particularly care for it, but it's money. That wouldn't be my choice of income, but right now it is.

I'm hoping that I can finally get some furniture work done now that I've got my shop cleaned out and my wood is all dry. I have spent years just collecting. Of course, I used to work all the time, but now I've got

PLATE 114 The wood-drying room with a large variety of great wood
ready to be worked

lots of free time. I've got lots to work with. I'm hoping by this fall [2014]
to have quite an inventory.

Everything that I have sold has been basically by word of mouth.
People have made design requests, and I will give a little bit. They'll say,
"I want this and I want this," and I'll say, "Well, here's what I got to work
with." I mean, I give a little choice, but not really. I don't want to get
into that, somebody to say, "Oh, make me this." At some point, I might
change my mind, but right now, I want to make it into what I see in it. If
they don't like it, somebody else will.

My friends down there in Rabun County have been real helpful
about getting the word out. I'm just now getting to where I can really
start, and I'm not into production either. I might work on a piece and
set it aside for a few months and come back and say, "I don't like that"
because you have to match up legs to the top. I might let a piece sit for
six months and come in there one day and say, "Hey, that'll work." Then,
I will put it together. Like I said, I'm not into production. It takes the
fun out of it. It's a fun hobby right now. I found that people want to pay
good money for it.

I try to use glue, and I use pegs, but I also use screws because, with
something that big, you have to have [strong joiners]. But I hide all my
screws and stuff. You can't see a screw; it is all hidden. You know the

screws will be underneath, and even though the screws will be underneath, I try to plug the holes. I don't want you looking at a pretty piece of furniture and seeing a screw. I try to hide everything in my joinery.

I use a clear sealer. I actually use floor sealer. It's a Varathane; it's water-based. It doesn't color, like polyurethane, which will yellow over time. This Varathane doesn't color with age, so you don't have to worry about it turning yellow in five or six years. It's just natural. I don't use any kind of stain. I'm a purist when it comes to leaving wood natural. I use a clear finish, and that's it. I don't see the point in staining something. The clear brings out the grain, and that's what I want people to see is the wood grain itself. It just brings it out.

Do you feel a kind of connection with the wood you are using?

Sure. Yeah. That's just it, and a lot of that stuff in there [the drying room]—I helped load the logs on the sawmill, and I have actually seen them when they come off. It's like, "I got to have that!" I mean, to me it's like a picture just waiting to be brought out. I'm definitely connected. If those trees could talk, the stories they could tell. I'm definitely connected in that way. It's a work of love; it ain't about production. It's about taking a piece of what people call trash or firewood and making something really cool out of it. That's where I get the most pleasure out of it. Just bringing out the beauty of the wood.

I've always worked with wood, but the first wood show I went to with the International Wood Collectors Society, I just started paying attention to the beautiful grain patterns, and it's like wow! I saw what could be done. When you saw the log and it's green, the grain really stands out. It's like, wow, that's what it's going to look like when it's dry and got a nice clear sealer on it. That's what you're going to see. So, that got me really started—just, wow, that is beautiful, and it just went on from there. I wish we could get in there. I got some really cool stuff in there. Like I said, it's so packed in there. It's something I enjoy doing. I enjoy seeing the finished product.

I've worked with wood; my grandfather worked in wood; my dad worked in wood. It's just always been in the family, you know. My grandfather lived just up the road. He made handles for people for many, many years—ax handles, shovel handles. People would come from all over. I've had people say, "Did you ever know an old man up by you that made handles?" and I said, "Yeah, that was my grandpa, Orpha Roper." It's an old name. We've been in this valley [a long time]; I've found deeds from

1877. It would have been my great-great-grandfather who purchased a hundred acres in here, so this is part of the original old homestead. We [the Roper family members] still own probably twenty-something acres amongst us. Back in that time, there was just four or five family names that lived in here. Roper was one of them.

We love [the homeplace]. It's grown up a lot. We used to know every neighbor in here, and, anymore, there's a lot of people living here that we don't even know who they are.

What tools do you most like to use?

I use Makita a lot, but like I said, I don't use a whole lot of power tools. I like Craftsman. I like the old Craftsman. You'll notice a lot of my tools are Craftsman from when they used to make them to last. But yeah, I use Makita and DeWalt when it comes to some power tools. Craftsman is probably my favorite, but it's the old stuff that I like best.

Where do you get the older hand tools?

EBay. I used to have a heck of a collection. I got rid of a lot of it, but I saved my favorites because, there again, I got obsessive with it. There are only so many [tools] that you can use. It's like, "Oh man, I don't need forty of these." But, you know, I use the old hand planers and the old drawknives because you can do things with them that you can't do with a power tool. You can get that drawknife into a crevice or whatever. If I could rig up a sander, I would use an old-time sander if such thing existed.

I guess shaping it is my favorite part of the process because I don't like to make square things. I like to use the natural edge as much as possible, but I like just giving it a good shape to where the grain and everything really flows. And like I said, I might look at a board, do something to it, and then come back and take a little more off. I guess the favorite part is creating it. Then, I guess the next favorite part is finishing it because when you put that finish on, everything comes out. Everything just stands out.

Nothing that I make—there's no two alike. That's what is unique. I might make a set of coffee tables or a couple of end tables, and they may be cut from the same log, but they're not exact. There are no two the same. One of a kind!

PLATE 115 John Roper with wood slab and hand tools

I'm a naturalist. I like the woods. If it was my choice, I would be in the woods right now, fishing or doing something. If nothing else, I would be just hiking.

I kind of go as [the wood project] progresses. I might plan something—say I'm making legs to match with the top—and I'll spend all this time making them. I'll dry fit it. I won't put nothing together permanently. Then it's like "Nah!" So, I'll come up with something else.

I do start with a plan, but it can change. I have a mental picture of what I want it to look like, but until you pair up the right pieces of wood with it, you don't really know. You know it when you see it.

A lot of the reason people like unique furniture is because there wasn't a forest destroyed or a tree cut down, and it's made by hand, which is something that normally doesn't exist anymore. It's made local; it doesn't come from across the pond. I find that people appreciate that it is handmade. I don't know if that is the correct term; it's not *handmade* but *made by hand*. It's not a production thing. Plus, it's unique; it's one of a kind. They don't have to worry about going to their neighbor's house and seeing the same thing. That's why people like having a unique piece, just something to be like "Hey, I'm the only one that's got one like that."

I think that's the biggest thing: handmade and unique because it's not a production piece.

I sign my pieces, and I number them. I've actually got a brand that I use to brand it on the back and underneath. I sign it and date it. I also write down the types of woods that it's made out of. It's always on the underside, where, unless you flip them over, you'll never see it.

I'm only up to like number fourteen. That's just because I've waited all this time for the wood to dry. Now I'm ready. I could kick it in, but I'm not really going to. It just takes the personal touch out of it when you do that because I'm not in it for the money. It's good, but I get satisfaction out of it. It's nice that people pay for it. It blows me away what people are willing to pay for a quality piece. And you talk about something [made by hand] versus [something else that] you go to the store and buy—all that has to do with their appreciation of how it came about.

I tinker with different types of wood. For instance, I own the mountain over there, and about five years ago, we had a serious fire come through, and it just burnt the whole mountain, and a lot of the mountain

PLATE 116 A coat rack made of laurel

laurel got killed. So, I found some mountain laurel lying around, and started making coatracks.

So, I just rescued the wood and was like, "Hey, wow! Those look cool."

Does your dog always follow you around while you work?

Yeah, I've raised him since he was a puppy. He's like a kid. He's about ten. He's got a lot of Plott hound in him.

Jake, look at the camera.

He was a rescue dog. I rescued him from the pound—the Humane Society. He was four months old when they got him, and I said, "I want a dog that nobody will adopt," and [the pound administrator] said, "They don't adopt the hound dogs." He was like four months old, and they said

PLATE 117 Jake seems proud to work with John Roper.

PLATE 118 Seat made of chestnut

he won't get no more than forty pounds. Well, he's about ninety now. Oh, he likes Grandma's cornbread.

[Mr. Roper points to another rocking chair and a seat on his porch before we go into the house to see some of his first tables.]

That rocking chair was rescued from a brush pile. Someone was planning on burning it. I said, "You're kidding me." I thought, "Man, you people are crazy." I rescued that [wood for the seat] from a brush pile. And that seat is made out of American chestnut.

It was piled up ready to burn, and I was thinking, "You got to be kidding me." People just don't appreciate the fact that, that wood is as old as it is. Plus, it's becoming rare.

[Mr. Roper invites us into his house to see the tables.]

These are like two of the first ones I've ever made. I was just experimenting with different things.

I liked that because it was petrified wood.

PLATE 119 One of John Roper's first tables

I think that [table] probably wasn't the first one I made, but it was either the second or the third. That's made out of camphor, and that's when I realized I liked camphor. And when I can, I like to leave the bark edge. It's really hard to get the bark to stay on unless the tree's sap is at its lowest point. The bark won't hold it and eventually separates. Appar-

PLATE 120 A camphor table with petrified wood on the lower shelf

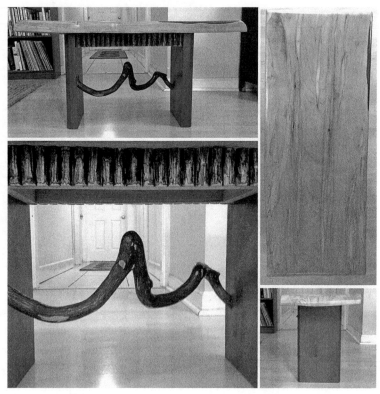

PLATE 121 Table with laurel center, courtesy of Bill Gridley

ently, those were cut at the right time [in the dead of winter] because that table has been here for probably five years or more, and the bark's not popped off yet.

But see, I've got the whole house from recycled wood. This is all chestnut, but it's from an old house I tore down or a couple of old houses I tore down. I like reusing stuff. Yeah, I made all the cabinets and stuff out of it. It was free.

STORYTELLING

Listen.

A crowd gathers at the Oconaluftee Islands Park in Cherokee, North Carolina: The people sit on stumps that surround a fire pit, and the ducks gather along the other side of the riverbank. The sunlight is giving way to the orange-red glow of a small bonfire. Even the traffic at the nearby road seems to tread lightly as a group of Native Americans in traditional dress take the earthen stage. They are storytellers, dancers, and artists, and they share their stories with all those who will listen.

As the sky and the mountains retreat into night, the stories intensify. Darkness removes anything not illuminated by the bonfire's light; the entire world has become only the storytellers and those who will listen.

A bond forms between the artists and the audience members, and as a group, everyone dances around the stumps and logs at the bonfire. As Foxfire student Jack Blackstock explained in *The Foxfire Magazine*'s Fall/Winter 2012 issue, "It always feels good to meet new people, and while holding hands and dancing in a snake line, you're almost forced to understand. If you connect the two, holding hands and dancing while understanding what they've gone through, this small group of storytellers can open our eyes to what has come and what is likely to come." Ultimately, everyone who attends the storytelling circle becomes part of the same tribe—everyone, that is, who listens.

Storytelling is tribal: it's an inclusive activity that invites everyone to be part of a community and share common values, even if for only a brief time. This experience is enhanced when the storytellers present their art in their natural environments. Whether listening to Jerry Wolfe tell stories as he points to the mountains where the stories take place or listening to Janie P. Taylor tell stories at the base of Tiger Mountain, the storyteller's art is one that builds community and invites everyone into that community—everyone who will listen.

—*Jonathan Blackstock*

TIGER MOUNTAIN'S STORYTELLER

An interview with renowned local storyteller Janie P. Taylor

Tiger Mountain is a source of my strength and inspiration.

—Janie P. Taylor

Janie Pleasants Taylor was born in the small town of Statesville, North Carolina, on November 18, 1930. Her parents, Mr. and Mrs. M. O. Pleasants, were both schoolteachers. When Janie was two years old, the Depression hit, and the Pleasants family moved to Tiger, Georgia, a small town here in Rabun County. Mrs. Pleasants, formerly Clyde Arrendale, was returning to the land where she had grown up and where her parents still lived. (In 1949, Mr. Pleasants died, and Mrs. Pleasants later married Carlton English. Foxfire students have often interviewed Mr. and Mrs. English for the magazine.)

Tiger is where Janie spent her childhood and youth, and where she raised three daughters and one son. She was very involved with our school system, serving as a science teacher, an elementary school principal, and a supervisor for our county's school lunch program. Her four children are now all teachers.

As we drove up to the Taylors' house on the outskirts of Tiger, Janie greeted us from her porch and invited us in. Her cozy living room offered warmth and security on a frigid, windy afternoon. She talked to us for about an hour, sharing things she collected or made that pertain to Tiger Mountain—watercolors she painted with the mountain in the background, a pitcher her uncle made of clay from the mountain, and, most of all, stories she heard. These stories were about things that had happened to her or were the retelling of those heard as a child. They are very special stories to her family and she enjoyed sharing them with others.

Then, we all walked up the road, where Janie showed us the remains of the old roadside zoo she mentions in the interview that follows. A short time later, we hurried back to the house, and Janie served us cups of warm spiced cranberry juice, a delicious treat on such a chilly day.

—*Scott Beck, Gina Hamby, and Erin Harrison*

PLATE 122 Janie P. Taylor with a quilt, telling a story in a classroom

When I was a child, Mr. and Mrs. Jabel Cannon owned the property right down the road from our house. They had a business there, Cannons' Cabins. The cabins were just for rental, as a motel would be today. As a little girl, I well remember that there was a zoo next door to the Cannons' property, right near here at the foot of Tiger Mountain. People stopped at the zoo as they traveled Old Highway 441, which was the main highway then. Today, there are still visible remains of the zoo buildings, broken cement sidewalks, and concrete foundations. The zoo was a well-built facility with a veterinarian, Ray Thomas, in charge. There were various animals, including two large black bears, one living in a cage and the other on a chain. There were other mountain animals, such as a fox, raccoons, and squirrels. There were several monkeys, snakes, exotic birds, *and* a large alligator who had his personal pool in the cage. I have a tale about this particular alligator I want to tell you about.

When I was about four years old, I was spending the day with my grandma Arrendale over at her house at the base of Tiger Mountain. As usual, I was sent to the mailbox over the road to pick up the daily mail delivery. It was a warm summer morning, and my dog Toddler, a white-and-black wire terrier, and I left Grandma's house, walked down the hill, over the creek, by the swamp and the old willow tree, up the hill, over the gap to the mailbox. I had been taught to count the pieces of mail so I wouldn't lose any. On this day, there were two papers and three letters. Toddler and I began the trek back to Grandma's—over the gap, down the hill—but when we came to the creek and swamp, Toddler began barking frantically and pushing me backwards! I looked for a water moccasin or some other snake, but didn't see anything. The dog continued to jump and bark—and then I saw it! A large alligator was lying under the old willow tree. He was opening and closing his massive jaws, showing the rows of teeth, and his beady eyes were staring at me! To get away, Toddler and I backed off and made a circle away from this "ferocious creature." I still had my two papers and three letters, so Toddler and I started up the hill.

I went into the kitchen and gave the mail to Grandma. I said, "I saw an alligator down in the swamp by the willow tree."

My aunt Ruth exclaimed, "That youngun needs her mouth washed out with soap for telling tales and making up stories. Her imagination is too real!" My grandma, who was busy cooking dinner for the family and farmhands, told me to go sit on the front porch and ask forgiveness for my naughty ways. Toddler sat on the porch floor beside me, and we waited. I knew that in a short while, the farmhands and my uncle Joe would be coming home for dinner in the wagon pulled by a team of mules. They would turn in at the gap, come down the hill, and see that alligator! Sure enough, the wagon came over the gap, down the hill, and when that team of mules sensed the presence of that large reptile, they went berserk and tried to run away! Pulling with all his might, the hired man, Luther, struggled to get control of the mules and wagon. My uncle jumped off, saw the alligator, and realized what was causing the trouble with the mule team.

Coming into Grandma's house, Uncle Joe shouted, "The big alligator from the zoo has escaped and is down by the road." When told of my encounter with this "wild beast," Uncle Joe and the others were amazed that I had not lost an arm or a leg, or that Toddler had not been eaten alive! The alligator was apparently suffering from heat prostration and lack of water, and thus was too weak to attack.

The menfolk went over to the zoo and got the veterinarian, who immediately brought a truck to load the alligator on. The alligator's snout was tied, and everyone heaved and strained to load that thrashing, bellowing, nine-foot-long alligator for the ride back to the zoo.

Later that day, I was rocking on the front porch at Grandma's with Toddler on the floor beside me. Aunt Ruth came out and sat down, and then she told me how thankful she was that I had not been injured by the alligator and that she was sorry I had been falsely accused. Finally, she made this plea, "Promise me, Janie, that you will never, never tell any tales again!" But I didn't promise; I just nodded my head. And that was over fifty years ago!

Janie felt a very close attachment to her homeplace and had a special relationship with the looming mountain behind her house.

Years ago, the people who lived at the foot of Tiger Mountain owned herds of sheep that lived and pastured on the mountain and that used the rock cliffs as shelter. Cattle also used to roam the coves and ridges before there were fence laws. I have climbed up to the cliffs many times, but the terrain is much more difficult now because of the undergrowth and ivy thickets. Today, the cliffs are perhaps home for the foxes and their young, but there is no livestock up there.

Several times, over the years, I have seen the light of the foxfire lichen around old rotting logs in various places on Tiger Mountain. This glow appears fairylike, and it seems to disappear when one approaches—almost like magic!

It is my understanding that there are veins of gold deep within Tiger Mountain. I recall hearing about Mr. George Watts, a good neighbor of ours who lived near here when I was little, panning enough tiny gold nuggets each summer from a stream flowing off the mountain to fill a wild turkey quill. He would then exchange these gold lumps for a winter's supply of salt and coffee for his family. In the sandy bottom of this branch [by our house], I have often seen the sun shining on bright gold flecks, but whether it's pure gold or fool's gold, I'm not sure.

On several occasions, I have felt movements of the earth's crust in this area. Once I heard a noise like the sound of an eighteen-wheeler truck climbing over the bridge to my house. This turned out to be the rumblings and shifting of layers deep within the earth—and below Tiger Mountain—caused, perhaps, by aftershock waves of an earthquake elsewhere. This area is near a fault line, and I have felt earth tremors at various times, enough shaking and trembling of the ground to cause candlesticks to fall over and dishes to rattle in the cabinet.

Although there are other ideas of how Tiger Mountain was named, I first heard this version as a young child, sitting on the porch steps at twilight listening to my elders talk. (Actually, this is oral history, but I have researched these facts.)

In the 1700s, the British fought the French for possession of territory of India. While in that distant land, the British soldiers became used to and familiar with the cry and scream of the Bengal tiger, a powerful animal of the Indian jungles. When these same soldiers returned to England after the victorious war, many of them migrated to the New World. With their families, they settled in this northeast corner of Georgia. Imagine their surprise and shock to hear echoing from the cliffs of a nearby mountain a piercing cry, as the dying scream of a woman—the same sounds as heard in India made by the black-striped tiger.

Because of these remembered sounds as recurring memories of far-away India, these early settlers called the mountain Tiger. The weird, frightening cry was, of course, not made by a tiger, but by a native mountain cat, a panther, commonly called a "painter." Today, the black, sleek "painter" no longer roams this mountain, for as civilization crept in, the "painter" slowly disappeared to more isolated areas and further into higher mountain elevations.

Nevertheless, the mountain is still called Tiger Mountain, and the neighboring settlement is now the incorporated town of Tiger, Georgia. Tiger Mountain is a source of my strength and inspiration. I am always reminded of the scripture verse "I will lift up mine eyes unto the hills, from whence cometh my help."

One afternoon in 1985, Foxfire staff member Mike Cook contacted my mother, Clyde English, concerning an old-fashioned quilting party, which would be filmed by Public Broadcasting [Service]. My mother quickly jumped at the chance for a "quilting" as soon as plans were made. The ladies of the community who are known as "quilting addicts" were contacted. Then the decision was made that a "Log Cabin" pattern quilt top would be pieced, and that the finished quilt was to be my very own—a Janie P. quilt!

On the scheduled day, the quilters all arrived with thimbles, needles, and thread ready to quilt. Soon the television crew arrived. The technicians covered the windows with materials for the proper amount of light, electrical circuits were checked, and television equipment was brought into the house. The living room at Clyde English's home near Tiger Mountain was filled with quilting frame, quilters, television crew, Foxfire students and staff, and all the cameras. Eventually the director announced that the actual filming time had arrived and requested that the ladies continue to talk and quilt in a normal manner as the cameras rolled to film this quilting process. The dialogue went something like this:

"Clyde, honey, does you roof leak?" asked one little lady on the left side of the quilt.

"No! My roof does not leak! Why?" replied my mother, most indignantly.

"Clyde, honey, there is a wet spot about the size of a saucer on this quilt," commenced the lady. All the quilters quietly pondered this statement amidst a few ohs and aahs.

"Clyde, honey, have you got a cat?"

"Yes, I've got cats, and the sweetest yellow kitten you ever saw! And it was sleeping in the middle of this quilt when I got up this morning!" Again, there was a busy silence as the quilters contemplated this last comment. Then . . .

"Clyde, honey, that cat has peed on this quilt!" Not an exclamation of alarm nor a word of apprehension from the group.

"Just rub a little Clorox on the spot and it will be just fine—no smell and no circle," suggested another lady calmly.

At this time, I interrupted. I could not bear the thought of my beautiful log cabin quilt having bleach used on it—for whatever reason!

And that is how this quilt got a very special name: the Janie "Pee" Quilt!

LEGENDS THAT WILL NEVER DIE

Storyteller Davy Arch shares Cherokee legends

I like to listen to older people. They've rehearsed their stories, and they've got it down to a science. They can really be dramatic and even act out their stories a lot of times when they're telling them.

—Davy Arch

As both a supervisor at the Oconaluftee Indian Village and a well-known storyteller in the Cherokee community, Davy Arch has often captivated Foxfire students. In addition to his storytelling talent, Davy Arch is a renowned Native American artist. He has traveled the world and has showcased his art, which has been inspired by the great Cherokee legends.

—*Katie Lunsford*

My name is Davy Arch. I'm Eastern Cherokee, and I'm the assistant manager of the Oconaluftee Indian Village in Cherokee, North Carolina. I am a storyteller, and, boy, I can tell some big ones. I tell mostly real-life adventure stories. I got into storytelling because of my artwork. I'm an artist by trade, and I do a lot of traditional arts, some of what I call pre-Columbian art. I make arrowheads, instruments, and weapons. I tan hides and do all that kind of stuff. I'm a sculptor. I carve stone and wood. I get inspiration from stories for a lot of my carvings. A lot of times, I'll go to an event, and I'll set up and demonstrate. I'll be working on a piece of sculpture, and somebody will ask, "What is that? Where did you get the idea?" Then, I would tell them the story behind the carving.

One of my favorite stories is about flint. You know, a lot of people identify Native Americans with making arrowheads. It's one of the few things that has survived over thousands of years. I'll be sitting around making arrowheads, and I'll think of its origin story. In the beginning, flint was contained all in the body of a giant that lived here in Cherokee country. This was in a time when all the plants and animals and human beings could communicate with one another. Everyone would talk about how much easier life would be if they could have some of the flint. They said, "We could make tools and weapons. We could build fire. You know, life would be much easier if we could just have some of this flint off the giant's body." But everyone was afraid of the giant.

One day, the animals were talking about it. The rabbit was kind of a trickster in our culture; he always liked to brag and boast. He said, "Well, I'm not afraid of that giant. I think I could get some of that flint." Every-

PLATE 123 Davy Arch tells stories outside the Oconaluftee Village.

body turned to the rabbit and asked, "Well, why don't you?" He realized he had stuck his foot in his mouth, but he come up with a plan.

In the history of our people, there have been times where it was so difficult that families didn't have enough to eat, but it has always been tradition to offer company or a stranger something to eat and drink. It's always been bad manners to refuse that. Even if you're full, you go in and take a little bit. The rabbit knew this, so he approached the giant and asked if he would come share a meal with him. Out of respect for the tradition, the giant accepted the rabbit's invitation. This was part of the rabbit's plan. He planned to feed this giant until he got so full, he'd go to sleep. He had prepared a hammer and wedge to knock a piece of the giant's body off when he went to sleep.

The giant came to the rabbit's house, and the rabbit had laid out a big feast for him. The giant ate and ate until he was full. He told the rabbit he was full and that it was time for him to leave. The rabbit said, "Wait just a minute." So, the rabbit went into his house and brought out another dish of food that was even more delicious than what the giant had just finished eating. Out of respect, the giant had some of that food, and each time he got ready to leave, the rabbit would do the same thing—go back in and get more food. He fed the giant until the giant was gorged. The giant went over to this huge chestnut tree and went to sleep. That's the moment that the rabbit had been waiting for.

The rabbit went back in his house and got the hammer and wedge, and he snuck up on the sleeping giant. He set the wedge on the giant's chest and was going to knock a chip of flint off of the giant's body. He drew back his hammer, and when he hit his wedge, instead of knocking a chip off the giant, the giant had gorged himself to the point that he exploded and went all over the universe. Now, in every country in the world, you can find flint. Flint stone is on every continent there is. They claim that the shooting stars across the sky at night are still part of the giant's body.

A lot of people wonder what happened to that rabbit. When that giant blew up, it didn't kill him. A lot of people thought that an explosion like that may have killed the rabbit, too. Well, it didn't, but a piece flew off and cut his tail off. The rabbit used to have a long tail. Since that day, he has had a short tail. Another piece of flint hit that rabbit right in the upper lip. If you'll look at a rabbit's lip, it still has a split lip. He carries that scar to this day.

After that, everyone had flint, and it made life easier. We used it for everything. We used it for tools. Men and women both learned how to make arrowheads and how to work flint. It's also easy to make fire with.

So, that's how we got flint. That's one of my favorite stories because I make arrowheads, and I can tell that [story] as I'm demonstrating what I'm doing.

Another story I used to tell a lot was about a carving I made of a half man/half bear. It looked a lot like a Greek centaur—a half man/half horse, but this has a bear's body and a man's torso. The story is about a boy who went to live back in the woods with the bears. He would come back home, but he got to where he was spending more time with the bears than with his family. The village got into a crisis and didn't have enough food. So, one day, the boy left and told his parents that he was going to live with the bears forever but that if they ever needed food, they could come get him and use him for food. That was one of the stories that I used for inspiration behind that carving, the boy turning himself into a bear.

I've got another story that was about the same, where a man was changed into a bear through magic and was condemned to roam the earth as a bear for the rest of his life. We have another story where a whole clan of people was transformed into bears to provide food for the rest of the tribe. They claim that, way back, we had nine clans. We had a Panther Clan and a Bear Clan, but those are two clans that don't exist within the culture anymore.

I've got several scary stories. There is one story I have told a lot. Everybody has ghost stories and scary stories and stuff like that, but when I was growing up, I hunted a lot with my grandfather. We'd be back in the mountains walking a trail, and sometimes, we would find just little piles of bone splinters in the middle of a trail. Grandpa would say, "Well, that was that Wampus cat eating something right here." I asked him one time what it was he was talking about. He said, "Well, thousands of years ago, the men had their own medicine, and the women had their [own separate] medicine." We still do, and this medicine that you are not supposed to talk about in mixed genders. One time, there was a young couple married, and the young man was a doctor. In the evening, he would leave and go talk to the men about the men's medicine. Well, he was driving his wife crazy; she liked to know everything. She couldn't bear to think that he was getting information that she didn't know anything about. One evening, she decided she was going to sneak down to the council and find out what these men were talking about. She disguised herself with a panther skin, but these old men knew she was coming. These old doctors know a lot of times before the patient does that they're coming to see them. The doctors waited on her, and when she snuck up on the men's council, they came up, caught her, and brought her into council. Because of her disrespect to the men's medicine, they condemned her to roam this earth forever as a panther. They changed her into a panther through magic because she had disguised herself with that panther hide. They told her that she would have to roam these mountains for eternity because of the disrespect. They also gave her the power to change back into a woman. They told her if she wanted to eat, she would have to change into this cat and eat while she was a cat. Sometimes, people see a woman walking back through the mountains. They believe that is the woman that shape-shifts from a panther back into a woman. If you ever hear a panther's scream, it sounds just like a woman screaming. My grandpa told me one time when we were back in the mountains and heard one, he said, "That's that ol' Wampus cat shape-shifting. It must be awful painful for her to shift from one thing to another." All through the woods, even nowadays, you will find those little piles of bones.

That's one of my favorite tales. I think about that a lot when I'm back in the mountains. I've never seen a big cat back in the mountains, but one time when I was digging up some Christmas trees way back in the mountains, a cat came down and walked around my truck in the snow.

I think a good storyteller is somebody who is telling real-life adventure stories, has a vested interest in that memory, and they get the enthusiasm of the time. They almost reexperience the adrenaline they had when they were living that story. I love to hear those kinds of stories from storytellers that research the information, have a good presence, and can relay a message that people can understand. I have heard storytellers who use big words and terminology that people don't understand, and to me, their story is not as effective.

I like to listen to older people. They've rehearsed their stories, and they've got it down to a science. They can really be dramatic and even act out their stories a lot of times when they're telling them. Younger storytellers sometimes add a little flavor that is really good because they're looked at as carrying on that tradition, especially if it is a story that has been passed down.

People have asked me if stories get changed around. You know, if you whisper a message and send it around the room, a lot of times it's a different message at the end of the line. A lot of people have wondered how true our stories are to the real story. In the past, it was kind of a rule of thumb that a story had to be told the same way every time so that it wouldn't be confused by the next generation. They taught lessons, so traditional stories are told the same way by a lot of different people.

I like humor and funny stories. Those seem to be the ones you remember—that and scary stories. The ghost stories and the funny stories seem to stick with you. I have several funny stories. One popular story around here is about the opossum losing the hair in his tail. That's one that a lot of people know. He was tricked by the crickets. They told him that they were preparing his tail for a dance so that he could brag on it. He liked to brag and boast on it. In reality, they were cutting the hair off of his tail in a way to embarrass him and teach him a lesson. That's a pretty good traditional story. [**Editors' note:** Native American storyteller Jerry Wolfe also tells an exciting version of the opossum's story.]

I'll tell you one of the funniest stories I ever heard. Where I grew up, over by where the casino is now, there was mostly pasture. We had a livestock barn down in the field there, and we had a barbed wire fence that went all the way around the field. Instead of the bridge that is there now, there was an old swinging bridge, just a footbridge across the creek. It was elevated pretty high out of the creek. Off the ends of the bridge, there were two wide boards—they must have been twenty feet long—that ran across into the field across the fence. A neighbor of ours was coming through there after dark. He said there wasn't a moon out, and it was dark.

He said he made his way across the bridge and started down the planks on the other side going down into the pasture. He said he stumbled and started running, trying to catch his balance. He ran out into the field and fell. When he fell, he landed on something big and warm and hairy. It moved. He said when it moved, it scared him to death. His imagination ran away with him. He jumped up and took off running. When he hit the fence on the other end of the field, you could hear the nails pop out of the fence posts all the way around the pasture.

What he had done was run out, and he fell on a cow that way lying out there in the middle of the field. His name was Bill Hicks. He was one of the chief's cousins. We called him Sweet William because he had those Sweet William flowers growing all around his place. Just to hear him tell that was a lot of fun. When he was telling that story, I could just imagine him jumping up from landing on that cow, taking off, and hitting the fence.

I've heard a lot of stories about people wandering around these mountains at night before there was electricity. There wasn't any ambient light anywhere. If you got away from town, you were back in the dark. It was just pitch-black dark. I've heard about people seeing lights and stuff like that. Grandpa said one time he was coming down off the mountain right before dark one evening. He said it was getting so dark that he couldn't really see. He had a little dog with him, and he had been fishing. The dog started barking at what Grandpa thought was a big limb lying across the road that had fallen out of a tree.

When he got up close to it, he could see the shadow or the image of something lying across the road. He began to smell a rattlesnake. His dog started barking, and he realized when he got up close that what he was seeing was a giant snake. He said it was as big as his leg. Its tail was lying up on the bank in the woods, and his head was lying off the bank and off the road going down the other way. It scared him to death. He didn't have a gun or anything, so he picked up a rock about as big as he could pick up and threw it at the snake. The rock didn't hit [the snake but] went past the snake and hit the ground. When the snake felt the vibration, it moved off the road. A log truck had wrecked, and that load of logs was still lying off below the road. He said the snake went over in those logs.

He hurried and got on around it and went home. The next morning when it got daylight, he got his gun and went back up there to see if he could find it. He said the snake left a trail across that road about a foot wide where it crawled. That was the second one that big that he saw in his lifetime.

A guy named Cub Calonahaski used to work with my grandfather. He lived on one side of the mountain, and Grandpa said that every morning, Cub would come across the mountain through what we call Jumper Gap and come down to Grandpa's house. They were digging up laurel roots to sell to the companies that make tobacco pipes.

Well, one morning, Cub came busting into his cabin just white as a ghost. He had gone up his side of the mountain, and when he had got into Jumper Gap, he stepped across what he thought was a pole lying across the trail and sat down on it. It was one of those snakes. When it moved, he jumped up and took off. Grandpa said he was scared to death. They took the gun out and went back up there. The snake was still up there, but they didn't kill it. In our culture, we don't kill things just to kill them. We call the rattlesnake our brother.

There's a story about the "Wrath of the Rattlesnake." A man came home one day, and he found a dead rattlesnake beside his dead wife. His wife had killed the snake, and the snake's mate had killed the man's wife. So, the snake and the man made a pact that day never to kill one another again. When we find a snake in the woods, we just tell it to go where people don't walk. Usually, they'll go out of the trail and leave. Once in a while, if we catch one in here in the village or something, we'll give it to somebody, and they'll take it back into the mountains just to get it away from people. I rarely kill them. Some people do kill them and eat them.

Grandpa said the snake Cub had set down on was about fifteen feet long. He said its head was as big as his hand. A rattlesnake will live a hundred years if you'll leave it alone. They have indiscriminate growth. If they have food, they'll keep growing, just like a fish. So, there were some monsters in this part of the world at one time. Land development has really taken a toll.

We have a lot of stories about giants and unusual creatures. How things got their characteristics is a big part of our culture. One of my favorite stories is why the inchworm is so small and why it has no legs in the middle of its body. They claim that in the beginning, the inchworm was a giant as big as a tree. They're carnivores; they're predators. They hunt and eat bugs and other things. When the inchworm was a giant, he started preying on the Cherokee. They said he'd come to the Cherokee village and stand straight up on the edge of it. They said he looked just like the bark on a tree. He'd wait until the hunters would leave the village, and he'd come down and catch the women and children and eat them.

The Cherokee got tired of that, so they devised a plan to kill the inchworm. They stacked up stone piles around the fire in the middle of the village to look like people when they know the inchworm was going to be there the next day. They waited until light the next morning, and the hunting party got together in the middle of the village so the inchworm could see what was going on. They left the village and went back into the woods and hid. Now, the inchworm, seeing that they had left the village, reached down, but when he reached down, he reached across the fire and grabbed the pile of stones he thought was a person. The stones were so heavy, he couldn't raise up. He kept trying to raise up, but while he was trying to lift that pile of stones, the fire burnt his legs off in the middle of his body. His body started to shrink. When he let go of that pile of stones to get back in the woods away from that fire, he continued to shrink down to an inch long. He had burnt the legs off the middle of his body, and they never did grow back. That's how the inchworm got his characteristics. There are stories like that about everything.

There was a giant serpent called Uktena that guarded a magic crystal. They said it had horns. On an old rattlesnake, the place over its eyes will turn into what looks like horns. They'll raise up and get a spike above their eye. I don't know if this was an old rattlesnake that looked like it had horns or if it was actually a serpent with horns. In Central America and down in northern parts of South America, they have the same image, a winged, horned serpent. Uktena was supposed to have guarded a magic crystal. They claimed that he found the crystal and killed Uktena down [. . .] on King's Mountain.

Up on top of the mountain, there is a stone wall all around the mountain, but on the back, it is a sheer rock cliff. Well, the Shawnee lured that snake up to the wall that he had built. He had oil about every eight or ten feet in a big pit, and he set that oil on fire once the snake got inside the wall. He couldn't go down the backside because of the cliff. It couldn't get out. The snake eventually tried to get out, and the Shawnee warrior doused him with oil and lit him on fire. The snake rolled down the mountain, then killed itself. He went and got the crystal. It was a clear crystal with a bloodred streak in it.

When they excavated Tellico Plains in Tennessee before the TVA [Tennessee Valley Authority] flooded that valley, we were able to go in and do archaeological digs on all the old gravesites. They found that old crystal over there.

In the old stories, when the doctors were using that, they had to feed it fresh blood. That's what the crystal required. There's a prayer, or what we call a formula, to put the crystal to sleep when you're not using it. To put it to sleep, you wrap it in a complete deerskin and bury it. When you want to wake it up, you go get it, take it through another ceremony, and feed it fresh blood. When they excavated Tanasi Village over there, they found the crystal. It had been wrapped in a deerskin and buried. When they got it back out and started handling it, it cut someone and got blood all over it. So, it got the fresh blood it needed to wake up. I think it is at McClung Museum over in Knoxville. A lot of the artifacts that they excavated are over there. Things like that, which have just been looked at as myths from the past, once in a while, they are confirmed through archaeology and science. A lot of what we talk about and the stories we tell are backed up through scientific evidence and archaeology.

The power of a crystal a lot of times is to reckon with the past or to tell the future. A lot of times, it's used to see what's going to happen in the future. Sometimes, it can shed light on how we can use the past as a lesson to make the future better. I think that has been our salvation—that attitude of looking to the past, no matter what has happened, as a lesson and not really holding a grudge.

We had a Day of Absolution a while ago, where everything was forgiven. Once a year, the day before Green Corn Dance, everybody was forgiven, and we started fresh. There was a lot of thinking like that to maintain balance. That kept feuding and fighting out of the tribe. We like to settle arguments with a ball game, a stickball game. That was the little brother of war. If you ever play, it's like war with sticks. I'm getting too old and slow to play anymore, but it used to be a lot of fun.

I get most of my stories from different people whom I have talked to here in the village. My grandfather, my mother's father, told me a lot of stories. We lived with them [my grandparents] until I was ten years old, and I was always out in the woods with him or on a creek bank. Later in life, he became a Baptist preacher, but most of his life, he made moonshine. He was half Cherokee and half Chippewa. His mother was from Wisconsin. She was a Chippewa, and she met his father at Carlisle, which is up in Pennsylvania. Used to, if you wanted more than an eighth-grade education, you had to go to Carlisle or Dartmouth or someplace like that. They had hooked up at Carlisle, so we're part Chippewa.

One of the most popular stories in our culture is about Spearfinger. She was an evil deity that roamed these mountains. She could shape-shift. Some people called her Stone Coat. She had the ability to move boulders with her mind. Her heart was in her hand. When we would attack her, she had almost like a force field around her. Our weapons wouldn't penetrate her coat. That's why they called her Stone Coat.

She loved to eat the livers of children. She would disguise herself as an old lady, and when children were around, she would beg them to come help her. When they would get close enough, she had a big finger-nail on one of her fingers that she would use to stab them and steal their livers. I've heard stories that she wouldn't kill the child, but they would turn into almost like a zombie.

One night, she was dancing around her fire and bragging that if only the Cherokee knew where her heart was, we would be able to kill her. The chickadee heard her and came and told us what he heard. [**Editors' note:** In Cherokee culture, the chickadee is a truth-telling bird.] So, the next time we encountered Spearfinger, one of the warriors shot her in the hand and killed her. They threw her into a pit and burned her to get rid of her body.

They claim a lot of the medicine songs came from that fire when she was being burned. Over around Looking Glass Mountain and Brevard, around over there is where she used to hang out. They claim that she is the one that moved those boulders around into place on some of those mountains up there.

The book Living Stories of the Cherokee *features many stories by Davy Arch and other great Cherokee storytellers. While the written word cannot replicate sitting with Davy Arch at a picnic table outside the Oconaluftee Village, which is surrounded by the mountains featured in the stories, this book comes closer to representing the experience than most.*

THE ORAL TRADITION: PRESERVING TALES THAT SHAPED A NATION

Jerry Wolfe shares stories of the Cherokee

We use the beat of the drum for prayer. When you have the beat of the drum, the whole community comes out for a meeting. Maybe it beat for a club meeting or whatever kind of meeting it is, but you hear the drum. You don't hear it now, but you would hear it a long, long time ago. The sound from the drum always carries up, and whatever's on your mind when you beat that drum will be collected by the sound, and that message will be taken up to the Creator.

—Jerry Wolfe

Jerry Wolfe is a very knowledgeable man when it comes to his people's history, and he gladly told us the legends that shaped the culture that we know today. Listening to him tell the stories of his ancestors as the sound of flute music played through the speakers at the Museum of the Cherokee Indian was an amazing experience.

—*Ethan Phillips*

When I was growing up, I heard a lot of Cherokee stories that were told by my father. We'd all sit around with him and listen to him tell the stories that shaped our tribe. When I was young, we didn't have a tube [television], a radio, or anything like that. All we could do was hear stories. For the most part, the stories were about nature, the wilderness, the animals, and the behavior of animals. They told how the animals behaved and why they have certain markings and stripes. There are so many things that relate to animals in our stories. All the animals are different, and there's a reason for that. That's what I used to hear when I

PLATE 124 Jerry Wolfe tells traditional stories to Foxfire students
Katie Lunsford and Ethan Phillips.

was growing up. Now, before we even get started, I want you to hear my language. We are the only tribe that I know of that has a true written language, and we also have a true written Bible.

We have a lot of Cherokee songs, and we use those songs for prayer. We use the beat of the drum for prayer. When you have the beat of the drum, the whole community comes out for a meeting. Maybe it beats for a club meeting or whatever kind of meeting it is, but you hear the drum. You don't hear it now, but you would hear it a long, long time ago. The sound from the drum always carries up, and whatever's on your mind when you beat that drum will be collected by the sound, and that message will be taken up to the Creator.

Of course, we also had the verbal Cherokee language for prayer. For years, the Creator used one hand to hear what is being said. The Cherokee like to say a little prayer and take a little moment of silence for our armed forces because our armed forces are our protectors. They're the men and women that protect us. So, I like to have a moment of silence, and then I'll do the Lord's Prayer in my language and also in your language.

*After we shared a moment of silence, Jerry Wolfe recited the Lord's
Prayer, first in Cherokee and then in English.*

The Lord's Prayer
Cherokee Translation

*o-gi-do-da ga-lv-la-di-he-hi
ga-lv-quo-di-yu ge-se-s-di de-tsa-do-v-i
tsa-gv-wi-yu-hi ge-sv wi-ga-na-nu-go-i
a-ni-e-lo-hi wi-tsi-ga-li-s-da ha-da-nv-te-s-gv-i
na-s-gi-ya ga-lv-la-di tsi-ni-ga-li-s-di-ha
ni-da-do-da-qui-sv o-ga-li-s-da-yv-di s-gi-v-si go-hi-i-ga
di-ge-s-gi-v-si-quo-no de-s-gi-du-gv-i
na-s-gi-ya tsi-di-ga-yo-tsi-na-ho tso-tsi-du-gi
a-le tla-s-di u-da-go-le-ye-di-yi ge-sv wi-di-s-gi-ya-ti-nv-s-ta-nv-gi
s-gi-yu-da-le-s-ge-s-di-quo-s-gi-ni u-yo ge-sv-i
tsa-tse-li-ga-ye-no tsa-gv-wi-yu-hi ge-sv-i
a-le tsa-li-ni-gi-di-yi ge-sv-i
a-le e-tsa-lv-quo-di-yu ge-sv ni-go-hi-lv-i
e men*

That was in the Cherokee language because we want the Creator to
hear our language and your language, too.

Another thing we don't have in our language is any kind of curse
word. We don't have any curse words at all in our language. We can call
somebody an ugly name, but we don't have a curse word. One time,
there was a young man, and he was talking to a group of people on a
tour. He told them the same thing. He said, "We don't have any curse
words in our language." Someone in the crowd said, "Well, what do you
say when you get mad?" He replied by saying, "We use your language."
So, that's what usually happens whenever Cherokees want to use curse
words.

The Creation Story

The Cherokee people believe that in the beginning, there was nothing
but water. The whole globe was water, but there was an upper room
where all of the animals lived. Well, this upper room was becoming very
crowded. The animals were running out of space because there were
so many members. Whenever they looked down, all they could see was

water. The animals decided that they needed to find some more land, so there would be more room. They wanted a volunteer with wings to fly down and scope out the water to try and find more land. They thought that they might stumble upon an island or something of the sort, so they sent animals such as the pigeon, the turtledove, and other birds to go down, but when they returned, they told the others that they were unable to find land. Then, they got the idea to send a diver to go down and search out beneath the water. Well, the first diver to volunteer was the Grandma Turtle. She told the animals, "I'll go and try to find some land." The other animals responded by saying, "No, you're too old, and we're afraid you'll never return if you go down because you're too old to make the trip. We need someone that's young that can go, make the trip, and come back up." This little water bug decided that he would go down, and they let him go. He went down until he ran into some soft mud. He crawled under that mud, began to pick himself up, and he brought that muck to the top of the water.

After that, they had to give it a few days to stay up and dry so it could become an island. When the mud finally dried, the animals looked down on the island to check on it. When they realized it was dry, they sent down the Big Buzzard to scope out the land. The Big Buzzard came along when the muck was soft, but he grew tired from all the flying. As a result, he flew low to the ground. As he flapped down, his wings made the valleys down in that muck, and when he pulled his wings back up, it formed mountains. Once he gave the other animals the okay, they moved down onto that island where there were mountains, but they soon realized they needed fire.

There was a small island across the water that had a few sycamore trees on it. Well, lightning had come down and struck those trees, and they caught on fire. The animals could see the fire burning, but there was water between the two islands. There was no way to get that fire over to the mainland. The deer and several other animals tried to get the fire, but they failed. The Big Hoot Owl tried, and he burned those round discs they have around their eyes. He also scorched around his eyes, and they became white. As a result, he has those white circles around his eyes. After the Hoot Owl tried, they sent the Raven. He told them, "I'll go get some of that fire." When he got over there, he was absolutely scorched by the flames. All of his feathers were scorched, and he turned into a big black bird. Then, there was another bird that went over and tried, but he failed, too. Well, the Little Spider said, "I'll go." So, they said, "Go and see if you can get some fire." Before he went, he made a little basket out of his web. When he completed that, he went right across the water over to that island, and he managed to get a burning coal in that little basket. Then, he hurried back across. He brought the fire to the mainland, and that's the reason we have fire today.

The Story of the Chipmunk

When I was younger, my dad always told me the story about the time when the animals had a big meeting, many years ago. The main topic of discussion in this meeting between the animals was the hunters. The hunters came in and shot their moms, dads, brothers, and sisters, and they never put anything back into the forest for payment. Well, the big bear was chairman of this big meeting, and he was listening to all the animals. Finally, he looked over on the little ledge, and there was the little chipmunk. Now, the chipmunk is a small animal. He was sitting on the ledge, and he was all hunkered over. The big bear says to the chipmunk, "What's with you? You haven't said a word in this meeting." Then the little chipmunk said, "The hunters don't bother me. The hunters are looking for bigger animals because they need meat to go on their tables to feed their families." Well, this didn't go over too well with the big bear. He grabbed that little chipmunk, took his claws, and scratched the little chipmunk down the back. Those stripes that were made back then are still there to this day. Our Cherokee people used to call the chipmunk *gi-yu-ga*, which means "seven stripes." That's what the chipmunk has on his back—seven stripes. The big bear put those stripes there. That's one of the stories that I'd heard from a long time ago.

How the Possum Got Its Tail

One of the stories I heard growing up was the story of the possum. In the beginning, the possum had a big, glossy, fluffy tail. It was a beautiful tail, the most beautiful of all the animals of the forest. Annually, they would have a contest to see what animal had the most beautiful fur coat or tail or whatever. All the animals would fix up their coats. They would shine them up, and they'd get up onstage to be judged. Every time, the possum won because of his tail. The day before this big contest was coming up, the rabbit come along and met the possum. He said to the possum, "I know you're going to be in our contest, and you always win that contest. So, tonight, I'm coming to your house, and I'm going to work on your tail. I'm going to make it more beautiful than it already is. After I'm through working on it, it's going to be shiny, glossy, and just a beautiful tail. Then, when I finish putting the final touches on it, I'm going to wrap it so it won't get messed up for tomorrow night. Then, at the contest, we'll unwrap it right before you go onstage."

The next day, the rabbit visited the possum, and he had brought company with him. He brought the little cricket with him. In Cherokee we call it *ta-la-du,* and that translates to barber. Well, he brought the barber along with him, and the rabbit came up to the possum and told him, "Just lie down, and relax. We're going to work on your tail." So, the possum lay down and took it easy. As he was relaxing, the rabbit pretended that he was really working on his tail. Right behind the rabbit was the little cricket, and he was taking all the hair off the possum's tail. The rabbit would rewrap the bare tail as the cricket was cutting the hair off. After a while, the rabbit got all of the tail wrapped up for the next night, which was contest night.

The next night, all the animals got together to have the contest. When it came the possum's turn to go up onstage, all the animals applauded, called, whistled, cheered, and did all kinds of stuff because he was always the winner. This time, before he entered the stage, the rabbit began to unwrap the tail, and as he unwrapped it, all the bare tail began to show. The possum had the ugliest tail of all the animals.

The possum didn't know anything was going on because all the animals were still making noises, shouting, and yelling. Then, he looked back and saw his ugly tail. It was so ugly, he fell over and played dead, which he still does to this day. Ever since that happened, he has had the ugliest tail of all the animals of the forest today.

The Story of the Snake and the Troublemaker

Another story I heard was the one about the snake and the troublemaker. The troublemaker was something that lived in our Cherokee Village and would go from one village to the next and cause a lot of trouble for the families. It would cause them to have all kinds of mishaps. It wasn't good, because it would lie. It told lies, tales, and all sorts of things. The Cherokee began wondering what in the world they were going to do with this troublemaker. It had caused them a lot of trouble, and they'd just let this troublemaker do it for too long, so they went to one of the leaders and told him the problem. The leader said, "There's a man down the way, and I think he can solve that problem." The tribal leader went to visit the man to see what he could do, and when he came back, he decided he was going to make a bunch of concoction (poison juice). After he made the concoction, they were going to send some men out into the mountains to get a snake and feed the poison to it, which would make it become venomous. They were going to take the venomous snake and set it down in the path where that troublemaker walked. That snake was going to bite the troublemaker on the leg, and from the bite, the troublemaker would die. Then, they'd be rid of the troublemaker.

As they were discussing these plans, they were sitting in a log cabin. Just outside, there was a snake that was listening. He was listening to all the details that were being said, and before they left, they placed the concoction in a container and sat it up on a shelf. The four or five men left, and they went to the mountains in search of that snake.

Now, it was a certain kind of snake that they wanted. They wanted a nonvenomous snake, so it was about three or four days before they found the right snake and brought it back to the little village. When they arrived and went to get the concoction down to feed the snake, there was nothing in there. It was empty. The snake that had been listening just outside had crawled in the cabin and up on the shelf. He drank that concoction and became venomous. When he became venomous, he went and killed the troublemaker. He went and laid just how he had heard them discuss, and he bit that troublemaker as it was coming down the trail. It soon died from the snakebite.

This snake was so proud of itself for doing the job that it came to all those people that had caught the nonvenomous snake, and he said, "Oh, I did the job. I did the job. The job's done, so you don't have to worry about that no more."

This didn't make the leaders happy. There was this one shaman that didn't like that at all. He said, "Now look; you are a sneaky snake. You eavesdrop, and you sneak up on people and bite them. You will be hated the rest of your life. As long as you live, you will be hated."

Today, the snake that killed the troublemaker is the copperhead. The copperhead stole that concoction, and that's the reason he's venomous today. That's the reason that he'll lay out, and I'll tell you, he'll bite you. That's how he came to be.

The Tale of Uktena

I heard this story before, and several different people have published it. It's the story about the big snake, Uktena. It was a big snake that was once here in this area. Uktena had a crystal on its head, and it was very powerful. The snake lived on a mountain that is referred to as Rattlesnake Mountain. In Cherokee, its translation means "Covered in Fire" because the mountain glows every so often. I've seen it glow, but it doesn't glow all the time. Uktena's crystal is hidden somewhere on that mountain, and that's what makes it glow. Many years ago, the Cherokees captured a Creek Indian. I'm not exactly sure what his offense was or why he was locked up, but they had captured him. He'd been here for quite some time, and he began to wonder how he was ever going to get out. He began to ponder that, and he thought about that big snake, Uktena. He said to himself, "I'm going to make a bargain with the authorities." He told the Cherokees, "If you will release me from prison, I will go and kill that snake and bring you the crystal from its head. You can use that crystal for any kind of power. You can use it for anything from healing purposes to whatever you might need." Then, they agreed to turn him loose. When he was released, he really didn't know where the snake was located, but Native Americans had ways of finding out where there was a big animal. They could foresee things.

Well, the Creek Indian began listening around, and he discovered that northern Alabama was home to a big snake. So, he traveled to northern Alabama, but when he arrived, the snake he had heard about turned out to only be a black snake. That wasn't the snake he wanted, but it was a great big one.

After that, he searched until he heard word of another reptile over in Tennessee, so he traveled from northern Alabama over to the mountains of Tennessee. This snake just ended up being an ordinary water snake. He said, "No, that's not the one I want. I want to find Uktena."

The next time he searched, he came close to the area where the Cherokee had released him, and he found that snake up in the Great Smokies. It was located up in the high altitudes. When he arrived, he just about fainted because the sight of that snake was so terrible. He grabbed some dry wood and surrounded that snake with the wood. When he finished, he lit it, and it all began to burn. The snake was consumed in the flames. He burned Uktena to death. After the snake had burned, he was able to get that big crystal. When he got the big crystal, he brought it back to the Cherokee. He presented it to them, and they took it.

The Cherokee people only had one man that looked after that crystal. He was a wise old shaman, and he was given the job of caring for the crystal. He had to feed that crystal and take care of it because it could be dangerous.

They did that for several years until the old man that was in charge of it discovered that he wasn't going to live much longer. As a result, he grabbed that crystal and carried it up on the mountain known to us as Rattlesnake Mountain, and he proceeded to hide it. We don't know the exact spot, but that crystal is hidden somewhere on that mountain. No one knows where it is, and just about once a year or so, that mountain will kind of glow. A certain place up there will glow because of that crystal.

My son told me he was out mowing the lawn one time, and he said, "You know, that mountain was glowing. I saw it glowing the other day." When he said that, it took me back to that crystal and the story of how it's hidden somewhere on that mountain. No one knows where, and I wouldn't want to know its location because it would probably be dangerous if you really found it.

Every one of the stories I know was told to me by my dad. We Cherokee have a lot of old traditions and beliefs. We always go through some rituals before we do anything. We go to the water for strength and for cleansing. We use a lot of medicine that comes out of the mountains. The medicines we use include things such as herbs that we drink to help our performance. All of the medicines that we use, we would drink to help clear us out. It would wash everything away.

The Story of Spearfinger

There was another story about Spearfinger. She was a disguiser, and she was very cruel to children. Well, the warriors got tired of her cruelness, and they went out to kill her. There was one bird that told them to shoot Spearfinger in the heart, but it didn't work. They began to call that bird Utsu`gï, which means "liar bird."

Well, the chickadee told the Cherokee to shoot her in the finger because her heart was in her finger. When they shot her there, it killed her, so from then on, [the chickadee] was known as Tsï'kïlilï', which means "true bird."

Story of Bingo

Many years ago, the foreigners were wondering what kind of games were being played by the Americans. As time went along, they discussed and decided to send a man over to watch these games after some meetings took place. When this man arrived here in America, baseball season was on. So, he went to every baseball game, and he used a little notebook to take notes on the sport of baseball.

Well, after baseball season was over, football season rolled into the picture. So, he went to every football game and wrote down some notes on football. After football, he watched basketball, and many other games. Once he had completed his research, he returned to Europe and made his report on all the games, but there's one game he didn't report on. He told the committee, "There's one game I didn't report on because I didn't quite understand what was taking place." He said, "Late in the evening, way back in the country, a group of men would set up a large tent. Well, under the tent they began to bring in tables and chairs. They would place cards on the tables, and the cards had letters and numbers on them. In a few moments, there would be a lot of people driving in, and the tent would fill up with people. As they came in, each one would grab a card and little grains of corn that had been placed on the table, and they would take them and find their seats. In a few moments, a man would come to a microphone and begin calling letters and numbers. It wouldn't be long after they started that you'd start to hear some heavy breathing and whispering. After that was over, somewhere in the crowd someone would yell out, 'Bingo!'" Then, he said, "All the rest of the crowd would say, 'Oh s#°+!'" So, he told the committee, "I didn't know what to call that game."

MAWMAW'S STORIES

Mountain tales told by Bonnie Shirley

I don't know if Mama made 'em up or if they were passed down from her mama. I truly don't know, but I know that when my kids were small, we'd lay in the bed at night, and I'd tell 'em these stories.
—Bonnie Shirley

Each story teaches a different lesson and has a variety of meanings. Mawmaw, my grandmother, Bonnie Shirley, has personally told me each one, time after time, in hopes of having them passed down to further generations . . . and to teach me a lesson or two.

I, myself, also use these stories from time to time. I remember going out and looking out in the woods for anything that seemed just spooky. A lot of the time, I also found myself running in the opposite direction of old ladies and blond-headed girls.

—*Taylor Shirley*

My mama used to tell us all kinds of stories when we were growing up. Sometimes, I don't really know if she told them to us just to scare us to death or to keep our attention and make us mind. I really don't know, but anyway, she told us several. I'll start off with the man on the bridge. My mama told us this story, and we tried it out one time to see if it actually was the truth.

Many years ago, it was raining really hard, and this man was coming around the curve to the bridge and he wrecked! It cut his head off, and when they found him, they found his body but not his head. So, on cold, foggy nights, you can go to the bridge and see his footprints because he was looking for his head.

When we were teenagers, we weren't allowed to go anywhere much, but me, my brother, my sister, and a group of friends decided to go to the bridge to see him. It was cold, foggy, and it was raining, so we went to the bridge. When we got over there, we sat at a church above the bridge—we were scared to sit at the church because of the cemetery, and we really didn't want to sit at the bridge either, but being the crazy teenagers we were, we parked the car. We walked and was looking around everywhere for his head, but when we got to the bridge, we were scared and cold from the rain. We waited and we waited and we waited, and there was just nothing there. All of a sudden, we heard a racket, and we turned around. We were all just absolutely scared to death, but it was my brother. He had left us and was sneaking up on us just to scare us. After that, we were laughing, and eventually, all of us went home.

When we got there Mama wanted to know where we had been. We told her we went to the bridge, and I asked her why we didn't see the man. She sat me down and said, "Well, honey, no wonder you didn't see him; there was too many of you. You have to be very quiet and not make no racket, but that man will come back out and look for his head one day."

There was another story, an old Indian tale my mama used to tell us about the light going up our creek.

She said this woman had lost her baby and never found out what happened to the baby, so every night, she would take a lantern and go down the creek and look for her baby. She did this for the rest of her life, and Mama said that on certain nights, you could see the light going up and down the creek. My daddy was a very religious man, and he didn't believe in ghost stories and other stuff like that. He always said that there was nothing to it, but my mama believed that light went up and down the creek. I never saw it, but the Indian woman's baby was never

PLATE 125 Taylor and Bonnie Shirley

found, so they never found out if it died or was just gone. Mama always said, though, that the girl was looking for her baby and soon thought that she was starting to have mental problems over seeing this light. Even though my daddy didn't believe in that light, he told us that he had heard about this light one time, and that it was the northern lights—the aurora borealis. He didn't believe in supernatural lights and whatnot, but when my sister was born, they named her Aurora. They named her after that light to keep her safe, and no matter what my mama did, she always believed the story about that girl looking for her baby, and she always retold it to us time after time.

One of the stories that she told us that I will never forget is about the woman who smoked:

There was an old woman that lived in a house deep in the woods, and she always smoked. She smoked, and she smoked, and she smoked. She would go out on her porch of a night, and she'd smoke her a cigarette. She'd always say, "Who's gonna spend the night with me tonight?" Then a voice in the woods would say, "I am. I am." She'd go back in her house and stay awhile, then come back out and smoke a cigarette and smoke and smoke and say, "Who's gonna spend the night with me tonight?" The thing in the woods would say, "I am. I am." Every time the voice would speak, it was getting closer and closer, but she still kept coming out to smoke a cigarette and saying, "Who's gonna spend the night with me tonight?" Eventually, it was coming up on her porch and the voice said, "I am. I am." This time she went back inside, and when she came out, she smoked, and she smoked, and she smoked. She didn't know the voice was that close and she said, "Who's gonna spend the night with me tonight?" The voice said, "I AM!" and it grabbed her and took her off.

Then she would tell us about the old woman that cut the old man's toe off and seasoned her beans with it:

One time, there was this old woman, and she was a mean old woman. She was cooking her some beans on the old wood cookstove. She didn't have anything to season them with, but she saw this old man walking down the road, and she lured him to her house. She said, "I'll fix you something to eat if you'll sit and talk to me awhile." And the man said, "Sure, I'll talk to ya." She gave him something to knock him out, and she cut his big toe off and put it in the beans. When he woke up, he couldn't figure out what happened to his big toe, and the beans were done, so the old woman said, "Would you like to have some of my beans? Would you like to eat with me?" and the man said, "Sure, I'm hungry." They started eating the beans. The man said, "These sure are good beans, but I can't figure out what happened to my big toe." He said, "It looks like it's gone." He decided he would leave, and he was headed out the door when something outside said, "I want my big toe back! I want my big toe!"

Then, there was the one where the lady was going to visit her neighbor through the woods. I truly think our mama told us this one to where we wouldn't slip off because we were bad to slip off as kids to go to our neighbor's house. They lived on the other side of the mountain, but she always told the story about this woman:

There was this woman who had a baby and was going to see her neighbor that lived across the mountain. There was a barbed wire fence that she had to cross, and my mama said that every day the woman heard a panther crying. My mama didn't call it a "panther," though; she called it a "painer." She said, "That painer would cry, and it sounded just like a baby." That woman never paid any attention to it, though, because she knew it would never come close. So, this one certain day, she was going to visit her neighbor, and she had to cross that barbed wire fence, so she set the baby down. She could hear the panther, but she set her baby down and thought that the panther was way up in the woods. When she crossed the barbed wire fence, she turned around, and her baby was gone. She went back over the fence and started looking for her baby. She couldn't find the baby, but she could hear it crying, so she started off in that direction. When she found the sound, she thought she saw the baby crawling in its blanket, but it was just a baby panther. She never saw her baby again.

My favorite story of all was about the little girl and the pears:

One time, there was a little girl that had beautiful golden hair, and she lived with her grandmother and grandfather. Her grandmother sent her to the store one day, gave her money, and she said, "I want you to get some beans, and I want you to get some flour, and I need a sack of milk." So, the little girl said "Okay, Grandmother, I'll go."

When the little girl got to the store, she saw these pears, and they were so beautiful. She wanted one to eat so bad, and she asked the owner of the store how much they were.

He said, "Well, how much money do you have?"

She said, "I have three dollars."

He gave the little girl six pears for her three dollars. The man put them in a sack, and she was on her way home when she decided she'd eat one. She did, and she said, "Oh my goodness, that was so good!" So, she decided to eat another one. She ate it, and when she was nearly home, she said, "Oh, that pear was so good that I think I'll have another." So, she ate one more, and her tummy was so full that when she got home, she was sleepy.

The grandmother said, "Granddaughter, granddaughter, where's the groceries that I sent you after?"

The little girl said, "But Grandmother, I bought pears instead. I bought six golden pears."

"There are only three pears here. Where are the other three?"

"Well, Grandmother, I was hungry, so I ate 'em."

The grandmother said, "Well, come out in the wood yard. I wanna show you something."

The little girl just kept getting sleepier and sleepier. She couldn't figure out what her grandmother wanted to show her in the wood yard, but she still went out there. About the time she got there, she was so sleepy that she laid her head down on a block of wood, and she went to sleep. Well, the grandmother took an ax and cut her head off. She buried it in the onion patch and went on about her business, but she was upset because the little girl didn't get the groceries she wanted.

She still had to cook her husband something for supper, and she didn't have the flour and stuff to cook the bread. That night, when the grandpa came home from working in the fields and cutting wood, the grandpa said, "Where's our little girl? Where's our granddaughter?"

The grandmother said, "Well, she's outside playing somewhere."

He said, "Well, you need to call her because it's time for supper."

The grandma said, "All I got tonight is beans. All I could cook was beans."

And he said, "Oh, that's all right. I'll just go out to the onion patch and get some onions."

The grandma said, "Okay."

He went into the garden, and started to pull up an onion, but it wouldn't come up. There was this little voice that kept saying, "Grandfather, Grandfather, please don't pull my hair because Grandmother killed me over six golden pears."

He looked around and said, "Man, I must be dreaming! That sounded just like my granddaughter, but I just can't understand why I can't get this onion up. I'll just try another one."

So, he tried another one and this little voice said, "Grandfather, Grandfather, please don't pull my hair because Grandmother killed me over six golden pears."

The old man said, "That has got to be my granddaughter, but I just can't understand where she is. I still can't understand why I can't get the onion up either! I'll try and get this one up. It's not as big."

So, he tried to pull the onion up again and a little voice said, "Grandfather, Grandfather, please don't pull my hair because Grandmother killed me over six golden pears."

So, the grandfather got up and said, "That sounds just like my granddaughter, but I can't find out where that voice is coming from."

All of a sudden, the onion turned loose out of the ground, and it was the granddaughter's hair. She had pulled her hair up from the ground, and he was so shocked that he started digging and digging until he found the little girl's head. He was so distraught that he went back into the house and yelled, "Old woman! Old woman! What happened to our granddaughter?"

She said, "Grandpa, she's out, she's out! She's outside playing."

Then, the grandpa came closer, and he said, "*No*, old woman, I found her head in the onion patch. Come out here. I wanna show you; I want to show you what I found!" She knew all along what he was gonna find, but she went out there with him.

About that time, he pushed her in that hole where he found that little girl's head, and the little girl came back to life. The grandma was gone. [The little girl] and her grandpa lived happily ever after.

Can you imagine having these stories told to you as a child, especially when you live in the mountains? We believed these stories. I don't know if Mama made 'em up or if they were passed down from her mama. I truly don't know, but I know that when my kids were small, we'd lay in the bed at night, and I'd tell 'em these stories. They'd laugh and say, "Tell me again; tell me again." Then, when I had grandchildren, I told them these stories, and they did the same thing. My grandkids and my children couldn't understand why my mother told me these stories, and like I said before, I don't know if it was to hold our attention, to scare us, or for pure entertainment. I grew up in the 1950s, and I lived in the country, and we didn't get to go to town every day or go to the store. We played in the woods, and we played in the creek, you know. We didn't have all the stuff kids do today. We didn't have a lot of toys or iPods. We did have a TV, but we only got to watch it at night because we had chores to do during the day.

My mama always found time for us, though. She always told 'em [the stories] to us. I think this reflects on the Appalachian culture because we all believe the folklore about ghosts and witches and stuff like that. I pray that when my grandchildren have kids, they pass these stories down to them.

After completing this article, Taylor Shirley wrote a play based on the stories you've read here. The play was performed during Rabun County High School's Fine Arts Festival in May 2013.

BLACKSMITHING

In olden days, when we didn't live in a throwaway or replace-it world, a blacksmith was fundamental to his community. His store was a gathering place for menfolk on rainy days. He made ox yokes, harnesses, nails, and tools, and he repaired damaged items.

In "The Hammer and the Forge," Dan Maxwell laments that blacksmithing may truly be a vanishing art. He says, "If we don't keep younger people interested or train 'em, it's goin' by the wayside." Former student Mike Ivey still practices blacksmithing and often demonstrates the art at our Foxfire Mountaineer Festival, and recently two Foxfire students have answered the call to rescue this critical art form. David Campbell and Eli Bundrick have not only taken an interest in the art, but they have also practiced the art and have both become well respected in the community for their talents.

—*Jonathan Blackstock*

THE HAMMER AND THE FORGE

An interview with Dan Maxwell

I guess I was born a hundred years too late because I always liked the old way of livin' when you had more time to visit and spend the afternoons, take a drive. The people are still the same. It's just the ideas.

—Dan Maxwell

When I pull into the Maxwells' driveway to conduct my first Foxfire interview, I immediately feel welcomed. I had spoken to Mr. Maxwell over the telephone a handful of times before we set the date for our interview, and I was already curious about not only the art of blacksmithing but the soft-spoken man with the hammer as well.

The Maxwells live in a log house with a wraparound porch that is, in itself, an invitation to sit and visit. With a view of a small valley and the mountains beyond, a visitor feels as if the busy world, just a few minutes away, has disappeared for a short while. A sign hangs from the mailbox—"Smokey Valley Forge"—and the driveway separates the lawn from the blacksmithing shop. Mr. Maxwell, along with his puppy named Georgia Girl, greeted me upon my arrival.

It was a perfect early autumn afternoon, which added to the feeling of "coming home." We sat at a table on the porch for the interview, and as Mr. Maxwell answered my questions with stories of his life and how he had become involved in blacksmithing, Georgia Girl joined us once more. Later, Mrs. Maxwell came home and gave me a tour of the log cabin, followed by a tour of Mr. Maxwell's blacksmith shop.

In a technology-based world full of cars, computers, and cellular phones, blacksmithing is a dying art form. Once a trade that enabled farmers to plow fields, carpenters to build homes, and many people to make a living, blacksmithing has become a trade mainly for ornamental pieces. This trade is a part of Appalachian legacy, and the Maxwells honor the memory and history of the blacksmiths of this area by helping to preserve this art.

—*Cheryl Binnie*

I will be fifty-eight years old this year [2002]. I was born and raised in Douglasville, and my father and mother used to bring us—my mother and kids—up here to Rabun County, so we've always known about it.

I was raised on a farm. I had one brother and one sister. They're all dead now, but we worked on a farm. It could get pretty tough. We lived on a little dirt road, and my mother would go down it once a week to buy groceries. We lived one mile from the main road, where she would catch the bus. She'd leave in the morning, and the bus didn't run back again until that afternoon. We knew what time the bus ran, so we'd meet her up there in our wagon and haul the groceries back. We had everything we needed.

I got interested as a kid in shoein' horses and mules on the farms. I did that all the way through high school. When I got out of high school, a friend of mine and myself went on an excursion: We bought a panel truck and went to Hialeah racetrack in Florida, and we shod horses all the way down. When we got to the racetrack, we shod horses, and we spent about three weeks there. 'Course, after every race, they'd need new shoes, so we'd make good money. Then, we'd come back a different way, and we'd shoe horses on the way back. People wanted their horses shod about every eight weeks. We'd make a loop and come back, and when we got home, it was time to go again, so here we'd go. We were never home. We were always shoein' horses. I had enough of that and went into the service, went to Vietnam, and got out of the service.

Metalwork and shoein' horses and blacksmithing were all in the same category. 'Course, a "farrier" is the name they give to a person who shoes horses.

I usually always had a forge, even shoein' horses, so I was used to a forge very early on. You have to put hot shoes on horses and heat 'em up and turn the caulks on the ends for pullin'. You make the shoe usually

PLATE 126 Dan Maxwell in his shop

for workhorses or draft horses, and you have to put the heel caulks and toe caulks on. You have to turn those in the fire. 'Course, blacksmithing is different. You just have to worry 'bout gettin' burned with the metal rather than gettin' kicked by a horse. There's quite a bit of difference, but the fire maintenance is the same and the procedures of quenchin' the metal are the same in any kind of forge fire.

I was getting a little older, and I didn't want to shoe horses all my life. I wanted to get into metalwork, and a blacksmith named Jud Nelson [**Editors' note:** See *Foxfire 9*, "The Jud Nelson Wagon"] wanted to see if I was really interested in blacksmithin' and keepin' with it, so he gave me a railroad spike, and he told me he wanted a spoon made out of it that was eighteen inches long and had the spoon out of the head of the railroad spike, and the other end had to have a hook on it so you can hang it up. I worked all day on it, and I finally had a piece of . . . Well, it was eighteen inches long, but it didn't look much like a spoon. He told me I'd do.

In the process, I learned how to use the fire and make things out of short pieces of metal, just like the old-timers used t' have to. The metal didn't come in sizes. It'd come in just pieces that you had to draw out, and this is a good example of the "peen" of the blacksmith hammer. The blacksmith hammer has got a face side, which is the flat side, and it's got a "half peen" on the other. A half peen is similar to a finger that's sideways, and that's how you draw your metal. Then, you do your flattening with the face of the hammer. You have to draw things, such as a railroad spike, out if you want it long; then you have to draw it out with the peen of the hammer. I learned fire maintenance and how to control the fire, to know when to add coal.

I moved to the mountains about fifteen years ago. We didn't have much money, and I was goin' to have to build my house myself, which I did. I never advertised, but somehow people found me. I sharpened plows and tools and reconditioned old tools. Then, I went to the John C. Campbell folk school in Brasstown, North Carolina, and studied the art of blacksmithing and made screens and fire tools. They taught me that. That kept me busy for fifteen years. I couldn't make it full-time, but I have a couple other different jobs.

I like sharpenin' plows and makin' tools. I really enjoy it. 'Course, you don't get to do that much anymore as a blacksmith. When I first came up here, I had a little blacksmith shop out on Highway 76 [Clayton, Georgia] in front of the hospital. I remember a fella on Scaly Mountain, North Carolina, an old farmer, came and had four plows and a scooter. He still plowed with mules up in Scaly. He wanted me to sharpen the tools he brought down, and he said, "When can I pick them up?" I said, "Well, about two weeks." Two weeks, he came back. 'Course, he was as old-timey as I was, and he says, "How much I owe you?" I said, "About ten dollars." Of course, when you sharpen a plow, you have to sharpen it, and then re-temper it, so there's a lot to it. I said, "About ten dollars." He said, "What?" And I said, "Well, it'll be twelve fifty." And he says, "I heard you the first time." So, I was goin' up on him again if he asked me again. That's the way the old-timers were. They didn't have much money, and they usually did it themselves, so that's changed.

Times have changed over the years. I still don't have a computer. I guess I was born a hundred years too late because I always liked the old way of livin', when you had more time to visit and spend the afternoons, take a drive. The people are still the same. It's just the ideas. Times have really changed, and as far as blacksmithin', people don't need their plows sharpened anymore. They don't need tools made because they can go now to the hardware store and buy the things they need. It's cheaper than gettin' 'em made these days. There's a lot of ornamental work to be done. That's what we blacksmiths have to go into now to make a livin' or to stay in the profession that we know and like. That's why I got into ornamental ironwork.

That's what we have nowadays, and as far as the history of blacksmithing, the blacksmiths now have to go into the ornamental ironwork rather than making tools and so forth. The things I made as a blacksmith in the year 2000 are fireplace utensils, fire screens, and chandeliers. I make tables and chairs. Just about anything you can make out of wood, we can make out of iron. That's about where we stand now as far as the history of it goes.

Personally, I stick to the old methods, but I've got some modern equipment down there in my shop. The old-timey way was nothing but a forge and an anvil and a hammer. It was a little difficult, but it turned out prettier if it was hammered right from scratch. Nowadays, we have power hammers and welders and things like that. You have tongs and hammers, different-sized tongs for metal. When you get a job, you usually have to make your own tongs for the type of metal.

The hardest thing I have ever had to make, I guess, would be an apple tree. It took about two weeks to make it, but the planning of it and making the tools to make it with took about two months. The most important thing is knowing and planning and getting your tools ready before you start a job because a lot of times, dependin' on what the job is, you have to make tongs to hold the metal. If it's a real thick piece that

PLATE 127 Mr. Maxwell's blacksmith shop

you're gonna draw out, or fuller, which is tapered down to the neck and shoulder, you have to make tongs to hold it while it's in the fire and to grip it good when it comes out of the fire so you can work with it.

That is a process all its own that you don't think about with black-smithin'. You think, I just need a pair of tongs and a fire and things like that, but, most of the time, you have to make your own tools to make objects that you're gonna create.

What's also hard to make are gate railings and fences. I made a fence to go around a flower garden in Otto, North Carolina. They wanted all the pickets hand-forged, spaced six inches apart. Every picket had to be different in its own design, have its own character about it. I had to make the tongs to hold the pickets, and then I had to make tools to form the top handrail. It had to be curved in certain places 'cause it comes around like a sidewalk. It's easy to bend a piece of metal on the face side, if it is flat, but it's much harder to bend it on the edge. To bend it on the edge, you have to expand one side and contract the inner side to make it come out flat. So, you have to make tools to grip the sides of the metal and to twist it when it comes out. It has to be quite hot all of the time while you are doing it, and you're continually havin' to put it back on the anvil and layin' it out to your template to make sure that it's the right curve. The molecules are goin' crazy and just changin' the whole time. It's better to have a template of the actual size of the gate out of cardboard or a drawing on a table, a big enough table that you could continually put it back and lay it down to make sure that the curve is right.

You have to do it all at once. You can make it in pieces, but if you are doin' it the old blacksmith way, if you make short pieces, you're gonna have to forge-weld it all back onto itself, and you're gonna have to hammer and chisel if it's got any kind of facet to it at all, if the top railing has any kind of design to it. Sometimes, it takes two or three people at the forge to help you hold these things. 'Course, if it's gonna be real long, you can do it in sections and then forge-weld it together. If you're workin' by yourself, you'll do it in shorter pieces, which I've mainly done all my work by myself.

Some of the chandeliers get pretty in-depth, sometimes. 'Course, I like to make chandeliers. There's a lot of different type things that people want that come up new to me that's real exciting and challenging— you know, to try to make something that you've never made before. I like to do that most of all.

'Course, I belong to a blacksmith club called ABANA (Artist-Blacksmith's Association of North America), and if I have trouble, which you always do, I can call a blacksmith friend, and maybe they've done

PLATE 128 One of Mr. Maxwell's chandeliers

something similar that could help me and give me advice. There's always something to learn about in blacksmithing. You may think people want the same thing of something that you have done before, but there'll be a different finial, an end piece, on it, or the design may change on it, so you go back to the drawin' board, figure out what you're gonna do, and draw it out.

You learn to work the metal, and your objective is to control the metal instead of having it control you. Unless you know pretty much what you're doin' when you get to the forge, and you practice, then the metal is gonna control you. You're gonna get frustrated and depressed because it's not gonna be what you want, and you're gonna spend more time correcting mistakes than you are workin' on your final piece.

For the old-timers, it was all pretty much standard. If you wanted a wheel or a rim for a wagon wheel, the only thing that changed was the diameter and the thickness, but it was all the same.

The history of blacksmithing, as I know it, is thousands of years old. People used to extract iron ore out of the ground and start making forge pieces. They'd make the cast of iron pieces. Iron ore, of course, is made out of phosphorus, trees, and wood. It came in big hunks, and if you wanted a little piece, you just had to cut it off and make rods or stuff like that. In the 1900s, they made wrought iron and roiled it into different-sized bars. It was like clay, and you could mold it like clay from the fire. It had what was known as a "silica fiber" in it, and it was real easy to work. They made wagon wheels out of it and farm implements and just any of the old nails for the houses, which you can buy nowadays. You used to have to make them.

After the turn of the century, they quit makin' the wrought iron, and they went to what is known as "mild" steel. Two types of that are "cold roll" and "hot roll," which has less carbon in it than wrought iron. What we got to work with nowadays is the hot and cold roll steel, and it's real tough to work with. It's not as pliable, and you have to heat it twice the temperature. Normally, cold roll had more carbon in it than hot roll, which was harder. The hot roll was easier to work with, but with less strength. The more you heat the metal, the more carbon you burn out. You try to get as much done in one heat as you can.

Coal is real hard to find for a blacksmith nowadays. There are three types of coal. The type that you use for heating is lignite. We call it a "stoker" coal, and it's got very little carbon in it and a lot of moisture and ash and sulfur. It won't burn real hot. Blacksmithing, you have to get it to a temperature in the fire of twenty-one hundred degrees sometimes to weld two pieces of metal together. So, lignite, the stoker coal, won't get it that hot. It'll get it to eight hundred degrees or something like that. The next type is bituminous. You can get it twenty-one hundred degrees. The next type is called an anthracite coal, which metallers [metal workers] just use. The coal a blacksmith uses is bituminous.

When I get started, I clear out the hollow of the forge to where you got a "duck's nest." A duck's nest is something that air comes up around it, and there's small holes that the air blows through and makes the fire hotter. It's called a duck's nest and a clinker breaker. You get deposits of slag material, and in the coal it forms over the duck's nest. Then you got your clinker breaker up so it'll fall on through so it won't obstruct your airflow. Then, you clear that out, and then you take about three sheets of newspaper and light it and then bring the coal to it, little by little—you don't put too much coal on it—and you'll start up real good. When it gets burning pretty good, you just put the air on it, and it makes it burn faster and hotter.

Most people are surprised, but when you get a good, hot fire, to make it hotter, you put water on it or around it. It helps the coal to melt

PLATE 129 Mr. Maxwell works at the forge.

together and makes a hotter fire. You sprinkle water on it, and it makes it more of a mass, a pyramid for your fire. If you want to get it to welding heat, you have to be about 1,800 to 2,000 degrees in the fire before you weld; so you add water, and it makes it hotter.

It'll get about twelve to fifteen hundred degrees, so it's real hot. That's just for normal forgin' work, or really any kind of metal, the normal forgin' temperature, and I've got a little blower with a rheostat on it. A rheostat is just like a dimmer switch on a light socket. You can increase the light by turnin' the dimmer switch, so that's like a rheostat, and that controls the amount of air. It's on the motor of the forge, the motor that blows air, and you adjust your air by that.

You get it goin' real hot, and then you put your metal in, and it starts gettin' black hot. You can see it change colors. The metal will get black, and then it'll get red, and then it'll get white. Between red and white is your normal range for your forgin'. If it starts sparkin', it means your metal's burnin' up, so it shouldn't be in there that long, unless you're doin' another purpose like weldin'.

If I get it out between the red hot and the white hot, I just bring it on the anvil and start makin' what I'm gonna make or start formin' it. In other words, like the leaf. I made it out of a half-inch-square stock. I put it in there, and I let it get nearly white hot, and then, depending on how long I want the leaf, I make the shoulder of the leaf. The shoulder is where it gets to the stem. I make that first, and then that determines the length of the leaf. Then I go ahead, and where I've shouldered it, I start drawin' it out from there to the end. Then, 'course, I make a point on the leaf end t' where it'll look like a leaf, and so I flatten it out into the design of leaf that I want.

When it gets nonworkable, I put it back into the fire. It should work pretty much like clay, and it has to be between cherry red and white hot, so you've gotta keep that heat to keep it from breakin' on the shoulder, 'cause if it gets less than that temperature, it becomes real brittle, and the more hammer blows you strike, if it's not cherry red or white hot, then it'll just crystallize; so you need to keep it heated all the time. That's one thing that's pretty hard to do when you start out blacksmithin'.

Usually, the least amount of "heats" that you can take is the best—I'd say no more than three heats—and a "heat" is every time you put it into the fire. You have to know what you're gonna do before you get there to the forge. Too many heats make it less durable; it's more susceptible to break after you finish with it. While you're workin' with it, sometimes you'll not know until you do finish, and it breaks at the thinner part.

In the first heat, you make the shoulder and the point. On the second heat, you form the leaf, the body of the leaf. On the third heat you do all your veinin' and texturin', and that would be your final heat. It's better to let it cool by itself because, again, if it cools too quickly, then it's more susceptible to breakage, so it's better to let the molecules expand, and they just go crazy. It's better to let 'em all cool naturally because you've modified steel, so if you were to quench it, it cools too quickly, and it becomes more brittle.

You usually wire-brush it just before you let it cool to get all the "slag." Slag is impurities of the metal and the coal that's formed during the heatin' process, and while it's hot on the last heat, you can wire brush it and then let it cool.

'Course, the final process is knowing when to let it cool naturally or to quench it and what to quench it in. Tools are usually quenched in oil at different heats, at different color heats, or go by a spectrum of colors, dependin' on the type of tool that it's gonna be used for.

The main thing when learnin' is knowin' what you're gonna do before you get to the forge. If you're gonna do any welding, you'll need a good, clean fire, and you need to do that first before you get all the impurities of the other metal in there. You've gotta master the hammer, as far as knowin' where to hit and how to draw out the body of the leaf and how to do the veinin'—stuff like that, you need to know—and you have to practice on other leaves so you know the process before you start in makin' anything that you wanna use. I'd tell a beginner to learn the different type of heats, knowin' when to bring it out of the fire, learnin' how to use your hammer.

It's a dyin' art, anyway, and if we don't keep younger people interested or train 'em, it's goin' by the wayside. Out of the whole North American continent, there are only three thousand of us that work full-time at it. That's not very many, so it's dwindlin' down.

DAVID BURRESS: THE MAKINGS OF A TRUE APPALACHIAN BLACKSMITH

An interview with a John C. Campbell Folk School ferrier

A hundred years ago, it might take a craftsman three weeks to make a wooden chair by hand, but somebody is still sitting in that same chair today because it was so well made. —David Burress

In the first week of September 2013, I participated in Celtic Iron, a black-smithing course that covered the basic techniques of early blacksmiths. The class was taught by David Burress and his son, Caleb Burress. The father-son duo has an extensive knowledge that helped me grasp a basic understanding of blacksmithing. For five days, we worked from morning till dusk making knives, axes, spears, and bottle openers. I was able to see firsthand what a true blacksmith was capable of as I watched David and Caleb turn a piece of metal into a work of art. I was privileged enough to find out a little more about Mr. Burress while conducting an interview with him later in the week.

—David Campbell

I grew up around a welding shop, so my brothers and I all grew up learning how to weld and work with metal. I kind of got into blacksmith-ing by accident when my brother and I were working together out on the road. We were between jobs when I met a lady at a dinner party who was a decorator from Atlanta. She found out I worked with metal and asked if I could make some iron furniture for one of her clients. I thought she just meant weld it together, so I said sure. She sent me the drawings of what she wanted done. I had no idea how to do it, but I needed the money, so we figured it out. I remembered, about fifteen years prior to that, I had read an article in the *Mother Earth News* about how to build a break drum blacksmith's forge, so from my faulty memory, we put one together. It didn't have a good air source, so we never got the metal over just a dull red heat. We had to make a table with one-inch-square bar that tapered all the way down to a quarter inch, but we could only get it to a dull red heat. We had to take turns, one of us holding it on the anvil and the other using a twelve-pound sledgehammer. That's how we did our first blacksmithing job.

I never had the privilege of training under anybody. The closest thing I got to an education was during the wintertime. When his busi-ness would slow down a little bit, Steve Kayne would teach a six-week course. It wasn't hands-on, but he would stand one night a week for six weeks and demonstrate basic techniques. We would take notes and then go home and try it on our forges the next day, but mostly I read books, used trial and error, and asked questions. You can learn from anyone, even someone who doesn't have as much experience as you do because

PLATE 130 David Burress works with a hammer and an anvil.

everyone has something that's going to make sense to them, and it is just going to click. I usually pick up tips from my students because they will be doing something, and I will ask, "What are you doing right there?" They will tell me, and it makes sense.

After we had done a couple of jobs and learned what we could from reading books and trying to apply what we had read, we eventually learned about a local ABANA chapter in Candler, North Carolina. The first Wednesday of every month, we would meet, and somebody would do a demonstration. Then everyone would stand around and talk to other blacksmiths. It was a really great environment because if I was trying something for the first time and couldn't quite get my head wrapped around it, there was someone there who had already done it.

We started traveling around, setting up, and demonstrating at the Scottish Highland Games and Renaissance festivals. That's how we got into the arms and armor. We consider ourselves a teaching forge, but we still do some little festivals and craft shows locally to keep our hand in it. We set up the portable shop at the festivals. I have a wood and leather great bellows I built to supply the air to the forge, and we offer lessons to people while we're there. I try to get people to come to the realization on their own that blacksmithing is something we've lost. It's true that a lot of stuff can be machined out, but it's all crap. A hundred years ago, it might take a craftsman three weeks to make a wooden chair by hand, but somebody is still sitting in that same chair today because it was so well made. It's still here, and it's still doing the purpose it was created to do. There will always be people that appreciate and understand the skill level required to do what you do. You have to educate people because the majority of people have a Walmart mentality. We just consume and consume and consume, and if we break it, we can throw it away and go buy another one.

As far as bladesmithing goes, that's probably the easiest niche market to fall into as far as marketing and blacksmithing. My advice to anyone who's looking to get into blacksmithing would be don't be so eager to make money with it that you rush the experience of learning. You have to be patient with blacksmithing; it's not a rush-job kind of craft. There's an ancient proverb that said, "Life's so short, and the craft takes so long to learn." That means if you learn something every day you go to light a forge, there's still going to be as many things to learn as you have days left on the earth. So, spend the time studying everything you can get your hands on. Read every book, talk to anybody who has more experience

PLATE 131 Foxfire student David Campbell works at the forge.

than you in the craft, and pay attention. If someone is willing to teach you what they know, even if it's something you don't think you're all that interested in, go ahead and learn it anyway. You never know when that might be the very thing that you need to pull out of your bag of tricks.

Experiences after the Campbell School

I can't adequately convey exactly how much I learned while at the John C. Campbell Folk School. The class taught me how to blacksmith, but the school itself taught me why to blacksmith. It instilled a sense of awareness, which can't be expressed through words alone. It taught me to see the beauty in my surroundings, great and small, and notice subtle details, which would have otherwise been lost to me. I have also noticed that everything has a soul. From the smallest blade of grass to a mighty oak tree, everything has a soul, which makes it unique. The same can be said of blacksmithing. Every knife, cloak pin, and bottle opener has a soul. When you pick up something that someone has made completely by hand, it feels different than anything else. I believe that this is what John C. Campbell was trying to preserve when he developed the idea for the Campbell Folk School.

After leaving the Folk School, I began to study various blacksmithing techniques and hone my skills. I soon discovered that blacksmithing was in high demand and began crafting pieces for people from Clayton, Georgia, to Franklin, North Carolina. I have been invited to demonstrate at the Taste of Scotland Festival, which will be held in Franklin, North Carolina, as well as at Old School Knife Works in Otto, North Carolina. I hope to return to the Campbell Folk School one day to continue studying blacksmithing. I still have a lot to learn.

HUNTING AND PROTECTING

In *The Foxfire Book*, Jake Waldroop shared a story about turkey hunting without the benefit of a call. "I was up at the head of Dismal [Creek]— see if I could hear a gobbler—an' I could howl like a hoot owl," he said. "So, I howled, an' this old gobbler answered me way down—he go, 'Cho-balobalob, chobalobalob."

When we talked with Jake fifty years ago, he used a call to attract the turkey to their hiding place. The calls were made of a variety of objects. The most popular was the small bone from the turkey's wing. Sharp sucking intakes of air through this bone produced a series of turkey-like yelps. Others used the hollow stem of an Easter flower bush, a new cob pipe, or even a blade of grass stretched between their thumbs.

Dale Holland makes quality turkey calls that are artistic enough for a mantel, but made for real hunting in the mountains. The sound that comes from Holland's box-style turkey calls is amazingly authentic. He shared these with us, as well as several stories about using them. In some ways it's hard to decide which art we'd rather witness—Dale Holland using the tools he takes pride in to craft turkey calls or Jake Waldroop mouthing owl and turkey sounds. Fifty years of interviews has certainly uncovered a wide variety of talents.

Like many of "The Vanishing Arts," the arts of "Hunting and Protecting" may appear to be vanishing because modern culture has developed other means of achieving the same ends. A modern family could buy a lot of frozen turkey for less than the price many hunters invest in becoming good turkey hunters. Similarly, there are many modern self-defense tools that take less time to master than shooting an arrow, especially if the time to make that arrow is considered.

However, none of those modern ways can replace the pride that

Dave Holland and William Swimmer take in their arts. Mr. Holland doesn't like to hunt turkey in the easier terrain of fields and golf courses because he takes pride in being a mountain turkey hunter. Similarly, when Mr. Swimmer discusses the history of weaponry, he shows a pride in his ancestry as much as in his own abilities.

—*Jonathan Blackstock*

THE ART OF MAKING TURKEY CALLS

An interview with Dale Holland, North Carolina turkey-call maker

My philosophy is that the Lord takes me with my infirmities, and he uses me if I want to be used, so who am I to cull out a piece of bad wood? It wouldn't be right. —Dale Holland

Upon our arrival at the home of Dale Holland, he welcomed us in without hesitation. While we sat in his living room, which was decorated with family photographs, mounted game, and turkey calls, he proudly displayed the four calls he considered his most memorable and sentimental. He also shared stories about past hunting trips and adventures he had taken with fellow turkey hunters. Later, we were privileged to enter his workshop, where we watched in awe as he made a turkey call step-by-step.

Mr. Holland has a humble and genuine character. He has a true passion for making turkey calls that both young and old hunters can use to "call a turkey up." This passion he conveys through his work makes each call infinitely more valuable. It also shows his love for nature and the ability to take something that would otherwise be counted as worthless and transform it into something that can be used and held close for years to come.

—*Ross Lunsford*

I started putting dates on them when I first started making calls. This says, "1/24/2004." That's when I made my first call, and all I had at that time to build a call out of was sandpaper and a table saw, so you can tell that it's quite rough. I hunted with it several years, and I guess it'll stay with me as long as I'm around.

I hand-build my turkey calls. For example, a builder might have a tool that he can run a piece of wood through to shape the paddle, but I wouldn't consider that hand-built. I get on my little sander here, and set in to sandin', and sandin', and sandin' until it's smooth. I feel like that's hand-built even though I used a machine. I could take a rasp and rasp it off, but I sand each one by hand. That's another part of the time that it takes to build one.

From start to finish, it probably takes me three to four hours to make a call. By the time I get them finished and everything, it takes probably five to six hours.

I learned how to make calls in my basement. The story behind the whole deal is that I worked for thirty-three and a half years for the U.S. Forest Service, and one of our fellas brought a turkey call in and set it up on his shelf. I said, "Where'd you get that?" and he told me who made it for him. I said, "You reckon I could get him to make me one?" and he said, "I don't know." When the fellow finally came, I asked him, "How much would you charge me to make a turkey call?" He said, "If you want a turkey call, make it yourself." That was it. He never made me a turkey call, so I came home and I said, "Well, if he can make one, I guess I can make one." I sat in on a cold January day and built this first turkey call.

The first turkey call I built was made out of separate pieces. I just looked at a turkey call and saw the basics. And pieces being the bottom as a separate piece, the ends are separate pieces, the sides are separate pieces, and the top is a separate piece. That's what my calls were for several years. Then, I started getting tools, and I started fancying the calls up a little bit. This is my 200th call. I kept it out of sentiment. This call is half butternut, it's half black walnut, it's got mulberry down the middle, mulberry on the bottom, and it's also got black walnut on the bottom. This is about the time that I started putting cork in my calls, and if you boys have ever made turkey calls, you know that they're a friction call, and you've gotta put chalk on the bottom of them. I started out just making a little chalk holder on my lathe to put my chalk in so that I'd always have it. I got to thinking one day, "Why not just go ahead and mount your chalk holder on your box call so you'll always have it with you?" So, this is my 200th call.

For my 300th call, I made a long box, I made a short box, and I made a slate box. I number 'em: 300a was my long box, 300b was my short box, and 300c was my slate box. I put my three 300th calls in a walnut presentation case and gave them to the Vietnam Veterans of America. They told me, and I don't have anything in writing or anything, that they made over a thousand dollars out of those three calls. They went to events and raffled them off.

For my 201st call, and I don't know if y'all have ever heard of Neil Cost, but he's an old turkey-call maker from South Carolina. Neil Cost's last call sold for eleven thousand and something dollars. The name of it was "The Fat Lady," because it was his last call, and you know, "It's not over till the fat lady sings." His calls now, gosh, I dare say, you wouldn't even find one of his calls now for less than a thousand dollars. I had a fellow, who had one of his calls on eBay, and there was a time when I had the opportunity to get one of Neil Cost's calls; he was at Helen, Georgia. Back then, I think he was selling them for like a hundred and fifty dollars. I didn't think I could afford a hundred and fifty dollars, but now I wish I'd bought one. But this fellow had one of Neil's calls on eBay, and so I just e-mailed and said, "Could you give me the dimensions on that particular call and tell me what he made it out of?" He said, "Well, he made the box out of butternut, and he made the top out of cedar." This fellow went to see Neil. Neil told him that his favorite materials was butternut and cedar. This is what they call a boat paddle. It's long like a boat paddle, and one of the fellows in the Turkey Federation, when Neil showed him this call, he told him, "Well this looks like a boat paddle." I made this as my 201st call. I made two of them, and I let a feller talk me out of one of them. I kept this one, and it, to the best of my ability, even though I wasn't able to measure it myself, looks like one of his boat paddles. It sounds good; it's got a good turkey sound.

The original man who patented a turkey call, a box call, was a Gibson fellow [Henry C. Gibson]. In his book, I looked at a picture that he had of his call. I saw all the pictures that he had put in it. I saw both sides and

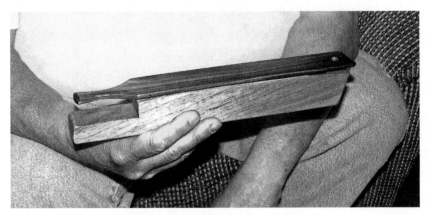

PLATE 132 Dale Holland's 201st turkey call

the top, and he had a man's name put on top, but I put "D. L. Holland" on mine because it's not a Gibson; it's a Holland. To the best of my ability, I built this call as close to the picture as I could find it. That includes on the sides. I tried to get it exactly as close as I could.

To write on the inside, I use a felt marker. It's simple, but this is my hobby. It's not my way of making a living. I worked thirty-three and a half years to have something to keep me going, and this is strictly just a hobby.

I do donate a deal of my calls, like if somebody has a benefit. They give me a call, and I give them a call! I am generous with my calls. I just rather one of my calls go to a benefit. Some of them go for two hundred dollars plus, and some of them sell for just fifty dollars. That's fifty dollars somebody gets. It kinda hurts my feelings if one of them sells for fifty dollars; I feel better if one sells for two hundred dollars.

Everything is like the Gibson, even to the little marks that he put around the edges, to the cork that he put in the bottom, which is where he put the chalk in this particular one. I try to do everything exactly like it, except I put my name on top.

It's a replica of the original Gibson; that's what it is. I've never made but this one, and I'll never make another one again. It was just something I wanted for me. It's in my personal collection.

I've got an Al Willis call. He's from South Carolina, and he used to be president of Keowee Turkey Calls. I got one of his calls in Helen, Georgia. It's a unique call. Instead of using chalk, he cut a section out and put a piece of slate in it. So, you never have to chalk it. I talked to him two or

PLATE 133 Turkey call signed on the inside

three times later, and he said he didn't make them anymore. Hopefully, one day it will be worth something. I say that [a call maker] has to die first, so I tell people when they get my calls, "When I die, they might be worth something."

I've also put, from the very first one, my name, the date, and the number of the call on the inside. A lot of call makers write on the top, but I just can't see, unless somebody wanted me to, messin' up that beautiful piece of wood right there by writing on it. That's just my feelings, you know? I don't know if I've got any more in my personal collection that I have made, but that's the four that I have kept. I'm on number 361 or 362 now.

Well, I've made more than that. I made a set during my low 300s, not this turkey season but last turkey season, for a handicap hunt that one of the churches had in April. The boy came to me the first week in April and asked me if I could have twenty-four calls by the last of April. I said, "There ain't no way." You can tell by the numbers that since 2004—that's ten years—I've made probably four-hundred-plus calls, so that don't mean that I make a whole lot every year. Like I say, it's just a hobby; I do it when I want to, and I don't when I don't. I told him that I didn't see any way I could do it, but I come home and got to thinking about it. I thought, "Well, it is for an awful good cause, you know, for those handicap kids." So, I sat in, and in less than, well, probably about three weeks, I made twenty-four calls. I worked way into the night several nights. Because I wanted to number them all 320, I numbered them 320A through 320Y. Anyway, I numbered them all 320 something, so that's why I say I have made more calls.

A few of my calls I haven't put my name on. I had a feller give me a piece of wood one time and he set in for me to make him a call, and it sorta bothered me, so I didn't name or number his call. One of my most enjoyable times was when one boy got one of my calls several years ago and put it in his glove box. A few years passed and I was with him one day. He was getting something out of the glove box and laid it on the seat and I said, "Where in the world did you get that thing at?" I mean, it was skinned up. He said, "Well, that's the call I got from you!" He'd been carrying it with him all those years, and I know he used it some, but he didn't hunt a lot. Really, if you think about it, that's what they're for.

Well, I want anybody, if they buy one of my calls or get one, to be able to hunt with it. A lot of people put them on their mantel.

I've got a first cousin that buys a lot of my calls. He's paid over two hundred [dollars] several times at benefits, and at the last one, I know he paid two hundred and ten dollars for it and gave it to another boy that wanted one of my calls. I had a boy, back in the winter, who came to me and said, "I want one of your calls. I have bought chances." I bought him a chance [at a benefit] and just gave it to him. I said, "Here, hopefully you'll win that call with this." His grandpa had bought five dollars' worth of chances. There was another feller that came to me and handed me seventy-five chances. He said, "Give 'em to that little boy." Seventy-five dollars' worth of chances, and when it came down to it, he didn't get it. It broke his heart. Later, he came up to me and asked, "How much would you charge me to make a call?" Luckily, I had a one-sided call. Most calls can call from this side [left side] and this side [right side]. That's called a two-sided call. But this particular call was a one-sided call. It just worked on this side. He asked, "How much do you want for this call?" and before it was over with, I gave that call to the little boy. His grandpa, who I saw two or three weeks later, said, "His grandma started to call you and ask you how much you would charge to come get that call." He was playing with it up into the night; they woke up and the little boy was up there playin' with it. I don't know if he's tore it up.

I used to go to Brasstown in the fall and sell calls, but they've gotten so high that I didn't go this time. I haven't fooled with it for the past few years. I was gonna go this year, but they're just too high, and I said, "I ain't gonna go." It's just a hobby, and I decided not to go.

A lot of them get torn up, and grown-ups are usually the hardest on them. I've had a woman, a grown woman, come and jerk a call this way [a way that the call can't go], and my girls were about to get her for it, and she backed off real quick.

You've got to treat a turkey call like a beautiful woman, and you don't just grab and jerk and shove a beautiful woman; you touch 'em tenderly. You take care of them. If you had a Gibson guitar that was made in the fifties, you wouldn't want to jerk and beat on it; you'd take good care of it, and that's what I try to tell people about a turkey call. You've got to take good care of it. Wood and water don't mix. They've got some of these calls now that have got sandpaper-looking stuff on 'em that say it'll work in water, and they make good calls, but when it comes down to it, wood and water don't mix. Durability? If you jerk on 'em and are rough on 'em, you're gonna tear them up. People have had turkey calls that they have hunted with for years and years; they've took good care of them. The boy that put his in the glove box won't last very long.

I like all types of wood. I like butternut. I'm like they said Neil Cost was, and I'm sure he's like me. I like butternut and cedar. As a matter of fact, this cedar came from Georgia. It came from Carnesville, Georgia. This butternut came from Swain County. This mulberry came from Cherokee County. I just have people give me wood. My wife gets a little bothered when I get to playing with them; I've got her drove crazy. I like all woods. People say, "What can you make a turkey call out of?" You can make a turkey call out of anything. I've made 'em out of white pine, yellow pine, holly, and poplar. Holly is a good wood; it's white.

I had a friend, an old farmer that worked for me years ago from Nantahala, and I said, "You ain't got any good wood, have you?" and he said, "I don't know. I might have a piece of poplar stuck up in the barn." He cut it up in pieces and brought it to me, so when I was making the call, I got to thinking. It had nails drove in it and stuff where rodents had been on it. So, I wrote a story about the barn board, and I wrote it as if I were the poplar tree, from the seed on, all the way up to thinking that I was really gonna be something. I ended up in a barn. Then, I ended up bein' torn out of the barn and stuck up in the loft, and the end of the story is I got given to a fellow that made me into a turkey call. I like to write. [**Editors' note:** This story appears in full on Dale Holland's website.]

I write poetry when I want to. I sent a poem one time to a Christian place up in Canada, and it didn't get published. The ones that won did some stuff that I can't figure out. Usually, the ones that win are like that, but I'm just a redneck poet. I'm really seriously considering writing a book after reading Herb McClure's *Native Turkeys and a Georgia Mountain Turkey Hunter*. A lot of things he said corresponded with a lot of my hunts. I've called a lot of turkeys up a lot of different ways. I've wrote one book, but I've not ever had it published. I've got a lot of stories and I've wrote a lot of poems, but that one book is *The Hunting Trip* and it's about my great-great-grandpa. His name was Anthony Holland. My great-great grandpa joined the Confederate Army as a cavalryman in Franklin, North Carolina, and went and fought in the battles around Richmond. He also had two other brothers that were from here that were sent off as cavalrymen. Now, picture Franklin, North Carolina, and Richmond, Virginia, and the only way you can get there is by a horse. I've wondered if they ever rode a train part of the way. Anyway, I wrote a story about him on his sixteenth birthday. He left out on a hunting trip by himself and went up to the right-hand side of the Cullasaja Gorge through a gold mine, through the flats, and he went into Highlands. He went to the Chattooga River. He came back the same way. This is my imagination, but I felt like it was something that could have happened. That's just something to think of.

Yesterday, I worked on some so that y'all could get an idea of how I do it.

I remember seein' my first turkey after I went to work for the Forest Service, and that was probably in the mid-seventies to late seventies. I really didn't start turkey hunting till the nineties. When I was a boy, I'd trail 'em and track 'em in the snow and try to kill 'em and stuff like that. We live in a time where girls and boys have a challenge and a good, enjoyable sport turkey hunting. In a way, it's kind of hard work. A lot of these people on these movies do their hunting on golf courses and cow pastures, but I'm a mountain turkey hunter. I've just about had to quit for a while, but this past year, I went to some places where I have not been able to go in four or five years, and there's nothing like in the mountains.

I took one boy hunting who was twenty-three, I believe, and he had never hunted in his life. I mean not just rabbits or squirrels; he had never hunted in his life. So, I told him I was gonna take him turkey hunting in the spring. He was a new hire that had started with us. During the winter, he bought himself some hunting clothes, a new shotgun, and a fanny pack. The first day we went out hunting we got out of the vehicle and he said, "Dale, do you think I have enough shells?" He had two boxes of ten, so he had twenty shells. I said, "Son, I don't think you need to take but just one box." I took him out, called a turkey up, and he killed it the first time he'd ever been hunting in his life. I took him back one more time, and later I asked him, "Have you been back by yourself?" and he said, "No." I said, "I ain't taking you. I'll never take you again. Unless you show the incentive that you want to go on your own, I ain't taking you no more."

This piece here is gonna be made into a bowl. I also make bowls on my lathe. I like little bowls, so I will turn that into a bowl. Most of them, I have given away. On my side of my family, I've given all my nieces a bowl that I've made. Some of them were different sizes, but I've given all of them a bowl. I don't have a whole lot of bowls, and I'll tell you why. My baby girl come in a long time ago, and the bowls were stuck up in the closet. She said, "Daddy, it's a shame for you to leave those bowls in the closet. I'm gonna take 'em home with me." She took six or eight bowls with her.

I had two different people do a senior project. I've mentored two young men, one right-handed and one left-handed. The left-hander didn't tell me he was left-handed, and I didn't figure it out for a while. I thought, "It just looks so odd." One night, I figured it out. I said, "You're left-handed, aren't you?" And then I started working with him as a left-handed person. He did a good job, but if you were watching two people that were left-handed and right-handed, it's really different. I've mentored people, but I don't know if I would do it again because what if somebody were to cut a hand off in my shop? Then, I'd wind up having to give away my house. Anyway, I taught them to build a turkey call.

The calls I make now, unless I make one like this, don't have a lot to hold them together. I take a solid piece of two-by-two and hollow the middle out. My first one was pieces that I glued, but what do I use now? Gorilla Glue. I have used Durabond, and it's waterproof, but wood's not, so I found Gorilla Glue as a good glue.

Well, if you were making a one-sided, left-handed call, you would call from the left side rather than call from the right side. On a two-sided call, you can call from either side, so it's whatever. You can put a rubber band around the call and make it gobble, too. There are, I'm sure, people who custom-build left-handed calls.

Lynch makes what they call a "Foolproof," and it's a one-sided call. I'll be honest with you. I don't have any idea why they would want to make a one-sided call, but when you push it together and put a rubber band around it, it might be easier to keep quiet. There's nothin' that bothers a turkey more than when the call squeaks. That's gonna alarm a turkey.

I've hunted a lot with my son-in-law over the years. He, my daughter, and their child are the love of my life. They've been married, I believe, thirteen years. Well, they got married in 1999, so I guess it's fifteen, near fifteen now. I took him turkey hunting because he had never killed a turkey before. I took him and called up a turkey the spring before they got married. When we're together in the woods, I like to put him out front, and I do the callin' and I let him do the killing. It's just as much enjoyment to call a turkey to me. We hunted some last year. I called one up and shot it. It flopped down the hill. He's more agile, so I said, "Get it, son!" He jumped up and run across the ridge and shot it. This year, I was by myself. Of course, if I'm by myself, I have to do the shooting. There's a feeling about it. I got into turkey huntin' because of some of the boys I work with.

I caught on a turkey one time in the mountains, and I had my mouth call in, and I called, and I heard absolutely nothing. Well, it was gettin' towards eleven o'clock, and I hadn't had any breakfast, so I got me out an oatmeal cake and was sitting there eatin' it. I got my slate call out, but I just stuck it back in my pocket. I thought, "I ought to have tried that. Here I am sittin' out in the middle of the mountains, you know?" So, I got that call out and I called. I heard a turkey down the holler. I'd already took my huntin' clothes off 'cause I was really hot, and I throwed my shirt on and set back against a hemlock tree. The branches swayed and about that time, the turkey came too far for me to shoot. He came up, saw me, and he went out of sight gobblin' at me 'cause he saw something he didn't like. Well, the next morning at daylight I was sitting at the same place. I got my slate call out. I called on it, nothing. I cut on it, nothing. I said, "Well, dadgone. He's not here." I put my mouth call in and called. He sounded, and I killed him. Two different calls is what killed that turkey.

Even back when they did the article on Aunt Arie, Foxfire was the same thing. We were friends to Aunt Arie. My daddy-in-law always worried about her when it got bad. It snowed and my daddy-in-law said, "I'm gonna go check on Aunt Arie, see if she's got wood." So, I went with him. We went in, and she was fixing breakfast. The night before, she had fried fatback meat, and it was just a big ol' thing of grease. She heated up the grease, and put the sugar in it. Then she poured coffee into that grease and stirred up this kind of syrupy-lookin' thing, and she was eating that on biscuits. That didn't look that good to me.

For one of my main jobs for the Forest Service, I worked with the Older American Program for thirty-plus years. I would work with senior citizens. I started out taking them out to work, and then, I would make sure to line up their work and do all the ratings in the latter part. Now I think they've lost that program. I really hate it because senior citizens can teach a lot of stuff. It's good for older people.

I think it originally started out as Operation Mainstream, and it ended up being SCSEP [Senior Community Service Employment Program]. You had to be fifty-five and older. I know that I had people working for me that were eighty years old. It was based on income. On our district, they went around picking up garbage and cleaning toilets. That may not sound good, but it's got to be done. We built things, laid rock, and we made shingle boards. We did all kinds of stuff with that program; it was a really good program. Then they financed them out of business. You had to make such a low income. A lot of 'em missed it by a hundred dollars, which is so foolish of a thing. It was a super program.

The Forest Service is not the only ones that had them. They worked in big cities, and I think they still have it. The program made it so hard that we couldn't hire people.

The National Wild Turkey Federation has a national convention in Opryland, Nashville, Tennessee. I've been out of the Federation for a while. I used to be in it all the time, but now I've got out of it. Next year,

I hope to have one to where I can send it to the convention and enter it into the contest. The old boy that won the contest, his call, just like this one, sold for five hundred dollars.

I don't consider a call finished until I bring it from my workshop and have it numbered, dated, and signed. Everything is inside a finished call that you need to know about this call. A 2013 Honda, two hundred years from now, might be worth something because they know it's a 2013 Honda. If you had nothing on it to know how old it was, it'd just be an old pile of junk sitting there.

A lot of people want to get into the inside and the heart of the wood. My mind-set is better calls come from sapwood. That's the outside. If you look right here, this is black walnut. You see the sapwood on that? I love to be close to the sapwood on a turkey call. I have a maple that is curly and rotten. That's some of the best wood I've ever gotten. A lot of my stuff is scrap wood that's been given. One particular call is made of the scrap wood from a man that makes tables.

I do little designs. I like to put a turkey on it. I don't like to do a whole lot of writing on my stuff. I had a feller come here during the first part of turkey season, and I showed him the one I had in my hunting vest. He said, "Boy, I'd like to have that," and I said, "Take it." He said, "I don't want to take yours. Then what would you do?" I said, "I will go into my turkey call box, and I'll get me one of them 'cause every call I got should be able to call a turkey."

The first thing on the mountains in the spring is service [pronounced *sar-vice*]. They usually don't grow big enough to make anything out of, but I happened to find this one that had fell. I told a fellow about it, and I had to be out, and somebody went to this place and had it sawed and gave me some boards out of it. They call it serviceberries, and it has a weird grain; the little dark places look like cracks in it. It's a heavy wood.

I also make slate calls, but I've not made any yet, but I will this summer. If you look in, I put glass behind it for a sounding board. The holes are what the sound comes out of. Since you could see in it, I couldn't put glass on it because you could see the guts in it. There were just fifteen kids at the handicap hunt this year, and I made them all a football call.

I saw this on eBay several years ago, and a game warden down in the eastern part of North Carolina made these calls, and so I figured if the game warden could do it, I could do it. It's a scratch box; it's what they call that. It's a small version that you could put in your hunting vest. I do things when I get in a mood because I think I probably made five of those.

PLATE 134 A call in the shape of a football

After showing us more well-made turkey calls outside, Mr. Holland took us down to his basement to show us his workshop. The setup he had in his shop was fascinating, and he used every single tool in it. Many of the tools he has would have been discarded and culled by others, but he managed to salvage them and is satisfied with the tools he has, as it is simply a hobby.

PLATE 135 Dale Holland's workshop

This is my shop. It's the only basement that I have. Everything in here I use. It's not expensive stuff; it's just hobby stuff, mainly. And it's getting like me; it's getting older and harder to deal with. I use the planer, too. As you can see, I do like to turkey hunt. These are the beards of the turkeys I've killed over the years. I've called up nearly as many for my son-in-law as I have killed. Here is a call that is made, but it is not a finished call until I take it upstairs and put the writing in it. I'll date it when I take it upstairs and when I do the writing. This one is made of black walnut and yellow poplar, and you don't find yellow poplar that looks like that. One of the boys I worked with years ago cut a poplar at his house, and he said, "When I split it, I seen that color. I told my wife, 'I've gotta take that to Dale.'"

My philosophy is that the Lord takes me with my infirmities, and he uses me if I want to be used, so who am I to cull out a piece of bad wood? It wouldn't be right. I could've culled this piece because it has three little wormholes in the handle. There are people that can sing beautifully even though they don't have arms and legs. They are willing to be used, so who am I to cull out things? Now, there are some things that you have to cull. Big knots in the middle of something or something, but that little feller [the call with the wormholes] will call a turkey up if the person who gets it wants to call a turkey up with it, so I just can't see being the judge that says, "No, you can't." That's my way of thinking, and a lot of it comes from sitting down here. The definition, I say, of a call maker is a grouchy old man that's down in the basement or out in the shop so that he won't be bothering his wife.

Have you ever heard of princess paulownia? They have a big ol' purple bloom on 'em, and they came from Japan. People from Japan, the older ones, want something made out of princess paulownia. It's a royal bush to them; everyone wants something made out of them. It's super lightweight.

Someone had American chestnut thrown out in their backyard, and they was gonna take it to the dump. He said, "Take it on." I've had it lying in my shop all this time, and yesterday I decided to make a paddle out of it. As a matter of fact, my first call that I showed y'all was American chestnut. For a little history, the one that's upstairs, right after I started working with the Forest Service in 1974, we were going and there was a piece of scrap two-by-six, or maybe two-by-eight, about three feet long. I've loved wood for all these years, and there it lay. They nailed it to two logs and put it on the ground to make a culvert so that water would run down it. I got to lookin' and said, "Dad gem, that's chestnut." So, I brought it home, and it laid there until 2004 when I built the first turkey call out of it. I made two more out of it. There will never be any more turkey calls made out of that little piece of wood.

I have some Spanish cedar that a boy ordered a box of. He was gonna make a humidor, which are made out of Spanish cedar. He said, "I'm never gonna make anything out of that, so why don't you just take it." If nothing else, it smells good. I could set here and roll and feel and look at the grains for a long time. That's just a love that some people have for wood.

On one call, you might get one that doesn't make a good sound. That service is a hard wood. It's hard to work with, hard to drill, and I think it makes the least-best sound. I think butternut, black walnut, mulberry, maple, any of 'em—I can call a turkey up with any of them.

It's enjoyable. I can come down here and get to workin' and go outside, and it's come the awfulest rainstorm. You can tell I like it 'cause if I can eat breakfast and come down here, I'll get to workin' some days and look out and it be dark. The day goes. It takes about four or five hours to make one, so I'm busy.

I've got a guarantee and I like to tell everyone this. I guarantee every call I make, and my guarantee is "If you cannot call up a turkey with one of my calls, I guarantee you you're not much of a turkey hunter." That's the guarantee, and I'll stick by it. I've had people that didn't call one up, and I'll say, "I guarantee you ain't much of a turkey hunter." If you catch 'em right and you do the right things, you can kill a turkey with a call. I will tell you; I like to use a mouth call, too. I made one [a mouth call] one time, but I buy my [mouth] calls from Mountain Callers in Cleveland, Georgia. A guy makes 'em over there, and I love his calls. I ordered enough the year before last to have for last year and this year.

How to Make a Turkey Call

First, I have to pick out the kind of wood I want to use. I personally like white walnut [or butternut]. I also like mulberry. I start out by cutting out a piece of two-by-two blank. I would make sure that it's good and smooth on the edges. Once I have the two-by-two, I bring it over to my table saw. By the way, it was my daddy's table saw. My dad's been dead for fifteen years. I went to see him one day, and it was in his barn, rusty and stuff. I said, "Daddy, what are you doing with that?" and he said, "Well, son, take it home with you." So, I brought it home with me, and it's been a part of my stuff for all these years. This table saw has got a

PLATE 136 Begin with a table saw

pretty easy life. I set the blade on five degrees. That's gonna form you a turkey call right here.

I then put it on this other machine [a lathe].

I mark the handle and mark out where the call is gonna be. It'll be cut out from there to there. This year, I put two little marks on the outside of the handle and three marks on the inside of the handle. I take a square

PLATE 137 Turning wood on the lathe

PLATE 138 Using a forstner bit to hollow the call

and mark the dimensions of the turkey call on the sawed two-by-two. I measure across the top, and I'd say right now, if I measure, it's gonna be about an inch and a half. Then I'm gonna mark me a line.

Then I hollow out the inside of the two-by-two with a forstner bit. I start out with an inch and drill that out. I put another bigger one in and finish it down. Then we have the makings of a turkey call.

Once I get that right there, I bring it over here to my table saw again. I set it on seventy-five degrees. I cut that on a seventy-five. You can pretty much see a turkey call in the making now. I don't measure a whole lot any more, but I mark where I just cut, and I'll sand a bit for a bit of decoration. I cut a good deal off with a sander, and this is the reason that you would call this a custom call. You can go to Primos and you can get as good of calls as you want, but this is, pretty much, what I would call handmade.

You have to make a place for the paddle to have a place to settle down in. Now I have to make the inside as pretty as I can and as thin as I feel like. The sides are actually thin. The thin wood makes it sound. You have to center the paddle up on the call.

I then take a Dremel tool and start working the inside out. The old-time turkey-call makers would take a chisel and clean the wood out. I work all the inside smooth. I won't quit till I get the sides and bottom smooth.

I drill through into the handle to make a place as a chalk holder. The drill bit I use makes a tapered hole. There's a lot of sanding that goes on

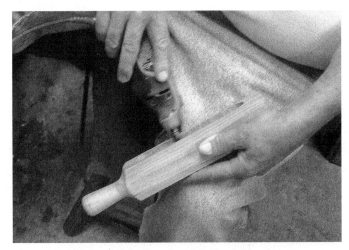

PLATE 139 The Dremel tool works the inside out.

to make this thing. Once the hole is in the handle for your chalk, you put a cork in it to keep the chalk in it. If you don't do anything else, in Georgia, a cork is gonna get people excited.

So, I measure over and get it as "in the center" as I can. It is important that you get the paddle to set as close to center as you can. If not, you're gonna have a paddle setting over here, and that looks like crap. It'd still work, but it looks bad. The paddle will be screwed into the center of the top.

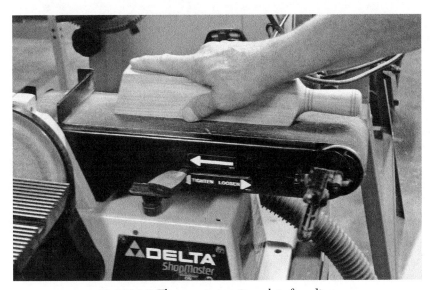

PLATE 140 The process requires a lot of sanding.

One of the last steps is to put three coats on the wood. I use a secret oil. I had a feller tell me, and he said, "Don't you tell nobody," and that's been somewhere close to 2004 when I started in Helen, Georgia. I believe he's from Georgia. I've gone through a lot of little bottles of this stuff, but I think if you're gonna build something like this, it needs to be quality enough so you can put it in your gun cabinet with your guns. I'll put at least three coats on. I'll come in and put a coat on and come back down here after it dries, and I'll sand everything down. Then I'll put another coat on it, hang it on these nails to dry, and they'll stay there until I come back. I always put three coats; sometimes I use more, but none less. When the last one dries, you can use a cloth. You'd think you'd need a piece of sandpaper, but you can take a cloth and just keep working that thing and get it just as slick as a baby's butt.

All these tools, I've bought one at a time. I buy some of my stuff from Harbor Freight, and just little knickknack stuff. I've built my cabinets one at a time. I'm getting it kinda the way I want it. I sit on this stool to do all my work. I use all these tools. I make 'em [calls] when I want to, and I don't when I don't. And you know, like I say, I've made in the neighborhood of four hundred calls in ten years. That's not averaging a whole lot of calls. A lot of people make four or five hundred a year, but it would take away my enjoyment and my hobby.

PLATE 141 Dale Holland examines one of his turkey calls.

PLATE 142 One of Dale Holland's beautifully finished calls

Butternut and cedar make good calls. Mulberry and walnut also do well. Good maple—some maple is harder to work with—makes a good call. If you get a good piece you hate to use it all. I had a piece of cherry given to me one time. I made two or three calls, and it grieved me to get rid of that last call because that was some of the best-sounding wood I ever got a hold of. Just remember—you can make a turkey call out of any kind of wood!

TRADITIONAL WEAPONRY

William Swimmer demonstrates construction of primitive weaponry

In the old days, our people were more of what you would consider perfectionists. —William Swimmer

William Swimmer's talents and artifacts can be seen on display at the Oconaluftee Village in Cherokee, North Carolina. Mr. Swimmer is a traditional Native American weaponry maker who takes pride both in making weapons by traditional methods and in using them accurately. The artifacts are authentic, as are the tools that consist of antlers and harder rocks to shape and sharpen the flint and obsidian arrowheads. William Swimmer learned this craft from respected members of his community and has developed his own skill so that he now shares his talents with others who are willing to learn.

In September of 2012, several of William Swimmer's handmade weapons were stolen, including a blowgun that Mr. Swimmer uses in competitions. While the stolen items had a great potential resale value, the blowgun was priceless to its creator. Fortunately, Freddy Bear Wilnoty, who appeared on the cover of *The Foxfire Magazine* Fall/Winter 2012 issue, found some of the items and was able to return them to their rightful owner. The Native American media network *Indian Country Today* featured the theft in a September 2012 article in an attempt to retrieve some of the unrecovered stolen items. While the egregious crime displays a gaping lack of moral fiber on someone's part, the effort made by community members and *Indian Country Today* remind us that a strong community can overcome some of the world's misplaced priorities. Bad things happen in the world, and the strongest weapon against those bad things is often a strong, supportive community like that of the Native Americans in Cherokee, North Carolina.

—*Jonathan Blackstock*

My name is William Swimmer, and I've worked at the Oconaluftee Indian Village making arrowheads for the past twenty-three seasons. I've been making arrowheads for about thirty-five years. I started making them when I was about fifteen.

To give you an idea on how to craft an arrowhead, you start out by finding a large piece of flint. Then take a large river rock, find a good place to whack it, and start flaking pieces off. This is how you start to form your arrowhead. They say you can use a smaller river rock to flake, but it depends on what you prefer or what makes the work easier.

You can also use various size deer antlers to do the flaking. I prefer to use an antler. I have various sizes that allow me to chip off different-size flakes. For example, a bigger antler knocks off a bigger flake.

You want to strike the flint at the point where it's worn down. After you get it chipped down to where you want it, you have to take the point

PLATE 143 William Swimmer crafting a dart for a blowgun

and do what we call "pressure flaking." That takes smaller flakes off the edge. Pretty much, that's what you use to put some degrees [for the angle] in the back.

The time it takes to make an arrowhead depends on the size you want to make. For example, you can make a real small one in a matter of twenty to thirty minutes. It just depends on how good the flint is working because, sometimes, it will break as you are working on it. That happens more times than you'd care for if you're not careful.

I learned how to make arrowheads from a few different people that have worked or still work here at the Indian Village. A couple of the people I have learned from are Davy Arch and Bob Reed; however, there are several more I've worked with that were fairly good arrowhead makers. I've taught a few people, as well. I gave a few lessons, showed them how to make the arrowheads, and they became pretty decent arrowhead makers.

In the old days, our people were more of what you would consider perfectionists. I mean this in the sense that, if we weren't pleased with how our arrows performed, we would trash them and start over. Nowa-

PLATE 144 A collection of flint arrowheads

days, we don't have that mind-set as much because they aren't as crucial in our life anymore. The only times we really trash them now is if we break them.

We also used some of that obsidian [volcanic glass] to make arrowheads. A long time ago, we had the means to acquire obsidian to work with. Most likely, they had to do a lot of trading to get the obsidian, but obsidian arrowheads have been found in this area. They recently found some over in Franklin, North Carolina.

Before our people had the bow and arrow to hunt with, we used an atlatl. They say the bow and arrow dates back three thousand years, so the atlatl dates way back. I actually found a banner stone that was used as the weight on an atlatl out in a tobacco field I was working in. When I found it, it was broken in half. I didn't really know what it was. Curiosity finally got the best of me, and I took it to an archaeologist. That's when they told me it was half of a banner stone.

We also made our own arrows. We used wild turkey feathers for the feathers on the end. We cut down half of them to make it spiral. We'd use what they call mountain cane for the shaft. It's the smaller cousin to river cane. It runs higher up in the elevations, and it grows a little smaller than river cane.

To make an arrow shoot true, you've got to make sure it's straight. A long time ago, they used a process they called conjuring the arrow. They conjured them, and that's pretty much how the arrow got to shoot straight.

I make other Cherokee weapons along with my arrowheads. One of the other weapons that I make is the darts for the blowgun. The original hunting darts were pretty much the same size as the ones we make today, but they used different materials to craft them. Back then, the shafts of the darts were made out of wood known as yellow locust. Nowadays, for convenience, we use wooden skewers when we show the public how to make darts. They still work just as good. To start off making a dart, you have to notch the end of the stick with your knife.

When this is completed, you will need the pods from a thistle plant. A thistle plant is commonly found in pastures or along roadsides. When they mature, a big purple flower grows on them. We go and harvest them, and then we tie them up to keep them from popping open until we need them. You harvest them before the color turns, and they start to wilt. That's how you know if you can use them or not. They have some burrs on them, and they can be tricky to work with, and they get in your finger. They're kind of like a cactus. Whenever you get the thistle, you have to pull it out of the pod and brush the seeds out of it.

Once this is done, you are going to tie the thistle to the dart. Our people used to use what they call an Indian hemp plant to make thread, but nowadays, we just use dental floss.

To get the thread from the hemp plant, our ancestors would strip the plant down, and the thread would be inside the plant. They would use this plant to make things, such as thread and rope, because it was a very strong material.

Tying the thistle is very similar to tying a fly for fishing. You put tension in it and then just spiral it onto the skewer. For most darts, it takes about two or three thistles to complete it. Once you have finished wrapping the thistle, just tie it off and cut the string. You should fluff the thistle up for more accuracy. Take it over by the heat, and it will cause it to fluff up. The heat is also used to straighten them out before hunting.

The Cherokees' darts were used to hunt small game, such as rabbits and squirrels, with pretty good accuracy. In fact, they were so accurate that when explorer Hernando de Soto came through here, he took note in his journal that he saw one of the old Cherokee hunters shooting the eye out of a wild turkey from approximately fifty feet away.

Surprisingly, it doesn't take much air to shoot these darts. It takes about as much air as it does to blow out a candle.

The darts would be useless if it weren't for the blowgun itself. Cherokee blowguns are crafted from river cane, which is an indigenous plant that resembles bamboo. When choosing a piece of river cane to make a blowgun, keep in mind that the longer the gun, the more accurate it will be. Before we had any kind of metal tools or anything of the sort, we used a big long stick with an arrowhead on it to hollow out the inside of the river cane. Once that was complete, they'd turn the stick over, put river sand inside, and work it back and forth to smooth out the joints.

Whenever you build one, you pretty much have to stay near a fire. You have to heat it up to get it straight because river cane doesn't grow straight. You've got to sort of bend it around on your knees to shape it. Sometimes, you'll think it's straight, but when you go to shoot it, it shoots off to one side. In a case like that, you need to heat it back up and reshape it. Keep in mind that when you are heating it up, you don't want to get it too hot because it will break the river cane or cause it to explode. Whenever you finish making it, you don't have to apply any preservatives to the blowgun; you just leave it natural.

I made my blowgun twenty-three years ago. It's got a little wear and tear on it, but it still shoots fair. I've got a nickel on the end of it because the end of it split, but other than that, it's been a good one. I shoot it down at the fair when we have competitions. I really enjoy it. They have competitions at the Indian Fair in the fall. They have the blowgun competition on the final day of the fair.

I think it's fun to go down there and shoot in front of a whole crowd. I've won more than once. I'm the current champ. I've been the champ for the last eight, nine, or ten years. At the competitions, we shoot from forty, fifty, and then sixty feet. During that time, you have to shoot six darts. That means you have six chances to shoot and hit the spot.

There's a story about how an elderly Cherokee man developed the blowgun. According to the story, the man was too old to go out hunting and fishing anymore, so he pondered how he was going to get some meat to go with his vegetables. The only food he had was vegetables from his garden, and he started to worry because he began to lose his vegetables due to the birds eating them. One night, he went to sleep, and what we know as the "Little People" came into his dreamworld. They showed him how to fashion a blowgun and the darts to shoot.

The next morning when he got up, he went out and gathered the materials to make a blowgun and darts. It took him a few tries, but eventually he made a dart that would shoot true. When he finally got it all put together, he went out and waited for the birds to come to his garden. When they began to appear, he started shooting the birds with the blowgun, and from then on, he had meat to go with his vegetables.

WISDOM
of
OUR ELDERS

Virtuous Living

I don't think it makes much difference what y' wear; it's how yer heart is.

—*Kenny Runion*

Appalachia is a unique community. A remarkable people with their own particular concept of life thrive within the boundaries of these hills. Full of strength and love for their fellow mountain folk, the vast majority of natives attribute their blessings to their Maker. Ideals of religion and proper behavior regulate life. This section explores what Appalachian natives believe about what virtuous living is and how one leads a virtuous life.

—*Katie Lunsford*

HOW TO LIVE AN HONORABLE LIFE

"I think the secret to good friendship is taking a sincere interest in your friends and not be in it just for what you can get out of it for yourself.

Also, do not hold grudges. Friends will almost always do or say something that you do not like, but you need to be forgiving. Grudges are too heavy to carry around." —Claud Connell (2006)

"I'd rather have friends as money. Anytime. 'Cause if I had a whole lot of money, an' if you didn't like me, I couldn't get you to do a thing in th' world for me. You'd say, 'I don't need the money. I ain't got the time; I got to do this; or I got to go over yonder.' But if you were my friend, if you were really a friend, an' I asked you to go do something, you gonna do it. Ain't no ifs and ands about it. When a friend asks me t' do somethin', I'm gonna do it for a friend, when money wouldn't get me t' do it."
—Lawton Brooks (1974)

"[Virtuous behavior is] doing the right thing and helpin' people. I've recognized that not to being worked toward. It's just inherited—the power to do what you are. It's just your nature. That's what I think. Because getting back to my mother, I helped her in the garden as long as I can remember. I would take kerosene in a snuffbox, and I'd go through there and pick out the bean beetles and put 'em in that little thing and kill 'em. I was the one that done something like that more than the rest of 'em. She needed somebody, and I don't reckon I ever remember her tellin' me what needed to be done." —Waymond Lunsford (2014)

"Work keeps people's mind occupied and keeps 'em from doing things they're not supposed to do. If they got their minds on their work, they'll be successful." —Annie Perry (1976)

"The Lord made trees a bit like he made people. They all have different characteristics, and if you look hard enough, you'll find something they're good for." —John Huron (2000)

"If anyone was sick, you'd chop up their wood and carry it in the house for them, and wash their clothes, clean their house for them, and do everything you could for them. 'Love your neighbor as yourself,' and you know, we believed that." —Aunt Nora Garland (1974)

"Another thing I would change is I would have turned to God quicker than I did. I was raised in a Christian home. I got lost from Him, but I found Him again." —Leona "Dink" Carver (1995)

PLATE 145 Foxfire student Rob Bailey and Leona "Dink" Carver

"Th' first thing is t' be honest and truthful. That's about th' best thing I could think of. Live their life; be honest and truthful and not steal. That's honesty, y' know. If you're honest and truthful, you're not a-gonna steal . . . I believe in tendin' to your own business and leavin' other people alone. If you tend to your own business, you've got plenty t' do without a-tendin' t' mine . . ." —**Maud Shope (1972)**

"Reach out to people; don't think about yourself so much all the time. Oftentimes, when you meet somebody else's need, you'll find your own needs met." —**Bob Thomason (2004)**

"Well, I oughtn't t' bother you, nor do no harm again' you. I ought 'a be a-tryin' t' lift you up instead a-tryin' t' down you worse 'n' worse. That ain't right. That ain't right, no sir. And you're not supposed t' get out and get pretty well fixed, y' know, and get t' feelin' that you're better 'n anybody else. That ain't so. They's poor people that ain't got a dime'll maybe get further t' heaven than we will—if they live right."

—**Thad "Happy" Dowdle (1973)**

"I wasn't raised in a religious home, but I had moral value that was instilled in me. I've never been a bad person. I've never robbed or stolen, but I've drank my liquor, and I've done this and I've done that. I've [attributed] that my relationship with God now is because of my moral upbringing, and like I say, I knew about religion and faith from the outside." —Carl Shoupe (2009)

"My religion is more important to me than all this house and buildings and things. My life and the way I live mean more to me than anything earthly because, you see, this life is here. But when this life ends, your soul has got to go somewhere, and it's either going to go where there is happiness and peace, or it's going to go to hell." —Carrie Stewart (1977)

"My faith in God, I think that probably would be my main virtue, to keep first my beliefs and my trust in God and not fail Him in that area, which we do sometimes. We strive, and I will use this scripture, which has been one of my favorites. People say you can't live a perfect life, but the Bible only tells us to 'strive ye, therefore, to be perfect even as your Father, which is in Heaven.' To me, that is a big goal because in ourselves, in our own nature, sometimes it is difficult to maintain the virtues that you hold as the way you've been trained up in life. To me, a virtue is being a good person to others. Do unto others as you would have them do unto you, and if people can't see those qualities in your life, there's not a lot there to me." —Maxine Darnell (2014)

"They [young people] think they can rely on themselves. It gets 'em to thinking that they can do anything within themselves, when you can't do that. They used to rely more on their Maker than they do now. They have learned so much that they think, 'I don't have to call on my Maker.' Things won't get better, not the way the world is going. I think Judgment Day is close at hand." —Annie Perry (1975)

"I was born to a set of Spirit-filled parents. I was born and reared in Mount Airy, Georgia. Everyone was a friend in the community. Someone else's parents were my parents, and my parents were their parents. You mind each other. You were taught the values. You were taught respect. I was taught growing up, first, to have respect for myself, and then have it for others. Treat others like I wanted to be treated. I didn't push my values on you, but we would sit down and talk with an open mind. I am still learning, I am still listening, and I am still trying to do the best I can.

PLATE 146 Baptizing at Camp Pinnacle

"You set a set of values that you're going to live and to do by. It's not what other folks expect out of you. It's what you expect out of yourself. I still live by it. That was the basis of how I raised my children. Before they made a great big decision, [I would tell them to] think about what you're doing. We have a lot of children today that don't give any thought to their actions.

"Look at other folks. You look at how others will see it [your action]. Other people, they have respect for you. They want you to do what's right. You want them to do what's right. We were just taught to treat each other and believe and obey each other.

"If I look back, and I would look back at how my parents reared me, they believed that if it was a good value in life to learn through a Christian experience, they would pass it on. I value that my father taught us that your word and a handshake was better than your name on a piece of paper. That was the thing when they grew up, and that was how I grew up. But now, it's a document with a name and a signature. Your word was what you were. If you said it, you did it. If you made an appointment, you kept it. If you made a promise, you did it. That was a value of ours. We stayed true to what we said.

"I was taught that if you went to school, you did your very best, that education was the thing that was going to carry us into the future. I grew up with a lot of children that somehow didn't want to go to school. On the wayside, on the way up the road through life, they matured and got into some other things that was not good for them. But for me, it was a wrong decision they was makin'. So, I knew I had to live my own life, and I had to do what was right, while doing what my parents expected and what the other elders of the community expected out of me."

—Willie Fortson (2014)

"Set a goal for yourself an' try not to follow everybody else. There's a tendency to be just like the others, but don't do wrong things because you see others doing them. Set a goal an' try to keep your life clean an' pure—you'll never be sorry." —Ada Kelly (1971)

"A virtuous person to me is one that has strong faith in God. Be diligent. If the Lord is tellin' you to do somethin', don't let it fall to the ground. You know, be obedient. Be good to people and if you can help somebody, help 'em. People don't take time for anything.

"This is one thing, and I guess you have to account it to both my parents goin' through the Depression. You didn't waste anything. You took care of everything you had. You worked hard. Do everything diligently. That's been my motto. Anything worth doin' is worth doin' well. I can't stand somethin' half done. I had an uncle. He was known to be a drunk. I think about him a lot of times. He would drink a lot, but he had integrity. If he told you somethin', it was the truth. He didn't lie. If he was drunk as a dog and came and borrowed five dollars from you, when he got sobered up, he'd come and pay you back, or he'd bring you his first mess a' beans outta the garden or somethin' like that. But these people who lie and go on, you don't want to see them comin'." —Sue Patton (2014)

THE WORLD IS WATCHING

They [Walt Disney Studios] was good to everybody, was real generous to us mountain folks then.

—*Doug Bleckley*

For centuries, the people of Appalachia have been viewed as peculiar, odd, inhospitable, and downright unfriendly by outsiders. Those views were shaped by encounters that did not take into account the idea that the people of the mountains were, with good reason, distrustful of outsiders. Historically, Appalachians have not been well spoken of by print, video, and audio media. They have been portrayed as inbred, lazy, shiftless, uneducated, backward, and sometimes violent. The stereotypes were accepted as truth by outsiders, and the negative labeling became fact in many people's minds.

The stereotype created by outsiders was hard to swallow and even harder to shake for the people of this region. Their distrust of outsiders was justified by a seemingly endless barrage of negative stereotyping, a categorizing that, until very recently, was still socially acceptable.

The following sections look at how mountaineers were portrayed and treated by various media from the 1940s to the present, focusing in particular on movies or videos filmed in or near Rabun County. The reader can reach their own conclusions, just as the people here have.

—*Ethan Phillips and Jesse Owens*

HOLLYWOOD COMES A-CALLING

THE GREAT LOCOMOTIVE CHASE

Local residents on the production of the 1956 film

Well, you know, they brought a lot of money into Rabun County.
—Randall Deal

I take great pride in how small and cozy this little paradise tucked away in the Blue Ridge Mountains of Northeast Georgia is. However, for one short summer in 1956, our "Smallville" label was put aside as Rabun County bustled with movie cameras, stage props, and actors. "Lights-camera-action" rang through the hills. The calm streets of Clayton were filled with people exclaiming fresh news of a famous visitor. People dialed four-digit numbers to brag about whom they had seen, and many soon found themselves on the "Big Screen," just like the movie stars they often paid to see.

Walt Disney had a lifetime fascination with trains and locomotives, which led him to produce a movie based on the Great Locomotive Chase. Before making the movie, Walt Disney and his crew had to find a suitable place to do the filming, and they chose the Tallulah Falls Railroad. After spending a little time in Rabun County, the movie crew discovered that the people of the area were genuinely good folks and would make perfect extras. What follows are their memories.

—*Erik Lunsford*

Johnnie Eller: I'm seventy-one years of age, and I played in the movie *The Great Locomotive Chase*. I was a stand-by one day and didn't do anything. They paid me ten dollars for my speaking part. My part was to stand there by Fess Parker. Fess was taller than me, you know; he stood there on my right. Kenneth Tobey was one of the movie stars on the left of me. Fess Parker looked up at the sky and looked down at me and said, "It's a cloudin' over. You think it'll rain?" I looked up at the sky and at him. Then I had to say, "Might could. Rains one minute and shines the next." Well, that was my part I had to say. They told me just to stand there and be an onlooker right in front of the depot when the train come in. They said, "You just stand there and weave back and forth like a daisy, and watch the people get on and off the train when it comes in and say your part when Fess asks you the question." I wanted to be in another part of the movie, but some of 'em told me I'd be too easy recognized. When they give me wardrobe clothes to wear in the movie, they gave me a string to use for my watch chain. They loaned out some great ol' big watches to use for that movie. I remember that the depot was there, where Keller's Furniture is at now [on West Savannah Street, Clayton, Georgia]. I remember there was a whole bunch of people standing around the depot from Atlanta: women and men, onlookers that come to see that movie being made.

PLATE 147 Johnnie Eller, forty years after *The Great Locomotive Chase*

Even when I was done with my part, I rode with them up in North Carolina on the train called the Ole General. They got that train out of a museum somewheres where they had them stored. I remember I stopped there in Mountain City. They was a-doin' different things there. I remember up there in Prentice, North Carolina [near Otto, North Carolina], they had horses up there they'd ride up over them banks. I sat around and watched 'em one day. I got to eat with a whole bunch of the movie crew. They took a picture that was in the newspaper of me and the engineer on the train. I think I was a-smokin' an old cob pipe that I'd made.

Jeff Hunter was in the movie. He was one of the leadin' movie stars with Fess Parker. Fess was a good-natured kind of a guy. Fess stayed in the Duncan Motel. His girlfriend was here, Betty Klingman. They come over here to my house once. One of the movie stars, Al Kramer, come here with Fess. Fess wanted a record of a song I wrote about Davy Crockett. So I made 'em duplicate that record. I think he said he had a collection of about fifteen.

"Fess wanted a record of a song I wrote about Davy Crockett."
—Johnnie Eller

Walt Disney, he come here, but he was a having a little trouble with his eyes. I think they was here about two or three weeks, way I remember it. They was here a good while. Howard Cannon, he hauled them movie stars around a whole lot. Some of 'em made good money, you know, being in the movie. After they made that movie, somebody sent me a telegram from New York—wanted me to come up there and be in one of 'em two-for-the-money shows. I never did go. I got somebody to write 'em a letter, but they never did answer.

Eula Parker: I'm eighty-nine years old. I remember some about when they made that *Great Locomotive Chase*. Lord, I see'd all of them movie stars. I talked to Fess Parker all the time, and I made a picture of him and my granddaughter Brenda. Oh, Lord, I went every day to watch 'em make that movie 'cause my husband played in it.

"Lord, I see'd all of them movie stars." —Eula Parker

Bob, my husband, was wearin' a Confederate suit and was a-leadin' the Southern army. He was a-tryin' to catch Fess Parker 'cause he was

PLATE 148 Eula Parker on the set of *The Great Locomotive Chase*

a-playin' the Northern part. I remember that they come right across the hill way up there in Dillard. They went through Dillard, and Bob's horse jumped that whole railroad track and run around up there on the hill. Bob and the army he was a-leadin' caught Fess and that bunch. Bob laughed and said he caught the movie star. When I talked to Fess Parker, he told me how they all come in here on a bus. When he was here, every-body called him "Davy Crockett." He come back here a lot of times.

Doug Bleckley: I was born in Rabun County, May 30, 1942. I was in *The Great Locomotive Chase*, which was filmed in Rabun County in 1955 and '56. In '56, I went to California and finished filming the movie in the Disney Studio. Most of it was filmed from Tallulah Falls back into Franklin. Most of the scenes were in North Carolina; the fightin' and all the horseback ridin' was done there. When they were here scoutin' for people to be in it, I was a-workin' in a lil' ol' café called the Pick Rick there in town. I was eleven years old at the time. They came in and got to talkin' to me and asked me if I would be interested in bein' in the movie. I didn't know really anything about it till I came home and asked my mother, and she had to give it a lot of thought before she would even think about lettin' me be in the movie. People were encouragin' her, so she decided she would let me be in it. They came back in the Pick Rick and asked me for an interview up at the Clayton Hotel, which is the Old Clayton Inn now. They assigned me a part and told me to let my hair grow out and everything, and they'd get back in contact with me. So, durin' that time they went back to California and came back to get ready to shoot the movie. They talked with me again and gave me another part than the one they had first assigned me to do. From then on, I was on scene.

I was in school then, and school had already started. They had me a tutor on the scene, on the set where they was shootin'. When they would get ready to shoot a scene, I would just have to leave my classroom and go out to that. They filmed then. I don't recall just how long they stayed here. I went out to California to the studio to finish filmin' out there. A year later, in the fall of '56, I went back out there for advertisement and was on "The Mouseketeers" for a week's series—Jimmy and Annette Funicello and a whole bunch of kids. I don't remember all of them's names. They're like me—they've all got age on 'em now. But we didn't have any TV at that time. Not anybody down Warwoman had one. We had to go into town when they previewed the thang. Cecil McClure's house could get the station out of Atlanta. We went and watched it out there on their TV. I remember that.

"All them things I had never seen, I probably never would have got to have seen if it w'u'dn't had been for that." —Doug Bleckley

I guess the highlight of the thing was I had never flown on an airplane, and we flew out there on the biggest airplane they had then. H. J. Ramey and myself, and we stayed out there for three weeks for filmin' the first time I went out there. I was out there at the studios. I visited a lot of people. H. J. had some people out there. We went up to Northern California to his cousin's, which was Wiley Ramey. Wiley eventually retired and came back here, and he passed away about two years ago. His mother was my first-grade teacher at Antioch School. That was the first time I had seen her in several years. He just took me sightseein' out there—we all went up to Yosemite National Park. All them things I had never seen, I probably never would have got to have seen if it w'u'dn't had been for that. And it was a great experience.

The second time out there, I stayed with a lot of the stars. Slim Pickens, he was real good to me—just took me places. All the time I w'u'dn't in the studio workin', he had sump'n planned for me to do—visited Rex Allen in Montana; he was a world champion trick roper then at the time. We went lots of places—went to Roy Rogers's house, but he w'u'dn't there.

Clayton has changed a great deal. At the time they were filming *The Great Locomotive Chase*, it was a boomin' place. Filmin' the movie, they put a lot of people to work that hadn't worked. They worked as carpenters. They had thangs for people to do, building props. I'd say at that time that the most money that was ever in Rabun County was brought in here by that movie. Back then, there w'u'dn't any textile plants here. The only thang was here then was the Shirt Factory. Most of the people that worked there was women, so that movie brought in a lot of money. There was a lot of money involved. They w'u'dn't a tight bunch of people. They really spent the money and paid people good wages. I don't know what they paid carpenters an hour, but they was a lot of people workin' that had never worked on a public job before. They was people that was goin' up and down the train track, and they had two or three flat cars; that was "meal cars," they called 'em. That was where they cooked. They had the cooks and everything. They fed people right on the scene. They had professional chefs a-fixin' meals for the cast and anybody else that wanted to eat. They would go by a railroad crossing, and there'd be children standin' there, and they'd throw dranks off by the cases and candy bars by the boxes—just stuff like that. They was good to everybody, was real generous to us mountain folks then.

I played Henry Haney; I was a fireman on the Texas. I only had a few lines to say. One was talkin' to Slim Pickens. He played the part of Mr. Bracken and was the engineer on the train. "Here's a coffee, Mr. Bracken." And the other line was to Jeff Hunter, who's dead now. "I'll fire for you, Mr. Fuller." He played the part of Mr. Fuller. That was the only lines I had in it. You know, I was in a lot of scenes where I was on the train as fireman on the engine. I just put the wood and stoked the burners. It was supposed to be a steam engine, which it really run off of diesel, but they used it as a wood burner.

They were all real nice. I met Walt Disney, and he'd talk to you about all the directors and all the other stars. Fess Parker and all of them. They was just plain, down-to-earth people. Fess Parker and them, they met me at the airport, and they had a limousine to pick me up and take me

PLATE 149 Doug Bleckley during the filming of *The Great Locomotive Chase*

to my motel room. They was some of the local boys who was out there that went back with 'em from here; Jimmy Heinz was one of 'em. He was good friends with one of the directors, Vince McEveety. They came out to LA Airport and saw me when I flew in out there. And comin' back, we rode the train. We had a choice that we could fly or ride the train, and I asked 'em to come back on the train so I could see the country. We came back the northern route through Illinois and all that. That was in the wintertime then, and that was cold weather—saw lots of sights that I'd never seen and ain't seen since. I enjoyed that train ride, too, 'cause it was an experience that took us about three days to come back. It was a lot longer than flying.

"I ate Thanksgiving dinner two years in a row with Slim Pickens."
—*Doug Bleckley*

Several years after I came back, I used to get Christmas cards, and we'd correspond sometimes with letters back and forth—I guess probably till I got out of high school and graduated—with especially Slim Pickens and a guy named Lennie Geer. He was a big star in a lot of movies with Rex Allen and Roy Rogers, too. Lennie was a comedian, and he was always a really nice feller. I thought a lot of him. I ate Thanksgiving dinner two years in a row with Slim Pickens. When I went the first time, it was to finish the movie, and the following November I went back to advertise; that's when I was on "The Mouseketeers."

We had to shoot scenes. In the movie we had to catch a runaway boxcar with the engine. We had to catch it right on the trestle. Them ol' wooden trestles would vibrate and wobble, and the train would jump up and down. That was a pretty scary part, and we had to do that several times to get the shot right. When the movie premiered in Atlanta, down at the Paramount or Fox Theatre, my mother and, I guess, one of my sisters went. Momma and 'em had to wear evening gowns and never been in one—that was the first and last 'un I reckon she was in. But it was real neat, and we was on national television then at the premiere. That was a big event there. All that was paid for, you know, an all-expense-paid trip. They treated us and lodged us when we went down there, had dinners and thangs for us. It was an experience for my whole family, really. I ain't had no high life too much except for that thang. I was one out of nine children. Well, at the time when they was filmin' and after we got through with it, Momma got a letter from Disney, asking us if we would move to California; they would put me under contract. But at the time they was still six of us livin' at home, and Dad had only been dead a year. So, Momma wouldn't hear of that. So, all of that blew over. My, I don't remember really a lot about what everythang looked like. I was really just footloose 'cause I was out of school and had the private teacher. Part of the time I would be in the classroom; if I w'u'dn't, I'd be out a-mixin' an' a-minglin' with them—you know, just young and like. I really didn't have no strings attached to me. I could get out and listen to them fellers just jokin' between the scenes, and sometimes I'd be in the classroom. They sung 'cause they was talented. They'd a-get actin' around like they was fightin'.

Jeff York was the big guy, and at one time he was a professional wrestler. They had a time keepin' up with him. He played in a lot of scenes with Fess Parker. He'd get to drankin' round here at night, and they couldn't find him for a day or two. He'd buddy off with these local fellers and get to drankin'. He was a huge man.

Frank Rickman: Way back when I was working with Roosevelt Coffee in the grading business and Walt Disney was making *The Great Locomotive Chase*, I became the go-between between the mountain people and the movie people. Walt Disney got me to go around and get the mountain people to let me take the board roofs off of their houses. We didn't have cedar shakes then, like we've got now, and I got people to let me take those board roofs off the houses and put a new tin roof or asphalt roof in the place of that. Walt Disney got to watching me work around there. When the Tallulah Falls Railroad [see *Foxfire 10*] was still in here then and when it came to bring the locomotives from California, they came to me. They had loaded them in California on railroad cars. They'd had to lay railroad track up on them flat cars because the locomotives were so heavy, they would have pushed them through the floor. They laid a railroad track up on the top of the car so they wouldn't push through the floor.

Then when they come back here to make it [the movie], the man was supposed to look over unloading them. He didn't do his homework, and then when the train come in, [he didn't know what to do]. Me and Walt Disney was standing up there at the old depot. We could hear the little train coming, pulling them in. It was just a-chugging along. Walt Disney looked over at the man that was supposed to do it, and that man turned plum green. He had overlooked that. There wasn't nothing here big enough to pick up a locomotive that weighed two hundred tons. I felt so sorry for that poor man. I was standing there hearing this and watching this man turn every color in the rainbow. That's the only time I saw Walt Disney lose his cool. He got all excited because they decided that they wanted to take them back to Atlanta and let two railroad cranes set them off the tracks. I felt sorry for that man that hadn't done his homework.

I said to him, "I can unload them things."

He says, "Shh, shh, don't let Walt Disney hear you say that. These locomotives is his pets." And he said, "If you was to scratch one of them, he'd have a heart attack."

I said, "I don't care. I can unload them safer than you can, taking them back to Atlanta."

Since they was fine antiques, Walt Disney didn't want them drove to Atlanta and unloaded and then drive them plumb back.

Walt Disney overheard me a-talking to that old boy. He said, "Frank, did you say you could unload them?"

I said, "Yes sir."

"Just how would you do that? They weigh two hundred tons."

I said, "I'll go up here on the railroad tracks and wherever we got a side track, I'll take up about one hundred foot of railroad track. I'll take my front-end loader and move that track over out of the way."

Walt Disney says, "Frank, just go ahead and tell me how you do that."

I said, "I'm gonna build an unloading ramp or dock. I'll start ramping down, and then I'll lay the track back in there. Next, I'll roll that flat car down in there. After that I can roll the locomotives right off on the line out through there."

He says, "Can you do that?"

I said, "Yes sir."

"You got yourself a deal!"

From then on I was the head knocker on that movie. He didn't listen to nobody else. He just listened to me. I done everything he had to do. When I got all that work done for the movies, [Walt Disney] eased around to me and said, "Frank, I found out what the local people think about you. I don't want to start no trouble, but I want you to go to California with me. I think I need you in my business. You need to talk to your family about it and see if you can get it worked out and let me know."

"I've been fooling around with movies ever since Walt Disney made The Great Locomotive Chase, *and that's been thirty-something years ago." —Frank Rickman*

I went home and told Sarah. I was a big [punk back then] and just had two babies. Sarah never had liked these mountains too good then, and boy did that tickle her, thinking we was going to get to go to California. In about a week, Walt Disney eased back up to me and says, "What's your family think about it?"

I said, "Everybody liked it but my daddy, and he didn't like it, but I think I'll do it."

Walt Disney then says, "Frank, I'm going to tell you right now. I know enough about you and I've done watched your work. I know what you'd be worth to me and I'll give you X number of dollars for forty hours, and all over forty hours I'll pay you time and a half and the amount that it amounted to." Me being born up here in the mountains, I didn't know nothing about big money, and I was the highest-paid construction man there was—I got paid $1.25 an hour—when he offered me that big money, I thought he was a crook just trying to get me to go to California. I looked at him and didn't say nothing to him; I say to myself, "The president of the United States doesn't make that kind of money, and if you think you're going to get me, my wife, and younguns out to California and us no damn way home, you got another think coming, partner." I wouldn't have nothing to do with him, and I dodged him from then on for a long time. Finally, he said that he wanted me to go, but I told him that I believed I wasn't going. I'd stay around here and do what come my way.

I've been fooling around with movies ever since Walt Disney made *The Great Locomotive Chase*, and that's been thirty-something years ago. Now, what's happened is that they have these unions. I'm not a union man. I believe a honest day's work is the way it should be, but the unions is not that way. The unions has made it so expensive in California and New York till we have worked at it in Georgia and had Georgia third in the nation in the movie industry.

"HE SHOUTED LOUD, 'HOSANNA, DELIVERANCE WILL COME'"

A community responds to the 1972 film

I'm just what I am, and I ain't no different. You can find me today just like you can find me tomorrow. —Mrs. Andy Webb

After *The Great Locomotive Chase*, many film crews were drawn in by the beautiful scenery of Rabun County. Possibly the most notorious of these movies is *Deliverance*. Written by James Dickey, the novel on which it's based follows four city slickers headed to the mountains for a weekend of white-water rafting. The men encounter mountain folks who are deformed, backward, illiterate, and almost nonhuman. One of the men is even raped by two hillbilly men they stumble upon in the woods. It is an understatement to say that the portrayal of mountain folks, in this book and movie, did not set well with Rabun County natives.

Over a three-month period of time, Foxfire collected material for an article concerning the movie *Deliverance*, which was filmed here. We felt the local people should have an opportunity to express their views on the movie. We also felt it was important to discuss the impact the movie had on our river and our county, since our state has encouraged other moviemakers to come to Georgia. In an effort to correct the stereotyping caused by the movie, we included a short personality sketch of Mrs. Andy Webb, who appeared in *Deliverance* along with her grandchild.

The title of this article, "He shouted loud, 'Hosanna, DELIVERANCE will come,'" comes from a Baptist hymn.

—*Laurie Brunson, Barbara Taylor, and Mary Thomas*

Mrs. Andy Webb: We lived around North Carolina. I was raised around Highlands. We was raised on the farm, and I've set down to bread and coffee, bread and water many a time, and got up and went on to the field and worked the rest of the day. My daddy plowed up the ground and made corn. We lived in a camp then. We moved to Whiteside, and it come a snow. The camp was just open; we didn't have no lumber to fix it. It come a snow, and that snow stayed on the ground till April. It come a warm morning and melted it all off. Oh, it was a hard life. We had an old steer. We rolled in logs beside the camp and set them on fire. That's the way to live. A' open camp and, boy, that smoke would put our eyes out.

My daddy made us trays out of black gum to wash dishes in. See, you had to make them out of something that wouldn't taste. Black gum and chestnut was all they could get. I never knowed to wash dishes in a dishpan. Well, we used to eat out of bucket lids and anything we could get ahold of. We didn't have any of these fancy things, never knowed what silverware was.

We'd make us tow sack bed ticks [mattresses] out of leaves. They grind up, you know, take them out, empty them, wash the tick [on a battling bench], and go and get another load of leaves and put them in. They felt so good.

I've been in the roughs. The neighbors knowed we was going to fix a house. They come and offered to help put up the house. We accepted it, of course. We got it up; then we moved in, but we just had dirt floors. We cooked on a fireplace. I didn't know what a cookstove was until after I was married.

I was borned on the old farm, and it was tough. We parched cornmeal and made coffee—it's pretty good. I've rode a steer many a mile to keep from walking. My daddy worked sometimes in the sawmill. We didn't have no money. We didn't know what money was hardly. I didn't know what a can was until I was growing up. We dried our blackberries and

PLATE 150 Mrs. Andy Webb

our buckberries and we dried apples. I've sat up many a night and bored holes through apples, stuck them on sticks, and put them up. I pickled barrels of beans and kraut.

I'm just what I am, and I ain't no different. You can find me today just like you can find me tomorrow. I ain't no high son of a gun. I guess you think we're the biggest fools there ever is. If these people that's a-growing up now had to go through with what I have, they wouldn't be here.

"If it's the Lord's will, I can do it." —*Mrs. Andy Webb*

I can stop blood; I can cure thrash. Anything I want to do. If it's the Lord's will, I can do it. Every time they get burned, they come a-running to me, and it's a mystery to me why. They ought to think the Lord has the healing power. They ought to get right with the Lord, so they can do those things theirself, but without that faith they can't do 'er. My dear Savior taught me how to do that; put my trust in the Lord.

There sets a baby I've brought through so far with prayers. She's going on fourteen years old, and I have to feed her and give her a bath. I tend to her the same as if she was six months old. And it's getting hard on me. She stayed in the hospital out yonder for three or four months. They never did do any good. Well, what the Lord does is right. And you can't tear up the Lord's work and make it over and make it any better. I told them all the time. I said, "They ain't a bit of use in taking that baby to the hospital. She'll be just as well off here as she will be there. And she's been better, too. She has been home about three months. I don't believe in the hospital business. Me and the Lord can beat them doctors to death. I wouldn't take a war pension for her. She's a lot of trouble, but I wouldn't take a war pension for her.

I told the children the other day that I didn't know what the Lord was a-keepin' me here for unless that was it [the child]. Mine is all grown, big enough to take care of theirselves.

I lost my husband. I don't reckon he had any enemies at all. And he told me where he was going, and that was a whole lot of satisfaction. He said he's a-goin' home. I said, 'To that good home?' He said, 'Yeah.' He didn't dread it a bit in the world, didn't seem like. Of course, I hated to give him up.

"I've done everything but die, and I feel like I'm a-goin' to die pretty soon." —Mrs. Andy Webb

I'm a-rubbing a hundred—pretty close. I ain't going to tell people my age, for I might want to get married again. That's just all fun. Ain't nothing to that. I still knit and piece up quilts and patch one thing, then another. I've done everything but die, and I feel like I'm a-goin' to die pretty soon.

Mrs. Webb is one of the half dozen or so people from Rabun County who appears in the movie Deliverance. *She has a small, nonspeaking part in the film. She works at patching a quilt while her fourteen-year-old granddaughter lies back on the bed.*

Mrs. Webb's home was used as the site for one of the movie sets. A country gas station was erected in her front yard, and a road was built. It was here that Burt Reynolds, Jon Voight, and the other actors came before they set out on their river trip, and it was here that the dueling banjo scene took place between one of the actors and a local youngster.

They come here, and they wanted me and the baby in the movie, and I was a-piecin' up quilt pieces. I couldn't see, but I was working like I was a-piecin' a quilt. I've got now so blind that I can't see to thread the needle. You can't get away from your old habits.

The crew was very nice. They wasn't but one thing they done . . . I had that little patch down there planted with taters. They was just a-comin' up, and they wanted to put a road through there, and they plowed them up. Yes, they paid me for them, but not what they ought to. You know a patch of taters like that is worth something. The taters was awful pretty, but I didn't grumble. I ain't too long here and when I leave here, I want to go in peace. Craving money—I don't do that. I spend my money as fast as I get it. Help out [my children] sometimes—they may be behind with their payments or something like that.

The crew was up at Mrs. Webb's about two months. Mrs. Webb enjoyed the banjo scene:

I like their music all right. They was a man a-dancin'. I like music if it's carried on right. It's got to be carried on right before I'll associate with it. No cutting up and acting a fool. It was lots of satisfaction to me 'cause my husband hadn't been took off too long and it was interesting to me. I enjoyed that movie picture very much.

We interviewed several other people who were in the movie besides Mrs. Webb to establish what the actual person-to-person contact was like between the movie crew and the local people.

Louise Coldren was the manager of a local hotel where some of the crew stayed:

One morning about five o'clock, I was serving breakfast in the dining room. Until that time, hippies were not as prevalent in Rabun County as they are today. I saw a man come in with his hair tied in a cord. He was clean, he was ragged, and he carried a briefcase. I think to myself, 'I'm glad he is coming in this early; maybe he'll eat his breakfast and leave before many people come in here.' I served him three eggs, bread, and a fruit. I did that for about three months. He was the assistant producer of *Deliverance*.

"Until that time, hippies were not as prevalent in Rabun County as they are today." —Louise Coldren

It was our first year of operation here in the hotel, and they had been here about three weeks before any of them came here to eat. They came back the next morning and wondered if I would cater food. And they wanted to know what I had to offer. From that day on, I began to cater their food, and then I began to cater their coffee breaks . . . after that, their special parties, like entertaining the Georgia Power company and the businessmen of Clayton.

We were also interested in finding out how the people of Rabun County felt about the way mountain people were represented. Louise Coldren commented, "They got some of the best of Rabun County and, of course, some of the worst."

One local man we interviewed, Ken Keener, had acted as a scout for the crew. Using his Bronco, he helped find locations for filming in wooded areas and on the banks of the river. He commented briefly on his impression of the crew, and then went on to give his impression of the movie's impact on the county:

They're like people everywhere; you can pick out the likables and the dislikables of the crowd. Some of them were really nice people, and some of them, well, like I said, dislikables. Most of them liked their drink, but as far as I know, it didn't interfere with their work, and it didn't bother me in any way.

Well, I don't think [the impact] was too good. I mean the local people didn't much like the impression it left on people, which I don't either. I think it would have been a whole lot better movie if they had left out two or three scenes; well, really the rape scene. Some people say that it left the impression the local people were very unfriendly. It brought a lot of money into the county, but it also left a bad image on the county. It hurt our pride, I think.

At this point, his wife, Mrs. Ken Keener, spoke up:

Now, I work at Empire Factory, and we had a new man come down from New York, and he said that he expected the people here to be as they were in *Deliverance*. And he was so surprised. Now, I don't know what he meant by that, but he said he would go away with an entirely different outlook from what he had gotten to see in the movie.

Edward Ramey was one of the local residents cast for the movie, and like most of the people we interviewed, he liked working with the movie crew. Edward played the part of the gas station attendant in the scene that was shot at Mrs. Webb's house:

I just walked around most of the time, and they had me a-dancing and making like I was selling gas and things like that. And I danced a little— they wanted me to dance some. I believe they thought I'd slide down that hillside. They poured motor oil on the ground, and they had it awful greasy, and I had to dance on that oil there on a sloping hill. I believe they did, but I didn't fall. They was just having their fun, I reckon.

"I believe they thought I'd slide down that hillside."

—Edward Ramey

We also asked Edward what he thought of the entire movie when he saw it after it had been released. His main comment concerned the rape scene:

They asked me what I did think about that. I told them, 'You may not like what I say, but I won't go around your back about it.' I said, 'I think it ought to be a violation of the law to show pictures like that of the act.' I told him, 'That was just a little too vulgarish.' I told him if a man was to take his wife and kids to see it, and then such as that comes up, it wouldn't look pretty. When them people stripped off down yonder on the river, that's the one I was talking about being so vulgarish.

Nell Norton appears in the dining room scene toward the end, relating a true story about a cucumber she grew. She thoroughly enjoyed and appreciated her contact with the Deliverance *crew and was quite frank in answering our questions:*

They didn't tell me what the movie was about. They said they'd like to take my picture and they interviewed me, and they said they would like to have me in the movie. They didn't tell me nothing. Anybody would enjoy being in a movie and meeting the movie stars. One of my husband's cousins, we was just fixing lunch, and I was just fixing to sit down, and this girl come across from there, walking. She said, "Nell, I'm so glad you was in the movie." Then she said, "Nell, is Burt Reynolds here?"

I said, "No, but out there where our dressing rooms are, his name is put on his door right next to ours, and you can go out there and put your hand on the door and maybe your heart will flutter a little." It wasn't me she came over to see. She wasn't that proud, and I wasn't crazy.

I enjoyed every bit of it. They just went out of their way to be nice to you. When they had the camera on you, they would tell you exactly when to talk and when not to. They got us at this table and asked us all kinds of questions. Ned Beatty—this was the man I really loved; Ned was so good—would say, "Nell, tell us something. What did you do yesterday?"

I said, "I worked in my garden and gathered cucumbers."

Ned said, "Nell, I know you never growed no cucumber seventeen and a half inches long."

I said, "You don't believe that damn cucumber was that big?"

If you liked it, you liked it. If you didn't like it, it ain't no use to say it. Lord, the first money I drawed, my refrigerator went bad, and I had

PLATE 151 Nell Norton

to buy another one. Next, my television went bad, and I had to buy another one. I've got to get in another movie. I like it!

Randall Deal, who played the part of one of the men hired to drive the cars up to Aintry, the fictional town in the story, where the canoe trip was to end, gave us this opinion of the film:

Well, you know they brought a lot of money into Rabun County. I wouldn't knock the film people for making it, because they put lots worse things in films than there was in that one. Still, the same, that wasn't one you'd show in church on Sunday morning. Some of the people in the county didn't like it, but I think most of them didn't really have much to say against it, I don't believe. Of course, there was a few didn't like it. I think that if they filmed another tomorrow about anything—Jesus, or whatever—there would be somebody that would find something wrong with it.

"I couldn't have said too much to them to make them change their mind." —Randall Deal

As far as the movie goes, I like it all right myself. They was all really nice people to me. I was with them about six days in all, filming that part I was in, first up on Mulberry at the Webbs'. I didn't like them filming that little girl up there, but I couldn't have said too much to them to make them change their mind. I guess out of that week, that will be one thing I always remember.

The River
People flocked to the famous river in droves, and all too many inexperienced tourists and thrill-seekers put in their rafts and kayaks and find that the unpredictable rapids and white water are much more than they bargained for. Thirty-nine people have died on the river since 1970.

Deliverance's author, James Dickey, warned, "That river doesn't care about you. It'll knock your brains out. Most of the people who go up there don't know about white-water rivers. They are just out for a lark, just like those characters in Deliverance. *They wouldn't have gone up there if I hadn't written the book. There's nothing I can do about it. I can't patrol the river, but it just makes me feel awful."*

Lindsey Moore was the head of the thirty-two-man rescue squad in Rabun County. Patrolling the river was something he is very familiar with:

We have been in rescue work for about six to eight years, and we didn't have too much trouble before. We had a little, but this movie has caused it to increase considerably. In fact, it has caused us rescue boys to have to do a lot of work. We've spent several nights on that river hunting those that are lost or stranded or whatever. And we've pulled approximately seven bodies out of the river, which had been drowned.

To my opinion, it's just got out of hand with people canoeing. Now, I might be judging it wrong. Of course, it's a man's privilege to do whatever he wants, wherever he wants 'cause this is a free country, you know, but it seems like that river has caused us a lot of hard work since that movie has been made.

"We get enough criticism . . . by just doing the best we can."
—*Lindsey Moore*

Some of the *Deliverance* film crew came down to Clayton, and they asked me if I'd take my men down there and drag the river for them, and I said, "No sir, I will not." Then he asked me how to drag the river and what to wear and where to drag, but he wanted to know if I'd take my men down there and help them out, and I said no. I didn't want to get in on that. We get enough criticism—the rescue squad does (you know what I mean)—by just doing the best we can, without getting into something that you know is not fit for the county anyway.

The river is a lot of trouble to get to. In some of these places, we have to use Jeeps to get to and tie a rope from one side to the other, and send a man out there on that rope with the drags to troll in there and pull. Lots of times we have to take those ropes and tie them to a boat or raft out on it and use it to drag with them. I had three men over there and almost drowned myself, looking for a body over there one time.

The people who float now, they're not familiar with the river. Well, some of them are, and some of them are not. Most of them are not familiar with it. They just come down there to get the sight of the river and where it's at, and they don't know anything about it.

They hear about it, and they want to come and try it to see what kind of a thrill they get out of it. Like I say, they don't realize what danger they're getting into.

Now, lots of them just come down there and camp on the river and don't float it. Most every camping area you go to has garbage all over it everywhere. It's awful littered up. It used to be that I could go down that river and catch a mess of fish most any time I wanted, but now it's lit-

PLATE 152 Lindsey Moore taking a break from work

tered up—the banks are slick—beer cans, garbage, and what-have-you scattered all over and in the river—and down by the bridge there, it's so cluttered.

Sheriff Chester York: I think more people have come to see Rabun County and to the Chattooga River since *Deliverance* was filmed. Because any side road—there's a lot of side roads that you can get into the river—you can try to get in with an automobile, but you can't get anywhere near the river. There's no place to park.

I understand from the Walhalla [South Carolina] Police Department that there are as many people coming from that direction as there are coming from this side of the line—from Atlanta and directions south of there. There's a steady stream over there through Walhalla like there is over here on the weekend.

The canoeists and rafters, or whatever, usually start there at US Highway 28 Bridge and go to Tugaloo Lake, which is probably twenty to twenty-five miles. They usually float different stretches there. Some of them are equipped right, and lots of them are not. They're just ama- teurs. If they've seen the picture *Deliverance*, it looks awful easy, but that water there is very treacherous. It'll even fool the local people, let alone the amateurs.

I think most of the accidents on the river are negligence and drinking because we found out from the bodies that have been recovered; there's only been one that hadn't been drinking, as I recall.

> *"People say, 'If our governor can go down that river, I can, too.'"*
> —*Sheriff Chester York*

I have been there helping to recover the bodies. The last body I helped recover was down north of the Highway 76 Bridge. When I arrived at the scene, it was probably five o'clock in the afternoon. There were at least twenty-five people passed before dark—canoes, rafts, and so on—and there being a body there didn't affect them a bit. They didn't even stop and ask what happened, even though there were some 100 to 150 people there helping recover the body.

I don't know why. It's just something new that the people like. To start with, they didn't realize we had a river that close by. Then our governor and some of our higher officials are kayakers, and the people say, "If our governor can go down that river, I can, too." It's a great sport, but so many people get on the river that aren't equipped and don't know

PLATE 153 Sheriff Chester York

what they're doing. That's when they get in trouble, most of the time. There's any number of people that lose their transportation, whether they're using a raft or kayak and walk out. Some of those places in the river will virtually tear a raft all to pieces—tear the bottom out if it gets caught under the water. There are a lot of these pools that once they get you under the water, you just roll over and over and have no sense of direction which way to go. It'll drown you before it eventually kicks you out. It's just got you. I've seen those rafts down there at Woodall Shoals on two occasions where there was a drowning. They got caught in one of these places, and half an hour later, it was still going. The raft was under that waterfall, and it was just like a flutter mill. There's hydraulic power in there. Evidently, there's a rock under there that causes the main force of that water to come right back over. You've got the force of that water going in there. If you stay on top, you're okay as long as you've got a life jacket on. On two occasions I've seen those life jackets stripped off of the body [by the force of the water], and you can imagine what kind of force that's got, but nobody realizes that. Well, most everybody goes over the top and thinks nothing about it, but once you go in it just right, and it catches you and takes the raft or boat under you, once you get under it, you're lucky if you just get out alive. You tell people that, and they still don't believe you. They have to find out the hard way. Quite a few of them do find out the hard way.

One Sunday morning three Foxfire staff members, Barbara Taylor, Mary Thomas, and Pat Rogers, began a raft trip down the Chattooga River with Payson Kennedy of the Nantahala Outdoor Center; his wife, Aurelia; and their daughter, Kathy.

They met early that morning where the Highway 76 Bridge crosses the Chattooga, one of the most overused spots on the river. The banks and beach there had a kind of tramped-upon look with half-dissolved Kleenexes, beer cans, and old campfires spread about, and there was a strange odor that they weren't sure we wanted to identify.

Mr. Kennedy had been running the Chattooga for eight years and worked as a stuntman with the Deliverance *crew when they were filming. He estimates that the number of people using the river had jumped in the two subsequent summers from one hundred a week to more than a thousand a week. "This summer I was taking around eighty people a weekend down the river, and the other outfitter was taking around one to two hundred a weekend. You can tell how the numbers of people have increased by the cans and bottles that are lying around."*

Before the Foxfire crew started out, Payson gave a talk on river safety that included things like what to do if they got thrown out of the rafts as well as a description of the hydraulic power of the falls at Woodall Shoals. And then we were off, life jackets securely tied and helmets buckled.

When they came to the part of the river known as "Deliverance Rocks," Aurelia mentioned "that Deliverance *syndrome," a term now given to people who have no reverence for the river, those who don't respect the power of the water and are just out for a joyride. They don't know what they're getting into, and they think they can imitate the adventure of that movie.*

Kathy added that many of the people who ride the rafts seemed to be frightened of the mountain people who are fishing from the banks of the river: "I get pretty tired of people asking about Deliverance. *Some of the rafters I have brought down here start squealing like pigs when we reach the part of the river where the rape scene was filmed. That, I don't care for."*

At the same time in the back of our minds, we could hear Chester York saying, "Don't go down that part of the river." We decided to walk around it.

It used to be that only a few trout fishermen, rafters, and campers visited the Chattooga, but now it is famous.

Even today, there are many in our community who cringe when they hear the word "Deliverance." Their anger at the portrayal of Rabun County natives as uneducated, inbred hillbillies has not faded. In 2012, an effort was made to hold a festival honoring forty years since the Chattooga was named as a wild and scenic river. However, when it was suggested that it also commemorate the fortieth anniversary of the movie, numerous local residents became upset. Tracy Speed McCoy, a former Foxfire student and owner and publisher of Georgia Mountain Laurel, *a regional magazine that celebrates art, food, businesses, and traditions of our region, wrote:*

"I am excited about a Chattooga River Festival but am disgusted by the resurrection of *Deliverance*. I wonder if we are that desperate to resort to promoting ourselves in the light that the movie did forty years ago. How can you take the same thing and make it different than it was then? The river is beautiful all on its own. It is a treasure in the mountains and enjoyed by so many. I am all for bringing people to the mountains and promoting our area. I do it twenty-four/seven and it is easy to show the beauty of our area, the richness of character of our locals and second-home owners and the diversity of our area. Because I oppose the stereotype the movie offers up to represent the mountain people, I am accused of not wanting businesses to make money. That has to be a joke. I just believe in the integrity of our people and don't appreciate the filth of *Deliverance*. How do we explain to our kids why this is something to celebrate?"

Attendance at the inaugural festival fell far short of the festival planners' expectations. The Chattooga River Festival has not become an annual event.

"I NEVER EXPECTED THE NOVEL WOULD BE PUBLISHED"

An interview with North Georgia native Olive Ann Burns

I look back and regret what I missed. —Olive Ann Burns

As a young writer on *The Foxfire Magazine* staff, Jenny Lincoln was fascinated by how authors accomplished their work. What inspired them? How did they think about their writing? She set out to interview one of her favorite authors: Olive Ann Burns, who wrote *Cold Sassy Tree*. This book tells a story about life in the South in the early part of this century [twentieth century]. The main character is the boy Will Tweedy; he and his family live in a little town called Cold Sassy, Georgia, where information gets around faster than a jackrabbit runs.

Olive Ann Burns grew up in a little town called Harmony Grove—located in the Georgia Mountains just south of Rabun County—whose name was later changed to Commerce; Cold Sassy was modeled on this village. She worked as an editor of *The Atlanta Journal-Constitution* for ten years before she wrote *Cold Sassy Tree*, her first novel. It was made into a made-for-television film in 1989.

Mrs. Burns worked on her sequel to *Cold Sassy Tree* up until she was diagnosed with cancer once again, after just having recovered from it not long before. She started chemotherapy treatments in 1987, which unfortunately led to congestive heart failure and prescribed bed rest. She sought the help of her neighbor Norma Duncan to help her transcribe her works she had completed up until that point. Mrs. Burns realized she wouldn't have enough time to finish her sequel, which was originally called *Time, Dirt, and Money*. We are sad to say that Mrs. Burns passed away on July 4, 1990, after many courageous years of battling cancer. She did, however, leave a legacy to us all. Her final wish was that her unfinished work still be published. In 1992, that wish was fulfilled. Her book was renamed *Leaving Cold Sassy* and is a testimony to Mrs. Burns's hard work and dedication.

—*Ethan Phillips and Jesse Owens*

I was born in Banks County, Georgia, in 1924, lived on the farm, and went to school through grade four in nearby Commerce. My early writing was in a diary after we moved to Dawson, Georgia, in 1933. About all it amounted to day after day was, "Got up, ate breakfast, went to school, came home, studied, ate supper, read my book, went to bed, and prayed for everything." In high school I wrote with passion about things I did that day, things I learned, things I thought, but I wrote nothing for weeks and months whenever I fell in love. I wasn't lonely when in love; I could tell my feelings to a person instead of to blank pages.

"In my day, young women expected to marry soon after college."

I went to high school in Macon, Georgia. By then I thought I'd like to be a writer, and the award-winning school newspaper was my training ground. A byline there meant something: no sloppy work allowed. It's the same process if you're writing for a school monthly or a city newspaper. It's just a different audience. The task is to write what people want to read.

I really wanted to be a doctor, but I knew I wasn't efficient enough to be a mother and a wife and a doctor, and I wasn't willing to study that hard. I was an A student at a good school, but medicine requires triple As. Besides, I was more interested in catching a husband. In my day, young women expected to marry soon after college. I'm glad I didn't only want a career.

I attended Mercer University and graduated from the University of North Carolina at Chapel Hill. I had read about a wonderful black teacher who taught black children in Mississippi. He said to them, "Don't just train for one career or one job. Try to get skills in at least two things, so if you can't get what you'd like to do in one, you can go on to the

PLATE 154 Olive Ann Burns

other." So I got a teacher's certificate as well as a degree in journalism. I was so practical, just awfully practical. My family had a long background in teaching—my mother taught, and my sister—and I had loved teachers all the way through school. My teacher's certificate was in social studies. I didn't take many English courses after sophomore year because I had to have the social studies courses, six education courses, six journalism courses for my major, plus courses in history, economics, and political science because the dean of journalism wanted us to know something of what knowledge was out there and where to look up anything needed to write a certain story. I also took about nine courses in French.

I never had any literature courses in my two years at the University of North Carolina, and I missed so much. The world's authority on Shakespeare was a professor there, but I didn't take any of his courses. I look back and regret what I missed. Certainly, literature is what I should have been aiming to teach.

I wrote one poem in my life. At Chapel Hill, I was very much in love with a Jewish boy. I'm a Methodist. The world has changed: many people marry today in that situation, but family pressures were stronger then. I never told my own family he was Jewish, and if you avoid telling your family something, you know there's a problem. Anyway, I started having nightmares about what I should do. One night I dreamed I was trying to get to an island. I could see this beautiful glass palace, and I craved to go there and claim it. I was swimming toward it when suddenly I saw the palace start disintegrating. It didn't take a psychiatrist to tell me that this dream meant the situation was disintegrating because it couldn't lead anywhere. I was very much in love, but I wasn't strong enough to face the difficulties with his family and mine. By the time I married at thirty-two, I would have been strong enough, but not at twenty-two. So, I wrote a poem about it and turned it in to the professor of a creative writing course. He submitted it to the *Atlantic Monthly*'s national contest for scholastic writing. It didn't win a paying prize, but it did get an honorable mention. That love poem was the end of my poetry career, but writing it was a wonderful experience. Anybody who wants to write poetry should try it. You learn a lot about expressing feelings and ideas, and you can make copies, bind them together, find a title, and give it to family and friends at Christmas. There are many ways young people can get started in writing. You don't have to wait for professional training the way doctors and lawyers must. While I was still in college, I edited a literary magazine.

After college, I got a job working for a company that published a magazine that went to laundrymen and to bottlers of soft drinks. A year later, in 1947, I became a staff writer for *The Atlanta Journal Sunday Magazine* [later called *The Atlantic Weekly*] under editor Angus Perkerson. I stayed there for ten years.

> *"You don't have to wait for professional training the way doctors and lawyers must."*

Margaret Mitchell had worked under Mr. Perkerson for four years before I was born. He was still the editor during most of my ten years there. He was a remarkable editor with a sure instinct for what people would read. He was shy, dour, profane, a chronic worrier. He had magnificent tantrums and was a great teacher.

Everything I know about writing began with Mr. Perkerson. He never rewrote a writer. You had to do it for yourself. You learned not to be sensitive about the x's he put in the margins. He'd go through the copy with you like this: "Don't you think a 'the' would be better than an 'a' here?" "Da . . . it, that whole page is boring." "This word is too long. We ain't putting out the magazine for PhDs." "You used the same word five times in two sentences." (Once, when I said I repeated a word on purpose, for emphasis, he said, "It's bad enough to be careless without being stupid.") If he said, "That's funny," he meant suggestive; being young and unworldly, I was often "funny." He never gave praise. You knew he liked your story if he put it up front in the magazine. He was obsessive about two things: being interesting and being accurate. Once he asked me when George Washington's birthday was. I said, "February twenty-second. Everybody knows that." "Well, call the reference department and make sure."

> *"Mr. Perkerson fired me three times in the first six months and scared me to death for five years."*

Mr. Perkerson fired me three times in the first six months and scared me to death for five years. Whenever he couldn't stand my pained writing pace any longer, he'd come over to my desk and yell, "If you don't finish that story by three o'clock, I'm go'n' throw it in the trash can!" After I got confidence that he had confidence in me, I could laugh at that, or at "Olive, you gnaw on a story like an old dog gnawing on a bone," or, "You rewrite so much, your copy looks like you wrote it by hand and corrected it on the typewriter." I came to love him very much.

The *Sunday Magazine* could really make a big byline out of a name like Olive Ann Burns—now magazines use these little bylines—and they sometimes stretched my name four inches across a page. So, long before *Cold Sassy Tree* came out, I was used to people reading what I had written.

I never thought I'd write fiction; however, I was always more interested in nonfiction. I believed I was writing *Cold Sassy Tree* just for myself. Who would publish a novel by somebody who didn't know how to write one? I never expected the novel would be published, so I wasn't sitting here dreaming about fame while I wrote it. When it happened, it was a great surprise.

I had gathered material about people, events, and attitudes at the turn of the century from many sources—relatives, friends, books, and newspapers. What hooked me on family history was not names and dates. It was the handed-down stories that bring the dead back to life. From my father, who, like Will Tweedy, was fourteen in 1906, I got a vivid picture of Commerce, Georgia, at the turn of the century. One of his favorite stories was about his grandpa Power, a store owner, who married three weeks after his wife died, and who (according to my father) said he loved Miss Annie, but she was "dead as she'd ever be, and he had to git him another wife or hire a housekeeper, and it would jest be cheaper to git married." I doubt Grandpa Power was much like Grandpa Blakeslee, and I know Miss Annie's successor was nothing like Miss Love, but I always thought the situation would make a good novel and that turn-of-the-century Commerce could be the model for a fictitious town.

I think the newspaper work helped me with the novel. I was used to listening to what people said and how they said it, quoting dialogue exactly the way it was said and paraphrasing dialogue only when a speech was boring or too long. Also, newspaper work made me always think and look for what was interesting. You know, if it's not interesting, readers put that newspaper down! And they may plod on through a book for three pages if it starts to get boring, but then they put it back on the shelf.

I had no idea how to construct a novel when I started *Cold Sassy Tree*. I didn't plan the plot in advance. I planned that Grandpa would die in the end, and I knew it was going to start with him marrying three weeks after his first wife died. That's all I knew. I started the book the way I would start a magazine article—trying to grab the reader in the first paragraph. If any passage seemed slow or boring to me—or to my husband or friends—I rewrote it. All I knew about plotting was to get the characters in trouble and then get them out.

I watched soap operas for a year, trying to see how the scriptwriters contrived to get new conflicts started while others were climaxing or being resolved. And where at first I made all my characters into people I could like and respect, I noticed the soaps had a main character that viewers could love to hate. (Hating is still a problem for me. I made Aunt Loma an unsympathetic character, and I hated how she was, but I kept trying to help the reader understand her.)

"I'm tired of books and movies full of paper-doll characters you don't care about, who have no self-respect and no respect for anybody or any institution."

When I started writing *Cold Sassy Tree*, I decided I didn't want to spend a whole block of time—which turned out to be eight years—with a whole lot of unsavory, awful people.

I don't think I'm the only person who is tired of sordid stories about unsavory people. I'm tired of books and movies full of paper-doll characters you don't care about, who have no self-respect and no respect for anybody or any institution. I hope this book is compelling and realistically sensual; I have great respect for human sexuality, but I'm tired of authors so lacking in sensitivity that they wallow in vulgarity and prostitute sex, making exhibitionists of the characters and Peeping Toms of the readers.

And I don't want to sound preachy or Victorian, but I'm tired of amorality in fiction and real life. Immorality is a fascinating human dilemma that creates suspense for the readers and tension for the characters, but where is the tension in an amoral situation? When people have no personal code, nothing is threatening and nothing is meaningful.

I wasn't exactly trying to write a "wholesome" book. Life is seldom wholesome, but I did try for "refreshing." I wanted to see if I could make a page-turner out of ordinary people doing ordinary things. Of course, it wasn't ordinary for Grandpa to marry Miss Love when his wife had only been dead three weeks. And Camp did kill himself, but that was the closest I got to violence in the book. Well, I guess the bandits did do a pretty good job on Grandpa at the end, but it was a funny scene.

As for the characters, Miss Love is completely made-up. Will is a lot like my father, but I realized I couldn't keep trying to re-create my father because then I couldn't let Will be himself—a person, not a reminiscence.

Several characters were composites. Everybody knows a Loma or an Uncle Camp. I wouldn't have believed anybody could be as hateful as Loma if I hadn't known somebody who was. I know several people like Loma, so she was a composite. The granny who died looked like a friend's mother who was a missionary in Africa. She met and married her husband there. When she was forty years old, she came home on leave and had all her teeth pulled because she didn't want to have a toothache in Africa, where there were no dentists. I thought she was remarkable. Will's granny was feisty like her, and small and wiry, but Granny Blakeslee's eyes—set wide apart—were like my husband's aunt's eyes.

Joyce Carol Oates says a writer is like a bird that picks up sticks and bits of string and feathers and anything else he can find to build a nest. A writer takes bits and pieces and changes them to suit the situation or the characters.

I had written several hundred pages before I learned to expand the characters gradually, instead of digressing from the story to describe a person and his life history. My neighbor Norma Duncan, who is very well-read and a very good critic, read the first two or three hundred pages of *Cold Sassy Tree* and said, "You're trying to tell all those funny stories your daddy told you. You've got thirty-five pages of Will Tweedy and the boys putting rats out at the school play while I'm wondering what's happening to Grandpa and Miss Love." That really turned me around. She said the story was about the grandfather and Miss Love, but half the time I had Will taking off on his own.

Then Ruth Herbert, a friend who taught fiction writing, read the same early chapters and complained that I had flashbacks within flashbacks within flashbacks, all of which digressed from Grandpa and Miss Love. Without this criticism, and suggestions from my husband, I would probably still be floundering around in a maze of incidents.

I had learned what a theme was in high school English, but I had completely forgotten about it. An English professor and publisher from Israel read my manuscript when I was about half through, and he asked, "What is your theme?"

I said, "I don't even remember what theme means."

He said, "Don't worry about it. You can make up a theme after you finish the book."

"I was just trying to tell a good story . . . I wanted it to be funny. I'm tired of a world so dead serious, in which silliness passes for humor."

I found out later that theme means what the book's about, what it is trying to say. My husband said, "This is a funny book about death." The publisher said, "I think it's a book about family." And my sister-in-law, an English teacher, said, "Oh, it's a book about many things. A major theme is prejudice." I never had any of that in mind. I was just trying to tell a good story. I thought stories ought to be interesting; I wasn't trying to preach or write a sociological study. I wanted it to be funny. I'm tired of a world so dead serious, in which silliness passes for humor. I wanted to present fictional characters who are human but fundamentally decent. I wanted Grandpa to be true to himself and care about work and goodness, yet be free of the burden of perfectionism. I wanted him to live with courage and gusto, and know how to look death in the eye.

In 1983, biographer Anne Edwards introduced me to Joan and Chester Kerr at a party in Atlanta. He was then publisher at Ticknor & Fields. His wife asked to see my manuscript. I worked it over for three months, mailed it, and received an enthusiastic letter that began, "Boy, howdy, ma'am, you have sent us a fine book." My joy at receiving that letter would rate at least twelve on a scoring of one to ten.

I've been working for a year now on the sequel. The title is *Time, Dirt, and Money*—the three things that most worriers worry about. All I have to worry about is finishing by January 2, 1991. That's what I promised when I signed the contract. It is the story of Will Tweedy and the girl he marries, beginning in 1917. I sent a hundred and eleven pages about a month ago to my editor. She liked it and said to go on with it, but our son was bringing his fiancée from Colorado Springs, and we were having some work done in the house. Then Faye Dunaway was filming the movie of *Cold Sassy Tree* in Georgia—I had to keep up with the goings-on there—and now our son is getting married here in October. I guess at some point I'm going to have to get back to the book.

Cold Sassy Tree has been made into a movie that will be shown on TNT cable television on October 16, 1989. Faye Dunaway produced it and starred as Miss Love. Obviously, they couldn't put all the characters and all the scenes into the movie. They used the scene with Will and Lightfoot in the cemetery, and God there in the polka-dot dress, but they cut out Will getting run over by the train.

Of course, they're using all the kissing scenes—Mr. McAlister kissing Miss Love, and Will in the cemetery with Lightfoot. They show Lightfoot telling Will good-bye, but they change Miss Effie Belle from an eighty-nine-year-old lady to a woman about Miss Love's age, so she could be jealous. In the book, Mr. Bubba is Miss Effie Belle's brother.

In the movie, they made him her father. "Bubba" means "Brother" in the South, but I guess the scriptwriter had never heard of "Bubba." In the movie, the man is Miss Effie's father, but she still calls him Bubba. A friend of mine, Charles Hadley, was the dialect coach. He said when the cast gathered around a table to read through the script for the first time, Richard Widmark, who plays Grandpa Blakeslee, had obviously never known a Bubba. He read it: "Well, hello, Mr. Boo-bah!" The dialect coach told him to put the accent where it would be in the word "bubble."

The scriptwriter, who was also the director, didn't put in any dialect. The dialogue was all educated talk. Not an "ain't" or a "git" in the whole thing. I was kind of distressed over that. She said, "I've never heard Southern talk, and I just can't write it." I think she was mostly in a hurry. TNT was really pushing her to get through so filming could start.

"Writing is kind of like gardening. Words come easily to me, but they are most often the ones I want. After the words are down on paper, I can see weeds and where new plants are needed."

About the mechanics of writing: in journalism school they said, "When you work for a newspaper, you don't have time to write a story out by hand first and then type it," so I'm used to thinking by typewriter. Two years ago, when I got too sick to sit up at the computer, my neighbor Norma Duncan said, "If you get dictating equipment, I will transcribe anything you put on it." At first I thought I couldn't dictate. When you're used to words coming out of your fingers, it's hard to make them come out of your mouth, but I learned to do it. For my new novel, I dictate; Norma puts it in the computer and prints it out; I scribble all over the pages; she puts in the changes and prints it out again. This may go on ten times or more.

Writing is kind of like gardening. Words come easily to me, but they are most often not the ones I want. After the words are down on paper, I can see weeds and where new plants are needed. To edit, polish, and rewrite a long book can mean thousands of pages of work. Norma once told me, "I had always wondered what was wrong with my writing. I would write something one night, and I'd think it was so good, and when I read it later and saw it wasn't good, I thought, 'Well, I just can't write.' But seeing how you rewrite and rewrite and really make it better, I know that writing is mostly work."

There are some lucky people who can plan their sentences in their heads. The sentences just come out, and they don't have to be rewritten. There's one author in Atlanta who says he never rewrites anything. He doesn't read the whole book through until it's in proof. Well, I just couldn't do that, as long as I can see that something needs to be added, or that the words don't say what I'm trying to say, and then I have to keep working on it. In *Cold Sassy Tree*, I've seen a few commas and one or two words I should have changed, but not many. Most of the rewriting was done before any editor ever saw the manuscript.

You might not want to go on forever trying to perfect one piece, but a beginner should write many stories or poems or essays and keep being willing to be criticized. Even professional writers need to be willing to be criticized. Writers are terrible about that. They don't want anybody to admit a story is dull, but if it's dull, somebody needs to say it. Critics shouldn't rewrite it for you but point out to you what doesn't work. In time you'll begin to recognize your dullness or clichés or dangling modifiers yourself. I'm a good editor. I edit my work every time I read through it. Sometimes a manuscript has to cool off before you can evaluate it, and after it cools, you may realize it isn't really good. That doesn't mean your idea isn't good, or what you're trying to do isn't good. It may just need more work. I know something I've written is good if I can read it over and over again, and it still delights me, or moves me.

I read a review in *The New York Times* of a performance by actors who were reading from authors' works. The person who wrote the review said the actors emoted too much, that they should have read the stories straight and let the audience feel the emotion for themselves. But when I read aloud from *Cold Sassy Tree* about Will and Lightfoot kissing in the cemetery, I get carried away. I'm afraid I emote. And I laugh every time I think about God standing there in the cemetery in a polka-dot dress, pointing a plump forefinger and saying, "Will Tweedy, you ought to be a-SHAMED!" I think I enjoyed writing that scene more than anything I ever wrote. [See page 246 in *Cold Sassy Tree*.]

"What's really important . . . is to be willing to work."

Talking to young writers, I find myself repeating and repeating that wanting to write and knowing you've got some gift at putting words together is not enough. What's really important, besides studying human nature, observing your own feelings, acquiring general knowledge from books and from living, is to be willing to work. A beginning writer needs to write and write and write, just the way a beginning pianist needs to practice and practice and practice before he performs a concert.

Writing is partly a skill. My husband took an art course because, he said, "I have so many pictures in my head, but I don't know the techniques to make the pictures I paint look like the pictures in my head." A writer may see a scene in his head and really want to reproduce it, yet not have the skill to do it. With practice and training, the skill comes.

But competence alone isn't enough. There are plenty of competent pianists whose music doesn't sound like Rubinstein's. There are competent writers without imagination. Many journalists can get an interview and write a story that communicates to the reader. Many fiction writers think up good plots and write adequately, but the artists are those whose words sing. My editor says, "I don't have to read a whole book to know whether I like it or not. I can read two or three pages and know if the writer has a voice." Writers speak of needing inspiration. Inspiration often comes from getting interested; on a newspaper, writing eight hours a day, you learn that inspiration comes fast if you have a deadline.

One important thing to remember is that writing is fun and exciting even if you never, ever sell it. It's a wonderful way to spend an evening. It helps you think. It helps if you know your priorities, but, as with acting, there's much competition. It's easy to get your heart broken if your main purpose is to get published. Nothing can break your heart if you say, "I want to be the best writer I can be, but I don't have to be better than anybody else." Whether I sell it or don't sell it, I'll have a good time writing.

"If you don't live, you can't write about life."

I knew somebody who said she got enough rejection slips that she could paper a wall. She finally became mentally ill worrying about all those rejection slips. It wasn't like that for me. The years I wrote for the magazine, I knew my stories would be printed and read. The magazine then had a circulation throughout the Southeast. I enjoyed the work, and I was blessed to have a way to make a living that I looked forward to doing every day.

To sum up, I think the most important qualities for a writer to have are a dedication to being interesting, the realization that writing is work, and dedication to the task at hand. I'd love to do ceramics, but I have to decide what I most want to do or there will be no time to write. However, that doesn't mean I should shut myself in a garret and do nothing else. If you don't live, you can't write about life.

I stay amazed at the sales of *Cold Sassy Tree*. There are now 365,000 copies in print; it is being taught in American Lit classes in high schools and colleges all over the nation, has been published in Germany and England, and is being translated into Hebrew in Israel. What means most to me is that young people like it and say they learn about life from it. In 1985, the American Library Association and the New York City Public Library included *Cold Sassy Tree* in their lists of books recommended for teenagers. The New York list had my name between Emily Brontë and Willa Cather.

Think of that!

THE MAKING OF THE FOXFIRE PLAY AND MOVIE

Foxfire students' experiences

It just so happened that Dean was there, thank goodness, and we got to play with John Denver. —Tom Nixon

In 1973, IDEAS, Inc. produced a twenty-two-minute color film focused on the Foxfire Program. The students worked very closely with the producers, and the film was full of students interviewing contacts, including Aunt Arie Carpenter. Foxfire hosted a previewing party at the Rabun Gap-Nacoochee School Library and invited the whole community. Aunt Arie came, and it was the first motion picture show she had ever seen! It is impossible to fathom what she was thinking as she watched herself on the big screen. Little did she, or Foxfire, know then that a few years later, a Broadway show based on her life would garner a Tony and be made into a Hallmark Hall of Fame Movie called *Foxfire*.

While working with Hume Cronyn and Jessica Tandy on a television special, Susan Cooper introduced the two to Aunt Arie via *The Foxfire Book*. They didn't use the piece in their TV show, but kept thinking about how they could use it. Susan contacted Foxfire about obtaining dramatic rights to that chapter. She was told that in order to get the rights, she would have to come to Rabun County and convince the Foxfire students that it was worth doing.

She and Hume came and were grilled by the kids, who made absolutely sure that the people of these mountains would be portrayed authentically. Hume Cronyn said, "Everybody sat on the floor in the office except Susan and me. We sat in the only two chairs, and they fired questions at us. Then they let us know that we could leave the room while they debated what they wanted to do. We went out and walked up the side of a hillside pasture and walked around and around, and waited and waited, and waited. Finally, one of the students came out and said, 'I guess y'all can come back now.'

"And we said, 'How did we do?' and he said, 'Well, we think maybe you're all right.'" By this time, *Deliverance* had come out, and many local residents were upset by it. The Foxfire students wanted someone to tell a truer story about us.

After numerous scripts and rewrites based on student input, the show was ready to go on. It was first performed at the Stratford Festival in Ontario, Canada. After some rewrites, it was presented at the Guthrie in Minneapolis, Minnesota, for a season, receiving a standing ovation each and every night. After going on the road and adding more rewrites, which included more student input, the production was ready for Broadway.

Eventually, Hallmark decided to make a Hallmark Hall of Fame TV movie. In April and May of 1987, Hume, Susan, Jessica Tandy, John Denver, and many others came down for filming, and the rest, as they say, "is history."

The following are quotes about the projects from former Foxfire students.

—*Ethan Phillips and Jesse Owen*

"Several years before Hume and Susan came to us about doing a play, we were involved in turning away a movie about the area that some other people wanted to film here. The script was really bad. They didn't know their butt from a hole in the ground when it came to mountain ways and people, but they didn't want to change the script.

"They went ahead and made the movie someplace else in the mountains, and a group of us went to watch that film in Atlanta, and it was the biggest joke that ever was. If you'd read any of the *Foxfire* articles at all, you'd know that what they were doing was impossible. It was so strange. They had new potatoes coming out of the ground in February and March—all kinds of crazy stuff.

"What I'm glad of is that we didn't have anything to do with it. The main reason we didn't was that they'd wanted to use the Foxfire name, and we didn't want the name to be put with something like that. There were kids in our classes who felt really strongly about this. We didn't take no guff off nobody. I would have loved to have a movie at that time, but not the way those people wanted to do it. They couldn't come up to our standards, and so we just said, 'Forget it.'" —**Faye "Bit" Carver Partain**

"After the decision was made to go ahead with the Foxfire play, I remember doing voice tapes for it. Basically, they'd set up a recorder and have us read certain things so that the actresses and actors could pick up our accents.

"My inner feelings on the script were that it pretty much told the story of Rabun County and this part of the country. The early, bigger families had a number of kids, and most of them have moved away and left the parents on the land alone. Then one parent dies and leaves the other, in this case Annie, alone. There's not a lot of interest among the kids in dividing up the land among them because there would be too many disputes between brothers and sisters wanting certain pieces and arguing over them, and none of them want to move back anyway, so what they usually end up doing is selling it and splitting up the money.

"That problem the play presents is real. That's really what's happening. The play gives the feeling that outsiders are taking over, and you do get that feeling in this area. It's a real problem, but what do you do? I went away to college, and when I graduated I came back, but the only way I could afford to come back was to be involved in my family's business, which is building supply, or in real estate. Or, I could have worked in one of the local factories. Although I like to maintain things in their natural state, I realize now, being in business, that's the only way you can stay in business is for the area to grow.

"In the play, I got frustrated with the outsiders, and it angered me that that land developer would bebop into Annie's house and try to take advantage of her circumstances and fast-talk her into selling what had always been hers. But what was she going to do? That's pretty much how I felt after seeing the play." —**Vaughn Rogers, Jr.**

"I remember going to see the premiere of the Foxfire play at the Guthrie Theater. My mama was out of town, and before the trip, I wasn't even sure whether I wanted to go. I was just so scared of flying, and I'd never been out of Clayton before.

"But it was fun when we got there. Everybody was so nice, and they treated you like an important person. That was the first time I ever realized how big Foxfire was. That's something that's hard to realize until you get out of school, go places, and see and talk to other people.

PLATE 155 Jessica Tandy and Hume Cronyn with Foxfire students

"I was in drama at the high school at that time, but that big theater just blew my mind! It was a huge, huge place. I was able to meet Jessica Tandy and Hume Cronyn. The play was great. Kim and I watched it twice, and we both just boohooed through the whole performance. Later, Jessica and Hume took us to our first French restaurant.

"Another great thing we did on that trip was to go to a school and give speeches. We also signed autographs at a bookstore. It was great to have people make you feel like you were somebody. The people really liked *Foxfire*, too. I loved every bit of it.

"There was a world of difference between the play and the Hallmark movie. I liked the movie, but I loved the play."

—**Donna Bradshaw Speed**

"Donna Bradshaw and I went to the Guthrie Theater. I've still got a blue T-shirt with 'The Guthrie' on it.

"I remember when they were doing the play and they took out the hog's head. Everybody in the audience started dying laughing.

"Donna and I were crying at one point. They made it that realistic. It was at the end when Annie knew she was going to live with her son and was going to sell the farm. At that time, everybody was having bitter feelings about real-estate people down in Rabun.

"I've still got pictures of where we were in the dressing room with Jessica and Hume. Jessica and Hume were real nice. We went out to supper that night, and you could tell that they were a close couple. It tickled you to sit and eat with them. They were equals, and they respected each other because they had been together a long time. One of them wasn't more powerful than the other one, and they were both real polite. I remember Hume smoked a pipe. You know, you wonder if some actors are putting on a front. Jessica and Hume weren't."

—Kim Hamilton McKay

"When they were going to do a production of the play at the Alliance Theatre in Atlanta, the producers came up and toured the land and picked out artifacts, like a wagon, that they wanted to use in the set. I remember a bunch of students loaded the things in a truck and got them ready to take down there. Then a group of us went to see the Atlanta production. It was real neat, with all the stage props borrowed from Foxfire.

"It was a very well-written play. Rural land is so precious these days and there isn't much of it left. I resent the developers that come in. I understand that there is an increased need for housing—houses on the lake, apartments, and condos. But there's so few people left who own the original land that they were born on, and that's something special that you should preserve.

"Every big town and every little town has its own personality. You have to maintain the individual heritage of every town. It's like Rabun County. There is only one Mountain City and one Clayton.

"You can tear down the condominiums, but you've already ruined the land, and the people that lived there have already moved on and died. Often the land is irreplaceable. A lot of people don't think about that. Change is good, but sometimes I don't feel like the price is worth it."

—Kim Oh Soon Shropshire

"My mom, grandparents, and I went to the play when it was brought to Highlands, North Carolina. Foxfire had fixed it so that a whole group of Rabun County people could go, including lots of the older people. It was good. I really liked it. It was sad because it was so true. Aunt Arie's land had to be sold when she died. There weren't any children to take it over.

"When they decided to make the play into a Hallmark movie and film it down here, I met the producer and took her to show her the Foxfire property." —Tonia Kelly McRary

"I remember a good bit about the Hallmark movie. I actually got to be in it, so that was fun. I remember when they came and showed us their script. I remember looking over it and suggesting some changes. I remember having correspondence with them back and forth and all that. When it actually came time to make it. I took a day off from school and went up to Highlands to try out for a speaking part. I went with Suzie Nixon and Darren Volk. We got to be in the music scene with John Denver at the Mountain City Playhouse.

"Being able to be behind the scenes and see how everything was put together, and how all the different people worked with each other to get every little thing done to make it all work and look natural, was real interesting." —Brooks Adams

"The filming of the Foxfire movie was a big experience for us. It's when John Denver was in town, and we got to back him up onstage. We were playing a benefit for a kid who needed a liver transplant, and John had been asked by the promoters to do a guest performance. We had played at a reception for the movie stars, and he had talked about having us play with him, but we didn't think much about it.

"The concert was at the stadium at the high school. John Denver wasn't there yet. We played a set to start things off. It was getting late, and a rock-and-roll band from Franklin was playing. Our banjo player, Dean, and his girlfriend were going back to Atlanta, and they had left. Well, here we are, and here comes John Denver in a helicopter from another concert he had had to do that evening. In the time he's getting ready, Dean's down the road but had to turn around and come back because his girlfriend had left something in somebody's car. Just then there's an announcement on the PA: 'Are the Foxfire Boys still here?' It just so happened that Dean was there, thank goodness, and we got to play with John Denver.

"We were also asked to play in a barn dance during the movie when Jessica Tandy was dancing. We were on the set and got paid like every-

PLATE 156 John Denver and several of the Foxfire Boys

body else. I had to look like I was playing the fiddle, and, of course, we were dressed up and had our makeup on. But it was a real important Foxfire experience to participate in the making of the whole thing.

"A film crew also interviewed my great-aunt Gertrude Keener about the Foxfire play when they were making the Hallmark program. She was filmed for a half-hour television special called *The Making of Foxfire*. Her situation is very similar to that of Annie in the play. She is a big land-owner, and she is a widow, and she has a son who lives down in Florida who sells real estate, except she's not moving. She's not going anywhere. She's held on to her land. She hasn't just sold it all. It means a lot to her to preserve it. It was the homeplace that she and my grandmother and all of their folks were raised on. She is eighty-six years old, but she'll get right out there and feed her cows and go on all day long. She and her family had to work in the fields, and everything had to be like clockwork from daylight till dark. They couldn't go in and sit down and watch TV and expect to turn on the dishwasher and washing machine. All that was done by hand. It took all day. They grew all of their food, and all the money they made was from labor—splitting rails and selling tan bark. A lot of my uncles made liquor, as they got older, just to make money. Values that make a person have self-discipline, honesty, and teamwork are values that Gertrude holds true to, and her religious beliefs are as big a part of her as anything." —**Tom Nixon**

"APPALACHIA GOODBYE"

*Laura Monk and High Cotton create a video
at the Foxfire Heritage Center*

Hopefully, the music I create speaks to you whether I wrote it, helped arrange it, or am just performing it. —Laura Monk

It's hard not to believe that Laura Monk was, through fate, luck, or divine intervention, meant to be a part of Foxfire. She is a lady with a mission. She loves music—all aspects of it—and her desire to touch everyone who listens to her songs is palpable. She seeks for them to create their own meaning from her art.

Having only "spoken" with her via the Internet, I wasn't sure what to expect. When she came to the Foxfire Gift Shop, her bubbly personality, candor, and sense of humor were immediately evident. Along with her sister, Anne, she shared how she and her band, High Cotton, came to make the music video for their song "Appalachia Goodbye" at the Foxfire Museum and Heritage Center.

Laura has a long history with the North Georgia Mountains and with Foxfire. She camped here as a child, and as a college student, she worked as a counselor at a camp in Rabun County. Her sister, Anne, spent her senior year of high school at Rabun Gap-Nacoochee School and worked with the Foxfire program. Through the years, she and her family and friends continued to visit the mountains anytime that they could. She lamented that she wished she had been born here, but if she had been, her story might not have been the same. I am glad that she came to the mountains in a different way—her way. These mountains called to her, and she answered by recording a song that embraces her love of these people and this place.

—*Kaye Carver Collins*

It is an interesting story how I came to know about Foxfire. When I was a freshman in college, I applied to work at Camp Dixie, near Clayton, Georgia, for the summer. I had applied for the stable job and got it. When I got up there, it was a lean year for counselors. My sister, Anne, who was still in high school, was a very talented artist. She knew a little bit about weaving, and Camp Dixie had these great old looms that had not been used in years. Ann Taylor was lamenting that she didn't have an art teacher. She was the owner of the camp. I said, "My sister is a great artist and she is only two years away from graduating from high school. She would be great being a counselor; they normally only hired college-age students at the camp. They agreed and brought my sister, Anne, up here. The camp used to get their sawdust shavings from Rabun Gap-Nacoochee School. On a journey to get sawdust, Anne came along for the ride in the pickup truck. There were some kids there from the school, working in the lumberyard. She starts talking to them about the school. I knew about Foxfire and the students were saying that this was where all the books and magazine took place. This was back in the summer of 1976.

"Guys, the only place to do this is on Foxfire's land."

We heard about the school, and Anne thought it was really cool. Anne gets home from camp and goes to our parents and said, "I want to spend my senior year in high school up at Rabun Gap-Nacoochee School so that I can work with the Foxfire folks." She is really the catalyst as to how I found out more about Foxfire. Long story short, Anne comes up here for her senior year and just thrives and loved everything about it. Fast-forward, many years later, we were doing the song that is all about Appalachia. My family and friends kept coming up here. We would camp and hike. I said, "Guys, the only place to do this is on Foxfire's land."

It was really an easy decision, for me, to use the Foxfire Center for our music video. Our drummer, P. J. Engeman, wrote the song "Appalachia Goodbye." He was watching the PBS special on Appalachia. If you saw the show, when you hear the lyrics to the song, you will hear a lot of the different people and their stories from the documentary. When he first sent me the song, I didn't have the music. He didn't send me a recording. I just read it and it was so beautiful. Then he later sent me a recording of him doing the song; the melody was just perfect. It just seemed to echo the feeling that it should. The way our band works, I am the main melody person. He said, "See what you can do with this." First, we birthed the song. We arranged it—figured out how we were going to perform it. Then when it came time to decide that we should do a music video, we just needed to figure out where to do it. The guys were first citing different places around Atlanta. I was just reading and practicing the song and it just hit me! We need to do this up at Foxfire.

None of the band had been to Foxfire. I told the guys that it was just perfect. They trusted me. We didn't have to take a field trip to check it out. All I could see was that first cabin, which is where we filmed most everything. It is the perfect setting. The way the light was coming in— that is how it became the place to do it. It was perfect and convenient because you had so many scenes in a small area. Which is, of course, I think, what the Foxfire village does, is to show what a community would be like, except much more spread out. That is how we ended up here.

I wrote Ann Moore, Foxfire's president, and said, "You don't know me, but every time we have out-of-town company, we come up to Fox-fire and show them this wonderful place. I also told her about my sister, Anne. Ann Moore writes back, "I remember Anne McInnis." I was so surprised, as it turns out Ann Moore came to work at Foxfire the year my sister, Anne, was there. My sister, Anne, actually did the artwork on the first Foxfire album cover and label and was in the studio while the album was recorded. She worked with George Reynolds. We had a deep and broad history with Foxfire. I was hoping that it would impress upon Ann Moore that we wouldn't abuse the setting and that our hearts were in the right place as far as what we wanted to capture and portray in the video.

I am an Atlanta native. I grew up coming to the mountains. We went up to Cashiers, North Carolina, as a kid. I loved this area. I camped at the bottom of Tallulah Gorge when you could still get away with that. I have been playing guitar since I was eighteen. I should be much bet-ter than I am, but I am just kind of a rhythm girl. I love to sing; I have always been singing. My husband is my bass player. I have always sung in groups and bands, but High Cotton is kind of the first thing where I have been at the helm. I was with a band; they broke up. My best friend, who sang with me, moved away. I don't mind playing by myself, but it is much more fun to have someone to play with. My husband, at that time, did not play an instrument. At Christmas, I got him a bass guitar. He learned quickly. We started playing as a duo called High Cotton. We did coffeehouses, a few festivals, and things like that. Then P. J., Patrick Engeman, saw us at a festival. He is a drummer. At the time we had been thinking about taking it up a level and adding either a lead guitarist or a percussionist. I got this e-mail from him, out of the blue, saying, "I saw you perform in Duluth; if you are ever looking for a subtle, nonintrusive percussionist, let me know. I would love to play with you guys." That was key for acoustic music; most percussionists want to kind of take over! We met with him and he was great. He also wrote "Appalachia Goodbye." We were doing original music and here was another performer who was interested in doing original music. We became a trio called High Cotton.

We put out our first CD, called *Pictures*. We had a pretty good response locally. In the studio, of course, we were able to layer it with instruments and have a bigger sound. We thought, if we are going to sound like the CD, maybe we should add that lead guitarist. Then we found Dan Foster, who became our lead guitarist and also started adding more harmony. We have been playing together for about nine years. Everybody else is from the north. My husband, John Monk, is from New Jersey; Dan Foster is from Michigan, and P. J. from New York. To their credit, they have been in the South long enough that they are pretty good Southern gentlemen. That is how we became High Cotton, a group. Then, about three years ago, the guys said that we needed something that made our name a little more unique. They decided to start calling it Laura Monk and High Cotton. When you do an Internet search for "high cotton," you get all kinds of things. It was all a marketing ploy, not a diva thing!

I have many, many influences musically. I was a huge Carole King fan; *Tapestry* is still my favorite album of all time. I still can sing every song on the album. A child of the late sixties and early seventies, a lot of those influences are there, which makes our music truly what the genre Americana is, which is a blend of everything. We are influenced by the blues and a lot of folk. I did Renaissance festivals for about eight or nine years as a street musician. I learned a lot of the old ballads. My husband is a big Tom Waits fan. He was also kind of into the punk era; there are

PLATE 157 Laura Monk and High Cotton [Photograph courtesy
of Alex and Sharon van Rossum]

things of ours that have a little more of an edge. Our market, the people that we speak most to, would probably be thirty years and up, as far as age and groups who enjoy what we produce.

We used other people in the music video because I am not the girl. It is not my story. I wish it was. I wish that I had grown up in Appalachia. Actually, I am in there—my arm. I am the older version, in color; it is kind of *The Wizard of Oz* thing, backwards. At that point, it is supposed to be her looking back and she is still playing the guitar. I couldn't look like a young girl leaving home. We wanted it to really have that feeling of telling a story in the present. Who knows where she ended up? My son, Alex van Rossum, and his wife, Sharon, were the videographers; it was truly a family affair. All the actors are Dan's grandchildren, and they did a stupendous job.

As far as actual filming, we did it in one day. There were visitors [to the Museum], and they were so kind. We tried to not be in their way. We did it on a Saturday; the Museum and Heritage Center were open to visitors. We got here early and we finished about five p.m. We got here as soon as Ann Moore would let us in.

"There is a visual in the video that is meant to represent the hard part of life in Appalachia. . . . We know that this life was hard— full of hard work, lack of luxuries, and oftentime sickness and loss of loved ones way too soon."

We had scenes that we thought we wanted to catch. Alex and Sharon were instrumental in saying what needed to be done. There is a visual in the video that is meant to represent the hard part of life in Appalachia. The video shows such idyllic images—happy faces, joyful games, faithful images—it all looks primitive, but still very beautiful and happy. We know that this life was hard—full of hard work, lack of luxuries, and oftentime sickness and loss of loved ones way too soon. I wanted to include an image that made a subliminal suggestion that it wasn't always so wonderful. Something that implied what these people struggled through and endured. When she comes through the door and touches the horseshoe, it is hanging upside down. For it to be lucky it should be hanging up with the "U" gathering all the luck—hung upside down, all the luck runs out. A few people have caught that it is hanging upside down and have called me out on that. I then tell them the reason and they usually go, "Ahhhhhh." [**Editors' note:** Watch the music video at http://vimeo.com/71473974.]

Alex and Sharon came up with the feather idea at the end. That was out of the blue. I brought all these props and I brought these feathers, hawk feathers that I found hiking one day. We were pretty much done, and Alex and Sharon were standing over on the porch. I kept seeing Sharon doing this thing with her arm, and they were dropping the feather and filming it as it fell. That was truly out of their artistic minds. Alex and I had spoken about what we wanted, but even still, no matter what you have planned, things change. I have got to say, what they ended up filming, because they had not ever been here either, sort of resembled what we originally envisioned. But, it still, mostly, developed while we were here. You see something, like the moonshine sitting on the porch railing. The sun was just right and Alex was like, get those jars up here. It was a lot of fun. The storyboard gave us our jumping-off point. It was better in a way that nobody but I had really been here before, because that gave everybody fresh eyes. They came in here, really, having no concept, except what the story of the song was. As far as telling it through film, it really was birthed right here at Foxfire. Some scenes just came together perfectly. For example, the one of the girls sitting on the porch and the little sister is brushing the sassafras girl's hair. That is such a sweet picture to me. The scene where we see just her feet—I love her feet because they are what moved her through her life in the mountains and what will eventually take her on her next journey. I didn't know they were capturing that, but it told the story beautifully. I go back and watch

PLATE 158 Scene from the music video for "Appalachia Goodbye"
[Photograph courtesy of Alex and Sharon van Rossum]

it every now and then and I am still moved by the story. . . . I find myself tearing up! We got inspiration just from being in this place.

I had always visited the museum when it was down on Highway 441. I guess the first time I came up on the mountain was the summer we hiked up here when our kids were little. It was while Billy Parrish was working here. That was a great story. We came up here to visit Camp Dixie; our youngest was maybe five. We walked into the old Foxfire office off the main highway, just to see the museum and find out if we could come up to the mountain. We were talking to whoever was greeting us, and a redheaded man walks in, and I see him out of the corner of my eye—I am looking and thinking, "That can't be Billy Parrish." But it was! He and I went to Berry College together, and that was so much fun to run into him at Foxfire. Every time I come up here, something interesting like that happens. That was 1991 or 1992. We drove up as far as we could, and we had permission to come on up and hike. We walked around, picked blueberries; we were excited. The kids loved it.

We did have copies of the *Foxfire* books in our home. I have this memory of my mom talking about them. I can hear her saying, "These kids, all they want to do is leave the mountains and then they got excited about their heritage. What a great story!" All of it is sort of serendipitous. Just being able to do the filming here and that it came out so great. You never know what you will end up with. Part of our deal with Ann Moore was that we would give Foxfire copies to use however they could through their programs. I really wanted it to be worth her while to let us invade.

Our group is not together anymore. Not a bad thing, just how life goes. P. J. moved to Wilmington, North Carolina. His parents are in their nineties. His mother is now blind. Their last visit, a little over one year ago, they realized that they needed to be closer. He is retired; he is the sibling who is best to do that. This past spring, he and his wife moved there. It was very sad, but he did the right thing. We took that as, fine, things just happen; we are moving on; that is how life goes. We worked as a trio for quite a while and tried bringing in a new drummer. He was great, but traveled all the time. We had a meeting. Everybody still loves everybody. It was not a bad band breakup. It just seems that maybe we are supposed to be doing other things. We are still going to get together in 2015 and record some more songs together as Laura Monk and High Cotton. We hope to still put out another CD. As far as being able to really play together, as the original foursome that is not going to happen anymore—unless a special occasion brings us together. We still maintain the website and blog; you can access it at www.highcottonatl.com.

I am still out there, still playing. I will have a website, just Laura Monk Music. I will keep the High Cotton website, but I will also have Laura Monk Music. I am doing several different things; playing with another little trio, with my husband and a friend. I am doing some music for kids. I did kids' music when my kids were little; I was a storyteller musician. I am getting back into that a little bit with some nonprofits. I told Ann Moore, of course, that anytime she wants me to come up here, I will. Dan and I played on the porch for the Folk Art Festival here at Foxfire. That was a lot of fun. Dan and I can still come up and do stuff. Music has been like my best friend. It is just therapy. It has always been there; even when my kids were little, I found a way to make a semi-living at it. I wouldn't know what to do without it.

I do think this place, the Foxfire Museum and Heritage Center, is amazing. When we have friends from out of town, we bring them up here to show them what a great treasure it is. I wish I lived closer, then I could volunteer here more. I live in Sugar Hill, Georgia. I truly love this place. I think that what you all have done and continue to do is incredible to save, to teach, and to inspire.

I guess my all-time favorite song I wrote is "Southern Belle Blues" because it is really my story. It is about being a Southern belle who marries a Northerner. I wrote all of it, did the music and the lyrics on it. Nothing and anything inspires me. I mean what inspires me is having a guitar in my hand. It is very rare that I write something and I am not holding the guitar. I usually strum some sort of chord progression and then the melody comes and then the lyrics will come.

My other favorite song is called "Pictures," which is about my dad. John's dad was very sick at the time, and we kind of knew he was going. My dad had died many years earlier. We had this old, wonderful dog named Whiskers. It was probably midnight; I was still up and had my guitar. There was this picture of my dad and the four of us siblings because my little brother had not been born yet. It was a Christmas picture. We are holding up our stockings. My dad would always run in to be in the picture. We are all laughing. I was looking at that picture. I was sad about John's dad, and our dog is probably dying. She was just sitting there. I started this little melody, and Whiskers came over and basically, literally, sat right at my feet. She put her head on my feet. I am looking at this picture of my dad and all us kids. I remembered these walks that my dad and I used to take. The song came out in five minutes. I put it down and recorded it on a little tape recorder and went to bed. I got up the next morning and said to John, "I think I might have written a pretty good song last night." I sat down to sing it for him, and actually got through it without crying because it was still mechanical. I am playing it for him. I look up at him, and he is crying. I went, "Is it okay?" He said, "That is a damn good song." Then I had to step away and come back to it. I couldn't sing it without crying.

What was really powerful, we were recording it in the studio and our producer, David Leonard, who as you record is sitting there with the cans on his ears—you can't see his face. I finished the song, and he just stays with his head down and hands over the headphones. I am thinking, "What is wrong?" I was waiting for the all-clear sign to talk. Finally, after about forty seconds, he wiped his eyes, looked up and said, "That is a good song!" It is a nice thing to see that your message is really hitting people. That is what you want. I don't really want people to just say, "That is a really good song. You are a really good singer." I want people who listen to my music to feel a message, even if it is different than what I think it should be. I guess as a musician and a singer, that is what I would like people to know. Hopefully, the music I create speaks to you whether I wrote it, helped arrange it, or am just performing it. Hopefully, in a positive way, it brings back nice memories, or makes you think.

I have to thank Patrick Engeman and Dan Foster; John Monk; and then all of Dan's kids; Dan's wife, Lynn; their daughter, Carrie; and son-in-law, who were kind enough to give us their whole day to film the video. The music we have been able to make as High Cotton has been a huge part of my life. I wouldn't trade it for anything. They are great guys. What I would love to have happen with this exposure in your book would be—I don't want to be a rock star. I want to still be able to go to the grocery store—the musician dream would be that somebody would buy some songs and record them. Spread the music that way.

Appalachia Goodbye
Copyright © PJ Engeman

I

A Sassafras girl and a banjo sings on an ancient moonshine night
A fiddle flies and a baby cries on a cold September first light
Coaxing hymns from an old prayer book
the ones nobody wrote
She'll fly to heaven on a feather bed, wearing songs like an old
*   patched coat*

She tied her heart to an old guitar
put her dreams in a mason jar
Touched the horseshoe hanging over the door
Appalachia goodbye

II

Mountain Laurel and enough blue sky to mend that old work
*   shirt*
Juniper and 'seng and deep woods magic brew on a floor made of
*   dirt*
A rough tanning hand cradles a bottle—it sparkles with
*   Grandpa's shine*
Her black eyes light up like fire in the night, scaring haints
*   hiding deep in the pine*

She tied her heart to an old guitar
put her dreams in a mason jar
Touched the horseshoe hanging over the door
Appalachia goodbye

III

She "played by air" that Cherry River Line and a song she called
*   "Old Long John"*
There's no chargin' for the lessons, she sighed . . . you just need
*   to pass them on.*
She sings harmony with the angels—you can hear them at her
*   old homeplace*
Every line she sings is somebody's life
every life a line on her face.

She tied her heart to an old guitar
put her dreams in a mason jar
Touched the horseshoe hanging over the door
Appalachia goodbye
A Sassafras girl and a banjo sings on an ancient moonshine
*   night.*

WISDOM
of
OUR ELDERS

Making Do with What We Have

We would go over to Popcorn. We would just run and play. 'Bout the only thing that we knew anything about was playin' that we was makin' liquor. Go ahead and laugh.

—*Waymond Lunsford*

When it comes to spirit, the Appalachian people have always been rich. When it comes to material goods, however, the people of this area have not been so fortunate. With this scarcity of material items, it has always been necessary that Appalachian folks be resourceful. It stands to reason that when one has little, one learns to make things work with what little they may have. Mrs. Janie P. Taylor called it "ingenuity." Numerous contacts have confirmed this idea with tales of their circumstances growing up and occasionally a story of how their family made do in a tight spot. Included in this section is just that: quotes from Foxfire contacts old and new on how they made do.

The rugged region of Appalachia instills in us that livelihood relies in its totality on labor. Contacts before and after 2000 stressed how imperative hard work was to making do. Even now, Appalachian children learn the benefit of hard work and are shown the strength of an honorable work ethic by the examples of their elders.

There is no doubt that this area has seen tough times. It was common to only purchase or trade for the things that were not producible. Food may have been scarce and the outlook dim, but contacts of both previous generations and newer generations showed a functionality and independence that aided in improvising to get by, shedding light on their remarkable resourcefulness.

—*Katie Lunsford*

HOW TO BE RESOURCEFUL

"Well, I had some hard times, all right. I can remember about the time I was to enter high school, and my parents debating very seriously whether or not they were going to get me in high school. I can remember my father was gone looking for a job, he wasn't home, and there was nothing to make bread out of at home, very little of any meal of any kind. Anyway, my brother came in and he happened to have a little bit of money, and he gave my mother fifty cents. She woke me up before breakfast and said, 'Here, take this fifty cents, and go get a pack of [corn]meal so that we will have breakfast.' That's how bad it got."

—**Woodrow Blalock (1991)**

"We had a small farm, so we could have a garden with corn. We just sort a' took what we had and made the best out of it. You have to accept what's handed to you. I've always had a faith in God. It's the little things that I try to make sure I'm thankful for because that's what you build on. Of course, with the large losses and all like that, you sure have to go to the Lord with your problems. I got strong faith. How to make do is to turn it over to the Lord. Then, it's one day at a time. You just have to know that the Lord will provide. Sometimes He has to teach you lessons. His answer may not come right when you expect it, but it's there. You can always fall back on it.

"Then there's opportunities out there if you look for 'em. Don't blame God for any tragedies that happen. There's a purpose behind it, and we may not know it, know what it is, but we know it's there. If we lean on Him, He'll see us through it. He can replace it." —**Vernice Lovell (2014)**

"It took all of us in the family day and night a-trying to keep food in our mouths." —**Melvin Taylor (1994)**

"As far as earthly goods, I got more now than I did back then, but you didn't have the worries then that you have now. . . . Things were better back then, but you didn't have no money either. 'Course, nobody else had money either. Nobody really had anything back then."

—**Berry Bray (2006)**

"We lived in Clay County, North Carolina, after the Depression hit. We got down to where I couldn't have no job. We just had cornmeal; you got it ground, and then we had to sift it out. And we made coffee, and a lot of times we wouldn't have nothing but onions and cornbread, and that coffee made out of grain; it was pretty good. We really had hard times.

"I know one time we lived on the head of Eagles Forge, over in Clay County. We stayed up there a long time and lived on groundhogs. I'd catch 'em. You know a groundhog is a woodchuck. I caught every one I'd come to. That's what we had to eat. It pleased her [his wife] to see me coming in with a big woodchuck. We'd cook that rascal. I'd dress him. She had a big ol' iron pot, and I'd dress that thing good, and then I'd go and cut some spicewood and break it up and put it in there. We had a pod of pepper, and we'd put it in. She'd cook it till it was good and tender, then take it out and put it in the stove, you know, and brown it. Boy, it was good! We lived off it! We went through some pretty rough times. I know that the second me and her got married, you couldn't get a job nowhere! Together, me and her peeled apples, filled seed sacks full of them. That was all we had to live on that winter—dried apples and groundhogs!" —**Oliver Meyers (1989)**

"I grew up just up here on the creek. They was five of us children livin' in a two-bedroom house. People act like they gotta have a room for ever' youngun. Mama and Daddy was in one room, and we had a big ol' room with lots of beds in it. I think that one time, years and years ago, they had a bed in the livin' room. Anyway, we made it. We didn't know no better. Now, them boys'd fight pretty bad. Me and sis fought some. We got put to doin' stuff we didn't want to do, but we did it, or Daddy'd got ahold of us.

"We didn't expect a lot. If you needed a new pair of shoes, you got a new pair of shoes, but that was once or twice a year maybe, twice at the most, I guess. There was no shoppin' done on no regular basis. Mama would make us—fix us a couple of dresses a year for school, and that done us.

"You had one coat and one sweater. That's the way everybody else was. You didn't have shoes to match everything you had. When you look around, there's always people that are less fortunate than you are. If you got a place to live that shelters you and plenty to eat and clothes, you are very blessed because there's a lot of people even in the United States that don't have enough to eat and especially in foreign countries. The Lord just really blesses us, and a lot a' times, we don't even realize it. We can go in there and get us somethin' to eat anytime we want it. It's just like this mornin', you wouldn't believe I threw away leftover stuff. We overcooked and had to throw it out. I said, 'This is shameful.' I hated to do it." —Sue Patton (2014)

"It's been tough, but I've made it with the help of the Lord."

—Harold Brown (1983)

PLATE 159 Harold Brown hewing a log

"I remember that my dad had to ride a bicycle back then. He worked for a dollar a day. That didn't buy a whole lot of stuff, though. We didn't have candy or nothing like that. All we bought was flour, sugar, and coffee. We had our own eggs, we raised our own meats, and we also milked our own cows. . . . That's 'bout all we had. We didn't have dolls or nothin' like that. Momma'd use rope and worn-out sheets of paper. She would roll them up into a wad and paint eyes on them with a pencil. That was our baby doll. She'd get out in the woods and make a playhouse with us."

—Azzalee Keener (2008)

"They was a long time that it was hard fer us t' get along without money. We didn't have any money—we just had somethin' to exchange. We had eggs, an' chickens, an' meat, an' corn t' take to th' store; t' trade fer what we needed. You raised yer own things, an' money was scarce. You'd pick blackberries an' blueberries, an' you'd cut stove wood. Most people then had their own lard. If they had a hog, they rendered their lard, an' ye got yer salt an' yer sodie [baking soda] an' yer sugar at the store. A lot of people made their own sodie out o' puttin' corncobs in one corner of the fireplace.

"Ya raised 'bout everythin', but coffee an' sugar, an' things that we had t' buy. You had th' other things yourself. You raised 'em in the garden—onions, taters, beans, and yer corn. Ye' put up stuff fer th' wintertime, either picked it, 'r canned it, didn't have no freezer, of course. An' you could dry stuff. We never did completely run out o' food—we'd been scarce a few times back when we had our children. We had four children, an' sometimes in the spring of the year, stuff would get out before the other come in." —Margaret Norton (1971)

"In the South, in these mountains in Appalachia, we were poor. You grew what you eat. If you went to the store, you traded for something you couldn't grow—like sugar, or something like that. You would grow your wheat, your flour, and your corn for your meal. We made our own soap and everything 'cause that is what you did." —T. J. Stevens (2014)

"Back when I's growing up, times was always hard. There was nothin' to bring in the money, hardly a'tall to plant corn, and most of the farming wuz just corn crops. If y' didn't have corn to sell, you didn't have much money. We wuz happy with what we had. They's a big family of us an' we didn't want the things, didn't worry about 'em, didn't even know they existed a lot of 'em that you have today. Our lives consisted mainly of playin', an' workin', an' goin' t' church. I never seed a picture show till after I's grown, and I don't know that I ever seen but two then."

—Fanny Lamb (1971)

"You didn't have any medicine. You had to do the best you can. Lots of kids back then had earaches. I don't know why. Mama would put a bunch of salt in a bag an' heat it—that salt retains heat, see—and lay it on their head. I can remember doin' that. Then she made sassafras tea and different kinds of teas—I can't remember 'em—out of herbs and things. We didn't have, like, headache pills and things. We had no medicine. You just toughed it out, I guess." —**Lois Duncan (2000)**

"We had a real hard time. We didn't really ever know what money was. We just had plenty to eat." —**Mae Cragg (1998)**

"We had gardens. We worked in gardens like all the rest of the families. We were just as poor as everybody else. We have a garden now, but not much. Age seems to creep in and a garden seems to become a thing of the past. But we had gardens. We farmed. Fifty or sixty years ago, people of the community raised their own meat. They processed their own meat, but they shared with the community. That was the thing. They shared. My community was close-knit. When one had, all had. When all came together for farming, they shared their products, and they took care of those who were less fortunate than they were.

"When I was a small child coming up, when there was no way, there was blessings. My father and them prayed that there would always be a way made, that things would work out for us. There were ways. Communities took care of each other. Churches took care of the communities. We didn't have much, but what we had, we shared with one another. That was a blessing, to teach us that we got along. We shared. We helped one another. It was just a blessing that we got along."

—**Willie Fortson (2014)**

"We made do when we didn't have, just the same as when we had."

—**Lillie Nix (1999)**

"We always had a garden. We had to, or we didn't eat. We didn't have the money to buy food. . . . If you didn't work, you didn't eat."

—**Effie Mae Speed Bleckley (2004)**

"We would go over to Popcorn [a valley in western Rabun County]. We would just run and play. 'Bout the only thing that we knew anything about was playin' that we was makin' liquor. Go ahead and laugh. We would have somebody playing as the one that was makin' the whiskey and somebody would be the revenuer. We would try to slip up on 'em. We couldn't. They would hear us. We was always looking around. If they saw us, they would take off runnin', runnin' them hills, mountains, wild.

"We would play Antie Over. You've played that, too. You might hear the name. You'd throw the ball over the house or you would have some kind of bat and throw it over. You couldn't afford to buy a ball, but you could keep a sheep. My grandmother Lunsford had a sheep. She would cut the wool, and they would clean the wool by washin' it. Then they would take what we called a spin wheel. You know what that is? And spin it into thread, but it was big thread. It 'as wool thread. Then, you could make whatever you wanted to with that. We didn't have any bought ball, so we made our own out of the wool thread that our grandmother had used. But they would knit socks. If you wore [the socks] out, you usually wore out the heel first. Then, they would patch it up by darnin' it. Most of the time, after you'd worn socks till they wadn't good enough to repair, they'd use it to make a ball out of. So, we would make the balls and we would play with 'em. It would surprise you how good they'd fly with a bat. [They would bounce], but not good like a ball today. We would play with those balls. Then, we would just do whatever we could do. We always were happy. Nothin' bothered us, because we didn't go anywhere, so to speak." —**Waymond Lunsford (2014)**

"Cash was hard to come by in those days. It was hard to get cash. People just didn't have any money, but, for instance, they [my parents] knew this friend, my daddy did, a college friend of his. He ran a sock factory up in North Carolina towards the coast. When they cut the top ribbon off of a sock, it's kind a' stretchy. You can imagine it's kind a' stretchy. They called it a clipping from a sock. Well, it was trash. My momma was up there one day, and she said, "What is this?" He said, "Lord, you can have all of it." So, Mama brought that back, and she called it looper clippings. Then, my mama found out that you could stretch 'em. You could do 'em in and out like we did the squares. You go in and out with a needle. Mama found out that you could use those and make spreads. You could make bath mats. It became a cottage industry, the looper clipping products.

We have some of 'em. There's some in museums now, looper clippings. That was just the way mountain folks thought. Make do.

"It [utilizing looper clippings] required a lot of time and a lot of hard work and, of course, when factories came in and started doin', that was it. It was a source of income for a lot of mountain ladies. That was the main purpose. That's one example of mountain ingenuity. We mountain folks used every available thing we could use to make do.

"Another thing you could make do is when they used feed sacks to make garments, chicken feed sacks. Now, mountain folks have always had to have something to carry something in. Now, remember, we didn't have these plastic bags fifty years ago, thirty-five years ago, a hundred years ago.

"Let's go back. Let's look at some of these early sacks. They [chicken feed sacks] were very prominent. They became very important, and this was called a croker sack. That was used to help keep grain in and whatever. This is the way that they made do. They used anything that was available.

"The salt came in this other sack. That was twenty-five pounds of salt. You didn't go get a little box of salt like we do. To make them usable, you usually unravel them. In other words, you took the seam out. When you unraveled them, you had a square cloth. Now, when you unravel these various sacks, you come up with what we call the raveling, and this was not wasted. This became crocheting thread or quilting thread. It became anything you needed thread for. [It was] very sturdy cotton. So,

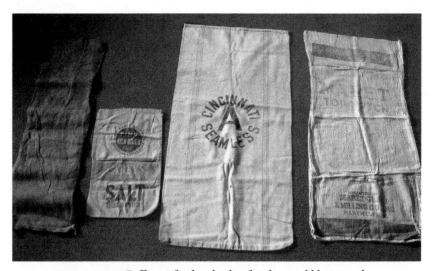

PLATE 160 Different feed sacks that families could have used

then we got salt bags. If I wanted to make this a square for a dishcloth, then I unravel it, and it will be a flat piece of cloth. That's when you have the raveling and you separate it, and that's the raveling thread and you can use it for crocheting, knitting, darning. That would be this wadded up—it's rolled up. Now, I've got two things to show you that are really beautiful and really to be treasured from cotton sacks.

"Now, my mother, she was a Depression person, and she made do. One day they wanted a new cover for the altar at the church, and so Mama said, 'Well, I'll get to doing that.' She used a feed sack, and it had also been used a lot, as you can see there. And so she crocheted from the ravelings; she did the cross. My mother did this piece. And it was down at our church at Tiger [Methodist] for years and years. Now, I don't remember what kind of sack this could've been. They starch beautifully. So then my mama-in-law, Mrs. Minnie, she had her a sack, and she made a runner. That's her dresser runner, and she crocheted this. She crocheted this with the raveling. Back in the Depression days, when there was no money, they utilized everything.

"At the end of World War II, the poultry industry came to Northeast Georgia, and all at once we had chicken houses, long chicken houses and big, growing chickens. There were different kinds of laying hens, and the

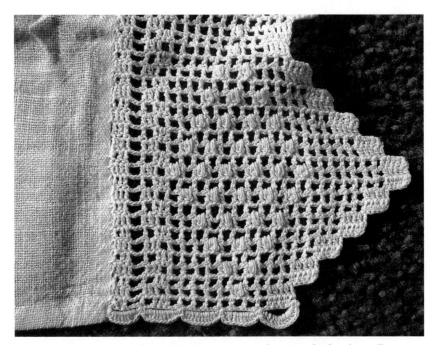

PLATE 161 Crocheted piece by Ms. Minnie Taylor using feed sack ravellings

ones that were raised in twelve weeks involved lots of chicken feed. It would come in a big truckload to a farmer. Well, one day someone had a bright notion. They said, 'We're going to please the homemakers. We're going to have pretty sacks.' It's one hundred percent cotton. The chicken feed sacks were very important." —Janie P. Taylor (2014)

Janie P. and her daughter, Dawn, discussed that these sacks could be used for dresses, shirts, bath towels, "winda" curtains, sheets, and pillowcases, among other things and spurred trading between homemakers for matching feed sacks to make larger pieces, such as sheets.

"The white people that raised my husband gave him a little spot of land. It had one little house on it, and they gave that to him, and we lived on it. You could lay down at night and look through the loft and see the stars. I remember once, one night it snowed and the snow had come through those cracks, and the bed and the floor were covered with snow. I waked up my husband and said, 'It's rained in here.' He made a light and looked, and everywhere in that room—even our bed—had just a little white coat of snow. It had come in the cracks overhead. It was fun to us. We got up and put some sheets up by the side of the walls to keep the snow from coming in. Well, it didn't keep it out, but it didn't go all over the house. We did things like that, and it was just fun for us."

—Beulah Perry (1974)

"There was some older ones [siblings], but I always had to build the fire. We had a lamp. Well, I'd set the lamp down and had done broke the globe on it—get my pine to start my fire and caught afire, I did. I went to screamin', and my daddy got up; he just grabbed my arm. I had on long sleeves, and he just rubbed it and put it out with his hand. Burnt me real bad. I don't remember if I went to the doctor or not. I think we just doctored it ourselves. I remember carryin' my arm in a rag sling. I just laid it in there and made a sling outta a rag."

—Effie Mae Speed Bleckley (2004)

PICKIN' AND GRINNIN'

I had a desire and a passion to really get out there. . . . Just like in life, give it your all.

—*Rodney Worley*

A place's value is often determined by big events or successful people who can call it home. In both cases, Appalachia is a very valuable place to be. Its deep, dark hills have a rich, flowing history and a long list of people who have achieved renown, especially when it comes to music. Like the Appalachian Mountains form the backbone of the East Coast, music forms the backbone of Appalachian culture. These mountains have always carried a song, whether it is the whistle of the trees or the lonesome call of a whip-poor-will. The Native Americans felt a close connection to the world around them and sought to create a harmony with nature's song. The beat of their drum echoed through the generations to a time when new settlers arrived. The Scotch-Irish brought with them a whole new sound that added resonance to the already existing melody.

Over time, the cultures flowing into Appalachia created a new and unique breed of music. Countless generations have carried down this tradition that gives everyone a sense of unity and pride. The Crowe Brothers, Dale Tilley, Curtis Blackwell, and Josh Crowe all shared their unique bluegrass sounds with us in *The Foxfire 45th Anniversary Book: Singin', Praisin', Raisin'* and accompanying CD. Many things separate us from other cultures, but if there's one attribute that defines us, from bluegrass to gospel to shaped-note singing our music is distinctive.

—Ethan Phillips and Jesse Owens

IN HARMONY

W̲e begin this section with a brief interview from two old-time bluegrass musicians, Oliver Rice and Curtis Blackwell. Both are Rabun County natives with long and distinguished music careers, and both have rubbed elbows with great all-time bluegrass musicians like themselves. They feel strongly that bluegrass should be played with acoustic instruments and each have made a living playing music.

—Ethan Phillips and Jesse Owens

OLIVER RICE AND CURTIS BLACKWELL

Two old-time musicians reminisce

I wasn't with Bill too long. It was around two and a half or three months. We were all about to starve to death by then.

—Curtis Blackwell

Oliver Rice: I've been playing bluegrass for around forty-three years. I was around eighteen years old when I first started, but I couldn't play very well until I was about twenty-three. I was mostly self-taught, but Dean Green helped me a lot.

When I started singing, we had a group called the Gospel Trio. I guess we played together for seven or eight years. I got the bluegrass group, which was the Blue Ridge Mountain Boys. Traditional bluegrass is what we played. I always played gospel with my act. I've never played anywhere that I can remember that we didn't play gospel music.

When I first started, bluegrass was totally acoustic music. There were

PLATE 162 Oliver Rice

no electric instruments, no amplified instruments in the group; it was all traditional. When I grew up, traditional bluegrass was all we knew. I grew up hearing Bill Monroe, Lester Flatt, Earl Scruggs, and the Stanley Brothers. They were all acoustic, and there were no electric basses or things like that for many years.

I've played with Ricky Skaggs when Ricky was—I believe—seventeen years old. He and Keith Whitley were with Ralph Stanley, and we played a lot of festivals. Out in the parking lot, we would get together and jam and pick and play with Ricky Skaggs. I was around him quite a bit back when he was in his late teens, before he went out on his own and went into more country music.

I play music because I enjoy it. Now we play mostly bluegrass-gospel music. I really enjoy the chance to get to play in a lot of places. We've been booked pretty regularly.

I could have gotten bigger. I played one summer—I can't remember what year it was—I played in Maggie Valley seven days a week. We started at ten o'clock in the morning and played until ten o'clock at night, with a few breaks in between. I had some booking agents come, and they booked me some shows in Kentucky and Tennessee. I could have gone from there if I had wanted to, but I decided that was too much and too far for me to go.

We do a lot of benefit singings. If we can help, we're gonna do it. We do a lot of that now. I still love bluegrass music, but there are some songs I can't sing. Traditional bluegrass tells a story about a tragic event or a love song. If they ain't got bad words in them, sometimes I'll be here at the house or somewhere, and I'll sing that old-time bluegrass music because I love it.

I almost had the opportunity to tour with Ralph Stanley one time, when I was playing at Maggie Valley, North Carolina. Ralph was without a lead singer at that time, and Raymond Fairchild had called him. Raymond called me and told me to call Ralph. I didn't call him right then; I hesitated for about two weeks. I finally called him one night and talked to him for a long time, but he had just hired someone else. I could probably have went there, but I was a little scared. I was afraid maybe I wasn't good enough to do that. Anyway, it's been fun down through the years, and I've enjoyed playing the music that I've played.

That was back when everybody played traditional bluegrass music, no electric basses or anything. I've had to play several times with an electric bass, and I didn't like it. I think it takes away from the music. I can't sing country music, but George Jones had a song called "The Window Up Above," and I used to sing that all the time.

I decided to just play traditional bluegrass and all gospel when I started preaching. I couldn't have an influence if I went and played like I used to play, so I quit and started playing all gospel music. I did it for the Lord 'cause that's what I felt led to do, but I've thoroughly enjoyed playing bluegrass-gospel music.

Curtis Blackwell was a featured musician in The Foxfire 45th Anniversary Book: Singin', Praisin', Raisin'.

Curtis Blackwell: Back years ago I had the Dixie Bluegrass Boys, and Al Osteen was our banjo player, and his brother was in the restaurant business. His name was Louis Osteen. He called me one night and said, "Look, Bill Monroe needs a singer and a guitar player. Why don't you go try out? I'll set it up for you." So, I did; we done it the right way, and I think that's what nailed the cast. I just wish I would've made enough money to stay with him a year or two, but I couldn't live on it. I could not feed two boys and their mother on what he paid me. I couldn't support my family, and that's the reason I had to go back to the house and go to

PLATE 163 Curtis Blackwell

work. When I left, I was working at a plant down at Pendleton, South Carolina. My boss told me, "I hear they don't make a lot of money with that type of work. Now, if you go on this job, and you can't make enough to feed your family, come back here and your job will be waiting on you." So, when I left Bill, I went back to work where I was originally at before I left. I wasn't with Bill too long. It was around two and a half or three months. We were all about to starve to death by then.

When I left Nashville, Tennessee, I had six dollars and some change in my pocket. I had a little Pontiac Tempest and the transmission had tore out of it. So, it only had low range. I put four dollars' worth of gas in that car, and you could buy a breakfast of one egg, bacon, grits, toast, and coffee for around a dollar eighty-five. I got breakfast and I still had a little bit of change left in my pocket. I headed out, and it took me all day long to get from Nashville, Tennessee, a little further than Murphy, North Carolina. It got me on home. I got home after dark, and I had drove that little car all the way from Nashville, Tennessee, in low range. It was pecking' a little bit, but it was still running. Before I left Nashville, I decided I'd put my clothes and my Martin guitar in the car, and if it tore plumb up, I'd get the Martin guitar out and go to hitchhiking. Luckily, I didn't have to do that. I made it home, and I thank God for that.

Music's been a big part of my life. I've quit several jobs to go pick. That's not real good for your family, but we made it. I've really enjoyed it. I've seen bluegrass music evolve since I've been involved with it. The music's been modernized. There's some of it I like, and some of it I don't like. I've seen some of the bands completely change and go off in left field. I'm a traditional bluegrass man, and people still seem to like it. Whenever I play, people come up to me and tell me they enjoy it. That's what I've always done, so we're going to try to stick with that for as long as I'm able.

I taught my boys the chords to the instruments, and I made them play rhythm at first to make sure they got that timing down before I'd ever let them take a break. It's seemed to work for all of them.

Shane just has a lot of God-given talent, to be honest with you. People come up to me and say, "Man, you really taught that boy good," and I don't have a clue what he's doing. He just had a lot of talent. Of course, I've helped him a little bit with what I knew, and there was a guy that gave him a set of training guitar tapes. That's where he got a lot of his guitar playing. Once he learned the basics of it, then he multiplied it himself.

Shane practiced all the time. He had bluegrass before breakfast. He'd come home from school in the evening, and he'd play until dark. Then, he'd get up the next morning and he'd play a while before he went to school. When he got to school, George Reynolds was teaching Foxfire, and Shane would play all day in there, too. So, he had a lot of practice he put into it. George helped him a lot, too. I'll give him credit for it.

I remember he went to a Tony Rice concert in Atlanta on a Thursday night, and that guitar was all we heard for about three months after that. He played when he got home from school and when he got up every morning. He just picked all the time.

When he was nine years old, we found out he had a hip Perthes disease, and he had to wear what they called the Greenville Brace. What it does is it puts your legs out wide, and it's got a bar that holds them out, and when you walk, you have to waddle. He went to school with those braces for nine years. Up until he got out of school, I carried him to Shriners Hospital in Greenville, South Carolina. He had to put up with that from the time he was nine until the time he was eighteen. Very recently—in 2013—he had surgery on his hips and got that fixed.

He went over across the water to Germany and stayed forty-four days. When he got home he said, "Daddy, I'm about burnt-out on music." Since then, he hasn't been with a band to that level. He plays banjo with me some, now, and a few little things here and there. He's played a lot of music in his lifetime, more than all the rest of us put together probably.

Editor's Note: Right in time with Foxfire, Curtis Blackwell will be celebrating his fiftieth year as a bluegrass musician soon. He will be releasing a 50th anniversary CD titled Then and Now *in 2016. Look for it at curtisblackwell.webs.com.*

THE BLACKWELL TRADITION

An interview with second-generation bluegrass musician
Shane Blackwell

Dad always played it, and it just got passed down to me. It's in my roots. —Shane Blackwell

Appalachian communities produce musicians with unmatchable talent. The Rabun County area is no exception. One of the most well-known musicians from the Rabun County area is Curtis Blackwell, who played with Bill Monroe and on the Opry throughout his career. He has made his impact on this area, but no impact was greater than the one he had on his kids. Shane Blackwell is the youngest child in this incredibly talented family. He has taken his passion for playing far beyond the front porch swing. He has performed alongside some of the world's greatest musicians at venues some only dream to perform at.

I got to know Shane while working at Reeves Hardware, and he and his wife lived in a house just above mine for a few years. He would come down and we'd sit around, goof off, and pick guitar on afternoons. I even have had the honor to have him perform with me at a few local shows over the last few years. It still amazes me how unbelievably talented he is. I've learned an awful lot from him, and he has helped me grow musically. He has definitely made his mark on this community through music, and we are very fortunate to have such a great ambassador.

—*Ethan Phillips*

For as long as I can remember, my dad, Curtis Blackwell, has played bluegrass. He and I used to sit on his bed and pick together. When I was nine I had leg braces, so I spent all my spare time learning to play. I'd be practicing something all the time. There wasn't much for me to do with those braces, so I had a lot of spare time. I told myself that I would learn to play everything the best that I could, and I've been fortunate enough to be able to do that. I had an advantage because I was around it all my life. Dad always played it, and it just got passed down to me. It's in my roots. There were always good musicians around me when I was growing up that I could learn something from.

I started out playing the mandolin when I was seven years old. Dad showed me a few chords on it, and I would take what he taught me and add to it. After that point, I started taking up more instruments. About three years after I started learning the mandolin, I took up playing the banjo. Then about another year after that is when I started on the guitar.

PLATE 164 Shane Blackwell (*right*) and his father, Curtis (*left*)

The last instrument I really took up was the dobro [a resonator guitar], when I was about sixteen. While learning each instrument, I would build off the foundation from the last. What I learned from one, I'd apply to the next one I was learning. The more I played, the more things would fall into place and I would get a better understanding.

Whenever I was learning to play, I would always practice by myself in the dark. I did that so I could learn the neck of the instrument without having to look at it. That way, I would be relying more on hearing it than seeing it. At the end of the school day when I got off the school bus, I'd go get an instrument and usually go into the bathroom because the acoustics were so good in there. I'd sit in there with the lights off, and I'd usually be in there about three to four hours a day practicing.

Back when I had just started, I spent every Saturday night at Cuzzin's General Store in South Carolina. For me, that's where it all started. I would go there with my dad, and a bunch of pickers would all get together and have big jam sessions. So, I would sit in with them and play along on the mandolin, listening to everything that they did. I'd pay attention to what they were doing and figure it out as they went. That was a real big help for me, that I had exposure to those pickings like that. Then, a little later on, I had an experience that changed my life. I went and saw Tony Rice live in Marietta, Georgia. That's all I need to say about that. After that point, I really took to playing the guitar because I wanted to play like him. I went and bought all the Bluegrass Album Band's and Tony Rice's records. I'd sit and play along with them until I felt like I had tried my best to learn all of them.

I started touring with my dad when I was about thirteen or fourteen. We played a lot of festivals and gigs during my teenage years. I can remember on the night of graduation dad had a gig at a bluegrass festival in Baldwin, Georgia. After graduation, everybody was going off to celebrate, and I headed straight to play the Hamby Mountain Bluegrass Festival. I played with dad full-time until I was in my twenties. Then, I got a pretty big opportunity. I found out there was an opening to play with Larry Stephenson. I auditioned for that job in Nashville. I guess you could say that playing with him was my big break. While I was with him, I played the Grand Ole Opry for the first time. It was pretty exciting to get to stand and play in that circle where so many great musicians had before me.

On the Opry stage, there is a six-foot circle of oak cut from the center of the Ryman Auditorium's stage. The Ryman is most well known for being home to the broadcasts of the Grand Ole Opry from 1943 to 1974.

PLATE 165 Shane Blackwell

The circle of oak was then placed into center stage at the new Grand Ole Opry House. Artists consider it a great honor to stand in the circle while performing.

I got to where I was playing so much with him, I ended up getting carpal tunnel. When I'd play, it would cause my hands to get really numb to the point I couldn't feel anything. It was getting to where they would get numb and the top string was cutting into my thumbnail and I couldn't feel it. It was hard on my hands. I ended up having to have surgery for it.

I stayed with Larry for about a year, until I got a job with Marty Raybon, the lead singer for Shenandoah. His bass player at the time knew me, and he set me up with an audition. I went and auditioned for him, and right after I got it, we loaded up the bus and headed to a gig in Michigan; a twenty-two-hour ride.

"I took all of his underwear out and put Icy Hot in them before a show."

When I was with Marty, I got the opportunity to go play the Opry again. When I was backstage before the show, the fiddle player, Glen Harrell, thought I had hid his shoes. So, he decided he'd pay me back by taking my khaki pants and wetting the front of them before we went out. He got them soakin' wet in the front. It looked like I had peed my pants. I ran to the bathroom, put them under the hand dryer, and tried my hardest to get them dried off in time. That didn't work. I went out onstage looking like I had peed in my pants. That was pretty embarrassing. I got back at him, though. For retaliation the following week, I took all of his underwear out and put Icy Hot in them before a show. He was on fire!

After about six years with Marty, I got a job with Bradley Walker. I played a few shows with him, including once at Disney World for a big company party. I stayed with Bradley for less than a year, then I got a job with Sierra Hull, who was seventeen at the time. I had known her since she was little. I had seen her at shows throughout the years, and then we just happened to have a jam session when I was playing in Florida. After I saw her that day in Florida, we stayed in contact until a few years later, she needed me to do some fill-in shows with her. We played a few shows here in the States, but then we went over and toured Japan for two weeks. That was pretty fun. It was no doubt the cleanest place I've ever been. We played bluegrass festivals while we were there, one of which had over a hundred bands there. They really enjoy listening to that kind of music over there.

I auditioned for Valerie Smith and Liberty Pike in Bell Buckle, Tennessee. I played with her for a couple of years. About eight or nine months into it, we went to play in Germany for two months. We played a bunch of different theaters and little pubs over there. We went through Switzerland, Austria, France, Amsterdam, and then, of course, places in Germany, like Nuremberg. There was a lot of nice people there and good food. One thing that really shocked me while I was there was you have to pay to use the bathroom. It was really awesome to see the autobahn. We drove down it on the bus numerous times. I got to see a lot of high-dollar Ferraris, Lamborghinis, and anything else you can think of on that road. Whenever we got back to the States, we played in Cumberland Caverns up in Tennessee. It's a set of caves that they hold concerts in three hundred feet underground. The caverns always stay a constant temperature, and the acoustics down there are amazing. Now, that was awesome.

After I played with Valerie for a couple years, I just decided I didn't want to tour anymore. That was the end of my touring days. It's hard on you when you're constantly moving around. I still play some with my dad at his gigs, and a couple other musicians here and there, but nothing on the scale that I was doing.

I've learned that if you play bluegrass music, you've got to play it because you love it. You don't do it for the money, because there's not much money in it. I really enjoyed it while I was doing it, but it was hard to make a career out of it. I've experienced a lot of things people don't get the opportunity to do through it, though. I've got to see the world from a perspective some work their whole life to achieve, and, even though it's had its ups and downs, I wouldn't trade it for anything.

"I'VE BEEN EVERYWHERE, MAN"

An interview with traditional bluegrass musician Rodney Worley

From that point on, I was hooked. I fell in love with it. I thought, "That's what I want to do." —Rodney Worley

Rodney Worley is an established bluegrass musician. In a generation that is captivated by a new wave of "music," he has joined a handful of others to preserve one of the unique characteristics most commonly associated with Appalachia: bluegrass music.

From humble beginnings, Rodney has felt a calling to the lonesome sound that defines this genre. He has performed at numerous venues within the States and abroad, something most people would never get the chance to do, while still remaining true to his roots. During the interview, Rodney demonstrated how important staying dedicated is when he said, "Don't ever get to the point where you think that you're good enough, because once you get to that, you'll never learn anything else. . . . Don't ever quit trying. Just like in life, give it your all." From the look in his eyes throughout the interview, it was clearly evident that his passion for bluegrass remained undiminished. It was reassuring to know that no matter how music may change, there are still those who cling to its heritage; that it, too, is not just another passing fad.

—*Ethan Phillips*

I was born in December 1983 in a little place called Nickelsville, Georgia. So, I grew up in a pretty small town. I come from a pretty big family. My grandmother had fifteen kids. I got to where, whenever I'd go over to my grandmother's when I was about five or six, I'd listen to her old records. She'd have ol' records from Bill Monroe, Flatt and Scruggs, and

Ralph Stanley and the Stanley Brothers. Well, I'd sit and listen to that. I never really knew I liked bluegrass, but I knew that I liked that. I guess I was too young to know what it was, but I just knew I liked it. I remember there was this one time I was over at my grandmother's house, and we were sitting there listening to a Bill Monroe record. It was a gospel song that he had recorded called "I've Found a Hiding Place." There are some parts on that where Bill Monroe gets really, really high singing the tenor on it, and when I heard them, I said, "Grandma, who's that woman singing?" She said, "That's not a woman. That's Bill Monroe!" From that point on, I was hooked. I fell in love with it. I thought, "That's what I want to do."

"She said, 'That's not a woman. That's Bill Monroe!'"

Nobody else in my family plays except Grandma's first cousin. She used to say, "He plays a guitar, but he lays it in his lap. I've never seen the likes." Who it was, was Josh Graves that played with Flatt and Scruggs. They were first cousins, and I guess that's where I get it from. Nobody else in my family plays, so that's all I can figure. I just kind of grew up listening to that. As I got into my teenage years, I tried to listen to different kinds of music. I tried country, rock and roll, and Southern gospel, but I just never really cared for it as much. It just didn't click with me. So I thought, "Well, maybe I'm just not into music," but I'd always end up going back to those old records. Then, whenever I heard them, I'd think, "Well, I really like this. This is what I enjoy listening to."

I took up a little part-time job after school. I was fifteen years old at the time. I saved up some money, and I told my daddy, "I'm gonna go buy me a fiddle, and I'm gonna learn how to play it." So, that's what I did, and I guess the rest is history. That's what I've been doing since. Whenever I'm on the road now, I play the mandolin, but I started out playing the fiddle.

I think what drove me to playing bluegrass was the fact that there's a lot of truth behind the music. You can relate to it as far as living in the country, the mountains, and rural areas. It really touches home. I guess that's really what calls me to it and emotionally connects me.

I'd have to say my biggest influences are Bill Monroe, the Stanley Brothers, the Osborne Brothers, and especially Jimmy Martin. I love Jimmy Martin. He's my hero. As far as the newer generation, I like Ricky Skaggs and Doyle Lawson, but I'm very traditionalist. I like the old stuff. So, I'd say those are my main influences.

PLATE 166 Rodney Worley

I consider myself more of a mandolin player than a fiddle player. I mean, I like to play rhythm guitar a little, too. I'm not a lead picker, but I feel that rhythm is just as important as lead. I don't hardly play the fiddle anymore. I don't claim to be a fiddle player. The thing about playing the fiddle is it's like a jealous lover, I guess. It's one of those things that if you don't play it every day and practice every day, it's not going to work with you. It's just not. Whenever I started on the road, I actually played the fiddle. I played it with Paul Williams, who used to be Jimmy Martin's tenor singer back in the sixties. I started out playing with him. I love to hear Paul Williams. He is another big influence on me.

It was funny. There would be times where I was standing onstage playing my fiddle, and I'd just stand there and watch him play mandolin. I'd kind of get lost in his mandolin playing, and then when it'd be time for me to take my break, Paul would just kind of look at me. Then it'd hit me, "Oh yeah, it's my turn."

I've got several instruments. The one I play now is a custom-built mandolin from a fella by the name of Pete Heart. He builds mandolins out in Ohio. Mine's called a Buckeye. I got him to build it for me about four years ago. I've got two older Gibson mandolins, too. I've got a 1927 and a 1943 F-style Gibson. I just kind of keep them under the bed now, though. They're so old, and I just decided not to get them out anymore. I figured I needed to have something to be my workhorse and actually travel with me. I've got somewhere around twelve or thirteen fiddles.

I've got a lot not to consider myself a fiddle player! I just got to where I'll go to antique stores, and I'll just find one. Then, if I find one, and I like the sound of it, I'll buy it. They usually aren't but thirty or forty bucks. I've also got two Martin guitars. One's a 1954 D-28, and then the other is a newer model. I really don't know what it is. It's got the large sound hole, and it's a dreadnought [an acoustic guitar body style that is common among bluegrass flat-pickers]. It's just one of those special models that they've started making. Then, lastly, I've got an old thirties model Vega banjo that I bought in a pawnshop for something like sixty dollars. I think that's about all that I have that I can think of. I've got a whole closet full of stuff.

"I've got somewhere around twelve or thirteen fiddles."

I've written a few songs that people's recorded. Three of my songs have been recorded and put on some people's albums. I don't say that I'm a songwriter, but I try to. I really enjoy writing songs and getting across what I'm feeling and what I think people would like to hear. It's pretty difficult for me to do that. You've always got to keep it in your mind that most of the time they come to you at two o'clock in the morning. Sometimes I'll be asleep, and I wake up and say, "I've got to write this down!" Then, by the time I find a pen and a piece of paper, I've forgot it. Now I've got to where I'll usually record it on my phone if something comes to me. I've got around forty-eight little clips of just me singing little snippets of stuff that comes to me. By the time I finish a song, some people like them and some people don't. It all depends.

The three songs that I've written and had recorded are all gospel, actually. I write a lot of gospel music. If it wasn't for the Lord, I wouldn't have this talent, so I've got to give Him all the honor and glory. I do have a few bluegrass songs that I've written. They're some of those pitiful lonesome ballads where you kill somebody, the kind of songs that people seem to love for some reason. I don't know why, but they love it in bluegrass. You just try to write what the people want to hear.

"I don't play scales because I actually don't know them."

I think songwriting comes just like practicing your instrument. I think it's one of those things you have to work at and work at. When I started writing, I remember I was writing one-syllable-word songs. It would be little simple phrases like, "The dog jumped over the log," or something along those lines. It would look like a kid was writing it. Then, you get more used to it, you start to understand there's no set way to do things. You may rewrite it over and over again until it finally becomes what you want. I normally don't write instrumentals. I've maybe written one or two, but I'm just not a big instrumental type. I'd rather sing and, really, back up the singer with my playing.

I'm one of those people that don't read music. I play by ear. I don't play scales because I actually don't know them. I'll be playing with somebody, and they'll say, "Oh yeah, it's in this scale." I'll look at them and say, "I don't know what that is. You're just going to have to play it. Whenever I hear it, then I can play it again." I can play what you play. You've just got to show me what you're doing. Sometimes I wish I knew how to read music because it'll just further my knowledge of music theory.

I love to sing. Ever since I've been playing professional, I've always sung some kind of harmony part. My favorite is to sing tenor. That's what I do with the band I'm with now. When I was with Paul, I sung baritone mostly. Paul is such a high singer that you don't tenor him hardly. It just wouldn't sound right. Most people just can't tenor him. He's just got such a high voice, we just sing two harmony parts under him instead of the traditional lead, tenor, baritone. So, I would always either sing harmony baritone or a low tenor part. We'd get out harmony that way, kind of similar to the way the Osborne Brothers done it.

"It's just a lot of practice and learning to listen to the lead."

There's not really a trick to singing harmony. If there are, I've not found it. I know this is going to sound crazy, but you have to sing with your ears. You really have to hear what the other person's doing. If this other man's singing lead, you need to figure out the melody of what he's singing and then follow him every step of the way. You have to get every phrase and nuance that he is saying down pat. You have to breathe the same. It's almost like you need to mimic everything that he's doing in your harmony voice. You want that tight blend that Paul used to call "the buzz." You want that tenor and that baritone to blend with that lead. He'd tell me about how he remembered playing with Jimmy back in the sixties. He said that you could hear the speakers buzzing because the harmony was so tight. That's what you want to get. So, as far as a trick to it, I don't think there's one. It's just a lot of practice and learning to listen to the lead.

There's been so many gigs I've got to play that I can't think of one right off that really sticks out. As far as venues regional to Georgia, I played the Fox Theatre in Atlanta. We went out west to California, up to Washington, and then Oregon back in February. There were a few theaters out there that I really enjoyed playing. I got to play the MACC (Musicians Against Childhood Cancer), which is in Ohio. It's like a benefit for childhood cancer, and everybody gets together and plays there. I got to play in a show with Tony Rice [a world-renowned acoustic guitarist and bluegrass musician] in Ellijay, Georgia, when they were having a little concert at Mountain Heart. I played backstage at the Opry with Ricky Skaggs one time. That was a big deal for me. I really enjoyed that. It's hard to narrow it down. There have been a lot of festivals I've played over the years. I love to play Bean Blossom; that's Bill Monroe's festival up in Indiana. As far as I know, it's the oldest running bluegrass festival. I've had the opportunity to play there several times.

I've played in almost every state. There's two or three that I've not been in. Of course, I've been out of the country and played, too. I've played in Nova Scotia, Prince Edward Island, Canada, and even Mexico. As far as out of the country, that's about it. It's kind of like that song says, "I've been everywhere, man." I really have, and I've enjoyed every bit. I'm really thankful I've got to see the country this way, especially to play bluegrass.

I always had a dream that I'd get to travel and play music. I had a desire and a passion to really get out there. I used to sit and I used to daydream about riding on a bus to our next big show when I was younger. Now, I do that. It's funny because people are always thinking, "Oh, you've got this big, nice bus, and you get to tour the country." It's kind of nice, but when you live with five other guys, it isn't as great after a while. You've got a little bunk that you sleep in. Of course, we've got the couch, the TV, and the kitchen, but it's a cramped space for five men to live on it for weeks at a time. It'll get to you.

How I got my start with a band is a pretty funny story. I'd probably been playing for about five or six years, and I had met some people up in Townsend, Tennessee. One of the people I met has become one of my best friends. His name's Jay Tipton. He had heard me talking about how I liked Paul Williams, and one day he got ahold of me and said, "You need to come to the house. Paul practices at a music store up here on Thursday nights. You need to come up and hear him." So, that's what I did. Jay and I got there, and we're sitting there waiting. I love Paul Williams, so I really wanted to hear him. He come walking in, and I watched without saying anything. His fiddle player had not showed up yet. So, it was just Paul and the guitar player, and they were going over their harmony parts. As they were practicing, I was singing the third harmony part in my seat with them. I started noticing that the guitar player was coming off of his harmony part onto the one I was singing. I looked over at Jay, and I said, "Jay, his singing's flat. He's not on his harmony part." Jay's the kind that's very skittish, and he said. "Well, don't say anything." I said, "Yeah, I'm going to." He said, "No, please don't." He begged me not to say anything, but when they got done singing that song, I walked up to him and I said, "Mr. Williams, I just wanted to let you know I was sitting here listening to y'all sing, and your harmony was off." He just kind of cocked his eyebrow and looked at me and said, "Well, do you know that other harmony part?" I told him I did and he said, "Sing it for me." So, we sang it and when we come to that part, his guitar player come down onto that harmony part that I was singing like I had said. Paul just kind of looked at me. He told me, "Well, you're right." He didn't really say too much after that.

> "I said, 'Mr. Williams, I just wanted to let you know I was sitting
> here listening to y'all sing, and your harmony was off.'"

About the time I went and sat down, his fiddle player and bass player showed up, and they practiced. We sat there probably two hours listening to them practice. When they finished, Paul came up to me and asked, "What do you play, boy?" I said, "Well, I play the mandolin." He said, "Well, I play the mandolin." I said, "I understand." Then he asked, "Can you play the bass? I think my bass player's leaving." I told him, "Well, I can learn. I play the fiddle, mandolin, and guitar." He said, "I'm going to give you my CDs, and if you can learn the bass and harmony on it, I may call you."

I went back home and I was doing all I could to scramble around to find a bass. I finally go to a music store, and they had one. Here I was about to shell out fifteen hundred dollars for an old Kay Bass. I was actually counting out the money to the owner when Paul called me. I answered the phone, and he said, "Rodney, did you say that you could play the fiddle?" I told him I could, and he said, "Well, I had to let my fiddle player go. Can you be up here Thursday and play a show with me?" I answered him real quick, "Well, of course I can!" He had called on a Monday. I didn't buy the bass. I went home, I got my fiddle, and I practiced probably ten hours a day until Thursday to try to learn all of his songs in time. I went up and stayed all night with him. The show went well. I was super nervous, and he come up to me and told me, "Don't be nervous. I understand where you're at. I've been in the same boat you're in. You'll do fine. If you happen to miss a lick or anything, it'll be all right. They won't notice hardly anything." So, he gave me a lot of comfort. I was scared to death, but everything just kind of went from there. He gave me a job.

Paul's a good mentor. He really taught me a lot about singing. I had always sung in church with my mom and my aunt when I was little, but he helped me further the knowledge I already had. He really showed me a lot of about phrasing, timing, the tone of my voice, and nuances. That way I could sing like him and with him. He's the one that honed that skill in for me.

"You don't necessarily want to play all these hot licks. It's fine to play those and to know those, but it's really all about playing from the heart and connecting with the people in the audience because that's what they're there to hear."

I've seen music change, but then as far as bluegrass music, it all depends on what kind of bluegrass you play. If you play the traditional stuff, it's going to stay traditional. A lot of people want to preserve that old sound with that way of playing and singing. Then, you've got this new generation of bluegrass. It's very modern and sleek. It's almost like they don't mesh together. Traditionalists will stay more true to the original. I was sitting there talking to Paul the other day, and he was telling me about an interview he did with a newspaper. The reporter had asked him about his thoughts on contemporary bluegrass. Paul said, "Well, it's in contempt with bluegrass. It's not real bluegrass." I have to kind of agree with him because I am a traditionalist. I'm not all that crazy about this new stuff. I don't think it's really bluegrass, but it is just another form. It's always going to evolve. It's never going to stop changing. You can try to preserve it as best you can, but you're still going to have influences from new people. I love the Bluegrass Album Band. To me, that's more contemporary, but I guess that's not considered contemporary anymore. It's already forty years old now. It's always going to be changing.

Whenever you play music, you always want to play to the audience. You don't play above their heads. You don't necessarily want to play all these hot licks. It's fine to play those and to know those, but it's really all about playing from the heart and connecting with the people in the audience because that's what they're there to hear. If you're going to play hot licks to try to wow these crowds, you're really just playing to other musicians because the average person sitting out there doesn't know music. They don't understand what you're doing. I was taught when you play a song, you almost have to play the words. That way, people will know what you're playing. So, I really try to stick to the melody. I mean I'll throw a few licks in there every now and then, but I really try to stick to the melody as much as I can. I try to get that through to the audience as best I can.

I'll let music take me wherever it'll take me. I love it. It's in my blood. I can't get rid of it. People ask me, "Well, are you going to quit?" I'll say, "No, I'll never quit. I may get tired of the road life and quit the road, but as far as playing, I won't." I started playing when I was about fifteen, and it's always been there for me. It ain't ever let me down. If I ever was feeling bad, lonely, or had the blues, I could always go pick music. It's always there. So, I won't ever quit. I'll play for as long as I can.

My best advice for an upcoming musician would be to always play from the heart. An audience will want to hear what's inside you. Never stray from that, because once you connect with an audience, it doesn't matter how well you play or how well you sing; that all goes away. You're connected with them, and they're connected with you. It doesn't matter. If you're singing "In the Pines," you have to put yourself in that situation. "The longest train I've ever seen went down that Georgia line." You've got to put yourself in a situation where your woman is gone, and you're never going to see her again. You really have to bring that emotion out and sing that to the crowd to let them know how you're feeling. Honestly, what you're doing is opening yourself up to everybody. You're vulnerable. I've laughed onstage, and I've cried onstage. It's this wide range of emotion that people see and love. So, if you're really going to start into bluegrass or any kind of music, just really play it from your heart. Learn what suits you the best. Just because someone else plays it, doesn't mean you have to play it like that. We all have influences, but you don't have to play exactly like them. Make it your own.

Bill Monroe said, "You've got to feel the notes you're playing." You may can play it note for note, but if the feeling's not in it, it's not doing nobody any good. He would say, "Hey there, boy, that ain't no part of nothin'." I think that holds a lot of truth to it. So, just play from the heart, and go with it. If you really desire to do that, then do what you can to be the best at it you can be. Don't ever get to the point where you think that you're good enough, because once you get to that, you'll never learn anything else. Always strive to say, "Well, I can do this a little better, make this a little clearer, and I can pull more tone out of this." Don't ever quit trying. Just like in life, give it your all.

THE ART OF A LUTHIER: MAKING THE LORD'S TREES SING

An interview with Danny White

I taught myself the whole process through a variety of ways.
—Danny White

Back in the 1970s Foxfire students interviewed Stanley Hicks, Tedra Harmon, Leonard Glenn, and others about banjo making. Foxfire had recently started a music class, and the students who were learning to play the banjo wanted to explore its origin and how it was made. They met some of the finest instrument makers these mountains have ever produced, many of whom used tools they had fashioned themselves. Their work is featured in *Foxfire 3*.

I have been playing guitar for about four years now, and I've really become interested in how the instrument I play works. Up until this point, I didn't know much more about the guitar than the songs I was playing. During the summer of 2012, I worked up at the Foxfire Museum. Foxfire's curator, Barry Stiles, informed me of a local luthier, or instrument builder, that might be an interesting contact to interview. Upon returning to school, I called up Mr. Danny White to set up an interview so that I could put together an article on the process he goes through when he is taking a stack of wood and transforming it into a work of art. Just like instrument builders Stanley Hicks and Robert Mize [*Foxfire 3*], Mr. White is painstakingly careful in his work and makes many of his own tools.

When I arrived, I was very anxious to learn but was also nervous that I wouldn't be able to capture such a detailed process. Mr. White greeted me with a smile and invited me into the workshop where he had built a business out of his passion of working with his hands. Right after I turned the recorder on, he began to explain his roots in music and how he became involved with the craft. With every question I asked, I became very interested in how intricate every step in the process was. He showed me examples of his finished instruments and even let me play one of his guitars, which had the most unique sound I have ever heard.

It was a great learning experience, and I feel very fortunate that Mr. White allowed me to talk to him. Like Mr. White stated in the interview, "A lot of people think it's just a box with a neck and strings on it, but there are a lot of little parts, and those little parts are what ties every-thing together."

He asked that I dedicate this article to his dear friend Harold Thomp-son, Jr.

—*Ethan Phillips*

I moved to the Rabun County area about the late sixties. We got in here by about 1965. I was born in Seneca, South Carolina, and raised in Oconee County, South Carolina, but I've spent the biggest part of my life here in Rabun County. I specialize in a flattop dreadnought guitar. It makes a great bluegrass guitar. That's 'bout all I've ever known when it comes to guitars, so that's what I build.

I grew up in a family that was always making music, especially blue-grass music. Ever since we were big enough to know what it was, we'd play. All throughout that time, I just never could get a guitar or anything that really sounded like I wanted it to sound. So, I said there's got to be a way to get one with that specific sound I wanted, so, shoot, I built one!

> *"It was all just a matter of trial and error really, plus all of what I had learned from other people, which was a big help."*

Nobody else in my family was a luthier. I took it up whenever I wanted to get that sound that I had always looked for. I taught myself the whole process through a variety of ways. I went and read all I could read on them, and I also talked to other builders over the years to learn all that I could to make a good-sounding instrument. They would point me in the right direction and give me good ideas, but I didn't have any experience whatsoever with the part of actually building one. It was all just a matter of trial and error, really, plus all of what I had learned from other people, which was a big help.

There are a lot of builders out there that don't even play. They have an ear for the way the instrument should be tuned when you're mak-ing it, but as far as playing, a lot of them don't even play. You also have some builders that won't build left-handed guitars because they like to test their instruments before they send them out. They can't play them, so they won't make them. Personally, I make them because there's not much difference in them. It's just a matter of turning everything upside down, really.

On Guitars

The guitars I build aren't necessarily anything fancy, but they make a good guitar. The thing that makes them iconic is their sound. They've got the kind of sound in it that I always wanted. They are almost identical to the guitars that Sigma by Martin makes. They are very similar as far as size goes and all. I have a 1970 model Sigma, which is the first year they came out. Sigmas are really good-playing guitars, and they sound real good. The thing about guitars is the older they get and the more you play them, the better they sound.

There's no set time when it comes to how long it takes me to build an instrument. It all just depends on what the person's wanting. Recently, I built one for a good friend of mine that goes to church with me. Neither of us was in a big hurry, so I took my time. I built him a mandolin to begin with, and come to find out that he had stage-four lung cancer. His daughter called me and asked if I had finished her dad's guitar. At that time, I hadn't even started on it. I had all the materials gathered up, but I just hadn't started. Right then is when she told me about the cancer. She broke down and went to crying on the phone. So, I got that one done really fast. It took me two weeks to build that guitar. The only reason I built it that fast is because of what was going on. I'd rather not build one that fast. I'd rather take my time and take at least a couple months to build one. That way, you're not pushed to get all your bracing just as accurate and the way it needs to be in a short amount of time. The trick to the guitar I built him was he wanted it to match the mandolin I had made him color-wise, wood, and all. I built the mandolin out of curly maple and put a sunburst finish on it. When I finished, the guitar matched that mandolin exactly. It looks just like the mandolin.

I built a guitar for a good friend of mine named Harold Thompson, Jr., and it turned out to be a beautiful guitar. It's got a 4-A [Wood is measured in different grades. 4-A is an example of these grades.] spruce top, 4-A curly maple sides, and a 4-A curly maple back. The neck is made out of a 4-A Mahogany. I was really proud of the way it turned out. I'd say that Harold's was the nicest one I've made. Another thing I liked about that guitar is that it will flat project. The curly maple back really throws

PLATE 167 Harold Thompson, Jr.'s guitar made by Mr. White

out the sound. Also, that 4-A top on that thing, it's just thin like I've got this one here. It's got the sound in it, especially bass.

My latest guitar is just a "plain-Jane" flattop. That guitar was made from a bunch of different parts I had made at different times. I built the body in 2009. Then it wasn't until 2011 that I built the neck and put it together. I had the body laid up in the shop. So, when I wasn't too busy, I'd work on it on and off for a little time. It's not that it takes a long time to do one, but you've just put your mind to it and build it. I usually prefer to build the body, then make a neck later on. I also make and put a truss rod [metal rod that runs down the guitar's neck so that you can adjust the string height] in the necks as well. It's inside, and then you just make an Allen wrench hole right in there. The neck and all is bolted on. It's a bolt-on neck, and I can take the neck right off of it. That way, if you need to do some adjusting, it ain't no big deal.

I cut the sound hole ring for that guitar out of scrap. I just took some scrap pearl that I had left over from other projects, and I just really hated to waste it. So, I made me a little pattern, and I used every little piece I could cut, and I put it in around the sound hole. The fretboard on the latest one I built is rosewood, and the body is walnut. The walnut I used came out of an old stump up on Hale Ridge [Rabun County, Georgia]. I've still got a bunch of the wood off that stump left in my shop. The neck is made out of cherry that I got ahold of. Pieces of wood like that have got seven layers of wood within it. Then, I made the peghead cover out of a knot out of that same ol' stump.

I built the neck of that guitar out of some cherry that came out of my mother's front yard. Cherry's a real good wood, too. It's a good stable wood. As far as building a body out of it, that wouldn't be your best bet, but it's great for necks or bracing.

"You might think flattop, but it's not really flat."

I order my tuners from Stewart-MacDonald. The particular ones I used on my newest guitar are Gotoh tuners. They're good tuners; some of the best I've ever used. I usually don't make the bridges for my guitars. I can make them, but it's just easier and quicker to order [premade] blanks. It isn't a big deal to make one, but it's just as cheap for me to buy a blank. I try to use bone everywhere I can. The nut, saddle [part of bridge that supports the strings], and everything on my instruments is bone. That's a key implement to getting your good sound, too—that and your top. I mean, your bracing's really where it's at. If you tapped on that top before you ever assemble it and put it together, you can pretty much tell what you've got before you ever put it together. A lot of people don't realize it, but there's an arch in that guitar's body, too. You might think flattop, but it's not really flat. I can also make pick guards to put on my guitars, but I hardly ever use them on mine. I always leave them plain unless a man wants one.

When I'm putting the necks on a guitar, I usually bolt them on. The old dovetail jobs work fine and dandy, but you've got what you got when you get it on there. You have to steam it to get it back off with the glue and everything. I always wondered if there was a better way. So I've found that bolting them on is easier on down the road if you have to have any repairs. My latest guitar I mentioned earlier and the other one I built Harold are bolted on, and it works fine.

"Getting the perfect sound is what it's all about. The older the wood is, the better the sound you're going to get."

When it comes to building the fretboard, it's not that hard. All the frets are pressed in. What'll happen on a radius neck is the ends of the

Neck Measurements

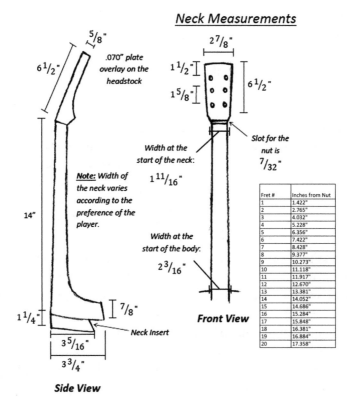

$5/8$"

$6^1/_2$"

.070" plate overlay on the headstock

$2^7/_8$"

$1^1/_2$"

$1^5/_8$"

$6^1/_2$"

Slot for the nut is $7/_{32}$"

Width at the start of the neck: $1^{11}/_{16}$"

Note: Width of the neck varies according to the preference of the player.

14"

Width at the start of the body: $2^3/_{16}$"

Fret #	Inches from Nut
1	1.422"
2	2.765"
3	4.032"
4	5.228"
5	6.356"
6	7.422"
7	8.428"
8	9.377"
9	10.273"
10	11.118"
11	11.917"
12	12.670"
13	13.381"
14	14.052"
15	14.686"
16	15.284"
17	15.848"
18	16.381"
19	16.884"
20	17.358"

$1^1/_4$"

$7/_8$"

Neck Insert

$3^5/_{16}$"

$3^3/_4$"

Front View

Side View

PLATE 168 Diagram of guitar neck, headstock, and fret measurements

frets will try to raise on you. So, what you do there is take superglue and just touch it up with superglue. Then, hold it there till it sticks, and you've got it. Usually, the ones down on the very far ends are the worst ones due to the fact they're the longest. The ones up towards the top don't give you any problems. I usually take a little ol' clamp, and I'll

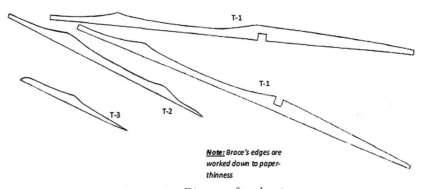

T-1

T-1

T-3

T-2

Note: Brace's edges are worked down to paper-thinness

PLATE 169 Diagram of top bracing

hold them on there with it. You'll put frets on before you ever glue your fretboard on the neck.

When I'm fixing the action of the guitar, I usually start by trying to get everything worked down as flat and as straight as I can without messing with the truss rod. Then, if it doesn't pull out straight when I do that, I'll pull it with a truss rod.

Getting the perfect sound is what it's all about. The older the wood is, the better the sound you're going to get. The tighter the grain of the wood, the better it does. Plus, another key factor is the location of the braces and how well they are tuned. When you're gluing braces in there, you glue them in while they are rough cut. Then you work them down and trim them after they're already glued on there. Then you can hold that rascal by one corner and take you a little hammer or small block of wood and thump it. You can hear it change as you trim it down. You can tune them as they sit in the guitar. They've got four tone braces in it, four bass bars, and two tenor bars, as well. Plus, along with all of that, you've got some back bracing and double-scallop bracing in it, too.

There are a lot of times where you run into problems with your bracing. You can hold the instrument up and look. If it's washboarded out and caved in, nine times out of ten, the ends of the braces are broke. It usually isn't too bad to fix them. As a matter a fact, I have a guitar in the jig right now that my son-in-law was going to build. He found himself a good deal on some rosewood. I bent his sides for him and everything, but he never did finish it. It's still sitting in that jig, and now it's starting to

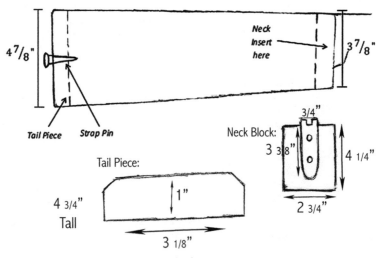

PLATE 170 Diagram of side measurements of guitar

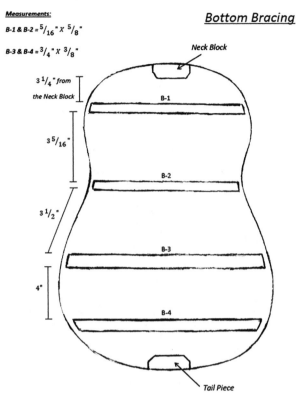

Measurements:

B-1 & B-2 = $5/16$" X $5/8$"

B-3 & B-4 = $3/4$" X $3/8$"

Bottom Bracing

Neck Block

$3 1/4$" from
the Neck Block

B-1

$3 5/16$"

B-2

$3 1/2$"

B-3

4"

B-4

Tail Piece

PLATE 171 Diagram of back bracing measurements

have bracing issues. He never put a top on it, and I told him, "You need to at least finish the body where it will be good and solid." He never did, and now the whole thing is flared out. I gave him a nice piece of pretty walnut to make the back out of and everything, but he never finished it. He'll come back one of these days and finish it, hopefully. It would be a good guitar if he'd get it done.

When you're putting pickups [electronics that you can put in acoustic guitars to amplify them] in acoustics, the most important part is working underneath your saddle. Since you are working around the saddle, you have to be very careful because that's such an important part of the instrument. You start by drilling a hole in one end of your saddle. Then just run the wire from the pickup through the hole in the saddle so that it's inside the guitar itself. You can put your battery pack and everything in the guitar body itself, of course, but that all connects back to that wire from the pickup. You might need to cut the grooves in the bridge a little deeper to compensate for the pickup being in there. It's real simple once you get past drilling in the bridge because that pickup isn't any bigger

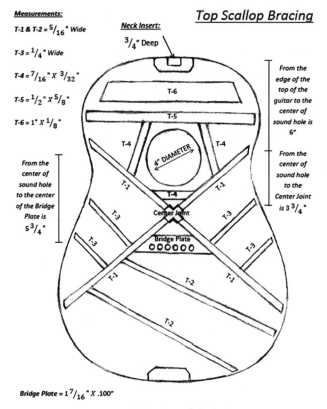

Measurements:

T-1 & T-2 = $^5/_{16}$" Wide

T-3 = $^1/_4$" Wide

T-4 = $^7/_{16}$" X $^3/_{32}$"

T-5 = $^1/_2$" X $^5/_8$"

T-6 = 1" X $^1/_8$"

Neck Insert:
$^3/_4$" Deep

Top Scallop Bracing

From the edge of the top of the guitar to the center of sound hole is 6"

4" DIAMETER

From the center of sound hole to the Center Joint is 3 $^3/_4$"

T-6

T-5

T-4   T-4

T-1   T-1

T-4

Center Joint

From the center of sound hole to the center of the Bridge Plate is 5 $^3/_4$"

T-3   T-3

Bridge Plate

T-3   T-3

T-1   T-1

T-2

T-2

Bridge Plate = 1 $^7/_{16}$" X .100"

PLATE 172 Diagram of top bracing

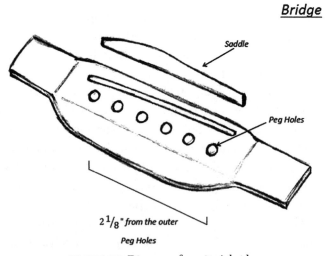

Bridge

Saddle

Peg Holes

2 $^1/_8$" from the outer

Peg Holes

PLATE 173 Diagram of a guitar's bridge

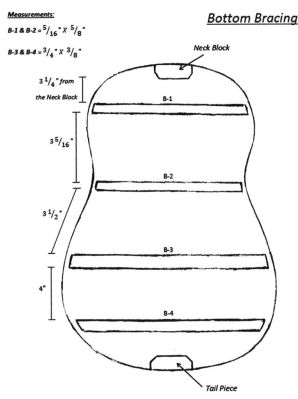

Measurements:

B-1 & B-2 = $^5/_{16}$" x $^5/_8$"

B-3 & B-4 = $^3/_4$" x $^3/_8$"

Bottom Bracing

Neck Block

$3^1/_4$" from the Neck Block

B-1

$3^5/_{16}$"

B-2

$3^1/_2$"

B-3

4"

B-4

Tail Piece

PLATE 171 Diagram of back bracing measurements

have bracing issues. He never put a top on it, and I told him, "You need to at least finish the body where it will be good and solid." He never did, and now the whole thing is flared out. I gave him a nice piece of pretty walnut to make the back out of and everything, but he never finished it. He'll come back one of these days and finish it, hopefully. It would be a good guitar if he'd get it done.

When you're putting pickups [electronics that you can put in acoustic guitars to amplify them] in acoustics, the most important part is working underneath your saddle. Since you are working around the saddle, you have to be very careful because that's such an important part of the instrument. You start by drilling a hole in one end of your saddle. Then just run the wire from the pickup through the hole in the saddle so that it's inside the guitar itself. You can put your battery pack and everything in the guitar body itself, of course, but that all connects back to that wire from the pickup. You might need to cut the grooves in the bridge a little deeper to compensate for the pickup being in there. It's real simple once you get past drilling in the bridge because that pickup isn't any bigger

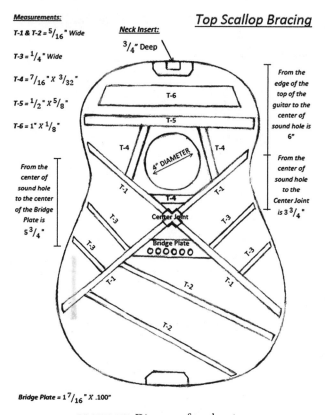

PLATE 172 Diagram of top bracing

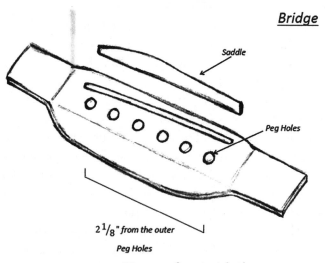

PLATE 173 Diagram of a guitar's bridge

than the saddle itself. It fits right in the saddle groove, and then the saddle sits right on top of it. If a man's going to go the route of putting in a pickup, he might as well go ahead and put the battery pack on it. A lot of them that they have now have the switch and everything you need sitting right inside the sound hole. That way you can control everything, and you don't have to take the risk of cutting into the body.

Personally, I'd rather have one that's "plain Jane" when I'm playing. I like the sound better when they're played through a microphone. They sound better to me.

One of my buddies asked me, "How in the world do you get the sound out of this thing that you get out of it?" I said, "It ain't so much that; it's what's written underneath that soundboard." He said, "What do you mean?" I went over there and got my mirror and said, "Just take a look." There are about twenty-five verses of scripture written on the underside of that soundboard. Every one I build is like that. Whether it be a mandolin, guitar, or whatever. Nobody will ever know that unless they take a mirror and check it out.

Nowadays, guitars are mass-produced so much, you can't even tell what you're getting. In factories, they've got a set of scales that they go by, and if it fits their jig, it goes out the door. It's like they aren't made to play; it's just made to get you started. Even the high-line guitar companies have this problem. If you don't go to them and tell them exactly what you want, it may not meet your expectations. There ain't no telling what might be slightly off if you don't talk to them about it beforehand. As a matter a fact, a boy told me not long ago about something similar to this happening to him. He's got a high-end guitar, and he paid a ton of money for it, but that thing discords [comes out of the tuning] like crazy. He would be playing and switch D to G, and it'd discord every time. I couldn't believe it, being from that particular company and all. He sent it back to them, got it back, and it was in worse shape than what it was before he sent it to them. So, he got it to a custom builder up in North Carolina to fix it. He stripped the fretboard off of it and completely reconstructed the neck, and now you can't beat it. It plays really good, but that was ridiculous to pay five thousand dollars for a guitar and it discord. Another good thing about a custom builder is you can pretty much tell them what style you play, whether it is fingerpicking, flat-picking, or whatever, and they can build a guitar that's best suited for that. In my opinion, getting a custom build is a better investment so that you get a guitar that best suits you.

On Wood

The choice of wood that you use really just depends on the individual you are making it for. I'd say spruce is the best wood to use for the top. Redwood has probably got a better sound than any of it, if you can find some that is really old. Also, Port Orford cedar is a great wood to use, too. I've got some right now that I bought that's two thousand years old. I'm planning on building some guitars out of it. Its grain is so fine, you can't even see it. It's so fine that it looks like plastic just about.

I got ahold of some redwood that came out of an old sinker log that had been sawed back in the day. The tree that it came from was cut back in the 1800s, and that log's been sunk for all these years. It's a pretty wood, and I believe it'll really sound good because it's real tight grain. So, when it comes to body wood, most people use Brazilian rosewood, a lot of people use mahogany, and there are tons that just built them out of plain maple. This latest guitar was made out of ol' straight Rabun County black walnut. It might not be the greatest wood to use, but it works. The age adds a lot to it. The ol' tree that this come out of had been dead for probably fifty years. It was just an ol' stump, and a guy that I worked with told me he was clearing off his old homeplace and ran across a walnut stump. Then he asked me if I wanted it for building material, and of course I said yes. I thought by the way he talked it was just a small stump. One Saturday, I heard something coming in here, and it was him in a big ten-wheel dump truck. A big ten-wheel dump truck. That stump was humongous. It was four or five foot through to the bottom of it. I looked at that thing and said, "I thought you was talking about a little ol' stump." He laughed and said, "It ain't too little, is it?" I sure did get some good wood out of that thing. I've still got a bunch of it propped up against the wall in my shop. There's a bunch of it that's already cut to make guitars out of.

I get the wood for my instruments from a variety of sources. I get it from local trees, and I'll order it, too. Recently, I made a guitar with some top wood that came from Washington State. It was from a spruce that was cut back around 1900. It's some old wood.

Other than what I get locally, I order all of my wood from a place out in Oregon called Oregon Wild Wood. There are a lot of other places that sell wood, but they've always been fair. They don't try to skin you just because they've got what you are looking for. Another cool thing about them is they'll shoot me an e-mail every time they come up with something they think I might like. If you order enough, they'll give you a good discount, too.

Even though I order stuff from out West, I like to use as much local wood I can. I've used walnut and curly maple from right here in the county. It works just as good, but it's hard to find top wood. That's the main thing. You could make a guitar out of cardboard, as far as that goes, if you've got a good top on it, and it's braced up right. I plan on making one out of some plain maple I've got. It's just as straight-grained as it can be, and it'll bend like butter. I've got some stuff here that I do a coat with the guns I make, and I'm going to paint that sucker stainless steel. I want to paint the whole thing like that to see what kind of looks I get out of people. When it's all said and done, it'll look like it's made out of stainless steel from one end to another. I believe it'll work well. It's a real pretty and smooth paint, and that stuff is tough. You can't tear it up, so it would be good on a guitar.

The cool thing about the place that I order from out West is I can go back to their website, run a number off that piece of wood I bought from them, and it'll send me back a detailed information sheet of where that wood came from, how old it is, who sawed it, and the whole nine yards. I have a certification sheet on all the wood I order. I like to keep up with that, too. That way, if anybody asks me what kind of top their instrument has got on it, I can show them everything.

When I'm preparing the wood to make instruments, I take my material and usually rip it down to a quarter of an inch thick. Then, I'll cut my sides to whatever the shape I'm going to make. Next, I run it through a furniture sander. One of my good buddies has a cabinet shop, and he's got one. I tell you, it'll sand that wood down to nothing. It gets it so close, it'll touch itself. I do all my inlay work on them beforehand and just leave it sticking up out of the wood. Then, by the time it's gone through the sander, it's cut down all nice and flat. You can't beat it.

I have some Port Orford cedar that's over two thousand years old. Whenever you tap that stuff, you can hear the vibrations going all the way through it. Judging from the way the vibrations sound, you can tell how good the guitar will sound when it is finished.

I'm planning on building a guitar out of red cedar next. I've never seen one that is made out of it. I believe it will sound good. The good part of it is I can get cedar off the hill right here at the house. I really like to try and make guitars out of the native wood that we've got right around here if I can.

Redwood is so different, it's pitiful. It don't compare to the sound of any other wood. I haven't ever made anything out of it, so I can't really speak from a firsthand experience. It's different. The grain is so fine within the big rays, so much so you can hardly see it. Also, it's stiff and durable, and that's what you need. It'll make a fine guitar. Probably one that's real punchy with a real high-top end on it. The redwood I have probably came out of brine water or brackish salt water. I think that's the case because it came out of the upper end of California. I also have some Port Orford cedar that came from Washington State, and it was already aged at two thousand years. I couldn't believe it. I said, "My goodness!" And the trees don't get much bigger than a five-gallon bucket. They're small trees. I thought they were big trees like the redwood, but they're actually really small. I couldn't believe it. That tree was alive back when Jesus was walking the earth.

> "I don't know why, but I save all my scraps. Eventually, every little piece can add up to something."

I've got some Bearclaw Sitka that I plan on using on a guitar. It was cut in 1920, and it was originally cut to be the soundboards for a piano. Then the company that made the pianos went out of business. So another company bought the wood and [converted] it into guitar tops. Since that time, they had been stacked in an ol' warehouse for all these years.

I don't know why, but I save all my scraps. Eventually, every little piece can add up to something. For example, I have some little pieces of walnut left over from a project that would be the perfect amount to make a pretty peghead [headstock of a guitar]. I've learned not to throw anything away. You'll need it somewhere down the line.

All in all, I like to experiment around with different woods and see how they sound. You find something that you like through trial and error.

On the Building Process

If a man wants to start building them, all he's got to do is get all his jigs and benders. Once you get all that stuff together, then just haul off and build one. All my jigs I use aren't store-bought. Everything I've got tool-wise I built myself. With that being said, really and truly, the guitars I build are one of a kind. Due to the way I build them, they don't match up with any other guitar's size, but they're pretty comfortable. They're not too big, it's not too little, and it's got plenty of sound. That's about all a man can ask for in a flattop guitar anyway.

I have a set of blueprints that I refer back to whenever I'm making an instrument. It shows your brace layout and the sizes of everything that

I put on my instruments. It has everything from your scallop bracing to your maple plate. The reason I really like my prints is because they break down the structure for the whole guitar. I've used them so much; they're about wore-out. It's the same set I've used since I started building them.

My bender is a critical tool when I'm making instruments. The bending process is as simple as pie. There isn't really anything to it, but you've got to be patient with it. There are some strings on mine that hold the wood in place, and of course you have to have clamps on there to hold everything steady. Once you get the wood folded in where you want it, clamp it down. I've got a set of stainless steel slats on my bender, and what I do is I take my wood, and I cut it to size. Then, I'll make a sandwich out of it. Next, I'll dampen the wood with a squirt bottle, roll it up in brown paper, and put it between the two steel slats. I bring it up and roll it to where it lines up with the waist [perimeter] on your guitar body. Once I've got everything situated with that, I've got a heat blanket that I lay over top of it. That blanket keeps it at a constant temperature. My heat blanket isn't anything special, really. It just looks like a piece of rubber mat. That thing gets hot in a hurry, but it's the best way I've found to bend the sides. You can do it the same way as the old-timers, and that is to bend them over a tube. I have tried it that way, but it's just slow going.

PLATE 174 Mr. White's wood bender

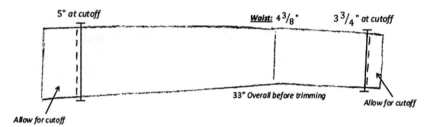

5" at cutoff   **Waist:** 4³/₈"   3³/₄" at cutoff

33" Overall before trimming   Allow for cutoff

Allow for cutoff

PLATE 175 Diagram of side measurements

If you plan on bending them over a tube, you've got to really watch what you are doing because you really don't have any control over the heat. You just have to take what's coming through the tube so the temperature varies. With that blanket I use, I can control it and keep the temperature constant. When the blanket hits 310 degrees [Fahrenheit], I'll stop it right there and run the timer on it. That way, whenever the timer cuts off, my blanket does, too, and my blanket won't burn up.

At this point, I'll crank down on the bender until the wood is pinched so that it's flush with the body and it's standing up in a "V." By this time, the heat blanket has got it good and hot, and I'll start rolling it over because with the heat you can bend it just like plastic. It'll just run right along the shape of the bender just fine.

They say by the time everything cools down that you can pull it out, but I always leave mine in there overnight. That way I can be sure by the time I pull it out, it's set. Then all I've got to do is go to my jig where the guitar body is, stick it in the mold, tighten her down, and it's there.

It's pretty interesting when you bend that stuff. The bending process is what kills most people. It takes some time and patience, and they'll give up. They can't bend it, especially curly. Curly wood is pretty funny stuff to work with. It'll bust all to pieces if you aren't careful.

I mark a line on the wood that indicates where the waist will be. The place where you mark is the same spot where it'll bend and make a "V." After that's completed, the rest of it will wrap around after it gets it good and hot. Once you hear it heating up, you better pay attention because it'll start frying. You'll hear the water getting hot underneath the blanket. That's when you can start cranking down [adjusting] the bender. I've got a temperature gauge that I always set on mine. Once the temperature gets up to 300 degrees on that gauge, I'll start to bend. Then, by the time my timer's about ready to turn off on that blanket, I've got it bent. It doesn't take ten minutes to do. The more time you have to spend with it, the better it will turn and the faster it will get done.

After you've got your sides bent, you've got to have a way to hold them in place. So, once that's done, I square the sides up, and I've got a little hacksaw that I cut them off with. Of course, you've got to have a bracing jig to do all your brace work with, and that's what this rig is right here.

The way my bracing jig works is I bend a set of fiberglass rods so that it'll hold all of my bracing in place. So far, that's the best way to do the bracing that anybody's come up with. The braces are probably the most important assets when you're building. Everything on the instrument is important, but it will always fall back on the braces. You've got to have them right because if you don't, you aren't going to get any sound out of that guitar.

If something cracks while I'm building it, I use this stuff called Acra Glass. I can color the Acra Glass and then fill the crack on the instrument, and you'll never know it was ever cracked after it's sanded down. It will completely hide the crack, and I've learned that it especially works good in walnut.

PLATE 176 Mr. White's bracing jig

You get the sunburst finish on your instruments by dyeing it. I use leather dye on my instruments. You take the leather dye and add alcohol to it to thin it down. Start real thin in the center of the instrument and work your way out to the edges, getting darker until you get the colorization just exactly how you want it. It's pretty neat. Now, a lot of the new ones have the finish sprayed on them. You can tell a difference when you look at them. If you look at ones that are handmade, real close, you can see the difference. I mean, it's blended in and there's no spray marks anywhere. It's just the wood itself.

The biggest step in dyeing them is getting it ready to color. If you're using maple, you've got to be really careful because it's so doggone touchy. The least little thing will scratch it up. You'll have to work the wood up to about eight-hundred-grit sandpaper before you even get to finishing it to where it will look right, whenever you go to dye it, because that dye will show every little scratch. That thing has really got to be slick when you dye it, so it takes longer to sand it to get it ready than it does to dye it. You can dye it in an hour. It doesn't take long at all, but it'll take two or three weeks to get it ready for that hour's worth of dye. You can dye them whatever color you want. Personally, I like to keep mine looking as close to the natural wood itself.

When you're dyeing the wood, you start out real light and thin with your alcohol-base dye. Then, you just work with it and get heavier with the dye until you get the look you're wanting. Roger Siminoff, the author of the instructional book I have, puts the sunburst pattern on his mandolins, too. It's a good chocolate color. It's not an off-the-wall paint like a lot nowadays. Now, he does airbrush his in the real tight spots that are hard to reach with the dye, but all of it, the biggest part of his, is hand-finished.

When it comes to cutting your pearl, a lot of people tell you it's tough to do inlays and stuff, but I like to do it personally. It's fun. I'll cut all kinds of different things out of pearl: crosses, names, animals, or whatever a man wants.

The abalone [pearl] is beautiful. Pearl comes in all kinds of colors. As a matter a fact, when I built Harold's guitar and mandolin, I made all kinds of pearl inlays in them. I made fish inlays for his fretboard. They ran all the way down the neck. On the backside of the peghead of his mandolin, I made a big eagle that was coming in for a landing out of white pearl. Then, on the front, I put a cross, and to top it off, I put a flowerpot on the peghead. I like to put a lot of pearl on one because it makes them special when you decorate them and make it unique. Sometimes, it might take a while if there's a lot of detail, but it's worth it in the end. I have a little jewel cutter's saw that I use to cut it out with.

"I tried for the longest time to get some boys to come and cut inlays for me, but they can't do it. I don't get it. It's not hard to do."

When you're working with a pearl design with a lot of detail, you start by drilling a tiny hole in the wood. If it's like the fish, you'll cut that shape out with your saw. It's a pretty cut-and-dry process. Once you've got your wood how you like it, then you've got your pearl to cut out, too. To cut the pearl out, hold your pearl down with your thumb nice and tight. I glue a piece of paper on it so I can draw my pattern on it. I'll draw my pattern on it and cut it out with the paper on it so I can follow my line. Then all you've got to do is peel that paper off. After that, it's good to go. I use the same wood glue for the pearl work that I use to glue the rest of the instrument together. The most detail I've ever done on an instrument is probably the pegheads on a mandolin.

I tried for the longest time to get some boys to come and cut inlays for me, but they can't do it. I don't get it. It's not hard to do. You just have to be careful not to cut your fingers all to pieces because that little saw, it'll get you. I really enjoy it. I've got a light and a magnifying glass in my shop that I can sit at and cut pearl. I can sit there and do a lot better job because I can see what I'm doing up close.

I'll get requests sometimes to do pearl work down the fretboard. It's not very difficult to do, since the wood is so dark. You can cut the design out and work with your materials so that there isn't anything showing once you work the pearl down [get the pearl flush with the wood]. It's not too bad at all.

As far as pricing my instruments, it just depends on who it is and what they want, just to be honest with you. The fancier the wood and accessories, the more it's going to cost. It just depends. Whenever I make my mandolins, I really try to do them up good with pearl. By the time it's done, I've probably got thirty-five to forty pieces of pearl in them, so that affects [the price]. There's a variety of different colors of pearl you can use. There's abalone, which I like to use in mine. It has a lot of red, green, and purple in it. It's really something. The stuff I have in this latest guitar is just "plain Jane." I've done a lot of pearl work in other instruments like Harold's. I like to decorate my sound hole. It needs a little something on it anyways.

You figure everything out little by little. There's a whole lot to it. A lot of people think it's just a box with a neck and strings on it, but there are a lot of little parts, and those little parts are what ties everything together.

You'd be surprised how many people like my son-in-law, John, make out like it's real easy. John is a real big music man, but he thought he could build one of them in thirty minutes. He found out right quick it was a whole lot tougher than he thought. You've got to have patience because if you don't, you might as well forget it. You'll never be able to make one. All you'll have is a handful of kindling. You can make them however you want, but I'll be honest with you, a real shiny, pretty high-gloss finish is easier to do than a matte finish. I can make one shine like, I mean, a piece of chrome. It'll be so shiny, you can see yourself in it. I'd just rather not do it that way. I like to be able to see the wood instead of the finish—put just enough satin finish on it to be able to see wood.

The hardest thing that someone has ever asked me to do is take an old one and put a new top on it. Now, that's a pretty tricky job. The guitar belonged to Doc Bennett. It was an old guitar that he and one of his buddies had built way back in the 1930s. They had gotten together and decided that they were going to be luthiers. They didn't get too far with that hobby because they only ended up building two. Doc had forgotten all about his, up until his buddy, who built the other one, died. After that, he started looking for that old guitar, but he never did know where to find it. He hunted that old guitar and couldn't find it. So, he brought it up to his mom and said, "Mom, you seen that ol' guitar I built way back?" She said, "Yeah! It's out yonder in the woodshed." He went over to the shed, and it was in the very back in amongst a bunch of junk in there. He dug it out and brought it down here to me. Of course the top of it was caved in and the neck, oh Lord, it was bad. I looked at it and said, "Gosh, I don't know about this, Doc. You got a problem there." He said, "I'd really love to get it going again if you can fix it." I took the ol' booger apart, put a new top on it, lined everything back up, and that's one of the sweetest-sounding ol' guitars you'll ever listen to. The age of the wood and all gave it a great sound.

The bracing pattern in the guitar is one that they came up with theirselves. It was really different altogether. When they had made their back bracing, they had cut little bitty pieces and fit them all together. By the time it was done, it was in a fan shape all the way around the back of it. It was laid out in a really unique way. It wasn't anything fancy at all. It was just all ol' rough sawed stuff, and I couldn't believe how good that thing sounded after I got the top on it. Man, it sounded good! Luckily, the neck was bolted on, believe it or not. They had taken lag screws, screwed them in the neck, and put nuts on the back of them to hold it on. Just by looking at it, I thought to myself, "This thing will never straighten up." Then, after I got the top good and straight, got a new set of bracing in it, and all the other necessities, it every bit just come right back just pretty and straight.

My preacher came up to me one Sunday morning and said, "Danny, come down here to the office. I've got to show you something." I said, "Oh, gosh, what have you found now?" He said, "You ain't going to believe this." I got to his office, and he showed me a 1941 model Gibson dreadnought that he found in a pawnshop in Clayton. He told me he had looked at that guitar half a dozen times when he was in the pawnshop. He'd bumped his head on it looking at guns. He said he moved it out of the way when it was hanging there and never thought anything of it. The last time he went in [and] bumped his head on it, and just happened to look through the sound hole, and saw an orange sticker in it, he made out a "G" on it. He took a good look at that thing again, and thought, "No, it can't be." It was as black as coal and looked really nasty. He said he asked that boy at the pawnshop how much he wanted for that ol' guitar. It had a price tag that was around seventy-nine dollars. The boy told him, "I'll give it to you for forty bucks, preacher." So, he bought that thing, took it home, and rubbed down the peghead with some Dawn soap. As soon as he did, the word Gibson just jumped right out at him.

He got a man named Bobby Downs to clean it and re-fret it. Bobby kept that thing for three or four months before he finally called Scott [the preacher] and told him to come get the guitar before he wore it out. By the time Bobby was done with it, you talk about a sweet guitar! He put a new bone nut and saddle on it and made a real nice guitar out of it. Scott told me he'd never get rid of it, and I'll be a son of a gun if he didn't mess around and trade it. He traded it for two high-end guitars.

I had a boy bring me a banjo a while back. I had redone his guitar and put a new fretboard and everything on it for him a little while earlier. He had me re-fret it for him. He called me the evening he was coming to pick up his guitar. While we were on the phone, he asked me, "Danny, have you ever worked on a banjo?" I told him I had before, and he said, "Well, I've got one and I can't keep the thing in tune for nothing." Well, a little later he came through the door for his guitar, and he was holding something behind his back. He pulled that thing out and said, "Here, tune this thing." I laughed when I first saw it because it's got a Prince Albert Tobacco can for the tailpiece on it. I thought, "Now, that's a man wanting to make music, wasn't it?" So, now I'm working on his ol' 1946 model Gibson Mastertone banjo for him. When he first brought it, it had big holes wore in it where it'd been played so much. So, I filled it and I'm going to redo it. I'm going to re-fret it for him, too. It still has the original inlays from when it was built. That's one reason I went ahead and filled it. I didn't want to mess the originals up. My plan is to re-fret it, and then I'll work it back down, smooth and flat. Then, once that's all finished, I'll put new frets on it. I've got the fret wire already.

I have an old Harmony guitar made back around 1940 that belonged to my good friend Henry Ezzard. He actually passed away last year, unfortunately, so I'm going to finish fixing up his ol' guitar and take it and give it to his wife. When I first got ahold of it, you wouldn't believe it if I was to tell you what shape it was in. You couldn't even tell what it was. It was as black as coal. He didn't have a case or anything for it. He had found it at a pawnshop down in Atlanta. It didn't have a bridge on it. So, I made a bridge for it. The doggone neck looked like a rocking chair's rocker. I got to looking at it, and he said, "It probably isn't worth fixing." I told him, "We haven't got anything to go by, but I'll do the best I can." It's got a big ol' piece of mahogany for the back on it. I believe it'll sound really good when it's done. A cool thing about it is the binding's made from red tortoise shell. The top is made from hand-carved spruce. You just don't see guitars like that anymore. I've just got a little left on it. I've still got to put a pick guard on it, and make a little piece that screws on the side and elevates the pick guard. I've got some blank pick guards that I use. It's kind of a unique guitar because this model was usually made from pressed plywood, but that is all hand carved. You can see the grain in the wood and tell that. He didn't give hardly anything for it, since it was in such bad shape. It didn't have any strings or a bridge on it, and that thing was black as soot. It'd evidently been hanging up in a room somewhere where it was exposed to smoke and got covered in it. I got the soot off of it with Dawn dishwashing liquid, but it took a whole bunch of time and rubbing.

My best advice for anyone who is getting into building instruments is you just have to go at it. There's a lot more to building an instrument than what you think. Once you've got all your jigs, and you understand all the basics and how everything works, it's not too bad. The most critical thing is your fretboard and your layout because if you don't do it right, you'll have major problems on down the road. When I first started, I was worried that bending the wood would've been where all my problems would be, but fortunately, I didn't have any problem with that.

WISDOM
of
OUR ELDERS

My Most Valuable Possession

I can tell you what a man ought t' want.

—*Mrs. Grover Bradley*

Throughout history, people have always found objects that they hold close. In the course of its fifty years, Foxfire has documented how seemingly simple, day-to-day objects can become much more than tangible goods. Driving through these mountains, you may see an old woodshed that is falling apart and fiscally worthless. However, the hands that built that lean-to shed found value and beauty in the same bowed-up wood. You may see a beat-up old anvil alongside a splintered hammer, but the blacksmith may see the shaping of his town, and the feeding of his family, with every ring of that same anvil. Significant items can be anything from a photograph to a house and serve almost as a time capsule to the owners. In 1970, students set out to find what each of our earliest contacts valued most. In this technological world, we found their answers fascinating, in their simplicity and in their resourcefulness.

—*Katie Lunsford*

OLD-TIMERS SHARE WHAT IS NEAR AND DEAR TO THEM

"Well, I think a cookstove would be the really importantest thing for a woman. I know when we children was at home, I can remember th' first cookstove that they ever bought. And a cow. That helped make th' livin' most of anything there was. We'd keep milk in th' spring, make butter, cheese, buttermilk.

"I think if a man was around th' house, a cow and horses and hogs would be th' best. That 'ud run th' home. You got t' have a horse on th' farm. And then you had t' have your cows, and you had t' have your meat. And if you had that, you could nearly live with a little bread. You sure could. I think that 'ud be the importantest thing for a man to begin with.

"A dog? Leave that dog out fer me! No, I don't want a dog. I always loved a cow, but never give me a dog. I like cats, but I don't want 'em in th' house. If you have 'em in the house, they'll sure get on th' table."

—Pearl Martin

"Back in th' olden time, why, it'd have t' be a horse or a mule or a yoke of steers t' do th' chores like gettin' th' wood, plowin', settin' th' crops. I imagine that'd be as useful a thing as they could a' brought in. In th' farmin' on up till I 'uz a grown man, all we had on th' farm with us was a yoke a' steers." —Jake Waldroop

"Families, whenever they'd move to a' isolated or unsettled part a' th' country, they had t' have an anvil t' beat their plow points on, sharpen 'em out. And lots of 'em then would want a spinnin' wheel. And a gun—they'd want a gun fer sure—and a' ax. That was four articles that I'd say took predominance over ever'thing else that they'd want t' bring. And mattocks to dig them Hoover onions with!" —Les Waldroop

"Well, I think the most important thing that I had was a good father and mother. When I was a small girl in a family of eight children, my father raised a lot of vegetables of different kinds in his garden, and he also raised a lot of hogs. And he had a big syrup boiler near th' garden that he cooked the vegetables for his hogs in. He usually did that late in the evening after the day's work was done, and he'd stand around the boiler and stir the vegetables." —Ada Kelly

"If you're startin' out, you need cooking utensils, and you'd have t' have a place t' sleep. Of course, that would say you'd have t' have a' ax t' cut your wood t' cook with and t' make a tent 'r some kind of shelter. I just don't know what comes first. I couldn't say that one could help without th' other, but I guess you'd have t' have an ax to begin t' cut with, and then we'd have t' find somethin' t' cook in.

"The pioneers carried very little. My grandmother came over th' mountain when my father was just a little boy and settled down on the Hiwassee River from Murphy, North Carolina. An' we lived in a log cabin—that's where I was born. Th' lake now, below Murphy, covers my birthplace. I went back there two years ago and couldn't get within two miles of th' place for th' lake. Oh, I could have in a boat, but I never had th' courage t' ride in it." —**Harriet Echols**

"Th' plow is just about the most important thing on th' farm. And a mule at that. Couldn't have had no crops 'r nothin' without it, th' land was so rough.

"Yeah, a mule, unless a man had a yoke a' cattle. They done plowin' and wagonin'. We used a mule to a sled and th' cattle t' th' wagon. Hauled th' corn. You know, people could make a livin', yet, wi' just a yoke a' cattle, when y' think about it. Be about th' best thing folks around here could use on th' plowin' field." —**Lester Addis**

"A good ax. Most people valued them so much they'd take 'em inside at night and put 'em under th' bed. Man I know kep' it there till he died. You could put up a house with one, hew crossties fer money, cut firewood, saw logs—oh law, law th' many things. It'd be bad doin' without an ax right now." —**Mann Norton**

"My butcher knife, my churn jar, and my quiltin' frame. You had t' butcher meat with a butcher knife. When they killed hogs, they'd holler fer my knife. I've wore out many a one." —**Mrs. Mann Norton**

"A Bible, clothes, and furniture. I'd take a Bible because it has all the directions for being a Christian, and you just might forget how to be one out there in the woods." —**Mary Brown**

"Water. You'd soon die without water. Cook with it. Wash with it. Takes water t' make wood; to put fires out. That was th' first thing that was ever made—the great seas. Read th' Bible." —**Jim Edmonds**

"Home. You got to have a place t' live and be." —**Algie Norton**

"A stove. Got t' cook. A quilt would come next. You'd want to stay warm when you went to bed. It really takes several things all at once. Got t' have somethin' to cook. And they ain't nothin' much better than a good cow.

"I can tell you what a man ought t' want. He ought t' have a home when he marries. Got t' have a place t' go to. 'Course, th' old people would say a horse and a plow." —**Mrs. Grover Webb**

"A horse. We couldn't a' farmed without it. Had t' plow, grind the cane inta syrup, bring th' logs in for fire. And had t' go t' town sometime. Couldn't a' made out without one." —**Deffie Hamilton**

"Th' plow t' plow with. Y' had t' have a single-foot and a cultivator. Couldn't grow any food—not without that. Man 'ud starve without them." —**Milford Hamilton**

"A bed, food, and a person. I'd want a bed to be up away from snakes and spiders!" —**Myrtle Mason**

"A Bible, clothes, and food. I'd take a Bible because it can tell you things that you can't find anywhere else." —**Mrs. Tommy Lee Norton**

"Consideration for others. Don't destroy for people to rebuild. Don't waste so that other people must spare. Take care of everything, whether belonging to you or anyone else so that they, as well as you, will have something to be proud of." —**Jim Heuser**

"I would think my father's mules because that's what he farmed—used to make his crops with. I would think that would have been his most valuablest thing. And he used them for going back and forth to market and hauling wood. That was the biggest way people had in getting around. They didn't have any other way." —**Beulah Perry**

"I'd a' thought it was a milk cow. Well, she gave milk, y' know. Y' make butter, drink the milk. Y' could save th' droppin's an' you could put it on yer garden." —**Jean Eller**

"Well, th' most important thing I had, I liked m' sheep. Yes, well, b'cause they were gentle; they were pretty when they were little; I liked all animals. That's why I said I wadn't no housekeeper! I've helped take care of the hogs, an' sheep, an' I've milked since I was twelve years old—that's the reason I like outdoor life." —**Annie Perry**

REMEMBERING WHEN THE WORLD WAS BLACK-AND-WHITE

Stories from a Simpler Time

What my part of Appalachia had in common with other parts, for a long time, was isolation from the mainstream of American life and neglect by both our state and national governments. The neglect has only partly been addressed. Yet things are changing—almost from day to day.

—*James Still*

When we was growin' up back then, people had more love for each other than they have today. People has lost their love for each other.

—*Lois Martin*

While working at Foxfire a few summers ago with leadership students from the current *Foxfire Magazine* class, Jon Blackstock and I were taking a much-needed, short break on the front porch of the Carnesville House cabin, listening to the birds chirp and enjoying the pure, unspoiled mountain air. Two visitors to the Foxfire Museum and Heritage Center approached. They stopped to listen to two brief excerpts from interviews, with two of our earliest interviewees, Luther Rickman and Aunt Arie Carpenter, which are set up on the porch for visitors to hear. Although Jon and I have heard them so many times that we almost know them by heart, we all listened reverently. After the last bit of Aunt Arie's voice faded into the stillness of the late afternoon, we began to converse.

The visitors weren't from here. Best I can remember, they were from South Carolina, but both were huge fans of Foxfire. The lady, whose name I regret not getting, began talking about her memories of the past. The stories were very similar to the ones Foxfire students have shared in the magazine and books for almost fifty years now. As they turned to go on down the trail to the next cabin, the lady said she remembered when the world was black-and-white, when you could count on your neighbors for anything, when you didn't have to worry about crime, when television shows upheld our morals. She pined for all she felt had been lost—the innocence, the trust, the random kindness shown to others—things she wanted her grandkids to know and to experience.

Jon and I looked at each other, and Jon said, "Wow! What a great title for a story!" Thus, the title to this chapter was created! So, random lady with a depth of feelings, thank you for inspiring us, just as countless others, both readers and interviewees, have done so many times over the years.

Much of our inspiration comes from the abundance of storytellers who seem to grow in our hills and valleys like mountain laurel on a creek bank. They weave their stories together with vivid descriptions, delightful characters, plausible events, and sage advice, capturing our attention and drawing us into their world.

Years ago, when *The Foxfire Book* was published, readers were introduced to Aunt Arie Carpenter. She lived alone in a log cabin without running water. She drew her water from a well and grew most of her own food. She taught us a lot about life, love, sacrifice, and dignity. There can never be another Aunt Arie. She meant so much to everyone she met, either personally or through the pages of *The Foxfire Book*. Her only mode of transportation was on foot, by wagon, or on the old Tallulah Falls Railroad. She had never seen a movie, but did occasionally walk to her nephew's house to see a television show. She and her contemporaries lived a life of simplicity, hardship, and sacrifice, but her sincerity, faith, and common sense were an inspiration to millions. In this section we introduce you to a few more of Aunt Arie's mountain peers: Edgar Owens, Francis Harbin, Johnny "the Big Cat" Mize, and Lois and Clarence Martin. There are still a few left who remember life in the early part of the twentieth century.

We also introduce you to another generation of Appalachians who grew up in the 1940s. They had more opportunities, further education, and greater exposure to the outside world, but still they maintained their Appalachian identity and values. Their connection to these mountains, these people, and the moral backbone of their forebears are evident in their life stories. They still see the world in terms of right and wrong, or black-and-white. They still embrace a love for their fellow man and give us hope that this thread of boundless love will be woven as strongly into future generations, as it was woven into them.

We also share here James Still's life story. Just like a lot of the people in our community today, Mr. Still wasn't born in Appalachia. Born in 1906, he came to Kentucky as a teacher in the 1930s. He fell in love with the people and place and made it his home for the remainder of his life. Along the way he, too, documented stories and sayings of the people around him, wrote eloquent poems and stories, and became an integral part of our deep-seated and enduring culture.

A lot has changed from Aunt Arie's day till now, but I take enormous comfort and hope in the fact that in this day and age, there are still people with principles, kindness, and life lessons to impart. In this chapter, you will encounter people whose stories are insightful, inspiring, and thought-provoking; people who feel blessed to have called these mountains home their entire lives; people who were born here, left, and had the good fortune to return; and people who were not born here, but have become an integral part of our communities and of this place we so proudly call home.

—*Kaye Carver Collins*

"I'VE TRAVELED A BIT, YET I KEEP COMING BACK LIKE IRON FILINGS TO A MAGNET"

An interview with James Still

I didn't own a camera either. Nobody in my community had one. What I did was to trace the hands of the old-timers, about a dozen of them. Next to the photograph of a face, I think the hand speaks volumes. —James Still

We conducted two interviews with James Still: one in our classroom and one in Hindman, Kentucky, where Mr. Still lives. He was very expressive in using his hands and changing his facial features to press a point he was making. His eyes may have seemed sad, but they were active, flitting from face to face and giving us each bright, keen glances as he answered our questions. His eyebrows arched and thickened on the outer edges, giving the impression that he was constantly surprised.

After we completed the interview and Mr. Still returned to Kentucky, we discovered that more questions arose from the material we had covered. We scheduled a second interview to be conducted at the Hindman Settlement School, where Still served during the Depression as the librarian. His house is a few miles away.

Although Mr. Still now lives inside the city limits of Hindman, he still owns the house on Dead Mare Branch that was willed to him by Jethro Amburgey. When he wants to get away to a quiet place to write, he still goes to the two-room log house.

Over the years, Mr. Still would hear phrases, stories, or anecdotes that seemed worth writing down. These were tidbits that came about through the natural course of conversation; he discovered things that could never be captured by a tape recorder on an interview. Still would make a mental note of these conversation excerpts, or jot them down on any available piece of paper and later record them in one of the many loose-leaf notebooks that he uses especially for this purpose. On occasion, he would use some of these excerpts in his writing, since the characters and locations were from the Appalachian region, the very same region from which he gathered the contents of the notebooks. From his "writer's notebook" he selected a varied sample of excerpts that exemplify the material contained therein, with the intention of producing a piece of literature that captures a distinct facet of Appalachian culture— oration.

When Still first considered allowing us to print quotations from his notebooks, he worried that spoken words and expressions could lose a certain value when written. The tone of the narrator's voice, his inflections, his hands, and his facial expressions all combine to give greater meaning and substance to words. A second reservation came from his concern that the majority of the notebook excerpts are not flashy or sensational but are rather homespun, quiet images of his community.

To the very last, we could only guess at the reason Still decided, finally, to allow the material to be published. On the last pages he sent us, he provided the answer himself: "The first notebook entry was recorded some forty-five years ago. Most of the participants are dead. Save for their gravestones, this is the only record for some that they lived and laughed and wept and had opinions like the rest of us. I have long tried to speak for them. Here they are speaking for themselves." The book, *The Wolfpen Notebooks*, published by the University Press of Kentucky, was the result of Still's decision to publish. What follows is the story of how he came to call the hills of Kentucky home.

—*Laura Lee*

My paternal grandparents were William Watson Still and Annie McClendon Still, and my mother's parents were James Benjamin Franklin Lindsey and Carrie Jackson Lindsey. My forebears from both sides first settled in Virginia during pioneer days. The Lindseys set down near Berryville and the Stills, what is now Lee County near Jonesville. There's a roadside marker at Jonesville noting the birthplace of Alfred Taylor Still, the man who conceived the medical system of osteopathy. Jonesville is up the road from Cumberland Gap, where I came to attend college in 1924. I didn't know then I was completing a genealogical circle. We've figured that my ancestors fought in the American Revolution and that frontier land was allotted them as reward for their services: the Lindseys in Georgia, the Stills in Alabama, and not many miles apart.

My mother, Lonie Lindsey Still, grew up on a farm near Franklin, Georgia. Her mother, my grandma, had been married before to a Civil War soldier who lost his life in the struggle to head off Sherman in the march toward Atlanta. Grandpa was an orphan; three years younger than Grandma and having never seen his father, he could cure thrush in children. Uncle Edd told me that during my mother's childhood the floor of their Georgia home where the cookstove was, was beaten earth. The move to Alabama, some three miles from the Stills, may have been spurred by the destruction of the home by a cyclone. Beforehand, Grandpa mined enough gold on his land to fill his teeth.

Grandpa Still fought in the Civil War and suffered a wound to the body and had a finger shot off by a Yankee bullet. I recall his discussing with a comrade the mining of the Confederate trenches by the North at Petersburg toward the end of the conflict. He regularly attended Old Soldiers' conventions in Richmond, Montgomery, New Orleans, or wherever held.

There were ten of us children, five girls and five boys. The sisters came first; I am the eldest son. There are only two of us left today. When my parents first married, they homesteaded in Texas in 1893, and two children were born there. I would have been born in Texas had my parents not come back to Alabama on a visit and one of my little sisters died of scarlet fever. Just before she died, she asked my mother not to leave her, and so Mama never would go back to Texas and leave her grave. The cotton farm Papa cultivated is now a part of the Fort Hood reservation, and I suppose is regularly plowed by tanks and heavy artillery.

I was born in 1906 on Double Branch farm just outside of Lafayette [Alabama]. Sometimes I tell people I was born in a cotton patch. Anyhow, I came to consciousness there. One of my first memories is of running about with a small sack on my back that Mama had sewed up for me. I'd pick a boll here and yonder and everywhere. Along about the time I was eight, I took the job of milking the cow. I recollect going out barefoot on cold mornings and the cow stepping on my foot. Before starting to milk into the bucket, I'd scoot a stream into my mouth, and a couple into the cat's mouth.

"A garden was her pleasure. She had a good one—a picture one. Some of that attitude rubbed off on me. Few people were ever able to suit me plumb in my own."

My mother was a worker. She had to be to raise ten children, to cook, to make most of our clothes, do the laundry and ironing, the canning and preserving, and keeping house. Besides this, she quilted, crocheted, embroidered, and tatted. When she could find a free hour, she joined us in the fields. She believed in children working as well, and could always find something for us to do, except when we were doing our studying.

My father was a "horse doctor," a veterinarian without formal training, and a farmer as well. He managed both by hiring a workhand to plow and lay by, and with the family's help. Cotton was the main crop—some corn, sugarcane, sorghum, and soybeans. And there was Mama's garden. Papa would plow it, and afterward she wouldn't let anybody else in it to work. A garden was her pleasure. She had a good one—a picture one. Some of that attitude rubbed off on me. Few people were ever able to suit me plumb in my own.

We children worked alongside our parents, hoeing and chopping, and picking and pulling. Fodder is not thought much of now as stock feed, but back then, we pulled every blade and tied it in bundles and hung it on the stripped stalks. My sisters wouldn't work within sight of the road. And to keep from getting a suntan and freckles, they rubbed their faces with cream and wore stockings on their arms and wide-brimmed hats on their heads. By the age of twelve I could pick a hundred pounds of cotton a day.

Before I was old enough to be enrolled in school, I'd sometimes go with my sisters. It was a two-mile walk, and they often had to carry me part of the way, usually on the way back. I was very small for my age; the only child to have to stand on a box to reach the blackboard. The teacher once asked me why I didn't come to school more often, and they tell me I replied, "I would wust Mama would let me."

I had a wonderful teacher in the first grade, a Miss Porterfield. The first day of school, she wrote my name in chalk on my desk, and handed me an ear of corn, and told me to shell the kernels and make an outline of my name. We did this many times over, and by the end of the day, I had learned its shape and could write it on paper.

Those were stirring and changing times. We soon had a T-Model Ford, a telephone, screen doors, subscriptions to the Georgia *Tri-Weekly Constitution*, *Farm and Fireside*, and the *Southern Cultivator*.

The boll weevil arrived, and nut grass. World War I was being fought. Schoolchildren gathered newsprint to take to school, where it was rolled into tight bundles, dipped in hot paraffin, and sent to France as trench candles. My sister, Inez, won the fifty-yard dash on field day, and the prize of a box of chocolate candy. After we had gobbled up the first layer, and found a second beneath, it was like discovering gold at Sutter's mill.

Aside from the Holy Bible, in our house there were three books: *The Anatomy of the Horse*, the *Palaces of Sin, or the Devil in Society*, and a heavy volume with a missing back, *Cyclopedia of Universal Knowledge*.

The *Cyclopedia* opened my eyes to the world. Many a subject was covered, such as you'll find in a modern reference work. And more still: how to prune a fruit tree, the language of flowers, rules for games, the art of social correspondence, good manners, twenty-five sample words in several languages, a collection of classic poems. I got the poems by heart.

I wrote my first story when I was eight or nine. I still have it. I titled it "The Golden Nugget," and it was written with a lead pencil on a school tablet—hard to read now, after seventy years. I found it recently, and I'll declare that I saw my future in the piece. A foreshadowing, you might say, of all the scribbling to come. You might not catch it, but I did. It was not going to be the last. The itch to write was there. Along about that time my teacher was reading poems and stories to the class from *The Youth's Companion,* and I had read my first classic, Robert Louis Stevenson's *Treasure Island.* Both undoubtedly caused me to want to tell stories and write poems of my own.

I started a little magazine when I was ten. I had one subscriber, my sister, Elloree, who was married and lived nearby. She had a box of folded stationery, and I used enough sheets to make an eight-page issue. I made up stories, which had to be pretty short, and I wrote poems for it. I wrote everything in it. I did a number of them; I don't remember how many. When I was eleven, I made a tent out of croker [burlap] sacks and pitched it in the yard and wrote a poem in it. I still can recite it except for one line. It is stilted and formal. I used the word "dawn" instead of "morning." Yet, considering my age, it wasn't too bad a beginning. I was trying.

When I was in high school, I started a novel. It was about the sea. I had never seen the ocean, but that didn't stop me. I remember I wrote a while every night. I don't know what became of the manuscript. One summer I kept a notebook, a diary of sorts. It's not what is there that interests me now; it's what I *didn't* mention, what I failed to put in. It

PLATE 177 James Still

tells an awful lot about me. I left out all the things I think are important nowadays. I never mentioned my parents, and hardly my brothers and sisters. I seemed not to be doing anything that summer except picking blackberries and going "washing" as we called it—swimming. And I was regularly playing baseball, the things boys do.

> *"I became an author without expecting to be . . . I just wanted to write things down, to play with words."*

The boys I ran with claimed they wanted to be either cowboys or railroad engineers. I don't think I made a choice that early. It wouldn't have been either. None of them followed through. The ones I know about became weavers, or mechanics, in a cotton duck mill in the town, except one who became a textile superintendent. He had us all skinned in the schoolroom.

I became an author without expecting to be. I don't recall the slightest encouragement from childhood all the way through my school years.

I didn't know about writing as a profession, something I'd be doing now and then all of my life. Nobody else in my family ever wrote or published anything. There was no precedent for me. I just wanted to write things down, to play with words. At first I had in mind writing a single poem—no thought of composing a second. Then, within a couple of weeks, another idea would pop into my head. The same with short stories; I'd compose one, and was satisfied for a while, an' along would come another, and another.

All that was in Alabama; I had started high school in Shawmut and attended two years. Then we moved to Jarrett Station, a short distance from Fairfax, a textile factory town. I attended Fairfax High School and graduated in 1924. I never got to read the great books until I attended Lincoln Memorial University, which was over the ridge from Cumberland Gap, Tennessee. I arrived with sixty dollars in my pocket, and I was starved for reading material. Every student earned his keep at LMU, and after morning classes, I worked afternoons in the rock quarry, feeding a rock crusher, and was the library janitor. When the library closed at night, I swept the floors and emptied the wastebaskets and rubbed up the tables; then, with the door locked, the several thousand books and collection of magazines were mine until daylight. Many times I stayed the night, too drowsy to make it to the dormitory, and slept on newspapers in the storage room. I was like a child in a candy store. I hardly knew where to start. Somehow, I found Thomas Hardy, Joseph Conrad, Hawthorne, and Walt Whitman. The library was what Lincoln Memorial meant to me. I was saved by it.

At the library I happened on *The Atlantic*, about the most prestigious publication in those days. The library received gift subscriptions of several copies of each issue, and after one was filed, I had instructions to put the others in the furnace. What I did was save copies for myself. Those were the times of the Great Depression, and I had no employment, so I spent the summer reading—all of them—every article, every poem, and every word. I practically ate the paper. I learned from them more than I can state, even the art of composition, if it can be said I ever attained it. I decided to write for *The Atlantic*, first and foremost. The odds were great, however.

I began sending verses to them. I kept getting rejection slips, but I didn't let them bother me. Eventually, I got a more personal rejection, which read, "We at *The Atlantic* have enjoyed reading your manuscript, but regret we cannot use it," and written in ink, "Try us again." Finally, they accepted a poem called "Child of the Hills," my first serious publication—sort of started at the top, you might say. Since then, they have published three poems and ten short stories.

The class of 1929, my class at Lincoln Memorial, was unique. Some ferment was at work. More than one hundred books have been published by its members, which include Jesse Stuart, who was to earn fame as a labor organizer and activist.

At Lincoln I was holding a work scholarship provided by a benefactor, as did most of the others. When I was a graduate, I found out his name and address and invited him to the ceremony. Although he had assisted many a student, this was his first invitation. His name was Guy Loomis. Afterwards, Mr. Loomis offered to pay my way to a graduate school of my choice in the South. He also said, "I'll make it possible, not easy." That proved to be the case. I chose Vanderbilt University.

On graduating in June, my benefactor offered one more term of schooling, and in September I was off to the University of Illinois. A year later I was back home with three diplomas, no job, and no prospects. One of my professors, whom I had in some way displeased, had predicted that I would end up driving a team of mules hitched to a wagon. The prophecy began to seem not too far-fetched.

Then, I came to Knott County, Kentucky, to help Don West and his wife, Connie, with a vacation Bible school and a recreational program. While in Knott County, I stayed a week at the Hindman Settlement School in the late thirties. When I returned home, they sent a letter offering a job as a volunteer worker. They would shelter and feed me, but couldn't pay me. I was willing, having no other prospects.

The teachers were mostly women—graduates of Wellesley, Vassar, and Smith. My assignment was the library. The library was rich in good books, and once a week—my own enterprise—I delivered a box of them on foot to some eight schools. A common cry from the schoolhouse door was, "Here comes the book boy."

"When I first moved in, I didn't know anybody. Getting acquainted didn't take long, for I began to attend community happenings, depending on the season—bean stringings, corn shuckings, molasses making, and hog killings."

I worked three years without pay. With the times improving, the fourth year I was awarded fifteen dollars a month. The publication of a few poems and short stories had kept me in razor blades and socks.

And I'd published my first book, a collection of poems reviewers were uncommonly kind to. As I tell it, I was so rich, I retired. On a day in June 1939, I moved to an old log house between Dead Mare Branch and Wolfpen Creek, facing Little Carr Creek. The log house I moved into was built in 1827; I went there to finish writing the novel *River of Earth*, for which the Viking Press had offered a contract. I had found a home.

When I first moved in, I didn't know anybody. Getting acquainted didn't take long, for I began to attend community happenings, depending on the season—bean stringings, corn shuckings, molasses making, and hog killings. Sam and John M. Stamper and "Shorty" Smith were my cronies. Sundays we would ramble the hills searching for ginseng, or pawpaws, or cane patches for fishing poles, or just looking. We visited old graves and half-forgotten home seats, and I listened to their tales. As I arrived in early summer, it was late to start a garden, but I did anyhow, and as the fronts held off until mid-October, I had a garden full of "sass"—sweet corn, beans, squash, okra, cushaw [squash], tomatoes, cucumbers, and cabbage. Come March, I had my own cornstalks to burn when everybody else set fire to theirs the same evening, and children danced about the flames, a rite of spring.

In those Depression days, the people on Wolfpen and Little Carr lived almost without money. There was no welfare, no food stamps—virtually no health services. Honestly, to this day I don't know how many

PLATE 178 James Still with Foxfire students at
Hindman Settlement School in Kentucky

survived. They did grow big gardens and potato patches and a lot of corn, and they had pigs usually, and most had a cow—not all. Still, you need more, don't you? With children in school, how did they keep shoes on their feet?

Later, I got to know the coal camps. Actually, I don't see how the miners made it either. They lived out of the company store. The coal companies paid them in script—their own money, so to speak. They couldn't use the script except in the company store, and the prices were usually jacked up. They received little in cash. At the end of the two-week period, they often owed the store all, or nearly everything, they had earned.

There are a lot of natural-born storytellers, and I've encountered them here and there. In Wash Vance's store—seated on lard cans and feed sacks at Bluestone in Rowan County—in churchyards—on courthouse steps—oral storytellers. I can't name the exact year I started jotting down things they said in notebooks. I did it only for my own eyes. You might say they were written to inform stories and poems to come, yet I never thumbed through looking for an idea or a quotation. To write it fixed it in memory. The purpose of the notebooks was to cover every facet of life in my community, as well as all of the county, and the counties adjoining. Nobody ever saw the notebooks until Foxfire asked to examine them. Before then I'd never considered publication. I did come to believe they might, in future, be of interest to folklorists and social historians.

I wanted only the meaningful, *telling* statement. I might extract a single sentence from a long conversation. As for a collection of oral statements such as I did record in writing, while many may not seem much in themselves, taken as a whole, I believe they offer a picture of the region not otherwise provided—another aspect.

I didn't own a camera either. Nobody in my community had one. What I did was to trace the hands of the old-timers, about a dozen of them. Next to the photograph of a face, I think the hand speaks volumes. Form dictates function, it is said. These are the hands of men who used them as tools to make a living on the land and under it—in the fields and in the coal mines. Missing are tracings of women's hands. At that time it was not what you would ask a woman to allow you to do.

"To be unlettered is not necessarily to be unintelligent. I've traveled a bit, yet I keep coming back like iron filings to a magnet. Here, we are more conscious of the individual. Everybody is somebody."

Now and then I still hear remnants of the language spoken by Chaucer and the Elizabethans, such as "sass" for vegetables, "hit" for it, or "fit" for fight. People here are more likely to express themselves in an original manner than any place I know. I think it is something to celebrate. I don't want or expect Appalachian speech to be like any other. It has its own individuality, its own syntax. To be unlettered is not necessarily to be unintelligent. I've traveled a bit, yet I keep coming back like iron filings to a magnet. Here, we are more conscious of the individual. Everybody is somebody.

Some of the people who come into the area expect to meet up with barefoot men packing hog rifles and wearing black hats plugged with bullet holes, the "hillbilly" stereotype. Naturally, if a visitor lingers a while, he'll notice regional differences in speech and attitudes. Yet, he'll find that human nature operates pretty much as elsewhere.

So, personally, I've never been bothered about being called a "hillbilly" or "briar." They're synonymous—the "samelike," as we say. I count it an honor except when used as a slur. I was pleased when talking to a "gear grinder" in a restaurant in Jackson who thought I drove a coal truck. After he had learned otherwise, and we had conversed a spell, he said, "You talk smart, but you've got hillbilly wrote all over you."

What my part of Appalachia had in common with other parts, for a long time, was isolation from the mainstream of American life and neglect by both our state and national governments. The neglect has only partly been addressed. Yet things are changing—almost from day to day. My nearest neighbor is spending the winter in Florida. There was a time when the road to his door was the creek bed. Many saw service in the three wars of our day. They've had a glimpse of the world.

Roads, telephones, and shopping malls—this would appear to be all good. It's opened up the world and broken down barriers. Most families have a car, or truck, and move about on roads as slick as ribbon. Jasper Mullins told me a while back he failed to make a garden because he had bought a television set and didn't have time to tend one. There are losses. A sense of community is lost. Around me natural gas wells have done away with the fireplace, which represents the cement, which holds family and neighbor together. Between me and even the middle-aged, there is mostly a "Howdy," or a "Hey-o." That's partly due to the generation gap. I'm considered an old-timer. There's only one other alive on my creek. We're survivors—yesterday's people.

I've always viewed myself as running toward the world, not away from it. I need people. They're my stock in trade. And I want a few of them to need me. William Peden in *The American Short Story* reported that my life span was 1906–1954. Could this be an error? As a neighbor once said, "Dead folks don't know they're dead." I think I'm still alive and kicking. Don't give me out.

Mr. Still passed away in 2001, but, as his poem "Heritage" states, "And one with death rising to bloom again, I cannot go. Being of these hills, I cannot pass beyond."

THE BIG CAT

Baseball star Johnny Mize recalls his raising in the Appalachian foothills

Back then baseball was more of a deal than it is now. Every town around here had a baseball team. —Johnny Mize

When Mr. Mize was a young boy, he lived on the edge of a park that sat just across from Piedmont Academy in Demorest, Georgia. There, he spent many days playing tennis and other games. Though tennis was his first love, he became involved in baseball through Piedmont Academy, and as many of you know, he became one of baseball's great stars. After he retired from baseball, he moved to Florida, and operated an orange grove. He then moved back home to Demorest, and for several years he has lived at his family's homeplace.

He was signed by the Cardinals as a seventeen-year-old and spent six years on the Cardinals' minor league teams before becoming a member of the St. Louis Cardinals in the thirties. While with the Cardinals he won the National League batting championship with an average of .349. From 1939 to 1948 he also won four home-run and three RBI titles. He spent the forties with the New York Giants, eventually finishing his seventeen-year major league career with the New York Yankees in the fifties. He is the only player to hit fifty or more home runs and strike out fewer than fifty times in a season.

Mr. Mize attributes his batting skills, in part, to "Peggy," a game he and his friends used to play at Piedmont Park in Demorest when he was a child. Following is a diagram of Peggy.

There are three essentials needed to play this game: a stob, a stick, and a "Peggy." All are just pieces of wood, but they are different sizes.

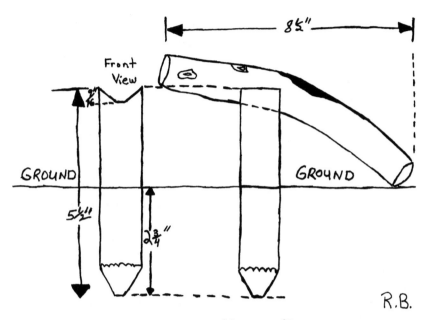

PLATE 179 Diagram of the setup of Peggy

The stob is a small piece of wood driven into the ground with a small notch cut into the top of it. The notch is so you can rest the Peggy, a piece of wood that is eight-and-one-half inches long, on it. With your stick (bat), hit either end of the Peggy so that it twirls up in the air. While it's twirling, bash it with your stick to send it sailing as far away as you can. Then count the number of running jumps it takes you to get to the Peggy. The first person to one hundred wins the game.

As Mr. Mize said, "Hitting that Peggy could be like swinging at a fastball that's probably up about ninety miles an hour. I think this might have helped me develop as a baseball player."

After the interview, Mr. Mize told us that he had a few plaques and awards upstairs and asked us if we wanted to see them. We eagerly agreed. Going up the steps, I saw several framed pictures of a young Johnny Mize. When I got to the top of the stairs, I didn't see just a few plaques and awards. I saw an entire museum devoted to Johnny "the Big Cat" Mize. The room, shaped like an L, had one wall filled with the awards he had received from being inducted in the Baseball Hall of Fame. Another wall showed newspaper clippings and caricatures. Near the ceiling was a row of baseball caps from several baseball teams. Mr. Mize's old baseball uniform hung proudly from the ceiling on the opposite side of the room. Several baseball bats hung on the wall along with team pictures. Mr. Mize lit a small Christmas tree for us that was decorated with miniature gloves, bats, and baseball figures. It even had a baseball in place of the star on top of the tree! As we talked with Mr. Mize, I noticed one wall that was covered with about a hundred letters. A closer look showed that they were fan letters Mr. Mize had received over the years. My curiosity overpowered me; I read every single letter tacked to that wall! Most of the letters were from fans in this country, but there were several letters from as far away as Australia and Germany. It was then that I realized how fortunate I was to interview a man admired by baseball fans all over the world.

—*Heather Manter*

I was born January 7, 1913, here in Demorest. I'll be seventy-six years old next month, which is not too far off. When I started playing baseball, I was seventeen. That was back in 1930, during the Depression, when banks were closed and things were a little rough. I guess the Depression affected everybody. I was living here with my grandmother and aunt. When the bank closed, your money was in the bank, and you couldn't get it. That was just about the way because most people that had any money put it into the bank. You got none of it back. It was just gone, and I knew my grandmother talked about making a deposit and how the banker looked at her, hoping he could say, "Don't put it in," knowing that the bank was probably closing that afternoon.

When I was growing up here, we had a broom factory, novelty shops, the saddle tree factory, post office, and bank. There was a barbershop, and then the doctor's office upstairs. There was a dentist's office, and, in the back part of the building, they had a meat market and a grocery store. I don't remember just how they got along, but I guess they continued to go on because that gave people a little money at the end of each week to spend in the grocery stores. Back then, they would allow you to charge stuff. You can't go in a supermarket or anything now and say, "Charge it to me, and I'll pay you at the first of the month." There was a notion store, where you could buy cloth, thread, et cetera. Now you can buy all of that stuff at one store. There was another grocery store beside that one, and a soda fountain. The saddle tree factory had an area where you could take your corn down and get it corn-milled and water-ground.

This community is different now. Now we have hardly anything in

PLATE 180 Mr. Johnny Mize

town. [We have] a little restaurant but no grocery store. The only grocery store up on this end of town is like a 7-Eleven. I drive either up to Clarkesville or down to Cornelia to get most of my groceries. Even before the college was here, there used to be a hotel. It was finally changed over to the girls' dormitory, which burned down. Piedmont even had a sawmill to saw their own lumber.

The railroad went through here and up to Franklin, North Carolina, so it could turn around. There were also excursions that used to come through on Sunday from Atlanta and go up to Tallulah Falls. [These excursion trains] would have ten and eleven coaches, and sometimes they would even run two of them on Sundays. My mother would sometimes come up on the first one because she worked in Atlanta. I think it was something like a dollar and a half, or two dollars for a half round-trip from Atlanta to Tallulah Falls.

Back then, people thought that in the mountains the water was healthy and the air, naturally, was cleaner because we didn't have all this electric stuff. With the railroads, it was an easy way for people to get here because the fares were very cheap.

We had one of the few telephones in town. People would call here, and they would want to speak to some professor here at Piedmont. Then I'd have to walk a mile over there to tell him that he was wanted on the telephone, and he would give me a nickel for doing it. People would call at night and say that their husband had beaten them up, and we would have to call the sheriff to come get him. They would call and say that some automobile was stuck somewhere, so we'd have to call the workforce, and we'd have to go down to the barn and get the two horses to pull the car out of a mudhole because, at that time, we didn't have paved roads. The main roads through here were dirt. We would charge them about a dollar for pulling them out. Now they go over there with a truck to tow you in and charge you about twenty-five to fifty dollars for it.

People would come up to go below the dam, to what we call an iron spring. They would go down every morning and drink that iron water. You could bring it back, like in a fruit [mason] jar, and set it in the kitchen. It would be just as clear as it could be when you put it in the jar, but after it sat for a while, it was just like you had a piece of iron in there, and it rusted and settled to the bottom. The springwater actually comes through the well; we just used it to water the flowers and things like that. We don't use it to drink, because it hasn't been tested.

"We had to take the cow and graze her. . . . Sometimes, we would leave her loose and look up and see her across the road grazing in someone's yard."

We had chickens and guineas. One thing about guineas, you could watch them and they'd fly over in the garden. You could see them walk down the row picking the bugs off of the different beans. We had a cow and a pig in the barn down there. We had to keep the pen real clean so the odor wouldn't get out. We had to take the cow and graze her. Sometimes, we would tie her someplace where she couldn't get loose and run off. Sometimes, we would leave her loose and look up and see her across the road grazing in someone's yard. I had to run over there and get the cow and bring her back. I'd go after the cow in the afternoon and hear the freight train blow. I would run over there when the train came by, and we'd jump on the side of it and hang on the side of the boxcars.

"Come to think of it, hitting that Peggy could be like swinging at a fastball that's probably up about ninety miles an hour."

We spent a lot of time playing tennis and other games in the park. One game we played I called "Peggy." I've asked people around the country if they've ever heard of it. I said that they ought to market Peggy or something, but it's a game that could be dangerous because you have to have enough room to play it. You go out here in the woods somewhere and cut a long stick. You would probably hunt all day trying to find a stick in the size that you wanted. You'd cut little pieces of wood about a foot long or less, usually out of persimmon. You had a peg in the ground, and you'd tap that peg. When it bounced up in the air, you tried to hit it. We would get down in the park and play there nearly half a day. Sometimes, you'd have ten, twelve, or fifteen [players], and you could play partners. If you lost, you had to wait your turn. A lot of times a Peggy would break in two. If a Peggy broke in two, the longest part of it was the one that counted.

Come to think of it, hitting that Peggy could be like swinging at a fastball that's probably up about ninety miles an hour. You hit the Peggy, which is on the ground, and bounce it up in the air. Then you have to get the stick and swing, before that Peggy hits the ground. That has to be a pretty quick swing, and batting [the Peggy] up in the air and then hitting it.

I always wanted to play baseball, but I played more tennis because, in the park, they had a tennis court, and it only took two of you to play tennis. Two of you playing baseball is not too much fun! About all you can do is play catch, or, if you had enough baseballs, one could pitch and one could hit. Anyway, when I started to play baseball, I was probably in about the fifth grade.

Here at Piedmont, the football coach was also the coach of the basketball teams and the baseball team. During baseball season, as soon as school let out, I'd go over to the baseball diamond and watch the baseball team. When they broke a bat, they'd give them to me. I'd take a needle and wax string and resew the balls or put tape on them. You could take the bats over to the broom factory, and they could run a row of wire around the bat, and then you would put tape on it. You could tap the bat against the ground, and it sounded like it was good and solid.

During the football season, I'd go over to the field on Saturday mornings and help them line off the field. Back then, you'd mix lime and water together and mark off the field. I was doing that during my sophomore year at Piedmont Academy. When it came time for baseball, the [college] team played a couple of games, and then this coach here asked me to come out for the team. I was in high school, it was Piedmont Academy then, and the coach, Harry Forrester, asked me to come out for the college team because any guy with Piedmont Academy could go out for the college team. I told him I'd think about coming out for the team. The coach said, "Well, come on out and get a uniform and work out with us." I finally agreed. He put me in to pinch-hit, and I got a base hit. Then he put me out in left field, and I played left field for the rest of the season.

Back in those days, you only played on Friday and Saturday. You had three months for baseball. You'd work out for a couple of weeks, and then play sixteen or eighteen games.

The next year the city took over the high school, and Piedmont Academy was out. Some of the baseball players from the college wanted to know if I was going to play with them, but I couldn't because I was in high school. They told me they'd fix it to where I could take a subject in college and play. So, I started to work out with the team. They never mentioned the subject again; I didn't either, because I was having enough trouble in high school without worrying about trying to pass something in college.

"It was amazing how you could foul a ball off down in those woods and how the people could come in there and come right back out with the ball. I don't think they ever lost one."

Back then baseball was more of a deal than it is now. Every town around here had a baseball team. A lot of these places, like Cornelia, Clarkesville, Demorest, Habersham Mills, Toccoa, and even a power company in Tallulah Falls, had a ball club. We had a fella, a plumber, that sponsored a team in the summertime. He went to Atlanta and bought us a sweatshirt and a pair of pants. We had to furnish our own shoes; we didn't use hose or anything, just a pair of shoes.

We'd go up there and play those teams this side of Tallulah Falls, just to the right going towards Clayton, over on a field down in the woods— just like they cut out a ball field right in the middle of the woods. It was amazing how you could foul a ball off down in those woods and how the people could come in there and come right back out with the ball. I don't think they ever lost one.

We'd ride in the back end of a truck, and then go down in the woods and change clothes and maybe put the uniform on there and go. You did anything back then when you're a kid growing up.

Toccoa would call me to come over and play with them, and Habersham Mills would want me to play with them, too. The Morris Lumber Company in Helen, Georgia, called and asked me to play with their team, against a team in South Carolina. If the team was going to South Carolina, they'd come by and pick me and Cy Grant up. Cy and I both played the different town teams whenever they had a tough team or something.

Someone connected with the ball club told the Cardinals in St. Louis that they had a guy playing for them in Helen that could hit a ball a long way. So, that's the way I started [professional] baseball. And Frank Rickey, the brother of the general manager of the Cardinals, came down to sign me. I was playing with Toccoa at the time he came down. I guess when you are seventeen years old, you just want to get away from home; I had just finished high school.

When I first went to Greensboro to play with the Cardinals' minor league team, we traveled in automobiles. We only had about fifteen players on the team. We only had about one [player] per position, and usually you had two catchers. The catcher usually played the infield and outfield, too. If somebody was hurt, the catcher would have to fill in.

Back then, the Cardinals had a baseball club in every minor league. The minors had several leagues. Double-A was the highest minor league you could get. There was also the International League, the American Association, and the Pacific Coast League. The Cards had a team in all of the leagues. There were about twenty-five minor leagues.

I could have made more money playing in the town league. I was only getting $150 a month in the minor leagues and paid all of my expenses. When I was in Greensboro, North Carolina, they paid my expenses when I was on the road, so living there didn't cost me much. A fellow living in Florida wanted me to come down and play for his town team. They would have paid more than what I was making in the minor leagues. They didn't pay much. I went to the major leagues with $500 a month. There were guys that went into the major leagues at $400. In five and half months, that is $2,700 in the season. Now the bottom salary is $62,000 for rookies.

I played in the minor league from 1931 to 1935. In the major leagues I started out with the Cardinals in 1936 and stayed there until 1941. During the winter of '35, I went to St. Louis and had both of my legs operated on. The general manager of the Cardinals said he was going to keep me in the ball club because I couldn't play regular down in the minor leagues. They kept me there so I could fill in at first base and pinch-hit. I said I was probably the only guy that stayed in the major leagues because he couldn't play in the minor leagues.

The first year I was with the Cardinals, I usually played first base, but I played eight or ten games in the outfield. In St. Louis I'd go out in the right field with the right fielder and catch fly balls. As soon as the first bunch was over, I'd go into first base, and the next group would come. One day the manager came over there and told me that I was going to play right field that day. It scared me to death because I hadn't played outfield in four or five years. That day, I hit a home run with the bases loaded and drove in five or six runs. We won something like seven to five. The writers all wrote the next day what a smart move it was to put me in.

"They were throwing the ball in the dirt, and the balls were taking bad hops. I managed to catch them. [Joe] came in one inning and told me that I looked like a big cat out there. So, that's where it actually got started."

I got the nickname "the Big Cat" one time in St. Louis, Missouri. A fellow named Joe Orengo, who died a few months ago, was on our ball club. They were throwing the ball in the dirt, and the balls were taking bad hops. I managed to catch them. [Joe] came in one inning and told me that I looked like a big cat out there. So, that's where it actually got started. All of the writers have changed it around to their own opinion.

In St. Louis I was hitting .349 and had about twenty home runs. The general manager said I should hit more home runs. Then in 1940, I hit forty-three home runs, which is still high. My batting average dropped down to .319, and I drove in 137 runs, and they wanted to know if I would take a cut in salary because my batting average was off. That's when I told them that they had better trade me. Now a guy hits .275, twenty-five home runs, drives in seventy-five runs, and they write up what a great year he's having.

I had been playing against the Giants for six years before I went with them. Playing first base, you meet each one of them, so you know all of them. I figured there was nothing I could do there to please [the Cardinals]. How could I ever get a raise? I was traded to the New York Giants in 1942. I played baseball in the service in 1943. I was in the Navy from 1943 to 1945. (After I got back from the Navy, I went back to the Giants.) In 1946 I hit fifty-one home runs with the Giants, and a writer called me one day to ask me if I had a farm in Georgia. (Someone had written in an article that I owned a farm in Georgia.) I told him that I was glad he asked because I did not own a farm in Georgia. I wished I did, but I didn't. So, if you'll put that in your article, that I did not own a farm in Georgia, I would appreciate it; I hate to have anything written about me that isn't true. That writer wrote that I had owned a farm in Georgia. I asked him why he wrote it, and I said it wasn't true, and he said it made

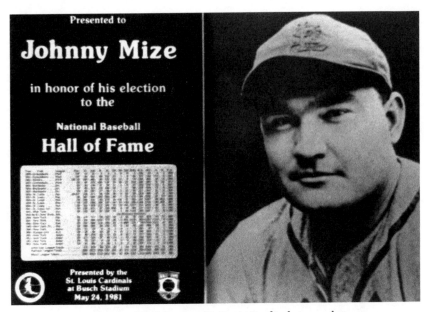

PLATE 181 Mr. Mize in a St. Louis Cardinals team photo

the story sound better. Yes, but it makes me look like a liar. It's a good thing that article was just going to stay in New York.

One time, when I was with the Giants, I played an exhibition game against the Yankees. I got hit on the right hand, and it broke a bone. I was out for three or four weeks. On Friday the thirteenth, they put me back in the lineup. Our manager came over and said that a lady [over in the stands] just gave him a four-leaf clover. He gave it to me. I put it in the brim of my cap. In about the seventh inning, I ran into the fence and broke my toe. I was out for the rest of the season. I missed about fifty ball games and a home run championship by only one home run. I used to have a small horseshoe [as a good luck charm]. I don't know if it came out of candy or what. I used to tape it on my belt.

The Giants trained in St. Petersburg, Florida, and the Yankees trained in St. Pete also. So, when I went to the Yankees, I was right in the same town with them. I knew the manager, Casey Stengel, from when I was with the Giants. I didn't have to give up my apartment when I was traded to the other ball club, so that made it easy. In the 1952 World Series while I was with the New York Yankees, I hit a home run in each of three straight games. I didn't play the first two games, but in the third game, I got a home run. Then, I started as a pinch hitter the rest of the game and was voted most valuable player.

My stance was not too wide; I could rock on one foot and rock back on the other one. I could stand there for two hours and never move. I see these guys that walk in there, and they spread way out and priss around. I guess it bothers them that the pitcher stands out there and kills time. It didn't bother me at all. It didn't make any difference how many times they stepped off of their rubber or threw to first base. I just stood there. I either got out or got on base. I think now, if you took a stopwatch, you'd find that a lot of these games are running an extra fifteen or twenty minutes, just because of these guys getting out of the batter's box. Then they have to practice their swings.

A curve ball, an overhead ball, and a forkball were popular back then. Now the forkball is a split-finger fastball. They get it between their fingers, and they called that a forkball during my days. They throw the curveball, and it goes down; they throw the slider that comes in; they throw the knuckleball, and it goes in every direction, an' if a guy has good speed, the ball will raise a little. There is also a sinker ball.

PLATE 182 Mr. Mize showing off his batting stance in his yard

When I played, the spitball was outlawed. Different guys threw spitballs, and you had guys that probably tried to scratch the ball. Now they make a big deal out of it. If they [were going to] outlaw anything, they should've outlawed the knuckle because more catchers have had their fingers broken by trying to catch a knuckleball. A spitball isn't going to break anybody's fingers, but it might because you don't know where it's going. George Earnshaw pitched to me and I hit a line drive. The ball hit him on the arm. A few days later, when he joined our ball club, he said that was the best spitball he had ever thrown. I nearly broke his arm with it, and I thought it was a fastball, but he said it was a spitball.

"What burns me up is to see these guys out there, a pitcher, or even a batter, stands out there, and he blows a big bubble while he's standing there."

Harry Forrester, the coach at Piedmont, was a spitball pitcher, and he chewed the slippery elm bark. It's just a bark of a tree. I don't know if it does any good or not, or how it tastes. I never chewed any of it. I chewed tobacco when I played. I was probably the first guy that ever chewed chewing gum and mixed tobacco with it. I used to put the gum in my mouth, and then after I chewed it a little bit, I put the tobacco in and worked it together. When I got ready to throw it out, it was all in one wad. You just throw it out and it's all gone. When you chew it [tobacco], it separates, it's all in your teeth, and it's hard to get out. What burns me up is to see these guys out there, a pitcher, or even a batter, stands out there, and he blows a big bubble while he's standing there. To me, that would be a distraction.

Now, if I had been hitting, way back when it was legal for them to chew that slippery elm and throw the ball, it might have come up and been a fast break or something. Now, the other guys, like Perry, they said he used Vaseline or hair oil or hair grease or something like that. They tried to catch him doing this. It was funny because he would be on one ball club and then on another. You figure somebody on the club he was on before should know where he kept it. If you get the reputation of throwing a spitball, every time you throw a strike up there and they miss it, they think it is a spitball.

It's an honor when you go into the Hall of Fame. Out of all the thousands that play, there are only a few hundred that make the Hall of Fame. The Hall of Fame is supposed to be the end of the line. The city of Demorest now has a monument in the park for me.

I don't think being a famous baseball player has affected my attitude. I just don't try to overpower anybody. I got picked up for speeding in Florida, and someone said that I should have told them who I was, but I just asked him how fast I was going.

SOCK SUPPERS, CAKEWALKS, COTTON PICKIN', AND A WATER LILY QUILT

Frances Harbin shares her memories

We were happy. We didn't have too much, but we had as much as any of our neighbors did. So we were wealthy in what was important, and that was love and a Christian home. —Francis Harbin

A quilt maker, Frances Harbin lives in Westminster, South Carolina. Mrs. Harbin shares childhood memories about the farm in her small community where family and neighbors always managed to entertain each other with ghost stories and games. Mrs. Harbin also recounts tales of her twin brother, the life of her two children, and the trust she has in God. Though she has had trials in her life, Mrs. Harbin says, "God knows best."

Mrs. Harbin also shared the story of a community project that drew folks together to accomplish a common goal: to raise funds to erect a classroom building for a church. Many women from Mount Pleasant Baptist Church lovingly volunteered to make the various squares, which depict water lilies in varying colors. Then, for ten cents, persons could have their name embroidered on the quilt. This project was one of many fund-raisers that helped to realize the goal of building on to the church. What happened to the quilt, you might ask? Wait till you see!

—*Ann Cross*

My name is Frances Ables Harbin. I'm eighty-five years old, and I was born September 7, 1919, in Oconee County, South Carolina. I was a twin, and my twin was a boy. My parents were John Benjamin Ables and Olive Barker Ables. I've lived in this area, well, a few miles of it, all my life. My parents were farmers. My parents didn't have too much formal education. I think my dad said he had about the equivalent of a second-grade education. I never did remember how much education my mother had. They both educated themselves through work and life. My dad was a pretty good carpenter. He did a lot of repair work for neighbors, you know, when something would go wrong in the home. He could figure board lumber quicker in his head than I could on paper when I finished high school. There's ten children in the family, and everyone finished high school at the same school. Because my parents didn't have an education, they were determined that their children were goin' to be educated as much as we could. They weren't able to send any of us to college, but, like our parents, we all learned from them and learned by doin' till we did fairly well throughout life. Well, we didn't have what you would call too much of this world's goods. We had plenty to eat, plenty to wear, and a roof over our heads. That's about all our neighbors had back in the early days.

Recycling is nothing new 'cause my parents recycled everything. Even the recycled feed sacks made dresses for the girls. There was seven girls in the family. My mother was a good seamstress. She could look at a picture on a catalog or paper, take a newspaper, cut out a pattern, and make a dress. They'd go to town about once a year in the wagon in the fall, after we'd sell the crops. Back then, you could buy a yard of good cloth for ten cents, and two yards would make a dress for most of the girls. She'd save every scrap and every string, and we made quilts out of that. They were savin' with everythin'. We didn't throw out anythin' that could be recycled or reused. I'm a pack rat: I never throw anythin' away. I try to make use of everythin' that I get. There was a thing that we had plenty of, though, and that was love. Our parents loved every one of us children. They showed it not only in words but in deeds, also. As we grew older, each one of us made a home of our own, and we tried to pattern our lifestyle after them.

When my dad bought this place out here, we had just rented and moved from the place before then. The government had set up a program during the Great Depression and was loanin' farmers money to buy farms with a home, livestock, and equipment. My dad bought it, and we all worked hard till he paid it off within less time than he was s'posed to. We grew just about everythin' we used on the farm. We had our cow for milk and butter, our hogs for meat, our garden vegetables, our fruit trees, and we grew wheat and corn for bread. We had just about what we needed at home. It was took care of to be used through the winter months when we couldn't go out in the garden and gather. My mother worked hard and canned everythin' she could. She also dried fruit. We had plenty to eat, but most of it was what we took care of and grew on the farm. We were happy. We didn't have too much, but we had as much as any of our neighbors did. So we were wealthy in what was important, and that was love and a Christian home. We didn't have televisions. We didn't have nothin' to attract us or to entertain us. In the wintertime, neighbors would visit each other and sit till bedtime, and they would talk 'bout growing up and things they did. I can remember a family that came to visit us one night. We always grew corn, for popcorn, and peanuts on the farm to have for snacks. We'd sit around the fire, and we'd pop popcorn, parch [bake or broil in the Dutch oven] peanuts, and talk. I never will forget one neighbor: he was the best at tellin' ghost stories. He said, "My daddy told me that he went courtin' one time, and he was in the buggy with his horse and comin' back home. It was late at night and dark. He was ridin' along close to a new ground; the people that had cleared that new ground had piled up brush and burned it. All at once, he looked down, and there was a big, white somethin' just a-rollin' along the road by the buggy wheel. He looked at it, and it just kept follerin' him up the road. He stopped at the next stop; he started over again, and it started. He thought it was a ghost. He was runnin' his horse; of course, an' he was goin' fast. The revolution of the wheels picked up the smoke from where they had burned the trash pile, and the smoke was just follerin' along there. He thought it was a ghost and it done had him, but it was smoke." They'd tell things like that. That's the only thing I remember him ever tellin' me. We had a lot of entertainment like that when we were growin' up, just listenin' to the older people talk like that.

When we started school, we started at Oakway School. It's a little town just two, three miles, a wide place in the road. It had just a small school to start with, but they kept addin' grades as the community grew and more children got in school, and they kept growin' until they finally got a high school. All ten children started in the Oakway School and went through Oakway High School. A lot of the grandchildren have graduated from West-Oak, which is a combination of Oakway School and Westminster School. In the last several years they combined schools, and they built new school buildings. Oakway is our home school.

We had a good school; we had good teachers. I mean, they believed in giving children an education. You didn't go to play, and you didn't go to cut up and disturb a class. If you did, you got your legs switched. Teachers had the authority to punish children when they were disobedient. I think that's one thing that ruined the schools; they took the authority away from the teachers that were in charge of the children under them. One unruly child can ruin a classroom to where the rest of them can get nothing out of it. We had good teachers and good schools, and we all got a good education.

My dad's family was kind of small. His dad died when he was just eight years old himself. My mother's family was a big family, and as far back as I can remember, her family all gathered together once sometime during the summer and had a reunion. That sticks with me more than anythin': goin' to that family reunion and seein' all the aunts, uncles, and cousins. I had one special aunt and uncle. They lived in Westminster. We were visitin' them one time, and all the boys were out in the pasture playin' ball. We were just little fellers then. One of my cousins gave my twin a stick o' chewin' gum, and he broke it half in two. He put half of it in his mouth and the other half in his pocket. One of my cousins asked him, he says, "What are you gonna do with that?" He said, "I'm gonna save it for Frances." Everthin' he got, he had to save half of it for me.

PLATE 183 Francis Harbin as a young woman

My twin—we called him J. B.—was named after my dad. My dad's name was John Benjamin. When my brother went to work, he was called Jake a lot. One time when we were in school, he had to stay in the fifth grade two years; I got a year ahead of him in school. He stayed in fifth grade two years 'cause he played the first year. He's always laughed. They couldn't afford but one set of books for the two of us to use. He's always told me that he deliberately played on that year so he wouldn't have to sit with me no more. One day there was two boys sittin' behind us, and one of 'em threw somethin' and hit a boy. The teacher was standin', writin' somethin' on the blackboard, and out of the corner of her eye, she saw it come from behind our desk, and she thought J. B. was the one that threw it. She came back there and she grabbed him out of that seat. She began whippin' him with a hickory. He said, "I didn't do it! I didn't do it!" I began to cryin'.

My twin died a little over a year ago, and I got a sympathy card from my cousin, and she said, "I can't forget the times that we used to visit each other when we were growin' up or the times that J. B. had to save half of everythin' that was given to him for you." I wasn't the only one that was impressed by his generosity.

First, let me tell you when the church was organized. It was organized in October of 1905. I don't know when that buildin' was built after the church was organized, but they didn't even have a buildin' when the church was first organized. I think there was about nineteen charter members that built the buildin'. The church that we were goin' to was a small country church. It was just a buildin'. A sanctuary was all there was to it; there was no classrooms for Sunday school or nothin'. It was just one long buildin' with a side door, a front door, and two rows of pews. A few members would gather by age groups in corners here and yonder all over the buildin'. They'd teach the Bible to the children, young people, and adults. In the latter part of the 1920s and the earlier part of the thirties, the women began to talk about needin' classrooms built onto the church. We started a plan about makin' a quilt and sellin' it to the highest bidder and chargin' a dime for everybody that wanted their name on the quilt, and this is the quilt that was made. This quilt that I helped make is famous. It's a "Water Lily" quilt, and that quilt has made history. I want to show you a picture of it. I'll show you the real thing later. Those names on it . . . everybody's names who's on it paid a dime. We embroidered their names in the corner of a square. Then the quilt was finished and quilted and sold to the highest bidder. Have y'all ever heard of a "box supper"? When I was growin' up, they used to have 'em when they raised money for anything. The young girls would get a candy box or something. They'd decorate it up, wrap it in crepe paper, and fix it to look pretty. They'd fix a meal (sandwiches and cake or cookies or somethin') and put it in that box. The boxes were sold, and the men did the biddin' on the box (he didn't know whose box he was buyin'). The highest bidder got the box, and he had to eat supper with the girl that fixed it. We had a "sock supper" when we was goin' to sell the quilt. Everybody, women and girls, brought a pair of men's socks, and we would put fruit in the toes of the socks. We'd put crackers, nuts, or wrapped candy and fill that sock full of something like that. The socks were sold. The men bid on the socks, and he had to find the girl that made his sock and eat supper with her. Then we had cakewalks. The women baked cakes, and they'd play music. The couples would walk around; when the music stopped, they would get a cake. The cakes, some of 'em, were sold to the highest bidder—we raised money like that. The main thing was the auctionin' of the quilt. My boyfriend's brother-in-law bought it for him, and he give it to me for a weddin' present. It brought seven dollars and a half, but this quilt was sold, I think, in 1933, during the Depression. Nobody had much money, but the Lord always blesses what you try to do. It got its name because this pattern is a water lily flower. We cut the pattern out of different colors of cloth and appliquéd on squares of material. We had yeller [yellow], pink, blue, and white squares of material. We appliquéd the flowers on those squares for the quilt.

There wadn't anything hard to me about it 'cause I was just about fourteen, I think, when we made the quilt. Our mother had taught all of us girls hand sewin', embroiderin', and quiltin'. It was nothin' hard to me, but a lot of 'em thought they couldn't do it. I don't know whether they did or not. This white square is one that I made. I made two or three squares.

The Blue Ridge Electric Corporation selects something for their calendars. On every month they show a picture, and that quilt is on one month. Another that I made, a "Cathedral Window" quilt, is on the back of the calendar. Laurel Horton, who worked with the McKissick Museum in Columbia, was in Seneca makin' pictures of old quilts to go in the museum. She made a picture of this Water Lily quilt and got the history of it, who owned it, and who it would be going to after I died. It will go to my oldest son; I'm goin' to talk to him and ask him to have it put in the museum. She asked me one day, says, "Would you let me have that quilt to send to Philadelphia? We're going to have a book printed about quilt making in America. That is the prettiest quilt that I have ever

PLATE 184 Water lily fund-raising quilt of pieced solid-color cottons,
75 inches x 65½ inches, made by women of Mount Pleasant Baptist Church
near Westminster, South Carolina. Back-to-front edge treatment machine
and blue quilting thread, seven stitches per inch, as well as colored threads in
French knot, outline, and buttonhole stitches. Collection of Frances Harbin.
Photograph by Terry Wild Studio (courtesy of Frances Harbin).

seen that was made for fund-raising." Usually, they didn't put that much
work in a quilt for a fund-raiser. She says, "I guarantee you, the quilt
will be taken care of and will come back to you in good shape." So I let
her have it, and she sent it to Philadelphia. That's where that book was
printed, and they made that picture and wrote up about it in there. It's
in that book *Quiltmaking in America*. It's really got a history to it. I have
really enjoyed it. There's so many names on there of people that lived in
Westminster at the time we made it. I carried it up there one time when
the senior citizens were havin' a luncheon at the church and was havin'
a show-and-tell, if they had anythin' interestin' to show and tell about. I
carried that quilt up there because so many of 'em's names was on there.

They knew some that had done passed on. Oh, they just had a fit over that quilt. They were so glad to see it. It was so nice to know that there's so many of their parents' and grandparents' names on that quilt.

We weren't the only ones tryin' to raise money to build the classrooms to the church. After the women got started, the men joined in, too. One man donated an acre of land, and the men got together and plowed, tilled the land, and planted it in cotton. Whenever it needed plowin', all the men would come and plow it up. The women and the young people would hoe cotton. When it was ready to pick, we all got together and had a cotton pickin' and sold that cotton to fund the classrooms. Back then, women in the country didn't go to work at public works. We had too much to do at home. About all the money we had was from the sale of butter and eggs and things like that. In the missionary meeting, the women decided they would save the eggs that was laid on Sunday and sell them and donate it to the church fund. They had a nest built up in front of the church. The women would bring the eggs that was laid or the number of eggs that was laid the Sunday before and put them in the nest. They were sold to grocery stores that agreed to pay the cash for 'em, and they put that money on it. They was just lots of ways we could raise just a little. We raised just ten cents here and ten cents there or a quarter till we finally got enough money to start on the classrooms. The men that had farms that had timber on it would donate logs; they carried 'em to the sawmill and sawed the lumber. There were several men that was pretty good carpenters and some that knowed what to do to help get it started. They got together and built the classrooms to the church. It was free labor, so we didn't have too much expense after so long. It wadn't like havin' to hand it all out at one time. It was over [several] years that we raised the money. Barbara, my companion, goes to the church now that this quilt was made for. The old church has been torn down, and they took over the area where it was to enlarge the cemetery.

My mother said that I was my dad's pick of the family. I was awfully sickly as a baby. I'm sure that's why he showed more affection to me as a small child, but he never made any difference. Very few times in my lifetime did I ever know of him doing something that he didn't for the rest of 'em. They loved us all, but I don't think he ever wanted me to marry and leave home. I had to slip around and do my courtin'; I had to elope when I married.

I married Oscar Harbin. He used to live below two miles from here. We went to the same church. Several years ago, people didn't go out of the community to marry and settle down. They just usually married their neighbors and settled down in the community they was raised in. I know when my son was researchin' family history, he said, "I have learned that we're kin to nearly everybody in Oconee County." You better not say nothing about nobody else unless you know who you are talkin' to.

People in Bible times married sisters, and they married close. I don't know whether that has so much to do with mixin' the blood. 'Course, God took care of things back then.

I had two boys. They finished high school in Oakway, both of 'em. We couldn't afford to send 'em to college, but they both went in service in the Air Force right after they got out of high school. I guess they got a lot of education while they was servin' four years in the service. When John got out—he was the oldest—he worked in several different jobs till he finally settled with Coats and Clark at Seneca, South Carolina. He worked twenty-nine, or I think it was 'bout twenty-seven, years there. He worked his way up till he was an engineer with the company through knowledge of what he was doin' and studyin' on the outside. Of course, math has changed, as y'all know. Two and two used to be four, but it's not anymore. I don't know how they did it. He took a class from a friend of his that was a professor, and he taught him to do math methods. 'Course, the answer always come out the same, but it was different. I don't know why. I don't know anything about it. He taught him math, and he took classes and become an engineer for the company. 'Course he didn't have a diploma from a college or nothin' like that, but he did go to Tri-County Tech and took some classes. He could've gone on to teach in a technical college, but he could make more money workin' for the company that he was with; so he stayed with 'em. He has traveled for the company all over France, China, and here and yonder—ever'where. He's still with the company, but the company has been sold two or three times. He'll be sixty-seven years old in June, but he's still workin'.

Jerome, the youngest one, went in the Air Force and served four years. As soon as he got out, he went to Washington, DC. He went to work as a clerk in the General Services Department, and he worked his way up. He started out as a grade four. I don't know whether y'all know anythin' about how the government grades the workers or not, but the lowest grade to start with was a grade four. He worked his way up. When he retired, he was a fourteen. There's a deaf college there near Washington. Because there was so many deaf people that he associated with in his work, he took classes in sign language. He was very good in the sign language. He taught night class at the University of Maryland in sign language to people that could hear but wanted to learn to speak to the deaf people around 'em. He did that for a while. Then, after he got tired of that, he wanted the time to go see plays and things that was comin' to the Kennedy Center. He got a job at night as an usher there so he could see all the plays he wanted to. He worked there at night for a while.

Jerome died. It'll be nine years this comin' September. We count 'em. He retired; he was plannin' on movin' to Florida. Two weeks before he retired, he was packin' up, gettin' ready to move, and he kept havin' pains in his chest. A friend that was helpin' pack told him, says, "You gotta see a doctor." So he went to see a doctor, and he put him in the hospital and operated that day. He said the main thing that brought the blood to his heart, it wadn't clogged. It just collapsed. And he says, "You come the nearest havin' a fatal heart attack than anybody I've ever seen not to have had one." He operated that morning and ballooned out that vein, and he was okay. He never did have any more problems with it, but in doing that x-ray in his chest, they found a tumor on his lungs. He had lung cancer. They just give him six months to live, but he lived a year. I stayed with him the bigger part of the year. He never was married, and I stayed with him after he found out he had cancer. He told me one day, he said, "Mom, you're not supposed to bury children. Children are supposed to bury their parents." I said, "No, God needs younguns the same as He needs olduns." It was hard, though. God knows best.

God didn't put us here to stay. He didn't give us children to keep either. It was hard to give up my youngest son, but I don't question God why 'cause he would really have suffered if he had lived on.

Advice that I think would be very important to give young people today is to be honest and sincere in whatever you do and seek Christ in your life 'cause life's nothin' without Him. I don't mean that everybody has to be a Baptist. I'm a Baptist. I fully believe in Baptist beliefs, but there's good and there's bad in every denomination. I think that God places in all of us a conviction to know when we need the Lord. I'll never forget the time I first heard God's call to repent and accept Christ. I was about thirteen when I first felt the need for repentance, but I was about fifteen before I ever really accepted the Lord, joined the church, and was baptized. It was the best decision I ever made. He'll never leave me. I think it's His Holy Spirit that convicts every individual when they need a savior, and it's up to that individual what they do about it.

Seven years ago, I had four major surgeries on my abdomen, and my stomach muscles never did gain strength where I could walk very good. I had to walk [at] almost a ninety-degree angle, all stooped over. I can't stand up but just a little while at a time. Barbara Martin takes care of me. She's like my adopted daughter; I never did have a daughter, but she's like my adopted daughter. She comes in at least one day a week and does what I can't get done. She takes me shopping every once in a while, whatever we need to do. The rest of the time, I live by myself and make out.

We were brought up in a Christian home. We wadn't sent to church: We were carried to church, and we worshiped together. It was a big part of our life. It's a good start when you get out and start a home of your own, too, 'cause a home is not complete till a man and a woman takes Christ into it. A lot of people don't like to hear you talk about things like that in schools. In a lot of places, it's forbidden, but that's what's wrong with our country this day and time. It's gettin' worse. I have to say it, but it's gettin' worse. I'm sorry for the children comin' up now 'cause parents don't carry children to church like we were carried. They may send the little ones, but their parents don't go. They don't set the example for 'em that should be. I think that's the biggest thing that's wrong with our generation comin' on.

FRONT PORCH STORIES

An interview with Edgar Owens

Nobody sees alike, and there's nothing wrong with expressing your opinion, and standing by your opinion, but it should be based more on what's good for your fellow man than what's good for me.

—Edgar Owens

Henry Edgar Owens, also known as Edgar, is known as Pa Pa. Between the months of April and September, you will find him and his wife out on the front porch talking. As a child, I would find my way into my pa pa's lap, asking him to tell me stories about the old days. I remember always imagining how things were and asking him to tell me more and more stories.

This past August, I was a new student in Foxfire, and I was told to find a contact to interview. It could be anyone I knew and found interesting who was not a previous Foxfire contact. Before the teacher was even through stating this, I knew that I was going to interview Pa Pa. I saw it as a great opportunity to record the stories I enjoyed as a child and share them with others.

That night I shared my idea with my grandfather, and he loved it. The next day I went to his house, which is not far from mine, and did the interview. To start off the interview, we each got a glass of tea and went to the porch. This seemed appropriate because that's where he told me the stories as a kid. I wish you could hear the interview on tape because you hear the crickets and dogs in the background, not to mention the passion of his voice as he told his story!

—*Alex Owens*

I was born on May 6, 1925. My favorite childhood memory would probably be me and my baby sister when we were little. We were real close; we played together and stayed together. The first year that I went to school, why, she pitched a fit every morning when I went out the door. I remember one incident when Mother had her sittin' up on the dresser trying to entertain her and keep her from crying. I snuck in and hid behind Momma to try and do a better job than Momma was doin' and Momma told me to get on out and go to school, she would be all right by the time I got out of sight. So that was what I had to do. We had a lot of things that I can remember us playing. My sister had a baby doll that she called Elvin, and she called herself Effie and I was Lewis. We played Effie and Lewis with that baby. There was twelve of us in my family. I had eight brothers and four sisters.

> *"Kids today don't know what it was like not to have running water, bathrooms, and lights. They'd have a hard time coping with a pine knot for a light or a dipper for a drinking cup."*

Four of us served in the Armed Forces, two in the Navy, and two in the Army. Their names were Riley Owens, Doyle Owens, Jesse Ray Owens, and myself. My oldest sister was Iva May Owens. The next one was Effie Angiline Laurel, then Frances Eloise. I also had a sister that died at the age of five with typhoid fever. Her name was Ovaleen. Most typhoid cases were from drinking water that was contaminated, or eatin' food that was contaminated. You had to carry all the water that you used to wash with. A lot of times kids didn't wash if they could get by with it from the parents. If you got by Momma, you didn't have to wash. So it wasn't the best of sanitary conditions if you didn't have running water.

Kids today don't know what it was like not to have running water, bathrooms, and lights. They'd have a hard time coping with a pine knot for a light or a dipper for a drinking cup.

Back then you didn't have any going to the hospital. There wasn't any hospitals close around. The closest was probably Anderson, South Carolina, or Atlanter [Atlanta] and gettin' there was another problem. People just didn't go to the hospital back then. They drove to the doctor or done the best they could. Sick people were kept at home and cared for by the family. That's how we cared for my sister before she passed away. When Ovaleen, my baby sister, passed away, Ivy, my oldest sister, come up where we were sleeping, upstairs of the old house, and woke us up. She told us that our sister passed away. It was about four o'clock that morning when she passed away. This was the first real encounter that I had with death. My first impression when I saw her, after she had passed away, was that she was well, because her eyes were open. I learn't later that wasn't the case.

Our food was different than it is today. Back then on the farm, we grew just about everything we ate other than salt, soda, and coffee. Kids didn't get any coffee, but their parents did. The basic things that are bought today we grew. We had our own chickens for our eggs and raised our hogs for our own pork. We produced our own milk, butter, eggs, meat, and pork. Occasionally, we would kill a beef. We canned our pork because we didn't have electricity. We grew our own vegetables. We dried them for summer and winter. We also grew potatoes, cabbage, dried beans, and green beans. We grew most of our food ourselves and put it up. Most of the time at our house, we ate cornbread three times a day. A lot of people had biscuits for breakfast, but our family wasn't one of them. Most of the time it was made of cornmeal. We had bacon, fatback, and eggs when the hens laid; applesauce and honey was our main source of sweetness. Sometimes Dad would work out things at work with other people who made sorghum syrup. We'd have sorghum syrup to supplement with the honey. We would swap out some with honey. Very little sugar was consumed on the table.

In my earliest recollection, my dad had a 1928 Model T Ford that you had to crank with a hand crank. If you didn't know how to operate it, you'd get a broke arm. It had mechanical brakes on it and no power steering. It was a crude automobile, but it was faster than a wagon and horse. We only went to town maybe two or three times a year, unless somebody had to go to the doctor.

"There was a man who pulled teeth for kids and grown people that lived in the community, but he didn't deaden it; they just held you down and pulled the tooth."

We didn't have the opportunity to go to the dentist. We didn't have the money to start with, even though it only cost a dollar to get a tooth pulled. That's the biggest thing a dentist done back then. You had to be rich to get your teeth filled. Dr. Taylor was the first dentist I ever remember in Rabun County. He done the best he could, but people today wouldn't have been happy with the best he could do. He pulled one tooth for me. He used Novocain, but he didn't give it time to work, so it wasn't good and dead, but he did pull the tooth. It hurt for a week after he pulled it and was worse than before he pulled it. There was a man who pulled teeth for kids and grown people that lived in the community, but he didn't deaden it; they just held you down and pulled the tooth. If you were a kid, or a grown-up, you had to be man enough to sit there and let him pull it. If you cried that was all right, too.

We didn't have toothbrushes until my oldest brother, Riley, went off to school over in Rome, Georgia, to Berry College. He was studying to be a schoolteacher. He had access to more stuff like that. He could get a dollar every once in a while, but he could buy toothbrushes for only a nickel. He bought us our first toothbrushes we ever saw. That was after half of our teeth had already rotted out anyhows. We didn't have any store-bought toothbrushes or toothpaste. Most of the time we used baking sodie [baking soda] or a mixture of baking sodie and salt. Salt disinfected and baking sodie cleaned. We didn't have access to what the children do today to keep our teeth cleaned and keep the enamel strong and keep the cavities out of them.

Most of our clothes were homemade. Momma knitted our socks out of wool. The wool came from sheep that we raised on the place. She spun and then we processed the wool into yarn. At home she knitted socks, caps, sweaters, and shoes. She made our overalls! She had a sewing machine that she pedaled with her feet. The only thing we bought was underwear in the winter to last us for the year. A lot of times, they were hand-me-downs. We passed 'em on down; the bigger ones to the little ones. If you could get by without buying, that's what you done in the hard times.

Christmas was far different from when we were kids than now. Times were a lot better when I was a kid. There wasn't any money to be had in the Depression. You could buy more with a nickel than you could today

PLATE 185 Edgar Owens with his mother's spinning wheel

with a ten-dollar bill. Most of the time at Christmas, at our house, we hung stockings up like all the other kids in the community. We were lucky if we got an orange, a stick of peppermint candy, and nuts mixed up like pecans and English walnuts. That consisted of our Christmas. We was a lot prouder of it than my kids were when they got their first bicycle.

We hit the woods every chance we got. We climbed bushes and rode one bush over into another bush to see how far you could go through the timber without hittin' the ground. We played fox and dogs. Some of us would be fox and the rest be dogs. We played hide-and-seek and games like that. We didn't have ball games. At school we did have a baseball made out of wore-out socks. The yarn was raveled out, so you just wound it up in a ball tight enough where Momma could sew it where it wouldn't unravel and that was our baseball. We played Antie Over (throwing the ball over the school from one side to another), and teamed up with so many on each side. You holler, "Antie Over," before you throw the ball and, if they missed the ball, you got to pick one from their side to come on your side. If they caught the ball, they could come over and whoever they hit with the ball had to go over on their side. Whichever side got all the players won. Our bat was a flat board. It had a shewed-down handle where you could hold it, and shewed-out just like a paddle. It was pretty easy to hit a ball that way.

We hunted rabbits, squirrels, 'coons [raccoons], and groundhogs when we were growing up. We first thought that we would get a little bit of money from possum hides, fox hides, as well as 'coon hides. We used 'coon meat for meat and then got a lil' money, too. Squirrel was a favorite dish. You couldn't buy meat. You either killed it or you didn't have any.

We walked to Glade Hope School through a trail way about a mile east of where we lived. This was during the Great Depression. When we were going to school, we didn't have shoes to wear. We got one pair of shoes a year; and we didn't get them until the weather got extremely cold. A pair of shoes doesn't last a kid, never has, over two or three months, four at the most. It was close to Christmas when you got your pair of shoes, and by the time the first day of May come, your shoes, why, they's pretty well worn-out. We went barefoot from the first day of May till way up in the fall. Some mornings we had to wait till the frost cleared in the old field that was between our house and the school. A lot of times our feet would get so cold we would find a sunny spot, and we'd sit down on our feet to warm 'em before we went on to school. I walked to school barefoot when there was icicles spewing out of the banks on the side of the road. Rain or shine, we still went to school.

We was in a one-room school. Seventh grade was the highest grade they taught there. All the kids was in that one-room school building. The teacher would take grades and teach her lessons. When she was teaching one class, the rest of the classes would be studying their lessons to prepare them to get ready for their turn while the teacher was teaching us. That was in the early thirties. I started school in 1930 or 1931. I finished seventh grade there in 1937–1938. We had a consolidated school in this community. A new school was built up on Highway 28 near the North Caroliner [North Carolina] line. They started running a bus up the highway. Kids that lived off the highway had to walk to the bus and catch it at the highway. My first teacher was Alvieta Hick. She moved and taught school my first year, and then she was called to Persimmon to teach over there. She taught one year at Persimmon Elementary, then married J. D. Wilburn, the son of the man she boarded with. She retired from teaching and stayed home to take care of her children and J. D.'s parents. The next teachers I remember were Miss Bonnie Walker, Miss Nicholson, and Mrs. Dorothy Davis. Her sister taught, as well. Dorothy taught one year and her sister taught two years. Mrs. Overholt taught school over there for three years. Most of the kids in this community graduated from somewhere between second and seventh grade. All of 'em just went one or two years. Some of us finished all the grades that they taught over there. For graduation all we had was a celebration. On the last day of school, the teacher usually gave us some kind of lil' gift, a pencil or something like that. Then she'd hand us our report card. The report cards were just about eight inches square, folded in the middle. The name of the school, your name, and age was all on the front side. The teacher's name was on the front as well. You open it up, and the subjects were listed on the inside of the folder. On the back, when you opened it, it folded back up where the parents signed it. When you brought it home they okayed it, then you brought it back. When the school year was over, they'd give you your report card and showed you that you were promoted to the next grade or retained in the same grade you were in. We studied reading, writing, geography, arithmetic, and spelling. That's all the subjects that I remember us having over at that school.

"Shirts were a nickel, and pants were a dime, but of course, nickels and dimes weren't that plentiful back then either."

I also went to school over on Highway 28. I took the eighth and ninth grade up there. After that, I got into Tamassee DAR [Daughters of the American Revolution] School, a residential boarding school in South Carolina. The school had a bunch of property that was farmland. They grew cotton, they had a dairy herd, they had a beef herd, they had chicken houses, they had swine, and they raised it and killed and cured it. They were self-producing when I was there. The DAR ladies would send a lot of clothes to the school, to where you could get pants or a shirt. Shirts were a nickel, and pants were a dime, but of course, nickels and dimes weren't that plentiful back then either. I could have got rich if I had been making ten dollars an hour back then.

The school sold the excess. They processed all the milk; they sold a lot of milk, but they took what they needed and sold the rest. They sold excess milk, hogs, and beef. Their cotton crop—that was a pure cash crop.

I was afraid that I couldn't pass the grades down there, and I took the eighth and ninth grades over. If I hadn't I would have graduated in the

1942–1943 school year, but I finished ninth grade and was drafted into the Army in August of 1943.

So I was eighteen when I got drafted. I had two brothers that were already in the service. The superintendent of the school begged me to let him get me deferred so I could finish my education—my grades would have merited it—he said, "I'll tell you right now, I can guarantee you with your grades, I can put you through Clemson College on scholarship, and it won't cost you a dime." I thought I should be loyal to my country.

I got a call for a physical examination in Fort McPherson, in Atlanta in July, about the fifteenth or sixteenth. We passed our physical, and we had a thirty-day leave before we had to report back to Fort McPherson on the seventeenth of August 1943. After that, we went to Camp Blanding in Florida and took basic training in the medical course for eight weeks. In the medical course, we studied the basics of medicine: dressing wounds, artificial respiration, cleansing wounds, bandaging wounds, and how to bandage a busted arm or busted leg. That was if they could not be transported to a military hospital from the battlefield—just the basic elementary things that a medic does on the field. Then our orders got mixed up in Fort McPherson. We were supposed to have went to combat engineer-training camp in August, but it took two months to get our orders cleared up. We were drafted as D-day troops, but we missed D-day by two months because of the mess-up in our orders, which in our outfit, we were grateful for. D-day was "jumping-off" day. That was the day we started invading the European continent. It was at three o'clock, June 6, 1944. American-allied forces went out on the beach in Cherbourg and Normandy, France, just across the English Channel, and it was a couple more beachheads east. The invasion went through France, Belgium, Holland, Rustenburg, and into Germany.

I was so glad to get home. One thing in Army training that you was taught was to conduct yourself as an honorable American and treat people in a way that showed friendship and love. You were trained not to bring disrespect to the Armed Forces. We never knew from one day to the next what we'd be doing, or what materials we'd be using. I don't regret my service in the military, not one bit.

There was times you'd like to run away, and times you thought you were gonna freeze to death. It wasn't all fun, but you enjoyed the people you worked with, fought with, and lived with. We had a bond between us; that part of it we enjoyed, and then there was the dangerous parts that none of us enjoyed. When we came in, we landed in a discharge center in New York, then we were discharged from up here in New Jersey. I think the name of the Army base was Fort Dick. After we were discharged, they furnished our transportation to our native states. I went back to Atlanta and caught a bus to Clayton, but at that time, Smoky Mountain Trailways was running buses through in 'bout all the rural communities. So I got on a bus from Atlanta and went to Glade Road off of Highway 28. We didn't have any telephones or no ways of communicatin'. You'd have to send a telegram and someone would have to bring it from Clayton to where you was at. It was cheaper just to catch a bus and come to the highway. I carried my duffel bag and all my personal belongings from the highway all the way home. The walk was about a two-mile walk, but that was all right, because I was young, stout, and ready to come home.

After I came back, I farmed for a year on the GI [Serviceman's Readjustment Act of 1944] program. Then my dad and I bought a tractor. I did a lot of custom work with it. I helped my dad on the farm, as well. I cut timber for a few months till I got a job at Raburn Mills [Rabun Mills]. I worked nearly eight years at that plant. After that I got into construction, and worked till I retired.

I first met the woman I married in 1948. I met her family then, but we didn't begin dating till 1955. We got married on February 10, 1956. On our dates we just rode around and talked a lot. She was stayin' and workin' with her sister and boarding at her sister's house, so I went down on the weekends and we'd go to church. We'd just get out and walk, or ride around and talk. We would ride in a '49 Chevrolet pickup that I had bought after I came back from the service. It was big and expensive; it was brand-new, for fourteen hundred forty-five dollars. It was the car I learned to drive in, although I did drive some in the Army.

When my kids was born, my wife went to Raburn [Rabun] County Hospital. To start with they had a maternity home out there for women having children. She stayed seven days in the hospital. They had doctors for all of our kids.

For our kids we had a Christmas tree, and we decorated it more with tinfoil, tinsel, and different-colored ropes. Back then you got to decorate Christmas trees differently. There wasn't electricity, so you didn't have any lights on before you decorated it; you decorated it with string and holly berries or string and popcorn. We used whatever you could make a string of. If we put a little color on the Christmas tree—it made it a whole lot prettier.

We had a lot of fun with our kids. We pulled pranks on 'em, and they did the same to us, but they always knew that we was their pal. We tried to be more to them than just a parent. We tried to be a friend and a pal, too. They knew that they could come to us with any problem that they had. They felt like they could have fun with us. We were always there for them, but we still pulled a few pranks on them. Tommy, Ralph, and one of the friends that they spent a lot of time with when they were growin' up needed a frog to take to school, so they went up to the pond to catch them a frog to take for a science project. They were going to bisect [dissect] it. They had a gas lantern. I slipped up to the edge of the pond. Back then, before I had my teeth pulled, I could make a racket that sounded kind a' like a bat-a-screeching. The neighbor's boy said, "Listen! Is that a mad bat?" And Ralph said, "It sounded like a bat to me." Tommy said, "Let's go!" They tore out down around the edge of the pond and had to wade knee-deep to get down around there. They put Tommy carrying the lantern, and Ralph and Melvin were with him. Tommy was trying to get one of the others to carry the lantern, and neither one of them wouldn't carry it; they just set it down on the dam and come around the pasture fence, run through the electric fence on to the house. I come to the house like nothing had happened, and they got to telling me about what an experience they had. I said, "What did y'uns do with your lamplight?" And Tommy said, "I tried to get them to take it and they wouldn't, and I sat it down 'cause I couldn't run with it. I left it sittin' up there on the dam." I told 'em, "Well, boys, y'uns gonna go back and get it, bats or no bats." So they started after the threat of a whoopin' [whipping] and got past a crib over there. They talked it over and they decided they would rather take a whoopin' than to go back up there and get that lamp. They started back to the house, and they didn't know I was hid 'side the road, and I shrieked again like a bat! It 'bout scared 'em half to death again. When they seen what it was, they had a lot of fun out of it. They've been deviled [teased] a lot since then. We had a lot of fun. You could make it fun with kids or you can make a hard time with 'em. We tried to see that they had a good time, best we could.

"The advice I would give to young folks is, first of all, we need to take care of our bodies. It's a gift of God . . ."

I retired when my wife got sick. I was sixty years old. She got disabled, and everybody on the mountain was working, so I couldn't leave her by herself. I had to quit work to stay with her for two years. We got by the best we could until I could sign up for Social Security—we wiggled around and got by.

The advice I would give to young folks is, first of all, we need to take care of our bodies. It's a gift of God; God gives us the ability to be born. We are also given all the measures to take care of ourselves, and if we don't, we are letting ourselves down. If we do everything we can to nurture our bodies, take care of our bodies—and that includes not being afraid to go to the doctor if we need it—that's what I'd say is key.

My advice for raising kids is that if they need discipline, I believe the parents should have the right and option of correcting their children anytime they need correcting. I don't believe in child abuse; I'm one hundred percent against child abuse, but there's a difference in a child being corrected and being abused.

"I've seen blood running in the ditches on the side of the road just like water after a thunderstorm, and it was American blood running, too. People don't think about war costing anything, but if they had been in a few places like that, they would realize that it's a price that nobody wanted to pay, but a lot of them did."

If there was anything that I would like to relive, it would be my youth. I think we lived in a good era, seen hard times, seen good times, and experienced sadness. We've experienced a lot of joy in life. I've done a lot that I wanted to do, but if I had it to do over, I'd do it a lot different than I done. I would walk a closer walk with God than I did. I knew when I was converted that God wanted me to preach, and the devil told me that I couldn't preach, and I listened to him for nearly twenty years. That's the biggest regret that I've got in my life—that I didn't go to preaching. I did everything I could to promote the Kingdom of Christ. I worked in the church, I worked with the young people, but I still was not doing what God called me to do. He wanted me to preach instead of what I wanted to do. Well, I surrendered when I was about thirty-five years old, I guess. I was ordained in either 1964 or 1965.

I'm glad we've got a two-party system [of government], but I think that we need to be loyal to one another. Nobody sees alike, and there's nothing wrong with expressing your opinion, and standing by your opinion, but it should be based more on what's good for your fellow man than what's good for me. We're gonna have to walk with God, and we've got to come together and trust God again. These cahoots we've got now don't even know what God is!

It burns me up that our government has degenerated to the point where we are losing all that we fought for. I've seen blood running in the ditches on the side of the road just like water after a thunderstorm, and it was American blood running, too. People don't think about war costing anything, but if they had been in a few places like that, they would realize that it's a price that nobody wanted to pay, but a lot of them did.

We have been blessed for fifty years together. I thank the Good Lord that I've had a long life and enjoyed most of it. There's been some bad, but there's been a lot of good. We've seen our kids grow up. We've seen grandkids grow up, and some of them finished college. We feel like we've been blessed with four beautiful lil' great-granddaughters. We are expecting another. We got five! If luck holds out, why we may have more great-grandkids than we have grandkids. I think we have seven. My most valuable possession is my family.

PLATE 186 Edgar Owens with his granddaughter Alex Owens

I pastored churches until the eighties. I had a severe sick spell in the spring of '89, and at that time I felt like I wasn't able to pastor a church. I have had the opportunity to marry some of my grandchildren, baptized some of them, and won some of them to the Lord. I thank the good Lord for their lives and the testimonies that they have today. We got one awful strong, young, granddaughter that's a great witness to the Lord. Her name is Alex Owens.

HEARTS TOUCHED AND HEALED

An interview with Lois and Clarence Martin

Now we don't have to watch for mad dogs. It's people. That's true. It's people we have to watch—sure is. I know some people right now that I'd rather meet a mad dog out yonder than meet them. I really had! That is the truth. —Lois Martin

I have always been interested in the "old times." I would give anything to go back just one day. Instead of being bored watching television, I could plow the field with a mule, walk into town with five cents in my pocket and buy a bag of candy, or even go swimming in the creek. The old times strike me as the "good times."

After a week of asking my fellow students for ideas about someone who could take me back in time, Mrs. Joyce Green, the Foxfire teacher at the time, recommended her aunt Lois and uncle Clarence Martin. This couple had many good years together, and they are never alone, for they take the Lord with them in their hearts wherever they go, and their hearts are "beating just fine."

—*Adam Hunter*

Lois Martin: May 1, in 1926, I was born in Rabun County. Back when I was born, they didn't send the mothers to no hospital; they done it all at home. My mother had me at home. I lived right around the York House, somewhere right in there. I think that the Will Grist family owned all that back in there, and that's who my daddy worked for at that time. He did a lot of farming and stuff like that. When I was two weeks old is when we moved to Habersham County, and I have been there ever since.

Lord, I'll tell you what—it wasn't good back then. We didn't have what you have today, not by a long shot. We didn't live in houses like we are livin' in today either. It was, I guess you could say, rough, 'cause back then my daddy worked for only about fifty cents a day. He worked all day long, about ten hours, for fifty cents. He worked over there at Habersham Mills, you know, when that mill was a-runnin'. People on the mill hill would hire him to do things, like cuttin' wood and cleanin' around the house for them and workin' in the garden and stuff like that. Later he worked in a sawmill. That's when I was a little feller and would go with him to work sometimes. I was little, but I still remember all of that.

"It was hard back then, but sometimes I think now I wouldn't mind goin' back over some of it that I already went through, even though it was hard."

Times was rough, but I get to thinking sometimes now: If you young people would have to go through back then, y'all would be a whole lots better off today than you are now. Now, I ain't saying you're bad—now, don't misunderstand me—but there's so much meanness out there in the world now. There wouldn't be half as much meanness goin' on as there is now, but the reason why a lot is a-goin' on is because the mothers work away from home. They are not home to see after their children like they was back then. You never heard tell of a mother cuttin' wood and cleanin' around the house and stuff like that, or workin' on a public job. Mothers just didn't do it. My mama used to take in washin' for the community. I mean, she went to the wash place and stayed here all day long, maybe for twenty-five cents, fifty cents, not over a dollar. Now, listen, that was good money back then. It went somewhere. I guess you've never seen a rubboard, but that's what she used to wash with. She put that rubboard in a tub, and she'd scrub the clothes with that. She also had a wash pot where she boiled her clothes. She had to draw water from the well. It was hard back then, but sometimes I think now I wouldn't mind goin' back over some of it that I already went through, even though it was hard.

When we was growin' up back then, people had more love for each other than they have today. People has lost their love for each other. Back then, if we had sickness in our home, the whole community would go and help them out. If they needed wood cut, and Daddy has took us and worked somebody else's crop because they were sick and could not work it. Now you get somebody to do that today! They won't do it. They have lost their first love. People don't love each other no more.

There wasn't much fun goin' when Daddy was raisin' us. We did a lot of farmin', and it wasn't just a little patch. It was acres and acres of farm. Back then Daddy growed cotton, if you know what cotton is. Well, he growed cotton, and from the time I was six years old, we was in the field a-workin'. We couldn't do much, but Daddy had us out there workin'. Maybe we'd get together at the house, maybe play, like hide-'n'-seek or something like that, little games like that. We made our toys back then, son! We'd go to the woods and cut down a pine tree and saw us some wheels off of it, bore a hole in that wheel, and make our wagons that we would play with. Whatever we wanted to play with, we made it. We made Tom Walkers [stilts]. Me and Marie has made a-many a one. They are things like crutches, only you put steps on 'em and get on them steps. Yeah, that's what we used to play with, and that was as famous back then, son, as it is if you was to get a new car today. We didn't have a car when I was growin' up. We walked wherever we needed to go. The first car I ever seen was when we lived next to where George Purdue's house is. Daddy told us when he left to go to work that mornin', "Now, children, watch about twelve o'clock. An A-model," or whatever, the first ones to come out, "will be passin' the road." At about twelve o'clock we was out there on the side of the road lookin' for it, and sure enough, it passed. I believe John Berry was the one who come by in it. He lived in Habersham. I guess I was around twelve when I saw it.

Sometimes Daddy would take us to church on Sunday, or if there was a tent revival goin' on, he would take us. Sometimes he would hook up the mule and wagon and take us in the wagon. Most of the time, we walked to church because the church wasn't too fer away.

There was four boys and four girls, and we all just got along together— wasn't no storytellin' done. We did not tell haint tales. We talked about mad dogs, but that wasn't a story. That was true. Sometimes mad dogs would get out in the summertime. We'd hear that there was a mad dog out, but, usually, someone would kill 'em before they ever got to us. When they said, "Mad dog," that scared all of us. It was good back then because when the community would hear something like that, they would get it across to the whole community to watch out. Now we don't have to watch for mad dogs. It's people. That's true. It's people we have to watch—sure is. I know some people right now that I'd rather meet a mad dog out yonder than meet them. I really had! That is the truth. Now, you wanted the truth. Well, you're gonna get it.

We always raised crops when I was growin' up. I went out there and worked in the fields. Honey, I've plowed a steer all day long, ten hours a day, many a day. Daddy would get us up and say, "Lois, now, we got to go to that field. What you wanna do—hoe or plow?" I said, "Daddy, I'll plow." It was easier to plow than it was to hoe, and I plowed a mule all day long, many and many a time. I love to plow. It's not hard, but hoein' an diggin' is hard. Now, a mule is faster than a steer. You get a steer too hot, and they'll lay down on you. Sometimes we'd have to bring it to the house and let it cool off, and it was all right, but a mule . . . You can go with them all day, and they just move at a steady go. I have plowed many of a day. I could do it now if I had a mule.

Life is much easier now because we have a lot more. You can make more money, and you have a lot more to work with. It's a whole lots easier than it was when I was growin' up. We have better clothes and everything than we had back then. Back when I was growin' up, you could buy material for about ten cents a yard. That is how we got our clothes. Mama would raise chickens, and we'd have plenty of chickens. We would sell eggs and buy cloth, and Mama made our clothes. We went to Clarkesville to Joe Stewart's store or Habersham Mills, where they had a company store, to buy the cloth. They wasn't any department stores close to us like we got today. They might have been some down in Atlanner [Atlanta], but around us, the biggest town we had was Clarkesville, and it wasn't as good as it is now. If we'd seen a place like Atlanner when we was growin' up, we'd a-thought we was in heaven. Now, it was rough back then.

The worstest crime that I remember in Habersham County, at the time I was growin' up, was a Brock man that killed his wife and throwed her in the river at the Cannon Bridge, and if I ain't mistaken, his wife was from Rabun County. She was a Bingham before she married. Sam McDuffie was the one that found her over here where her husband had killed her. [**Editors' note:** See *The Foxfire 45th Anniversary Book* for more details about the 1939 murder of Grace Bingham Brock.] I went to Cornelia to the funeral home to see her. They just had her on a slab, like a table, for people to view. You never did hear tell of nothin' like that back then.

We couldn't afford screen doors and screen windows, you know, so Dad would raise the windows as high as he could and open up the door and just put a chair in the door to keep the dogs from comin' in at night. Now, that's how people was livin' back then, son; you can't do that now. We have come through a lot, but still that was the best days for me because back then people had more love for one another. You had a friend out there you could go to, but you ain't got none today. So we are in that time that you can't trust nobody. They'll tell you anything.

I met my husband when I went home with my sister Icie to stay a week. She lived in Commerce, Georgia. While I was down there, I met Clarence. Then we started datin'. I think we dated about three months, and then we got married. I was eighteen. I have never been sorry about that because he has made a good husband. We have been happily married ever since, and we have never had a fuss because he stays out of my way, and he says "Yes, ma'am." I have a son named Jerry Martin, and I have a daughter Elaine Martin (well, she is a Norris now). Two is all I had.

Clarence is our pastor at the church. We started our own little church next door, and we have a nice little church. You should come and visit us sometime. You will hear the Word—I'll tell you that.

I have a lot to be thankful for. I thank God that my health is fine, but I have had three bypasses. I was not hurtin'. This is the honest truth: I had never had one pain. I never run no fever, and the doctor told me the third day, he said, "I'm gonna do something I've never let a patient do," and I said, "Well, I wanna go home." He said, "That's exactly what I'm gonna let you do." He said, "You can do just as good at home as you can in here. You're doin' fine." "Listen, Doc, I brought the Lord down here with me. He's been with me," and I said, "I do thank God for your help."

Clarence is seventy-seven. He has a pacemaker. He does anything that he wants to do. I had eye surgery the other day, and I'm a-doin' fine, and I feel real good. I am seventy-four years old.

I still work. I clean a plant above Clarkesville; I do sewin' for people in my home, too. I do ironin' for people, and I just do anything that I wanna do. There's nothing I can't do, but I'll tell you what I like to do best of all. You gonna laugh at this. I'd rather get out and do carpenter work than any work I have ever done in my life because if I take a notion to get up on top of my house, I get up there. Now, I am tellin' you, I had rather do carpenter work than any work I have ever done.

I have some advice for younguns—I sure do—if they'd do it. If all you young people would get y'self in a good church somewhere and turn y'self over to the Lord—I'm talkin' about gettin' saved, start servin' God—we'd have a good country to live in everywhere. That's the advice I'd give them today, and that's the only hope we have. If they don't turn

PLATE 187 Lois and Clarence Martin

to God, it's gonna get worser, and time is gonna get worser than what we see right now if people don't come back to God and do their first work. You just can't get that across to people today. God will always be with you through good and rough times.

Clarence Martin: I was born in Madison County and raised in Madison and Banks County, Georgia, till I was sixteen years old. I was in Banks County up until me and Lois married. She dragged me on up here to Habersham. That is how I ended up here. She did not want to leave the mountains, praise the Lord!

I never went to school in my life except a day or two. They was thirteen of us in the family, and we had to stay at home and work. There's days once in a while that I would get to go to school. I was so old that they let me go into two other grades, and I didn't finish a grade, not nary a grade, but I do thank God for what God has given me.

Our parents kept us out of school to work. It was true of most families then. They wasn't a law back then when I was a goin' to school to make us go, and Daddy, he kept us out to work. I got to the third grade, and that is when I quit. I can remember the last year I went to school that they furnished the lunch. I can't read anything but the Bible. I cannot even write my name or write a letter. I can read a little bit more than I used to, and I went through the Old Testament three times this year. I want to go through the old Bible because I want to know the Word of God. The Word of God is what sets us free, and I still say, "Praise the Lord."

I will tell you one thing for sure: I do the work that God wants me to do because God called me to preach the Word without education. I ran from it for six months sayin' that I couldn't do it. I finally said, "If you give it to me, I will preach it." I woke up one Sunday mornin' readin' six verses, from the fourteenth chapter of St. John, and I went right on to the church that night and asked the pastor to let me have the service on Wednesday night. He give it to me on January 1, 1964. I have been preachin' ever since.

A SELF-PROCLAIMED "BLACK SHEEP"

Mischievous antics with Malcolm Dillard

I had to find things out the hard way. It's unfortunate that every generation has to learn over and over again. —Malcolm Dillard

I chose Mr. Malcolm Dillard for my interview because for the last year and a half that I have lived in Dillard, Georgia, Mr. Dillard has been a close friend to my family. When I moved up here to Rabun County from Macon, Georgia, I had no family or friends in the area, but the Dillards made my family and me feel very welcome.

As I approached his house on the day of our interview, I thought about all the questions I would ask. Once I arrived, I was not surprised to see him outside waiting. He strolled over, opened my door, and welcomed me with a comfortable, friendly smile. Not only did he have plenty of stories that would make for an interesting article, but I enjoyed benefitting from his knowledge of the area, as always.

Mr. Dillard told me of William F. Dillard's leaving for the Civil War and the family's recent discovery of his fate. He told me about the old Revolutionary War rifle used by his great-grandfather and ultimately willed to him, and he also told me of his family's founding the Dillard

House, famous for its down-home Southern cooking. However, Mr. Dillard shares not only some of the family's history but also some of his own mischievous childhood antics and personal anecdotes and warns us to be wise enough to listen to our elders and heed their instructions.

—*Rebekah Carson*

I was born on December 24, 1934. Guess I messed up several people's Christmas that year. My daddy and mother lived with Granddaddy and Grandmother in the old original Dillard House. Joe, my brother, was born in 1936.

Joe became very ill a month after birth, and Mother had to stay right with him around the clock. My daddy, Barnard Dillard, was the local pharmacist and worked seven days a week and was on call even at night. My granddaddy and grandmother, in addition to running the Dillard House, tried to take care of me.

Some of the first things that I remember are the big snows in winter and then being in the garden with my grandmother in the spring. I idolized my grandfather, who was near eighty at this time. I followed him around, bothering him all day long. I lost his tools and took a lot. Later, I started getting into mischief: damming up the branch that ran in front of the house, backing up the water in the springhouse, and turning over milk jugs. I caught fish and put them in the dam. I would catch fish at the dam pond over again and put them back. I know that they had a big case of sore mouth. Old water moccasins would also find my fish and eat them. They were nonpoisonous snakes that looked a lot like cottonmouths, but they were not. I learned to grab them by the tail and pop their heads off. One time I caught several over two or three days and put them in a bucket with a ventilated lid. I carried the bucket of snakes up to Dillard right in front of the drugstore and dumped them out. Dillard was a busy place on Saturday afternoons at the drugstore and Dr. Neville's office. You could hear ladies screaming quite a ways that afternoon.

When my granddaddy and grandmother were in their eighties, they realized that they could no longer run the Dillard House and take care of all the guests. They placed their regular guests with Boxwood Terrace and Oaklawn. These boardinghouses were run by Aunt Sally Powell and Arthur Dillard, Granddaddy's sister and cousin.

Jim Dillard came down to our house and asked Granddaddy [Zack

PLATE 188 The house where Mr. Dillard's grandfather was born

Dillard] if Oaklawn could take the name of "The Dillard House." I remember this, and I think my granddaddy was pleased. He told Jim, "Sure, we are done."

This was just at the end of World War II, and I remember all of my cousins coming home. I remember my daddy and grandfather following the events of the war. My granddaddy was a very authoritative person. I thought that he knew everything, and I also thought I knew everything.

My granddaddy and grandmother died in 1946 and 1947, and I felt lost. Mother had gone back to teaching school, and Daddy was busy in the drugstore. Joe was better, but having suffered several years left its mark on him.

I had a hard time growing up. When I was very young, about three years old, Mother had warned me with a switch about going up the steep steps in the old house. One day, I said, "Mother, get your switch, I am going up the steps."

"I absolutely could not behave, even though I tried."

Later I had a few friends, Fred Jolley, Edward Dillard, Gene Vinson, and others. I managed to get into trouble and get them in trouble, too. We greased the railroad track with lard; when the old steam engine of the Tallulah Falls train would pull out of Dillard, the wheels would slip, and we would sit up on the bank and laugh. I remember one time we got a soft cow patty [manure] out of the pasture and packed it right under the track where the brakeman had to switch the tracks to leave railcars in Dillard before going on to Franklin, North Carolina. We set up on the bank and watched the brakeman stick his hand under the switching track and then sling his hand vigorously. We laughed, and the brakeman threw rocks at us.

When I was in the first grade, my mother taught the second grade. When time came for me to go to the second grade, Mother asked Miss McKinney, the principal, to let her switch grades for one year, as she had enough of me at home. I dodged the bullet, and she did, too. I absolutely could not behave, even though I tried. I remember one time, when I was in the fifth grade, I got two whippings in one day. Mrs. Noah Grist, my teacher, said she would have given me another one, but she knew that my mother doubled the licks when I got home.

Since I worshiped my grandfather, I heard a lot of history about the development of Rabun. My grandfather, Zack Dillard, was the son of William F. Dillard. William F. Dillard was the youngest son of James Dillard, the son of old John Dillard who settled this area.

William F. Dillard left for the Civil War, and nobody here ever heard from him again until recently. Ann Dickerson and Odelle Hamby found out that he died in Lynchburg, Virginia, with pneumonia and is buried in a Confederate cemetery.

William F. Dillard built the old home several years before the Civil War. This home later became the original Dillard House. My grand-daddy, my daddy, and I were born in this house, which is now owned by my son, Zack.

My grandfather willed me the old rifle that was used in the Revolutionary War by his great-grandfather, John Dillard. Along with the Revolutionary War rifle, Granddaddy left an old Hopkins and Allen drop-block 12-gauge shotgun in the old house. I took over this gun and hunted all over the valley. We ate a lot of rabbit and squirrel. Mother would cook anything that I brought in just to please me. Then I started fishing all up and down the Little Tennessee River and Darnell, Mud, and Kelly's Creek. One April, my cousin, Edward Singleton, Joe Ed Brown, and I went behind Rabun Bald and camped. We got over there later and built a lean-to. That's putting a pole between two forked stakes and leaning brush over the pole. The temperature dropped so low, the red worms froze in the can, and we had to break them in pieces to bait our hooks. We caught the biggest mess of old native speckled trout in Holcomb Creek that you ever have seen. This set me on fire for trout fishin'. I started goin' up Darnell Creek by myself, all the way to the "Beasley Fields" whenever I had a chance. I would walk down in front of the Dillard House, across Mr. Herschel Burrell's pasture, then all the way to the Beasley Fields, located above where the firing range is now. This was a distance of about eight miles from home. A lot of Sunday afternoons, I would walk there—two hours—and then walk home.

Rabun Gap high school was a good school with excellent teachers. I was real interested in vocational agriculture and had already learned to love the woods. Somehow, the good teachers at Rabun Gap managed to get me out of high school in 1952. I had been awarded a small scholarship to the University of Georgia through Agricultural Education.

"My parents, not impressed with my grades, asked what was wrong; I told them I had just spent too much time on one subject."

I left for the University of Georgia in September of 1952. After being there a few days, I realized I was where I should be, but was concerned because I had so little money. The first quarter was fine, and the grades were okay. The second quarter was rough, and the grades were rougher. The third quarter, I barely stayed in school. I think this was the time that I came home with three Fs and one D. My parents, not impressed with my grades, asked what was wrong; I told them I had just spent too much time on one subject.

I decided to change my major to forestry at the end of that spring quarter. The Forestry School got me a job in Oregon that summer in the Willamette National Forest of Oregon. Leaving for Oregon was a low point in my life because of other disappointments that erased some of my hopes and dreams. Realizing that I was tough physically, but not enough mentally, I had to do something with myself.

As I was arriving at McKenzie Bridge, Oregon, the ranger told me that he was sending me to Rebel Rock [part of Willamette Forest], since I was from Georgia. They packed my food on mules and left me for the summer. I had no lookout tower, but walked a rimrock each day to look for fires. The total trail for one day was ten miles. I lived in a cabin one and a half miles from the main vantage point on the rimrock.

I was not allowed to have a firearm on Rebel Rock. I came to realize, after a while, that I didn't need one, although there were cougars, bears, elk, deer, grouse, and other wild things. They had packed me a bunch of rice, which I didn't care for very much. I would throw it out in front of my cabin for the grouse to eat. I got a hard stick and threw it into the middle of them, killing two grouse. I reported to the ranger station that I had Southern fried grouse for supper. The fresh meat was packed and was kept in a snowbank that lasted all summer.

In late summer we had a dry lightning storm that set sixteen fires in the forest at one time. One big one was between my cabin and the rim-rock. I was on the rimrock when it happened, and from the smoke over the hill, I thought it was my cabin. I called it in to the ranger station, and they told me to stay on the rimrock and record the bearing of lightning strikes as determined by compass. In a few minutes, the station called back and told me to leave and fight the fire. They further said they were sending in a crew to fight the fire because it was a big one. I was able to get a line dug in front of the fire toward the top of the hill, and when it reached the top, the head of the fire fizzled out. The sides of the fire, "the flanks," were not burning fast and were easy to put out. The fire crew came in and mopped up the fire and brought all kinds of food and supplies that you could imagine. They asked how I stopped the fire, and I told them that it was just our old Southern way of doing things. The crew was the first people that I had seen in forty-two days.

> "I also told them South Georgia boys that when we heard of a drought in South Georgia, we always flushed our commodes to help them out."

The second year at Georgia, I got a job working in the cafeteria at Snelling Hall, so I ate good. I had to drop out spring quarter because I had run out of money. The junior year was good at Georgia. I had saved money and had a lot of forestry courses. A lot of the forestry students were from South Georgia around the Okefenokee Swamp. I made life-long friends there. Those flatwood South Georgia boys were a lot like us mountain people. They were independent, honest, funny, and would do anything in the world for you. They kidded me about being a "North Georgia Yankee." I responded, "When Sherman broke through Atlanta, you South Georgians let him go straight to the Coast of Savannah." I also told them South Georgia boys that when we heard of a drought in South Georgia, we always flushed our commodes to help them out.

My cousin, Edward Dillard, joined me at Georgia that junior year. Edward and I are not as much kin as we are friends. I did pull a rough trick on Edward that year. In 1955, we had a "panty raid" at Georgia. The panties came floating down from six stories of windows at three of the large dormitories—hundreds of them. One of the girls stuck her head out the window and said, "Why don't you boys go home?" Another girl stuck her head out the window and said "Shut up, you old heifer!" That would be nothing now, but then there was a full page in the Atlanta paper.

Edward had told his parents that he was studying during the time of the panty raid. I had to come home to get the car to carry all of our clothes home for Christmas. I told Mother and Daddy that I wanted to fix Edward up with a large pair of panties to go in his dirty clothes. Mother really came up with a fine pair. I knew when Edward was taking his final tests, so I slipped over to his boardinghouse and put the panties in the bottom of his dirty-clothes bag. I left undetected and came back later to pick him up to go home. The next morning, I made a visit to Edward's house to find him beside the heater with his head between his hands. I told Edward that we needed to get out and about. Edward looked up at me and said, "Mother found the biggest, raggedy pair of panties in my clothes bag, and I can't go anywhere. I'm grounded!" I had to confess to get Edward off the hook.

Finally, all of my college course work was completed at Christmas, 1956. Georgia Kraft Company hired me to begin work on January 1, 1957. In June of 1957, I went back to Georgia for the official graduation. I was drafted into the Army right after graduation and went to Fort Jackson, South Carolina, for my boot training. After a battery of tests, I was advised to apply for Officer Candidate School. With only one interview to go, my buddy discovered that if we went to OCS, we had to stay in the service for two years after becoming a second lieutenant. Mike Dutton, my friend, and I signed a waiver to block OCS training, and immediately we were sent to Italy. We were placed in an artillery unit to fire the "Honest John Rocket." I wanted to see all of Europe that was possible. I ended up going to France, Austria, Switzerland, Germany, Portugal, Greece, and Spain.

In June 1959, I was discharged from the Army back through Fort Jackson. I immediately went back to Georgia Kraft Company in Rome. Georgia Kraft kept me on the road all the time. I had started dating Charlotte House, a secretary at Georgia Kraft, but didn't get to see her very much because of traveling.

In March 1960, a big ice storm hit Northwest Georgia and tore up a lot of Berry School's timber. Georgia Kraft had an agreement with Berry to salvage all of the damaged timber. This took me off the road.

Staying in Rome afforded me the opportunity to do serious courting.

PLATE 189 Malcolm Dillard while stationed in Italy

I asked Charlotte to marry me early in 1961. We got married on July 9, 1961, and I was moved to Marietta. A son was born to us on January 13, 1964. We named him Zachariah Barnard, after my granddaddy and daddy. I left Georgia Kraft and went into the wood business, buying wood for yards. We had a little girl born on October 3, 1967. We named her Carrie Louise, after both our mothers.

In August of 1965, I took a job with the Georgia Department of Education as the vocational forester for North Georgia. I loved this job, working with vocational teachers like Mr. Jim Burden, Mr. Jack Martin, and Mr. Cabe at Rabun County High School.

Our children grew up and are married. We have five grandchildren. Zack had two boys and girls. Carrie had one daughter. Charlotte and I both retired in 1996. We planned a trip out West just after we retired. Our plan was to sell our house and move back home to Dillard when we got back. However, things didn't work out that way. Our house sold while we were gone on the trip, and we came straight to Dillard.

"Growing up in a small town like Dillard had its advantages, but it doesn't make the person."

I had been growing balsam fir and white pine Christmas trees at Dillard for a good while. When I got home, I planted more (too many). I have cut way into my fishing time. People come from everywhere to buy trees this year. I don't know if I ever will quit growing trees.

This area has begun to change a lot. There is still beauty all around us, and we have got people moving here. Growing up in a small town, I guess, does have an effect on your life, but it doesn't dictate who you associate with. To be honest, many of my friends were city boys. I just like good, down-to-earth people that do what they say they are going to do and are honest. Growing up in a small town like Dillard had its advantages, but it doesn't make the person.

Well, as far as religion in my life, I joined the Methodist church when I was nine years old. Jack Waldroop was our preacher. He took a lot of time with me. I guess he realized that I needed help. I believe just like the Bible verse says, "Raise up a child in the way that he should go, and he won't depart from it." I think that is true. You can kind a' lose your way every once in a while, but then you find your way back and realize your mistakes because your conscience is always there. You know when you're wrong.

My parents taught me to go to church, listen to your preacher's counsel, and obey your parents. The main thing that impressed me was the way they lived their life—not full of greed, but willing to help people— and the way they overcame hardships. We were in debt for a long time because of my grandfather lending out money to people and not getting paid back. Finally, we paid every penny off. That's what made me learn to work hard and pay off debts. I had a hard time growing up because I was so mischievous, but I survived.

My advice to the younger, upcoming generation would be to listen to your mother and father. Try to be truthful, not only with everybody else but also to yourself. We have to spend some time thinking what the end results are going to be. We need to always think about that. Also, what are our actions going to lead to? If it's something constructive, it will lead to something good. I had to find things out the hard way. It's unfortunate that every generation has to learn over and over again. Some people are wise enough to heed their instructions and listen to the older people. We really want to set you people of today on the right track. Some people are wise enough to do that.

"IT HAS BEEN WONDERFUL, REALLY!"

The unique life of Beanie Ramey

Working as a waitress, meeting people, and interacting with them contributed to my self-taught education. —Beanie Ramey

Beanie Ramey is a remarkable woman who has led an abundant life rich in people, places, and experiences. She graciously and candidly shared many of those experiences with us. Her ready smile and comfortable manner made all of us feel welcomed. As we approached her door, a slew of bunny rabbits hopped around in her flower beds and yard. We learned later that those bunnies were one of her late husband's favorite hobbies.

As we entered her home, we immediately noticed the artwork adorning her walls. She told us that most of the art, which depicts Rabun County scenes from years ago, was done by her brother, Broderick Crawford. She also showed us some of her own artwork. We were surprised that she had the time for creative endeavors because she is the head of Ramey Enterprises, a very successful family business. In her son Horace's office hangs a picture taken by Beanie's son Tom. He and some other students went to interview Beanie's grandmother, Carrie English McCurry, for an article in 1977's summer issue of *The Foxfire Magazine*.

Just like her grandmother, Beanie is an industrious, determined woman. She is modern in many ways but still adheres to the old-fashioned individualist nature of her forebears. Her exuberance and quick wit entertained us for hours. Near the end of the interview, Beanie said, "I have seen a lot of changes. I've done a lot of things. I have been on long rides, and I wouldn't trade it for anything!" We wouldn't trade our time with Beanie for anything either.

—*Kaye Carver Collins*

Marvenia is my real name. I don't have a middle name, so I use C. from my maiden name, Crawford. I was born on August 16, 1939, in Tiger, Georgia, right on Main Street. That's where Delmo and Caroline Patterson live now, in my mother's old home. The white house on the left, coming from Clayton, is where my grandmother lived across the street. She moved there when I was six to eight years old; before that time, she lived on Hollifield Connector. Right when you start up Hollifield Connector, there's a little house on the right, and that was her home for many years. I used to have an uncle that would put me in a bicycle basket—I don't know how old you have to be to do that—and he would ride me down to her house.

My father, M. L. Crawford, was much older than my mother. He was born in 1886. My mother was born in 1917. My granny, Carrie Holcomb, was born in 1888. There's just a couple years' difference in their age. My father was one of the old lumbermen here in the county. He always had his horses and did sawmilling. He also raised and sold hunting dogs all the way up into my high school years. He shipped them all over the country. My mother raised little spitz puppies and little fox terriers. I helped my father make shipping crates from broom handles, rejects from a small factory in Tiger.

My dad's and mom's names were M. L. and Eva Crawford. My mother was Eva English, and at the time of her death, she had remarried after my father died. She was Eva Brown. They lived all their life right there in that house in Tiger. My daddy built that, and I can remember in the early, early years we didn't let dogs in our house, but if Mother's dog had puppies in the wintertime and there was a chance they might get cold, they got put in a box and set by the heater, and we had wood heat in the house. My mother would take care of them and wouldn't let anything happen to them. They could stay in a big box by the heater to stay warm, the same as she always did for us. There were five of us in the family other than our two older sisters. It was my father's second family, so the older sisters were married and had children our age. Along with that wood heater, she always warmed a blanket and put it around our feet in the wintertime so we wouldn't get cold. You sleep better with warm feet.

There was a preacher who lived behind us when we were young, and my mother had the preacher's wife make us dolls. They laughed at my doll, 'cause one was dressed in white and one was dressed in beige. They told me that my doll had dirty clothes because it was beige. So, I got rid of it! Don't know what I ever did with it. I think one had blond hair and one had dark hair. Carolyn got the one with the white dress and blond hair. When I told Tom [my husband] that one, he bought me all the Gorham dolls—beautiful dresses—like Christina and Rosemary— one of those really pretty dolls. He said, "Since you don't have dolls, I'm giving you dolls for Christmas." He gave me about twelve of them.

When I was probably in fifth or sixth grade, there was a big fire in

Tiger at the looper factory. Do you know what a looper is? Have you ever seen a pot holder made of loopers, those round things, those little round circles? We used to weave them together, you know. Lay them out and weave them together. It was next door to my mother's house. It was just a big white building, and there was a lady named Mrs. Phillips—that was the woman that ran it. I asked somebody the other day if they ever knew anything about her, or who she was, or whatever happened to her or anything, but Mrs. Phillips ran the looper factory.

"When I got to the Texaco station, I saw all of our furniture out in the yard, and I thought our house was on fire."

I really don't know who owned the looper factory, but they said a boiler blew up in it and it burned. It had some kind of big boiler down in the basement. I believe I was in the fourth grade when that happened. I could see the smoke, and I could hear people saying something about the fire. You could look out the schoolroom at Tiger School and see the smoke coming up from around my mother's house. At that time, there was a Texaco service station on the corner, across from the post office. I remember running because it was in the direction of our house, running home that afternoon. When I got to the Texaco station, I saw all of our furniture out in the yard, and I thought our house was on fire. I can remember just running until I couldn't run anymore, but they were spraying water on our house, to keep it from burning, because the looper factory was already on fire.

Then I can just remember I couldn't sleep that night. I would sit and watch, and I could smell the smoke! All of a sudden I would see a flame start back up, and it just practically burned all night. You know, it's just a memory about that fire; I could just see it all night long. It'd just flame up, and then, all of a sudden it'd kind of die down, and it was just reflecting in our window, and our house was real hot. They had to move our furniture back in that night, and I can remember my mother being up. She was afraid to go to bed. She was afraid it'd start back and catch our house on fire. So we just couldn't even sleep that night.

One of the most fun things I remember in grammar school that they did was at the fall festivals. Everybody would make boxes; they would take a box and decorate them with crepe paper, roses, and ruffles, and they would fill them full of a meal. They'd put sandwiches and cakes, or candy, or something like that, and then they would take them to the Halloween carnival. They would auction these boxes off, and the prettiest one, of course, would always bring in the most money for the school. Then they had a meal whenever they bought the box to take home, and that's an unheard of thing I guess at this time. Sometimes a young lady would make a fancy box, and her boyfriend would buy it, and they shared it—he could check her cooking out. It was like a picnic, kind of. They used to always look forward to Halloween carnivals because it was all at the school, and the fishponds they would have, and the witch telling the fortunes, things like that. Each little room had a certain thing they did in it. The ladies would bake cakes to auction off and there was a cakewalk.

My mother and father would take their vacation in the wintertime, and I always stayed home. I always stayed with a relative or someone. I had one lady who taught me how to make biscuits and chocolate pies, and I sold the dogs, if I could sell any, while they were gone. My parents liked to go to Bartow, Florida. Because my daddy loved sulfur water, they went to Bok Tower, of all things, and there was sulfur in the water. They liked to go to the center of the state, and they always talked about going to Bok Tower and staying a week.

Bok Tower, you know where that is? It is right below Ocala. It is just a tower that was out in the citrus groves. Florida didn't have Disney World and all that stuff then. My daddy always loved sulfur; I never will forget seeing it in the early years, before all the environmental stuff with water. You could see just old slimy stuff that would come out of the water faucets and things. He loved that sulfur in that water; I don't know why. He'd say, "I can't wait to get to Florida and get some of that good sulfur water!"

One time, we went to visit some of the Wattses, Carol Reeves's relatives (her mother was my half sister), in Bartow, and they wanted us to try swamp cabbage. I don't know what it was, but we tried it! They grew strawberries and did farming. I will never forget that we had swamp cabbage to eat that night. I don't even remember if it was any good. I don't even remember if I ate any of it. I just remember going to Bartow, Florida, and having swamp cabbage.

I lived in Tiger all through my years of school. I had a sister that was a teacher there at the high school. Her name was Zella Ramey, and she taught on Persimmon, Tiger, and then in her later years Tallulah Falls. She took me to school with her when I was five years old. I got spoiled because I wouldn't drink milk, and she would go home at night and make chocolate syrup, so I would drink chocolate milk at school. She was my teacher in my early years and first grade. She lived in the little green house next to my mother's in Tiger. It's vacant now. My half sisters were Della and Zella—Della just passed away at 102.

Then Louise and Bill Wilson moved to Tiger. They built 'Tween Lakes Motor Court [1940] and the Tiger Drive-In Theater [1954] and all that. I babysat with their daughter. We all hung around the motel down there and cleaned rooms and did anything we could. Then, when I was in the ninth grade, I started work at the Bynum House. I worked a short time at the Clayton Hotel for Mary Greene, but I got a summertime job at the Bynum House. We worked seven days a week from nine to two; we were off if we had all of our work done. Then we went back in at five and worked until it closed around nine at night. We made fifteen dollars a week. Now that's one change that's happened here. We made good in tips because we had a lot of wealthy people come and stay at the Bynum House in the summertime. One week, I even made forty-five dollars in tips. That was seven days a week. Working as a waitress, meeting people, and interacting with them contributed to my self-taught education.

"We were married fifty-three years—he passed away May 20, 2013. The love of my life!"

I graduated high school in 1957. The year before that, my mother went to work in the shirt factory, and she was making a dollar an hour at the shirt factory. It started as sixty cents an hour then went to a dollar an hour. She bought a new '56 red-and-white Ford. So, I got my driver's license at sixteen, and I was always able to put a dollar's worth of gas in it because I could get three to four gallons for a dollar.

After I graduated from high school, I worked a couple of weeks at the shirt factory until I got a good job at Burlington Industries. I was the switchboard operator up there and a receptionist. I had Broderick, my little brother, with me everywhere I went, and I would buy my gas over at Ramey's Super Gas. Tom saw what a good babysitter I was, and he asked me if I would watch his daughter at the same time. There was twenty-nine days' difference in their age, so I would take both of them out a lot of times. Then, he asked me, "If you aren't doing anything else when you take them home, I have some books that need posting over here. Could you help me get my books posted?" And that went into a love affair. We were married fifty-three years—he passed away May 20, 2013. The love of my life!

Tom did a lot of good for our county. I think he will always be known as being good to people and a fun person. He tried desperately to do what he could for our county. He was very interested in the water, the sewer, and saving money. Whatever he could do for our county was in

PLATE 190 Beanie Ramey

his best interest. He was mayor of Clayton twice. Our son Thomas, Jr., is mayor of Tiger now.

He liked to develop property better than he liked to run a finished business. We would run it until we could sell it. He was hoping to get things developed up there where Ramey Boulevard is. That was the reason for putting that much more money into it. We paid heavy for the farm. We did all the filling and piping. We put a lot of money into that piece of property. It is going to be hard for us to get out of it because the property values have just dropped down.

We had heard from many Rabun residents that Tiger, Georgia, used to be a tourist destination. It was hard for us to imagine, as the Tiger of today is a sleepy little town with four or five businesses and a four-way stop. Beanie shared her childhood memories of what Tiger looked like in bygone days.

In Tiger, the present post office was put there in the fifties, and I remember there was an old service station there. Roane's Store was still there, and we would walk out there all the time. And where Tiger BP is, that was the packinghouse. I have a big picture of Tiger that Broderick did that's just exactly like it was when we grew up.

Bob Massee's packinghouse was where they packed apples for roadside selling and shipping. It burned when several buildings were burned by an individual. The changes in Tiger were not that much—other than some of the buildings from the motel there at 'Tween Lakes Motel; they're gone. They had shuffleboard, close to where the walkway is now. Most of the Drive-In has been put back like it used to be. North of the Drive-In, where Cannonwood Assisted Living is, that was just a house where one of Cheryl Majors's grandparents lived. Mrs. Cannon had little cabins, little white cabins that would be smaller than my living room, I'd say, just big enough to hold a little bed maybe and a bathroom, or maybe one down in the woods.

There wasn't motels then; everything was individual cottages with a bed and bathroom in it. That is all you could find anywhere. Motels were later in life. That's what Clyde's Place was—cabins and a restaurant. It was little brick cottages around a circle, and it was what Cannon's Cabins looked like. Later on, they got people to come spend the entire summer in those cottages. They had little kitchenettes in them, and that was just how it was. You children are used to seeing high-rise motels; you wouldn't even know what one of those places looked like.

And then on down at Tiger, we saw the end of Clyde's Place. That was Tom's father's place, and there was a restaurant. The depots were where the train went through, and then there were two big stores. Mr. Taylor had a store, and then Mama Ramey, as we called her, Tom's grandmother, had a store. The post office was in the back of the store, and then later,

PLATE 191 Clyde's Place in Tiger, Georgia

they shared a little place off to the side, and it had another little shed roof with a little post office. There were two stores just alike, white with pointed roofs. They had white boards, and there was a walkway between them. Then, out in the back there was a well that was an octagon shape, with a gazebo over it. The two depots were over on the other side of the railroad track, where the road is that you go up to the school. There were two buildings. There was one like a warehouse, and one was like the building, where they did the book work and all that—the regular depot.

'Tween Lakes Motor Court was between my mother's old house and a brick building; it was all between the drive-in theater and the packing-house. Right next to my mother's house, there was a place that had five little brick units. That house was the original house on the property that Cheryl Wilson, or Cheryl Majors's, family, lived in. She had an uncle who lived there years and years ago named Von Cannon; his mother was the one who had the Cannon's Cabins. That property used to have stairs in the front, and a fishpond, and stairs to the highway, but they took that out, and he put four more units on the side of the house. There was a lake behind it with a swinging bridge across it. There were two little houses in the back that they bought. There was another row of cabins and it had a circular road all the way around it. There was a small, cute cottage in the back, and it was the honeymoon cottage. And the building closer to the highway was a restaurant, and that was very active.

We had been told that there used to be several juke joints in the Tiger/Lakemont area, as well as The Clayton Club, which was not only a juke joint but also a "house of ill repute." When we asked Beanie what she knew about those places, she began telling us about establishments that we had never heard of and also about Piano Red, a legendary singer whom her husband's family brought to Rabun County to perform.

See, Tom's daddy had Clyde's Place that had a nice big restaurant and dance hall, and that's how he got involved with Piano Red. Piano Red came up from Atlanta, and as a matter of fact, I just got his life story. I've got it right there. We had it done by a boy with a movie company. He gave it to us probably ten or fifteen years ago, and we just left it on an old reel-to-reel tape, and the tape almost deteriorated. Tom's daddy helped Piano Red get started in the music industry. He's just an old blues piano player, Dr. Feelgood and the Interns, that used to play the circuit. He was an African American albino. On the tape he starts telling the story about Mr. Clyde Ramey, which was Tom's daddy, coming to Atlanta and getting them to come up here to play in his restaurant—honky-tonk, I guess is what you'd call it.

Then he keeps telling more. I listened to part of it, and he said that he would go over into part of Clayton where the black people lived, and they would let them come to their place to play for them on Sunday afternoon. There was a man named Harley Penland that had a little house. It was low to the street, but that's where Piano Red went, was over to Harley's. They would go play for the black folks on Sunday afternoon. Then they started charging a nickel, or a dime, or something like that, and they would come down and sell cold drinks to the people that would come over there to listen.

This kind of ties in to the place on Lake Rabun called the Clayton Club. Tom said he remembered going down there and watching them when Piano Red went out there. Piano Red [continues his story] with how he got his other pair of pants and packed to come up here. The man had two pairs of pants to get ready to go on a trip for the summer to play! That's the first thing he said: "I got my other pair of pants! We left and Mr. Clyde picked us up in Atlanta." He played with that Blind Willie [McTell] and mentions him in the tape and everything.

Piano Red, he was a friend of ours. We bought him a home in Atlanta one time 'cause he told us he couldn't afford a house anymore. His family, you know, paid for it. We went to his funeral. His funeral was right in downtown Buckhead, where 103 West Paces Ferry and all that is, in the little downtown Buckhead area. He was in a little church out there, and my mother and her husband, and Tom and I went to the funeral. We got in there, and they had the ladies dressed in white like nurses, with the fans, and it was summertime, and they'd fan us. Then all of a sudden they asked Tom to get up and speak and do his eulogy. He was not prepared to do that, but he did it!

"We could have been Las Vegas here; just think about that! If they'd just kept going!"

I didn't know much about [the Clayton Club], but it was right in the area where Mrs. Kate Worley, the schoolteacher, lived. Right up in the little road that went up in front of her house down there. It was on Lake Rabun before you get to Lake Rabun Hotel, and it was just a little club where they were playing the pianos and the music, and doing the singing and everything. Tom said they always went down to the Clayton Club, because in the latter years, they had a lot of people to come from Atlanta, with the maids and the butlers, the wealthy people down in the Lake Rabun area. At that time, Lake Burton wasn't even developed. The old money was at Lake Rabun, and that's where they would bring them, and they would go to the Clayton Club for their entertainment. Tom didn't know that much about it, but he said he remembered going there. He remembered seeing Piano Red there. Tom was born in '30. And this was in the thirties when he was down there. So, Tom had to be just real young and would probably ride down there with his daddy. I certainly wouldn't doubt [that there was a brothel there] because I've also heard just a little bit about that there might have been one at Cannon's Cabins, Jabe's Place, at the Red, White, and Blue, or some of those places that they might have been able to find a lady hanging around down there. I don't know! It is only hearsay. The Red, White, and Blue was down on the river, where you turn off to Lake Rabun, and you kept going before you get to Joy Bridge that's there now. And then there was also a place on the corner. It was called Jot-Em-Down. I think it was just a service station where you turned off to the lake, but I think Cannon's Cabins might have been Jabe. I believe it was Jabe's Place; Red, White, and Blue; or Clyde's Place. We could have been Las Vegas here; just think about that! If they'd just kept going!

They had painted pictures back in the dance hall part of it, back in the back of Clyde's Place. The restaurant had a big horseshoe bar up front, and then they had some little rooms and that was the poker rooms from what I understood. And then they had the band and the dance floor back in the back. I can just remember seeing pictures that was painted on the wall behind their stage where they played. And I never got a picture of it. Never did get that. And I never did get any history much from Thomas's mother and daddy. I didn't get interested in it till I got older.

I would say Clyde's Place stopped having dances in the sixties, but I've got a picture of Clyde's Place. People mostly from the lakes patronized Clyde's Place in the summertime. Clyde always had barbecues. Now, the locals would go to the barbecues they'd have down there. My granddaddy worked for him, and I just remember him saying that he would carry loaves of bread, like wood, in there. I guess they made the barbecues out of sandwich bread instead of buns or something back then. They had all these barbecues, and it was probably all of it in the summertime when the tourists were here, instead of wintertime. I don't even know whether they were open in the winter or not; I just never heard them say anything about that. When the State put in new [Highway] 441, Tiger started kind a' drying up, and it was just hard to keep a business going.

Beanie and Tom Ramey are well known in our community for their entrepreneurship. They have owned a tremendous amount of real estate in our community and have developed much of it. They have provided jobs for many, paid taxes that support our community, and helped numerous people throughout their lives.

It was a lot of work. We had that service station, Ramey's Super Gas, and that's when the roads were changing and going over to the bypass. Then he and I built the Heart of Rabun Motel [now the Days Inn of Clayton, Georgia] and opened up in the summer of '66, and we did sell and develop the property there where McDonald's and the old BI-LO shopping center is—it was the Tom Duckett Farm. We sold that, and we're still going up the road developing more of it. We ran the motel. That's how my boys got started working. They were real young when we built the Heart of Rabun, and we took them over there, and Tom said, "When you have a place like this, you gotta work everybody, and everybody's gotta work as much as you can." They nearly worked me to death, but he made the boys work on the weekends. Sunday was always the busiest time. He'd make them empty the trash, and pull the sheets, and take them to the laundry room, pick up the wet towels and help in the yards, sweep the dust out of the parking lots, ride go-karts. They did a little of everything over there. That was an interesting time in our life. I mean, I could go on and talk the rest of the day on stuff we did over there. We had a good business.

Tom bought Kingwood at one time. That was another thing! We bought it and got involved with that fellow from Naples, Florida. And we finally saw the writing on the wall and got out of it. It was a nightmare. He had it going good; people were joining, business going good, and then he was away for the summer, and when he stepped in at about August, he decided that he was gonna run it instead of their general partner running it, which was Tom. Everything went downhill from there on. We got out of that mess. We've tried it all.

Our taxes are tremendous on our property because we bought the Wilson Farm, which is where Ramey Boulevard is. We put that road in and paid for it ourselves; Ramey Boulevard cost us about three hundred and fifty thousand dollars that we put into the road and bridge. You know, you don't get a whole lot of thanks for stuff like that, other than heartaches and "did you do it right?" Then we ended up buying the farm right next to it, the big white Smith house. That was Judge Smith's house. That was an interesting place because of Judge Smith, his dad, built that house. It started out as a square log cabin. After we bought it, there was one of the relatives that lived there named Harry Smith. He was the last one that lived there, and they put it up for auction. It was Nancy Schaefer's father's house. [**Editors' note:** Nancy Schaefer is a former Georgia state senator who served from 2004–2008.] When we got in there and started restoring the building, they had to just kind of gut it out on the inside. It had just the square log cabin that was still there. They had to take most of that out because of powder beetles. They had to stabilize the whole building. [Mr. Smith] just kept adding on, year after year. He would have more in his family, and he kept adding on. A day or two after we bought that, Nancy Schaefer came to us and wanted us to give it to her for a foundation she was trying to start for a children's home. I thought, oh my God, we have just spent all this money on this piece of property here, and she is wanting us to give it to her! I threw the paperwork on it away the other day because of her death. It has not been successful as a business place.

We had one lady that put a spa in it, but unfortunately, she didn't do well. She put a lot of money into the building herself. She said that she ended up spending eighty thousand dollars on the inside of that building. She spent a lot of money. She put a lot of stuff in it. She went big-time. Then we ended up on the losing end of it. So, we just closed it, and I have got storage in it right now. We built it hoping a restaurant would go in there. It has the largest walnut tree east of the Mississippi, in the yard. I've got some history on it that Preach Parsons did, and it was done by the Forest Service. Some of the limbs are as big as trees, and a lot of the limbs keep breaking, and I think it is getting so old that it has just about had its day.

We have got apartments in seven places, and we are probably at about fifty percent [occupancy] on all our apartments. Houses rent pretty good, but we found out that if there are no jobs available, some of these people who lose their home, they find a place to rent, and then they find out they can't get a job to even pay their rent. A lot of people are just moving out of here. I think we are two or three years behind. Atlanta and the larger cities are coming back [from the recession]. I think we are way behind that. That is just my opinion because of the way it seems like in our business. People can't stay, you know, any length of time. Just about everybody that calls has been people that are in the waitressing, cooking, or something in the restaurant business. We don't get any big firms—anybody coming in—so that gets into a real big issue.

"Prices don't get lowered down. Grass won't quit growing; you still got to pay somebody to cut grass."

I was out of town and someone introduced me to a nice man and woman. They asked, "Where are you from?" I said, "Clayton, Georgia." They commented, "Oh, the 'home of the speed traps'!" There is not that much coming in. The people on the lakes are not spending the money that they used to. I think we went through a very high-end part four or five years ago. We may not ever see it again. It may be a long time before we see how money changes hands here.

See, we have got the same taxes, the same maintenance to keep up, and we are making a lot less on our profits on all our rentals and everything. I am going to continue working with our place and trying to sell land because we have got a lot of property. We are loaded with non-income-producing property that we need to get rid of. Some of it didn't develop as fast as we thought, and we are kind of stuck with it. It makes it really, really bad, the taxes you have to pay with it. So, I've got to think about our future because of what it is costing us in taxes. It could get us in trouble when you start paying seventy-five or a hundred thousand a year for taxes. We don't have that type of income anymore. Prices don't get lowered down. Grass won't quit growing; you still got to pay somebody to cut grass.

Beanie's family was involved with several of the movies filmed in Rabun County. They met and socialized with many famous celebrities.

When [Disney was] here, Tom was going to be in *The Great Locomotive Chase*, but he had the station here, and he started doing transportation for them. He would bring all the cars in, check the batteries, fill them up with gas, wash them, and have them ready for the next scene. The stars stayed in the Bleckley House and the Duncan Motel in Clayton. They usually ate at the Clayton Cafe. That was like going out of town to eat because they had steaks and seafood. Fess Parker bought a dog from my mother during that time.

The movie crew would go down on the ball field and play touch football, and just wander around town. I saw Fess Parker a lot. Tom's daddy was in the movie as an extra, and Jimmy Hines that lived with them was in the movie, and Tom was, too. They became friends with some of the people in the movie. Lennie Geer was here from California. He's been in a lot of westerns, and Tom and I visited them in California and went to their home. Tom went back with the movie crowd for three months and stayed in California with them. We've got movies of Lennie's home, and he was the one that had Mr. Ed, and he did all of that training out in his yard. He has pictures of the boys from home riding Mr. Ed and watching him at their house.

I played Carol Burnett's stand-in for *Four Seasons*. That was interesting. They came back to do some more filming, and we were filming out at Johnny and Natalie Howard's house on Lake Burton, and then the orchards over in Long Creek. We'd get on a bus and go in the morning. When that car drives up the hill and Carol Burnett gets out of it, that's me driving the car up. That's the way they did a stand-in. You did all of the work for them, but we got to meet them. There was Carol Burnett; Rita Moreno; Jack Weston; Alan Alda and his wife and girls; Len Cariou; and Sandy Dennis. All of them were nice except for one person. She was hateful to us all of the time and wouldn't talk to anybody, and it happened to be Carol Burnett! She was the bad one, the one I had to work with! It was fun because when they were doing a scene, everyone else just got to sit around where we were filming.

Some of our boys—Jeff and Tombo, and maybe Horace—played in *Grizzly*; they had bit parts. Horace's daughter just did a bit part in *Goats*.

When asked what advice she would give to the young people in our community, Beanie had several ideas.

If they don't want to go to college, if they can't afford to go to college, try to go to some technical school and learn a trade that you could use in some of the businesses here. I think we have got enough beauty shops. There is a beauty shop in every house! That wouldn't be my advice. Work hard in your athletics, and see if you can get a scholarship to go on to further your education. That is about the only thing that I would know because I have watched two granddaughters, and that is what they did. One got a soccer scholarship to North Georgia, and the other one has just graduated from the University of Georgia. She graduated with a 3.8 grade point average. She is going to school in Dahlonega for her Physical Therapy doctorate. She has got three more years to go. So, she spent four years in Athens and three years at North Georgia. There is not much future here. The only thing you can do is try to get a job at Ingles, work in the movie department, or cashier, or coffee, or a restaurant job. And as soon as summer is over, you know that is going to die back down come November. Parkdale, one of the factories here, are now hiring—someone is telling everyone to rent in Franklin, [North Carolina,] because of the law stopping everybody.

I don't know; we have got the same thing with our grandson. He is working for us cutting grass, doing whatever. He was sitting here listening to us, listening to me talk a little bit. Maybe he can remember some of the things I have told him. There is nothing for young children to do! Nothing! Nothing! They won't even let them sit at BI-LO [a vacant store parking lot] anymore now. They have run them off from there. They have been over to Ramey Boulevard, and they have been to the Regions Bank parking lot, and what do they do? I mean, they can go rent a movie, and go home, and watch the movie. They get tired of doing that. People won't hire them. Now, you tell me what would you say? What do you plan to do when you get out of school?

"We didn't have fast food, big box stores, four-lane highways, or traffic lights."

I may be running for mayor myself! I went up there to run for mayor the last term when David Phillips got the mayor, and Horace said, "Mama, you do not need that right now!" David was standing at the front door of city hall. Horace said, "David, what are you doing over here?" David said, "Fussing about my water bill. They have got it too high, and I can't get anybody to change it!" I was going in to sign up to run, and Horace turned around, got David by the arm, and said, "Let's go in here a minute." He walked back to Pat Bussier's office and said, "David's here. He wants to sign up to run for mayor." Horace left me standing there with my mouth open. I said, "Horace, I came over here to sign up." He said, "You don't need it. Let's let David have it." David signed up with ten minutes left to go before the deadline. So, I walked back out the door. I was going to do it, you know, but David ran and got that. I been hearing a lot today about politics, but I have had two or three people ask me if I was going to go try and run again. I don't know; I'd have to think about that.

The biggest change in Rabun County is we have got into a divided thing with so many newcomers. If we were in a big city, I could see it. Here, it is almost like some of the people want everybody to think they are the money people, and they kind of look down on the locals. I wish they were more like normal people. We are kind of the poor Appalachian group that was here when they came. We didn't have fast food, big box stores, four-lane highways, or traffic lights. There were no castles on our lakes. We had good farms and moonshine.

They come in here and try to take over. We have so many people that come from different parts of the country in here, and that was one thing that made it real hard for Tom, the different people just like we have got in our politics now. They try to change everything, and we don't need to change. I wish that everybody in the government could be more honest. I feel like there is a lot of dishonesty. You see too much about people embezzling money—people just doing things wrong. They are just not honest anymore. The morals of the country and the morals of the children growing up here—that is one thing, you all need to be taught good morals. Drugs are the worst thing that we have at the present.

I wish we were just like we were years ago. We have got definite changes in life. It makes a big difference in our county. I hate to see a little town like this divided into groups. I don't like that. I want us to be a whole, like we were when we were growing up. We were plain, old-fashioned, down-to-earth, God-loving, Appalachian hillbillies. It was a better life then. I have had a very different life, and nobody in the county really knows probably everything I have done all my life. It has been wonderful, really.

"EVERYWHERE THAT I HAVE BEEN, I WAS ALWAYS ON MY WAY BACK HOME"

An interview with the Honorable Zell Miller and Mrs. Shirley Miller

If you have room in your heart, you have room in your house.
—Zell Miller

We were very fortunate to have the opportunity to conduct an interview in February 2015 with former governor Zell Miller and his wife, Mrs. Shirley Miller, who have retired home to Young Harris, Georgia, after Zell's long, distinguished public career. The first interview, with the then governor Miller, was conducted in 1996. He agreed for a Foxfire student, Candi Forrester, to meet with him in the governor's office in Atlanta. These two interviews have been combined below to present a portrait of this esteemed man and his wife. He is a person who, although he is well-known, respected, and admired, never lost touch with where he came from or who he is—a true son of these mountains!
—*Kaye Carver Collins*

Senator Miller: My great-great-grandfather, Thompson Collins, came into Union County, Georgia, as one of the very first settlers in 1830. He was there when they made it a county. He was there when the Indians were being pushed out. He had a dozen children. Most all of them married other persons who lived in Choestoe. I am kin to everybody in Choestoe. I have two cousins; we are kin to each other about seven different ways. When I was about ten years old, my mother took me and my sister across what is known as Track Rock Gap into a land called Choestoe—this means land of the dancing rabbits. That is where my father had come from. She wanted me to see where my father walked to come from Choestoe over to Young Harris College to get an education. It is a corner over here in Union County. It is a big, beautiful valley. My mother came here to teach art and my father came here directly from WWI, still wearing his uniform. It was a good eight miles, and some of it is kind of steep.

Bud Miller, Zell's grandfather, wanted his children to have the best education he could help them acquire. As Zell said in his book The Mountains Within Me:

There was no high school or academy in Choestoe, but he was aware of Young Harris College a few miles away and began to plan to send his children there . . . He would not borrow money. However, he had made a loan to a neighbor and decided that the interest from it would be used solely to further his children's education. Each child could go one at a time 'on the interest' . . . When the money gave out, they would return home until more was available. While not attending, they worked in the fields, helped tend [my grandfather's] store and taught in the schools in the valley. My father's first teaching experience was at Pinetop, a one-room school located at 'the head of Stink Creek.' He lived with his parents and rode there on a mule.

As you can see, Zell came from a long line of teachers.

I was born in Young Harris, one county over from Rabun County. I was born in a house that was owned by Young Harris College because, at that time, my father was teaching there. He died seventeen days after I was born. He passed away from mastoiditis. It is a thing behind your ear, up here in your head. People don't die from it now, but they did back then.

My mother then moved us out of there, and we lived in a house that she built. I still live there. My father left her a thousand-dollar insurance policy, and that was it. She took two hundred dollars of it and bought a piece of land, and then she had eight hundred dollars left, so she started building a house. She had seen these beautiful rocks in the creek not far down from the hill where this property was. All during the summer of 1932, she put me on the bank, and my little six-year-old sister watched after me. She got down in the creek and got these beautiful brown and amber and gold and white rocks out and put them up on the bank. Then on Saturday, some of the menfolk would go down there with a mule and a sled, and they would haul them up to where she was building this house. She hired somebody to build the house and make it out of rocks, and she did that until the eight hundred dollars gave out. Then, we moved into the house, and it was not even completed. The outside was beautiful with those rocks, but the inside was where we could look right down through the cracks and see the ground. Of course, when we first moved in there, we didn't have electricity; the electrical outlets were bare, and the rafters were just naked. She says that the first night that we were there, a dog came in and ate the butter off the kitchen table. I used to say that she got all the rocks out [of the creek]. She would get on to me and say, "Don't say I got all the rocks out! I didn't! I had a lot of people helping me!" But then she would add, "But I got most of them out!" This wall behind the fireplace was just raw oak plank. When we added sheetrock, they found these little tacks with cardboard on the wall. Do you have any idea what that is? My mother had gotten brown paper, like you would wrap stuff at the grocery store. She made this and put that on the walls; if you just used a tack to hold it, the wind would blow them off, but if you had this little piece of cardboard behind it, it would hold it. I remember making them out of cardboard from a Premium Cracker box.

Little by little she finished the house over the years. That's my home. That's where I lived whenever I was a baby. That's where I grew up and went to high school and college and lived whenever I was a young state senator and a professor there at Young Harris College, and that's where I came back to when I was no longer governor.

"We were just like everybody else. We didn't know that we were poor." —Senator Miller

My childhood was a wonderful childhood. I guess now if you look back, they would say that we were poor, but we weren't poor. We were just like everybody else. We didn't know that we were poor. I had a wonderful time. I had rabbit boxes that I would go to every morning during the fall and winter. I can remember I had eight at one time, and you got ten cents for every rabbit that you would catch. I could take it to the local store and sell that live rabbit for ten cents. On mornings that I caught two rabbits, I thought I was really making the money. I had a lot of playmates, and we fished in the creeks and we swam in the old swimming holes, sometimes, a lot of times, without any clothes on. It was a wonderful childhood.

> *"You know, you can get anywhere in the world from here."*
> —*Senator Miller*

My uncle Hoyle, back when we were growing up (he married my mother's sister), was a big hunter. He would come home with squirrels in his hunting jacket. One of his jokes that he would play on us kids, he would come in and we would want to know, "Well, how many did you get?" He would pull one or two out, then pull three or four out; our eyes would be getting bigger and bigger. Then, finally, he would have about eight squirrels that he had killed. He trapped one time and got a mink. You could sell a mink hide for twenty dollars. Muskrat is what he usually caught; they were two dollars a hide. A possum hide was worth fifty cents. They weren't very valuable. My aunt made fried squirrel and gravy, but she also boiled them sometimes. They were very good. I liked them. They also cooked rabbits much the same way. I didn't like the rabbits much, but I loved the squirrels. There may be a few who hunt and sell hides still, but not like they used to.

Back then, when this house was built, [US Highway 76] was not there. It became a road there when I was a very, very young child. I remember when they made it. My mama gave them a lot of her front yard. In one of my books, I write about how we would take a piece of chalk that we would bring home from school, and we would draw the hopscotch formation. We would play hopscotch out there. Maybe every ten minutes, there might be a car run by. In fact, I remember sitting on this front porch with my mama and a car would come by at night with its lights on. We could watch that car as it made its way up the mountain. You could see the headlights as it went up this mountain over here. I remember my mama saying to me, "You know, you can get anywhere in the world from here." I always thought that was just great.

I think that my inspiration as a child—I have thought a lot about this, especially as I have gotten older—came from three main people. These three people played a big part in what I became. One was my mother.

Then, when I was about fifteen, I had a high school English teacher whose name was Edna Herren. I had never thought much about anything scholarly. I had never thought about books much; I didn't study much. I was just interested in baseball.

I took an English course under her, and she just completely opened up a whole new world to me. She was the advisor to the school paper. I had never written anything or thought about writing anything, but because she was the advisor, I went out for the school paper and became the editor of it. She was also the debate team coach, and I was scared to death. I had never said anything in public and was scared to death to try to, but because she was the debate team coach, I wanted to please her. So I went out for the debate and learned how to speak a little. She had a tremendous influence on my life. I doubt if I would have gone to college without her. I don't know what would have happened to me, but I have often thought about what would have happened with my life if I had not had her in high school. When I was inaugurated governor, I had her sitting right down in the front row because I knew that I wouldn't be up there going in as governor if it hadn't been for Edna Herren. She died several years ago, and I told her many times how much I appreciated what she did for me. I used to think (I guess this is how students are) that she thought that I was something special, and she paid all this attention to me. Later, I met student after student that felt the same way about her, but to me she was able to project that she was interested in just me. That was just the kind of teacher she was, and she inspired many of her students the way she inspired me, and that makes a great teacher.

Then my wife—I married early—I married when I was in the Marine Corps. We had children early. We have been married now for sixty years, and she has played a tremendous role in my becoming what I did in my life. My wife is the most valuable thing I own, although she is not my possession. She is anything but my possession. She was a student here at the college. She is from Andrews, North Carolina, which is not far from here. I met her at a square dance, really, one of the first times we were together. She had to be home at a certain time, but then we might could go riding. So, she took me up to her house and we crossed two branches [creeks]. It was just the worst road you have ever seen. I was following her, and I thought, "Where in the world is this girl taking me?" You drove up the creek bed to get to the house! So, those three women played the largest role in my life.

Shirley Miller: I came to Young Harris, Georgia, when I was fifteen and never left. There was a sprinkling of us from Cherokee County. I was the only one from Andrews, North Carolina. I grew up way back in the sticks. There had been a polio epidemic, and we moved out of Andrews. A little girl I had been playing with had polio and died. We drove up the creek. We didn't have a decent road till I moved over here. We never went back to town. Zell and I still have the house that I grew up in. There is a road to it, and they paved it last year! Andrews is an old town and it is not like here, Clayton, Hiawassee, none of those. We were really, really out in the sticks. In our holler [hollow], there were twenty-some-odd people. My daddy was the only person that had any cash money. He did construction work. There were two other girls about my age in the community—one who lived and worked with us—one that lived in one of the houses in the community. If I had a new dress, so did they, or a pair of shoes, or anything. My father bought for them, too. They had what I had. I didn't have anything that they did not have.

Back then when I was a kid, there was open range, and on one of our first dates, Zell came over to see me on a Saturday. My daddy said, "It is our turn to take the salt licks to Nantahala Lake. We rotated with families that had cattle there. So, we went off in an old beat-up farm truck with the back end full of salt licks. The old licks are hard to get off the posts and the new ones hard to get on. I thought, "I will never see him again. This fella will never come up here again!"

Senator Miller: Like I said earlier, I had not even thought about going to college until I became a senior in high school and certainly had not thought about being a teacher at all. Then later, when I did go into college, and when I was in the Marine Corps, I thought that I would come back and that I would study law and that I would be a lawyer. That's kind of what I wanted to do. Then, when I came back out of the Marine Corps, and I started at the University of Georgia, I had a history teacher whose name was E. M. Coulter. Here again is a person that touched my life, although not in the same way those three women did. He was a great history teacher and an authority on Georgia and Southern history. I really loved his teaching, and I took everything that he offered. I decided that I wanted to be a history teacher instead of a lawyer, so I became a history teacher. I was working on my PhD and teaching part-time. I was a teaching assistant at the University of Georgia for a Georgia history course. That is what I was doing when I got an opportunity to go back to Young Harris and teach. So, I left and came back here to teach.

"My mother would make us get quiet because Harry Truman was about to speak or Franklin Roosevelt was making his 'fireside chats,' and we would all huddle around and listen."

—Senator Miller

I went into politics because I'd always been fascinated with politics. My mother had been on the city council for a long time, and she was one of the very first female mayors in Georgia. In fact, when she was the mayor of Young Harris, there were only two females that were mayors in the whole state. This was back in the late forties. I can remember, as a little boy, going out to where they were holding the election when they were counting the ballots late at night. I can remember being huddled over in the corner, and she would be the only female in that whole room. I can remember kind of how they respected her and were nice to her. Anyway, it was interesting to me; it was fascinating to me. So, I always had an interest in politics. I am sure that her sense of civic duty inspired a lot of what I did. We listened to the conventions on the radio. My mother would make us get quiet because Harry Truman was about to speak or Franklin Roosevelt was making his "fireside chats," and we would all huddle around and listen. So I grew up with an interest in politics.

When I was teaching at Young Harris in 1959, I went to a University of Georgia football game one Saturday afternoon, and when I came back, somebody came to the house there and said, "Guess what? You've been elected mayor of Young Harris." Well, I didn't even know I was running. I wasn't running! They just kind a' drafted you back then. You didn't run for mayor of Young Harris. They just kind a' drafted you into doing it, like they had my mama. Then in 1960, when I was twenty-eight, a vacancy in the state senate came up. Back then you had senatorial districts of three counties, and our senatorial district was Rabun County and Towns County and Union County, but you just ran in one county. Like the one before me had been Senator Cannon. Mr. R. E. Cannon had been the senator from Rabun County, but he represented the three-county district. It was time for Towns County to elect a senator, and there was a man running—I was young and idealistic—and I doubted this was the kind of man that ought to represent our county down in Atlanta. That's how I thought at that time. Now that I look back, I might have come up with some other reason that I wanted to run. Anyhow, I went to the president of Young Harris College, and I said, "I want to run for the state senate, and if you'll let me and I get elected, I'll teach four courses." What you taught was three courses a quarter. I said, "I'll teach four courses spring quarter with fall quarter off. I'll teach whatever you want me to—summer school—if you'll just let me have the winter quarter off to go down and serve in the legislature." To my surprise, he said, "All right, go ahead." As I look back on it, his name was Dr. Charles Clegg; I think what he thought was that I would get defeated, and then I would get this silly idea out of my head and settle down and make him a good teacher. But I got elected by 151 votes, which is not much, but I got elected, and so, in 1961, I came down to the legislature. I still taught at Young Harris, and I kept that up for four years in the senate—teaching at Young Harris and also serving down in Atlanta in the legislature at the same time. During that time I served with Carl Sanders in the senate. I also served with Jimmy Carter in the senate, and so I got to know these men, and they later played a part in my career, too.

There were a lot of things in between offices that were not that easy. The only reason that I was the governor of Georgia—it wasn't because I was the smartest person in Georgia—it was because I was persistent and I would not give up. I would say most of your teachers in Rabun County are smarter than I am. I wasn't the governor because I came from a big city. [At the time,] Young Harris had about 222 people. I wasn't the governor because I was rich. My family was always a little . . . I wouldn't call it poor, but we sure weren't well-off. I wasn't the governor because I looked like a governor. I'm pretty average-looking, probably below average, in my appearance. See, I ran for Congress after I had served as a state senator for four years and was beaten. Two years later I ran again, and I was defeated. If a man had any sense, he probably ought to have quit, but I didn't, and then finally I made it to being lieutenant governor. Then, later, I ran for the US Senate, and I was defeated, and everybody thought, "Well, this man can't be elected statewide. Here he's tried all these different times." I just kept trying. My favorite story was *The Little Engine That Could*. I can remember my mama reading that to me, and I have just always been very persistent. I think that persistence is more important than being smart or good-looking or anything else. Being persistent, I think, is the most important trait a person can have.

One piece of legislation that I worked hard on as Georgia's lieutenant governor was the Mountain Protection Act. [**Editors' note:** See *The Foxfire Magazine* Spring 1988 issue.] It didn't work as well as I had hoped it would. I had to keep watering it down to get it passed. I was almost lynched because of that act. I am exaggerating, but I was kicked in the fanny very well over that act. The people here didn't want anybody messing with their land. They did not want anybody having any say-so about what they did with their land. We have already had one house that was built out [on the mountaintop] that slid off the ridge over here. There will be others. I saw how they were cutting down some of these mountains. In the very beginning, they just built on them in any kind of way. The part we finally got [approved] was nothing like what I started out with. I started out much stronger about what they could not do. I had to give in on some of it, to get a very weak version of it passed. I wasn't happy with their version we have, but I think it is about all we can do now.

In 1980, when I ran for the US Senate against Herman Talmadge and got defeated, I looked at it two ways: I could either get drowned in alcohol and self-pity, or I could get drowned in Appalachian history. That is really when I went all up into Kentucky, Berea, and Tennessee. It is when I first got the bug to really study this Appalachian history as a scholar.

Shirley Miller: We had already visited Cratis Williams at Appalachian State [in Boone, North Carolina]. We went up to Western Carolina and saw what they had in their library, and then we went to Virginia. You know, there are the Seven Sisters colleges in Virginia. They are a group of seven small colleges, and we went to all the Seven Sisters to see what they had in their libraries. Last year, we went to Cades Cove [outside Townsend, Tennessee, in the Great Smoky Mountains National Park]. I read yesterday about the 110 families that eminent domain was used on at Cades Cove. On both sides of my family, there were Reagans and Carvers from the first census at Cades Cove. While that was really bad for the government to move 110 families out of Cades Cove, yet now it is a treasure for the whole country. More people visit that park than any other.

Senator Miller: If you want to understand Southern Appalachia, read anything by a man named Horace Kephart. He is really the first scholar of Appalachia. He wrote a lot of books in the early 1930s about it. He had a problem with alcohol and wanted to come south to try and shake it. He came as far as Bryson City, North Carolina. That is where he stayed for several years, and that is where he wrote most of his stuff. There is another one named Purvis Williams [that Shirley mentioned earlier], which is a very good friend of mine who taught at Appalachian State. Another good friend who has written a lot about mountain humor—I got some of my stories from him—is a man named Loyal Jones, who is from

PLATE 192 Zell and Shirley Miller

down here in Brasstown, North Carolina. That is where his family lives. He went to Berea in Kentucky.

"If a man had any sense, he probably ought to have quit."
—*Senator Miller*

If I had not entered into politics, there are some things that I would have liked to have become—even more than being a teacher or a governor. I would rather have been able to play a banjo and write songs, and I had rather been able to have been a good baseball player, a professional baseball player. I've always just been nutty about music and about baseball.

I really miss the music. I loved the music. I loved it. I used to hitchhike on Saturday nights to go to the square dances at the Mountain City Playhouse. One time my friend and I got a ride from Mountain City to where you turn down to go to LaPrade's on Lake Burton. So, we started walking, thinking somebody would come by and pick us up. It was between twelve and one o'clock in the morning when we set out walking. We walked till daylight! We had to walk all the way into Hiawassee! I will never forget that! It was worth it! I miss that!

One of the great Georgians I did know was Johnny Mize, who came from Demorest. He was inducted into the Baseball Hall of Fame in about 1983–1985. I went with him up to Cooperstown when they inducted him into the Hall of Fame. I got to know Mickey Mantle because he spent a good deal of time here in Georgia, and I admired him greatly.

"History is not just all wars and elections." —Senator Miller

I heard about Foxfire as soon as that first book came out, or maybe before. I served on the Foxfire board as long as you could because back then they used to have a rule that you would rotate off after a certain time. I stayed on until they rotated me off. I've always loved what the Foxfire program did for the boys and girls. I thought that it was a wonderful program that could be copied and that whether you came from the mountains or not, it would apply to other places. So, I was glad to see that happen because there is so much rich heritage and history out there that is just unrecorded. It's people like the people that work with Foxfire that go out there and get the history. I'm a history teacher, and history is not just all wars and elections. History is how people lived, and that is what Foxfire tells us about. It is how people really lived.

This is kind of an unusual thing for me right now. I haven't had a talk like this with any folks in seven years. I got out of Congress in 2005, and I came home and I got shingles—from my toes up to my hip is scar tissue. When I got over that, I was a little crippled. I then fell down these stairs out here one morning about five a.m. I was coming down here to work without bothering Shirley. I broke six ribs, collapsed a lung, and moved my heart over. Then two months after that, I fell again and broke my back. I used to be real active, but I haven't been able to do anything. I couldn't say no to Foxfire, so for better or for worse, this is it.

I have written a few books, but I hadn't written anything about life here in particular. I have always been interested in the mountains. I think I tell in *Purt Nigh Gone: The Old Mountain Ways* how when I was a little boy, I didn't have a father at home. So, as a little boy, I would go to all the loafer's benches. There were three stores, but two of them had really good loafer's benches. Early in the evening, after the men came in from the field, they would come up to get them some coffee or something, and they would sit around and talk. My mama just hated it.

She thought I would learn cuss words, and I did, a lot of them! But I just always had an interest in where I came from.

There were terrific storytellers at the loafer's bench. One of the stories they told was the Fuzz story. This is pretty much a true story, although it has been embellished some. There was a big store right out here on the corner, and one night it caught on fire. This is before we had any kind of fire system or anything. So all we could do is just gather and watch this store go up in flames. While we were watching, out of nowhere came this old, beat-up pickup truck, one fender off, the other one almost off. The windshield was halfway busted out. It came up, and the man driving it was a man named Fuzz, who was a local character around here, and he had his wife in there with him, and his maw-in-law, and there were about four kids in the back. They drove that pickup up to where the fire was going and looked like they were going to keep on going. Then all of a sudden, he just veered into this fiery mass of a building being burnt up. He got out, and he had a couple of other grown-ups in the front seat with him. They got out and they had this old blanket in the back. They started beating on the fire with it. They grabbed some brush and started beating on the fire with it. They put that fire out. When that was over with, the mayor passed the hat and took up a collection. He went up and gave it to Fuzz. He said, "Fuzz, we think that is one of the most heroic things we have ever seen in Young Harris. We want to give you this little bit to help. It is not much, but it is a little." He said, "By the way, what are you going to do with it?" Fuzz said, "Well, the first thing I am going to do with it is get some brakes put on that pickup!" I miss the old storytellers. It is quite an art—quite an art.

Shirley Miller: Zell got some great stories from Mr. Ensley before his death. He was a great storyteller. Tell them one. He was one of our neighbors when I was growing up. He was the one who got up most early in the morning, and would go build a fire where we all caught the bus. He would have a fire going where we all gathered to wait for the school bus. Tell them one of his stories.

Senator Miller: You know, the men would go out on Friday nights fox hunting with foxhounds. This crowd—there would usually be three or four men from different families—one of them had lost a leg many years before. He had a wooden peg leg. So, they went out, and usually they would have them a little white lightning to drink during the night, too. This night was no exception. They all went to sleep. All of a sudden, a big commotion awakened them. The wooden leg had gotten into the fire. The one with the wooden leg was down below the road and was saying, "I want you to come down here, but you have got to watch it. There is a helluva hole every other step!"

We had white lightning around here when I was growing up, very much so. One of my best friends was a young fellow, who from the time he could get a driver's license, he started hauling it. One of my first duties as a state senator was going over to see the judge to see if he couldn't be easy on him. I don't know that it worked. He knew he was a good boy.

I miss those loafer's benches—those stories! But, I see Young Harris College and the advancements it has made. They now have 1,215 students there. When my father taught there, there were about 300. It is, of course, much better than it was in some ways, but I miss knowing all my neighbors. I can still name all my old neighbors, starting down here at the end of this street and going all the way through town, and even out the side roads. I don't know them all now. Back then, of course, I knew them all, and they knew me, too.

I wish my grandchildren could know how close neighbors were. They are not that close anymore. It is not like it was when I was growing up—having a relationship with other people. When they got sick, you tried to help them out. When you killed a hog, you would share the meat. When hog killing time came along in the winter, a neighbor would string it up, cut the meat out. I can remember my mother in here, grinding up meat to make sausage; also, we could have some sausage that night the hog was killed. All the neighbors shared that meat from that one person's hog. Then when another one would kill his hog, he would share his meat with them.

I think the reason so much of our culture has been lost is economics. You couldn't make a good living working around here. You could go to Marietta and work, and many of them did. Some of them had carpools. They would go down there every morning and back to Marietta. A lot of people here went north, to Michigan. In Marietta, they worked for what we used to call the Bell Bomber plant, Lockheed. My mother worked there. When we moved to Atlanta, she wanted to help the war effort out. She was just that type of person. She was waiting to go overseas to join the Red Cross when the war ended. But, anyway, a lot of the folks that go off finally do come back. I never intended to live anywhere else in my life. Everywhere that I have been, I was always on my way back home.

The thing I miss most are the relationships that people had with one another. If somebody got sick, they would try to help them and look after them. My mother had a family that was pretty bad off, and she was all the time helping them in some way. We had a visiting teacher here, named Mary Will Hunt Phillips, and she tells the story of taking some clothes that her sons had outgrown, and she went to visit this family whose children had not been coming to school. She left those clothes there with them. She said, "I thought this might help." Well, they didn't come to school and she went back two or three weeks later, and the clothes were right there on the front porch where she had left them. They did not want her giving them anything. So, she figured it out and talked to this woman and said, "I tell you what, come help me some at my home." So, the lady worked for her and the teacher gave her those clothes for helping her. That woman did not want them given to her without her giving something back. I miss that kind of thing.

I think even the people who grew up here don't have that sense of neighborliness; they are too busy. We didn't have television. We didn't have all these other things to take our mind off others. Not much of the old stuff remains; it's purt' nigh gone.

There is, in a way, still *some* neighborliness. The people my mother bought this land from, their grandson now is a doctor and lives next door. He has told me more than a dozen times, "If you ever need me, know all you have got to do is just holler! I'll be there."

Shirley Miller: Their phone number is on our refrigerator, the one they will answer in the night, in case someone in their family calls. Funeral etiquette among the natives, I don't think that has changed a whole lot. When we hear that someone has died, we go to the funeral home. We go to the funeral. We take food to the family.

Senator Miller: The thing that surprises me the most about the world today, I guess, is how money-grabbing it is. You can't blame them. They want things that are good for their family. That is what they are trying to do, most of them, trying to have a better family life, and being able to do things they were not able to do when they were children. But, sometimes, those things could be better left undone.

I've had a pretty good family life. We have two boys, so we have grandchildren and great-grandchildren, and they are all close by. We still all get together at Christmas and on birthdays. I have tried to keep that kind of tradition going in this family. I think we have done pretty good so far. I don't know how the other generations will do, but they are good. They know they are supposed to be at Papa's and Nin's at Christmas to open up presents. They know they are supposed to be here at birthdays.

Shirley Miller: I think we are very close-knit. I can see it in my oldest grandchild, Asia, who lives over in Franklin, North Carolina, now with her husband. She was a teacher. Murphy, our son who is the father of all our grandkids, came back from Atlanta. I think he wanted his kids to grow up like he had. Not as Huck Finn a life as his daddy had, but still it was a pretty good life. Our granddaughter, Asia, who has four kids of her own, and who works with her husband, took in a homeless boy—a kid who had no one in the family to take him. So, Asia took him. So, now she has added one that was fifteen last spring, when he came to live with them. He is a ballplayer. Her husband loves sports and knows the coaches. She knew the teachers. She found out about this boy and that there was not a foster family available. She heard that he was going to be put somewhere else, and so now he lives with Asia. He fits in just like her own kids, I think. Mama Bea always said, "If there is room in the heart, there is room in the house." Seeing Asia do that shows that she has learned by watching. Maybe the values they saw influenced them. Kids do what they see.

Senator Miller: I think some of the values from the old-timers have been passed down, though not near as much as it used to be. But I think you still find that in the current generation here.

Shirley Miller: Multigenerational families, being together, have a relationship with parents and grandparents, aunts and uncles, and other older people around them all the time; I think that makes a difference. I know it made a difference with our children. Being around Birdie, Zell's mother, influenced them. Murphy is our oldest. He is a superior court judge now. He went to Emory. He went to law school in Atlanta. He worked for the DA some in Gwinnett County, and he clerked down there for a couple of years for a Fulton County judge, even bought a house inside the perimeter that they had redone. So, we thought he would be an Atlanta lawyer forever, but he came back home. Our youngest, Matt, has worked at United Community Bank in Hiawassee, and I think he would have come back to Towns County even if he had to take a deep hit. He came back about two or three years after he got out of college. Zell Miller, no matter where you were, if he decided that he was sleeping in Towns County, you had just better be prepared to go!

Senator Miller: When I was in in Washington, in the Senate for five years, I came home every weekend. I had two yellow Labs I had to look after. That was my excuse. I heard the mountains calling me. Everywhere I have been, I was planning to come back home to Young Harris; I knew I was.

Shirley Miller: Several people asked me, especially when we were in Washington, "Where are you going to live when you retire? Are you going to stay here? Are you going back to Atlanta?" We said, "No, we are going to Young Harris."

Senator Miller: I think there are some that do still have that deep sense of belonging to these mountains. My two sons were that way. They intended to come back here. I don't know, but I think some of them do have that sense of belonging. I think what creates that sense of belonging is a sense of security. It gives them a certain type of security to be among these people they have known all their lives and to be in an area where they are known and have been known since they were just little kids.

I would tell today's generation to remember where they came from. If it is not a good memory, then try to make it a good memory. I realize that not every kid has a mama like I had. I know that. She was remarkable. I see some mothers that don't have that same level of love for their children, but a lot of them do.

There was a personal code of ethics and civility here. It has to do with having a good work ethic. It has to do with looking after your neighbors and your family. It is a thing that you have deep inside of you that says to you, "They looked after you when you needed it. Now, you need to look after them when they need it." That is about it.

The advice that I would give to young people who are still trying to decide what to do with their life is that it's not anything to worry about if you are sixteen or seventeen and have not decided exactly what you want to do with life. Like I said a while ago, I'd come back out of the Marine Corps before I actually thought that I knew what I wanted to do with my life, and that was to be a history teacher. I think, more than ever, a college education is important. It was important when I came along, but now it's absolutely essential that you have some education, a good bit of education, beyond high school.

Of all the things that I have ever been involved with, the thing that I am most proud of having accomplished was helping to create the HOPE Scholarship. That enables people to go on to college, and it is just so very important. So, what I would do at this age is I would continue to be interested in a lot of things and learn about a lot of things and just know that high school is not the end of education. It is really just the beginning; you need to go on and get more education. Then it will come to you what you want to do with that life of yours.

One of the most valuable lessons I learned was to treat everybody with the same love and dignity that you would want yourself to be treated. I saw that by example. I hope that I will be remembered for never forgetting where I came from. I came from a God-fearing, God-worshipping, hardworking family who had to work for everything they got to begin with. I thank God for having a mother like I did.

"A LITTLE GOOD IN EVERYBODY"

An abundance of love from Susie Hembree Dockins

I would say that we had a better time back then. Children today never know what's enough. We never knew enough because we had everything that we needed. —Susie Dockins

Susie Dockins grew up skinny-dipping, sewing, cooking, and going to church. Between her four brothers and five sisters, the ten of them could always find something to do. They were very creative, using big logs as horses and large stumps as stoves. They could even buy a Coke for a nickel and then return the bottle for two cents.

The brothers and sisters loved to play together, but they also had their own special roles. Mrs. Dockins told me she loves to cook. At the age of four, she began cooking biscuits for her brothers and sisters. After eating supper with Mrs. Dockins, I can assure you that her cooking talents stayed with her throughout her life.

I met Mrs. Dockins through my very good friend, Whitney Dickerson, Mrs. Dockins's granddaughter. I've learned a lot from Mrs. Dockins just sitting at the kitchen table talking about life. She grew up in the ways of the people of the foothills of the Appalachian Mountains.

Through our talks and this interview, she helps to preserve our heritage. She teaches us much with an abundance of love.

—*Christina Mitcham*

My name is Susie Hembree Dockins. I was born in Nantahala, North Carolina, on December 21, 1949. My daddy worked on the railroad at Tallulah Falls. He would walk to work. He would get up and start walking at three o'clock in the morning.

When I was a child, there was ten children in my family. I had four brothers and five sisters. Going down the line, they are George; Barbara Jean; Carlie; Joanne; Harold; Susie, which is me; Hoyt; Katie; Melinda; and Carlene. We worked real hard. We worked on a chicken farm. We would get up at three thirty in the morning, get things ready for Mother, carry water, milk the cows, and slop the hogs before we went to school. We didn't have toys, but we had a lot of love.

All my brothers slept in one room, and all my sisters and I slept in another room. We had an outside bathroom. We bathed in the creek, but we always went clean. We had a wringer-type washer, and we had homemade soap. We killed hogs in the winter. We put up [canned] all kinds o' canned stuff.

When I was a kid, I was always in the kitchen with Mother. I loved to cook. I still love to cook. My oldest sister, Barbara Jean, she liked to sew. Joanne, the next sister down, she liked to can. I always learned to cook. I can remember the first biscuits that I baked. I was four years old, standin' in a straight-back chair, standin' up and makin' 'em [biscuits] in a dishpan for my brothers and sisters.

Me and my brothers and sisters made a playhouse out in the barn. We would take squash and stuff that were too big, and we would can 'em up and act like those were our canned stuff that we would put up. We would make a stove out of concrete blocks and corncobs, and we'd just play with everything. We had cow-pile [dried cow manure] fights. We rode a wagon, and we'd pull a wagon that a mule pulled, but we would pull it and ride it ourselves. We made toys out of corncobs. We made corn silk dolls; we made zingers [toys] outta can lids; and we made yo-yos. We made everything we played with. With all of this, we never got bored.

We pulled a lot of mean stunts on my younger brothers and sisters. We did do that. We'd go to the swimmin' hole. We'd go in our skivvies [underwear], and we'd tie our younger brothers' and sisters' clothes up together so they couldn't get 'em untied. If my mother had to come lookin' for us because we weren't back in an hour, Mother would punish us because we knew we had only an hour to swim. She wouldn't let us go back to the swimmin' hole, but the children knew they couldn't come home without their clothes either. Me and my brother, who's two years younger than I, we played a lot of bad tricks on my younger brothers and sisters.

One time, my sister got a diaper rash. Mother was in the cornfield, and I was left to do the cookin' and to take care of my baby sisters. This is not funny; this is mean. Me and my sister Katie had homemade diapers. They were nice and white. We didn't know what to put on Carlene's bottom, so I put something that burnt very bad. It cured it up! I put rubbin' alcohol. I played that trick on her, but that wasn't no trick. I got a spankin' for that.

I would say that we had a better time back then. Children today never know what's enough. We never knew enough because we had everything that we needed. We would break down trees and play like they were our horses. I remember my brother Hoyt standin' on the hog lot preachin' one time. He fell off backwards and broke his arm. We had to have that fixed. I was a song leader and two of my baby sisters, they were the congregation. We just always had stuff to do. We never run out of anything to do.

My first job was when I was nine years old. I stayed with the deacon of our church. I cooked and cleaned his house 'cause his wife wasn't able to get out of bed, and that's what I did.

I broke two records here in Clayton, Georgia. I was the youngest girl that ever went to work at the hospital. I went at the age of twelve as a candy striper, which was really a nurse's aide. Dr. Turner pulled me in there and made me help deliver the first baby. I was workin' at the Nicholson House. I worked for Mrs. Nicholson at the hotel. I worked for her for a year and a half. Nobody had been able to work for her for over two months at a time, but I worked for her a year and a half 'cause I was makin' seventeen dollars a week, and that was good money. I gave most of the money I made to mother, and I used the rest to buy school clothes. Four dollars a week back then would buy a lot of school clothes. We could only wear dresses, and they had to be down below your knee. They were conservative, very covered, with black-and-white oxford [shoes].

We never got to wear pants to school. We had dresses. We didn't get to date when we were young. That's a reason I think I married the first boy that I ever met. I can remember one time I was in a talent show. Mother wouldn't let us dance, so my daddy learned me how to dance in the chicken house. There was ten kids in the talent show, and it was cloggin' to it and singin' in it. Well, I didn't know that Mother was going to surprise me and be in the audience. I told her I was just gonna tap my foot. Well, I took an award that night, and I spent the night with Jan Queen over at the jail. [**Editors' note:** Jan's father, Lamon Queen, was the sheriff in Rabun County.] All the time, my mother was in the audience. I didn't see her, but the next day I got a spankin' for dancin'.

Goin' to church with my family was very memorable to me. Church molded my life and made me a better person. It made me love people. I can survive when other people will give up. Church back then was a wooden floor and wooden pews. It was Pleasant Hill Baptist, of which I'm still a member. When I was five years old, they would set me up on the piano. I was song leader at five years old, and I remember one time the preacher preached a black snake out from under the pulpit. My daddy picked it up and was gonna carry it out, and the whole congregation ran. My mother was very angry at him for a while, but he was just gonna carry it out of the church. I played the piano by ear in the church. We couldn't afford one, so I'd go out to the church and just play by chords. I learned how to play when I was probably around seven.

As the song leader, you just led the congregation. We had one man who would sing by "do, re, mi, fa, so, la, ti, do." His name was Julius Speed. I never will forget him. I remember right there where he sat in church, and he would sing by chords.

I loved church at Christmastime. I love the smell of home at Christmastime. We didn't get toys. We always wondered about Santa Claus, but we didn't have a Santa Claus. Our "Santa Claus" was going to church and puttin' on a Christmas show. We would get a little bag with an apple and an orange and stick of candy, and that would be our Christmas. My mother would make homemade applesauce cake and things and put 'em in the bin over the old woodstove. They would smell so good. So, Christmastime was a good time for me.

I was in the Christmas plays all the time. I was Mary one time. To tell you the truth, acting out the Christmas story and playing the roles just came natural to us because we read it in the Bible. Mother read it to us.

I was fortunate enough in the fifth grade to go to Tamassee DAR School, which taught me a lot. School was strict, very strict. When I went to Tamassee, I wore uniforms. All of us dressed alike. Mother canned 250 cans [of food] for my tuition to go over there to the boarding school.

Going to DAR school made me understand better the way that I was livin', and made me understand also how I could prosper in life by the way that I was taught to do things. Going to the girl's school, I stayed in the kitchen most of the time. We had chores we had to do. My chores were to set up two tables before we ate. We all ate in a big dining area. I stayed in a building called New York. We'd have to make our own beds, do our own laundry, and press our own uniforms.

My best friends were Lura Jean Speed and Yvonne Justus. We nick-named Lura Jean "Speedy." I was with her or she was with me every weekend. We did all kind a' stuff together. We smoked rabbit tobacco; we smoked grapevines. I remember one time ants came out of the tobacco and got on my tongue. They bit it an' it swoll [swelled] up! I couldn't tell my mother what had happened. I had to sing a special song in church, but I couldn't sing, couldn't talk, and couldn't tell Mother what happened! I was afraid my tongue was gonna come off!

I know it would have been different if I hadn't gone to school because you're always gonna need school. A lot of people say, "I can make it with-out school," but you can't. You have to learn the basics. I could not have survived in my job that I had for thirty years without going to school. I learned the main part of my job, which was management, on my own, but I needed to understand numbers percentage-wise. So [education] follows you all of your life.

"You can look at a lot of people that's still livin' today the way that we lived way back then, and they are very, very happy."

The saddest time in my life was when my dad died. I was at school. Mr. Brookshire was the principal. He called me and my brother to the office. He stood up and said, "I'm sorry. Your dad was killed this morn-ing at eight o'clock in Waukegan, Illinois." So he let the school out at lunchtime and got the buses in line for all of 'em to go down and help my mother because our road had caved off.

I started dating at the age of sixteen. I was slippin' and goin' out. Mother didn't know. I started bringin' Boyd to eat with me, and then I married him. I told her, I said, "Mother, I love him, and I'm gonna marry him." When he would come over, Mother would make me and Boyd stay in the same room with her. We couldn't go out. I couldn't even walk with him on the porch and say bye to him.

We had a very small wedding. We were married in Walhalla, South Carolina, by the justice of the peace. We had our honeymoon up in a little trailer in Mountain City, Georgia. We stayed one night, and we had eighteen dollars in our pocket. We spent twelve dollars the next day. I was workin' at the hospital as a nurse's aide, and Boyd was workin' at Rabun Mills.

I was fortunate enough to marry at the age of sixteen. I moved away from Clayton and stayed gone thirty years. I learned a lot out there. I moved back, and you still see people that's livin' here tryin' to survive, to make a livin', and still just tryin' to get along the way they always have without all the fancy things. You can look at a lot of people that's still livin' today the way that we lived way back then, and they are very, very happy.

Leaving home, believe me, was an adventure, and I was scared. One or two times I would a' liked to go back, but I wanted to learn more, more, and more. I never wanted to quit learnin'. I moved to Cumming, Georgia. I lived there thirty years and raised my children there.

Graduating high school was a present that I gave to my mother in 1976. I had lacked two and a half units graduating. I got my GED from Pickens Tech [in South Carolina] and I wrapped it. I gave it to my mother for Christmas.

All of my children's friends were my friends. They would come to my house instead of Angie going to their house. We had a very good relationship; I always taught my children, if you wanna smoke, bring it home, and we'll try it. If you wanna drink, bring it home, and we'll try it.

PLATE 193 Susie Dockins (*far right*) with her husband,
his two sisters, and their daughter Angie

Anything you want to do, you bring it home, and we'll try it. Don't you sneak around and do it, because if I find out you do, you'll never get out of this house again.

I think having smaller sisters and feeling like I had to raise them when I was growing up, and then leavin' them so early because they were still small, helped me and my daughters' relationships a lot. My oldest daughter was my baby doll when I had her because I was nineteen when I had her. Having the husband that I still have forty years later has not all been perfect, but we've tried to make it. Me and my husband always try to talk things out. We don't like to go to bed mad. Always talk to your mate. Keep everything out in the open.

You think your children are something, but wait until you have your grandchildren. There's nothin' like those grandchildren! I hope I live to see my great-grandchildren. My grandkids sure have put a lot of love into my life. Throughout the years, the Lord's and my family's been good to me. I'm proud of my children, and very proud of my grandchildren.

"If a job is once begun, never leave it till it's done. Be the labor great or small, do it well or not at all."

I would like to see Rabun County just like it was back then, but now I know that it's gonna grow. There's a lot more people. There's a lot more people from away from here. The older generation's dying out, and we've got to accept that fact. We're gonna be the ones to pick it on up [Appalachian traditions], so we have to get involved with things to pick it on up. Even though the changes are good, I'd rather see some of this area back the way it used to be.

I think Rabun County is going to remain basically the same. We're still gonna have the tourists. We're gonna have a lot more, which I'm glad to see. We'll have more restaurants, which I'm glad to see. I wish I could've made it a little better on my mother. I moved away from here, and I've learned a lot more. I learned how to do things and how to just live life easier. We had to do and live the hard way. That's the way that we were taught.

I remember a lot about when my daddy was around. I was fifteen [when he died], and I'm fifty-seven now. I can hear words my daddy said, so I can say that you should always listen to whatever an elderly person says to you because it'll always be there with you. He always told me a sayin' that I'd like to pass on to you: "If a job is once begun, never leave it till it's done. Be the labor great or small, do it well or not at all." He meant every word.

You can survive on anything you have. You don't have to have a kitchen full of food to put a meal on the table. You can walk in my house and not see a thing in my house to cook, and I can put you a meal on the table. You can learn to survive without fancy soaps and lotions. There's a lot of things that you can find other things that's more expensive. I think that's one thing that's wrong with the world today: We're tryin' to live way too rich.

I write poetry. I started writing when I was a little bitty thing. It just came to me—a blessing from God. Most of the poems are about the olden times, Christian poetry, grandbabies, and things to make people feel better when they've lost a loved one or something. I always have to have something to inspire me about what I write. Altogether, I think my poetry does affect others, and that's my big reasons for writin'. Here is one of the poems I have written:

Whatever happened to the days of old?
When work was hard, and life was gold.
We'd work the fields, in the morning sun;
At the end of the day, our work would be done.
We'd sit on the porch, hear the wind whistle by,
In the far yonder, see the stars in the sky.
Oh the aroma of Mom's apple pie—
She'd work so hard, it would bring tears to our eyes.
Those days of old are here and gone,
And the new generation is now our own.

WISDOM

of

OUR ELDERS

Women and Children

[You] teach your children about God these days, and you teach
'em to work.

—Sue Patton

Child-rearing is a challenge for every parent, and different cultures
give value to different kinds of behavior. In Appalachia, old-timers and
new generations alike are particular about how a child should be raised.
They want to instill in the child a sense of faith, family, and neighborliness, as well as a reverence for the land. Being from these mountains
has always provided some protection from outside influences; although,
today that is changing.

The methods of child-rearing in Appalachia are paramount to the
culture. The people of this community remain adamant about the importance of parents in raising a child. Women of this area and elsewhere
believe that more time should be spent at home with the children, regardless of their work outside the home. The Appalachian women ensure that this extra time is spent with the children, so much so that it has

become a priority. However, the influence on the child is not limited to the child's parents. Most of our contacts reiterate the role that the community plays in child-rearing. Elders and neighbors provide additional instruction to the child. Moreover, quotes from each time frame regard religion as essential to the proper rearing of a child. Christianity and morality many times influence a child's life because the parents' moral convictions oftentimes determine how a child is to be raised.

In an interview with James Paul Wooten—a friend of mine—he shared a little story with me about his grandfather. Reminiscing about his childhood, he said this:

> "He, Grandpa, rode a mule to town. One time, I was a little bitty boy, just barely even big enough to walk. As he come back by, I was out in the yard. I started cryin' 'cause I wanted to come home with 'im. He didn't even get off that mule. He said, 'Stick your hand up here.' So, I stuck my hand up 'are. He reached around my hand and pulled me up in front of 'im. He told my mother, said, 'When you want 'im, come and git 'im.'"

Simple stories such as this embody a childhood spent in Appalachia. Living in such a rural area allows for a deep bond to form across generations. Those lessons learned from our elders stay with us, influencing us throughout our lives.

—Katie Lunsford

"TRAIN UP A CHILD IN THE WAY HE SHOULD GO"

Advice on child-rearing

"That's one thing that is wrong with the world today; the parents are not home when the children get there, and they're not trained to go to school, to get to bed or get up in the morning."

—Willie Blalock Elliott (1992)

"I had a good childhood. My parents were God-loving people. They taught us the ways of the Lord. My dad was such a humble man. He was a man who really gave us a Godly example in our home. I actually grew

up way out in the country. The town nearest to where I lived was Independence, Virginia. The town was about midway between Bristol, Tennessee, and Roanoke, Virginia, right in the heart of the Appalachians."
—**Reverend John Bagwell (2005)**

Happy: "The parents 'ave changed an' they growin' 'em up different. That's what changes the kids. Her [Sarah's] children's raised up to respect old people and anybody they come to. And y' go round quiet and tend yer own business. Wouldn't bother people . . ."
Sarah: "And now you have the younguns telling a lie to his daddy."
Happy: "No sir! You never heard them going back at their parents. They know'd better. And now, well, they'll stand up and argue with 'um, a little old eight- and ten-year-old boy stand up and argue with his daddy. Well, now, my daddy would a' wooped the dickens out of me if I'd a' started that early." —**Sarah and Thad "Happy" Dowdle (1971)**

"It is important to raise your children to help with chores. I am a firm believer in that. Don't make slaves out of them, but they need to learn how to run a household. They are going to be in that position one day, and I think it's giving them a leg up in life down the road to teach them those values, principles, and duties at home by letting them help and pitch in." —**Jan Lunsford (2011)**

PLATE 194 Hillard Green teaches former Foxfire student Paul Gillespie to hew logs.

"Parents keep lettin' kids go and don't control 'em. Their parents hadn't been controlled in their time. They'll let their kids go on that way. Why, sure, kids are ungrateful. Why, sure, they are. That's th' way they was let go all th' time. There's just too much toys—too much playin'. They run together—too many of 'em. They're too close. Th' town's full. Th' country's full. And gettin' inta trouble—one takin' off after another. And one'll take off after another just th' same as a dog will. And kids will do the same thing. Yeah, I know parents are makin' it too easy."

—Hillard Green (1970)

"My dad, he could be your friend, but he could be your parent. He could be soft and gentle, but he was stern. He wouldn't tell you to do something he wouldn't do. When he told you to do something, it was right. He thought about it. We grew up as children that you mind your parents. My mom, I guess you could say she was the easiest one to talk into doing something for us. She was it. She was the best. She loved her children. A little 'Mama, please, we need this.' It would come, but Daddy was kind a' stern. He said, 'No.' He'd hold the line. A little on down the line, he would give in, you know. He knew what we needed and what advice we needed." —Willie Fortson (2014)

"We all got along fine. I always loved my parents, and they always loved us and were always good to us. They weren't generally strict. They just was particular about where we went, especially my dad. If there was some place we didn't have no business, why, he'd just tell us that he didn't think we oughta go, and we'd always abide by it.

"I guess the way my parents taught me helped me a lot. The most important thing they taught me was to tend to my own business and stay out of other people's business, not to meddle. They always taught me to let the other fellow alone and live. That's the way I've always tried to be. I never did wanna do anything that would hurt someone else. I mean, what other people done, that isn't nothing to me."

—Jesse Edmonds (1992)

"I might have used a word I shouldn't have used, or I might have done something I shouldn't have done, and it wouldn't be odd for a neighbor to pick you up and shake you and say, 'Boy, you better straighten up or I'm gonna tell ya' daddy.'

"My advice to these young people is to keep doin' what you're doin'! This is so important, guys. In your life, establish morals. I don't know if all of y'all go to church, but I would recommend you give your life to God. Be active in your community, and support your community."

—Carl Shoupe (2009)

"I think teenagers will be teenagers, and there is a lot of pressure on them, and there is more things for them to deal with. They have so many pressures put on them that we did not have back then, like drugs, alcohol, and school. I only went through the eighth grade. I think that staying in school is the best thing for young people to do while they have the time. . . . Knowledge is something that no one can take away from you, and you need to get all the schooling that you possibly can."

—Roberta Hicks (1994)

"I want to be remembered by lots of things, not just one thing in particular. Number one would be that I was always honest, truthful, direct, and lots of fun. I want to be remembered as fun, and when others think of me, they laugh. I want to be remembered as someone who loved for others to come to my house at any time. The door was always open, and people could come in and get something to eat, and make themselves at home—very Southern, I guess you can say, you know, Appalachia-style. The main thing I want to be remembered by is my name, Joy. Joy stands for Jesus first, Others second, and Yourself last. That's how I've tried to live my whole life and make sure everyone else sees that in me because I believe that if you live the kind of life that God would be proud of, then other people can see it in you. You don't have to go around advertising it. They comment on it, and that's where the Jesus first always comes in. That's what I've always tried to teach my children. That would be my legacy I leave to them—a challenge to always have joy in their lives."

—Joy Phillips (2014)

"I'll tell you kids something: Take care of your health and your reputation. That's the main thing. If you have good health and a good reputation, nothing else matters." —Woodrow Blalock (1995)

"Then I had a son. M' boy said, 'Dad, I smell liquor on you!' I had 'bout a pint and had just took a drink 'r two. I got it up and shook it good. I said, 'If I'm gonna raise that boy, that'll be a poor way t' bring him up. I'm done!' So I took that bottle and poured it out right then. I've never touched it since, and that's been thirty years.

"I've heard folks say that they couldn't quit this and they couldn't quit that. They can quit anything they've got a' ambition t' do. And when m' boy was goin' t' growin' up, I decided that [alcohol] wadn't a good thing t' bring out in front a' him." —**Thad "Happy" Dowdle (1973)**

"Never get over your raisin'. Always be yourself. Never put on a front to anybody, because one of these days you're gonna have to live it down. Always try to keep a good name. Stay in church. Once you quit goin' to church, it's hard to get into the habit of going back. Always listen to your mom and daddy. . . . Never feel too young to work. Don't be wasteful."

—**Susie Dockins (2008)**

"I came from a family where there was a lot of love and understanding and discipline. There are some deep-seated things in our culture that have affected children. Many children today are coming from homes where they do not have that. The children can come and go as they please and when and how they please. They lack this discipline. The home is the basis for encouraging a good education."

—**Louise McKinney (1986)**

"Raise 'em around a good environment, good people. Take 'em to church. Teach 'em about the Lord. I guess the older I get, it's more about teaching. You teach your children about God these days, and you teach 'em to work. Eat better than we do. We have rich foods. We have fried foods. It's not healthy for kids to eat just old junk all the time. We have a record of overweight kids. [In previous years] you did the work. You were healthy. Back, years ago, you had to walk where you went. So, you didn't have to [make an effort to] exercise. I remember one day I walked with my grandmaw to Dillard and back, which wasn't that bad. It was a good distance. There was a drug store, a grocery store, and a feed store. That's where we went and done most of our grocery shoppin'. Then one day we walked and went fishin' at what they called the Quarry Pond over here. It's across the highway over there.

"When it come to disciplinin' us, Mama was firm, you know. We didn't talk back to her. I got the worst whoopin' of my life for talkin' back to her one time. I just smarted off at her or something, and she said, 'You come here.' I run, and she caught me. Every time I took a step, she warped me on the way back. It wadn't all that bad. I didn't do it no more. It was my worst fault, my mouth.

"I believe Appalachian people have become more lenient. They take things a little bit easier than they did. Like my mama said, her daddy would whip her for trivial things. If someone told a lie on her or something, she got whipped whether he found out it was the truth or not. He just believed what people told him. It's getting a little more where people will listen to their kids more than they did. That's the way I think. I think they were just raised that way. I think they were raised rough and carried it on, passed it down, I guess. I think that when your children are small you're more studious with them, and you're more strict with them.

"Daddy didn't give many whippings, but when he did, you wish you hadn't crossed him. Mama was more of the mouthier one, you know, but she'd get you after a while. She'd say more about it. I remember Daddy was with me one time because I wanted to go somewhere, and I was defiant on going. He said, 'No, you're not,' and he got a flyswatter and whipped me.

"'Course, I don't know how my parents were treated when they was young. I don't remember Daddy saying much about how his parents whipped. I remember that Mama said that she found a pair of shoes one time—I'm talking about in the twenties—a pair of tennis shoes. I don't know what they looked like back in the twenties, but she found them, and somebody told her daddy that she stole them. She said she got a whipping—she called it a beating, though. I don't know what the circumstances would've been if I brought home some tennis shoes, but I guess it would've been fine. You didn't have things like that back then, but she got a whipping over it, you know, and he didn't even ask her I don't guess." —Sue Patton (2014)

"I think children have freedom [in the country] that they don't have in the city or a town. Now you can't just turn a child loose in town; you can turn one loose in the country. I just know that a child in the country has freedom, but they don't have as many advantages. They do have advantages enough. They won't be near as mean. They can have their minds occupied with something else besides badness." —Annie Perry (1975)

"My relationship with my mother and father could not have been better. They tried their best to teach me right from wrong and how to act. They also had sufficient restraint to leave me alone and let me make some mistakes, then let me suffer the consequences. They did not protect me from reality too much. If I did something I should have known better than to do, I just had to take what was coming. I don't think my dad spanked me but three times, and I still remember to this day what they

were about. He did not have to spank me. He had instilled respect for
him in me, and when he spoke, I almost always replied, 'Yes sir.' He was
able to do that because he was not always on me for every little thing.
He let his children be children, so to speak, but let it be known when he
drew the line. The line was unmovable.

"I was very fortunate to have two very dedicated and loving parents.
They taught me what love was all about. I know of no man that had
more love and respect for his wife than my dad had for my mother. I
never heard him say anything disrespectful to her or even raise his voice
against her. I am not saying that they never disagreed, but if they did,
they did it in a respectful way, not violent. . . .

"Parents now do not provide a respectful role model for the children
to follow. Parents also tend to protect them from reality and not let them
suffer the consequences of their actions. It is always somebody else's
fault. There are lots of problems with discipline at school because children are not disciplined at home.

"I think the best advice I can give young people is to encourage them
to take responsibility for their actions, to prepare themselves to be able
to support themselves and their family if they decide to have one, be
responsible citizens by obeying the law and taking interest in government, especially by voting, and to take care of their physical body—not
to abuse it with drugs, smoking, alcohol, or excessive and junk food and
lack of exercise." —Claud Connell (2006)

"And they's not a thing in this world in my life that I'm ashamed t' meet
nobody with. You all remember that, children. That's th' first advice I
would always say t' them younguns'd be, 'Always do th' right thing.' And
one thing t' do for sure is never t' do nothin' they don't want their mother
t' know. Now, that's about the best advice you can give a child—I mean,
little children—is t' never do nothin' they don't want their mother t'
know. For, nine times out a' ten—ninety-nine out a' a hundred—if y' do
anything wrong when you're young and that way, your mother will find it
out." —Aunt Arie Carpenter (1972)

"Well, Daddy and Mother, they were strict in a way. In another, they
wadn't. They let us have our freedom. They taught us right from wrong.
They took us to church ever' Sunday mornin'. I can remember, back in
those days, Mother made all our clothes, all the boy's clothes. The shirts
and the little pants and the short pants. To church we'd go. When we'd
go to church, Mother and Daddy would sit on a pew, and we'd sit on

the same pew. You didn't get up and run around. You set right there, just like a little feller is supposed to do. Clark's Chapel—see, I went to the Methodist church all when I 'as raised—had a bell. When Sunday school come, they rang the bell. If we's out in the yard playin' around, before them bells started, we'd better be going up the steps. You get in the house. Get in the church.

"Daddy did very little whipping. He knew how to talk to us, and we did whatever he said. Mother—bless her heart—she'd get aggravated at us, and she'd send us to get a switch. We'd come back with the puniest-lookin' thing you ever saw in your life. That'd make her mad, and she'd send us back to get a good one. Then she'd whoop us with both things then. Oh, well!

"I guess the biggest thing I remember, our daddy and mama raised us up like somebody. We just wadn't thrown to the dogs. We wasn't on drugs. We didn't drink. I never saw my daddy and mother take a drop of anything. We just wasn't raised that way. A lot of people can't say that, and that's bad. I am proud that I've got a heritage like 'at."

—James Paul Wooten (2014)

WOMEN OF APPALACHIA

Thoughts on their changing roles

Oh gosh, we were tough as nails. All mountain women were tough as nails. Appalachian women are hard workers. —Janie P. Taylor

They weren't an individual, they were the family. . . . She didn't have time to be just a woman. She was always a mother.

—Andrea Burrell Potts

As I searched through Foxfire's archives, it occurred to me that there was a clear absence—never has Foxfire dedicated a section to mountain women. Appalachia is a community built on custom and tradition. In a region that is rooted in its beliefs, it is normal for a man to be considered the head of the house, as is biblically instructed. However, in Appalachia, women are the backbone. They are the cores of the homestead and the families.

Mountain women are strong. Their bodies may not always match their spiritual strength, but their toughness compensates for their lack in

PLATE 195 Nora Garland making a pone of cornbread

physical ability. From personal experience, I can attest that the women of my home are more capable than those of other areas. Given their commonplace participation in hard labor traditionally considered to be men's work, they possess a know-how lacked by women who grow up in a more urban area. As I child, I was taught to keep a clean house and fix cornbread, but I was also taught to hang siding and split wood.

"Women of Appalachia" acknowledges and commends the labors and abilities of an unparalleled body of women. Unique and tough, the women of Appalachia can be a source of strength to people everywhere. Within the pages of this section, you will find quotes and excerpts from interviews that exhibit the astounding cultural structure of women's roles years ago and the remnants of those roles that exist in today's Appalachian women.

—*Katie Lunsford*

"I think, to a certain extent, women have a right to go [out and work], and they have a right to stay home and let the husband carry on [working]. Somewhere I read the woman wasn't supposed to speak in the church service. She was supposed to speak to her husband and let him take care of it. It seems to me that women now have the lead in more things than they've ever had before.

"When it comes to the home, the woman has the whole responsibility of raising the family, and the man brings in the food."

—Carrie Stewart (1977)

"I had to do the cooking and the washing and the ironing. From the time that I could remember, I had to work. My mother was sick; then she died when I was ten years old. I could not reach the table, so I had to stand on a chair to reach the table to cook. My baby sister, Viola, was just one year old when I had to tend to her and do the cooking and the housework, too. I did all the housework that was to be done. It wasn't too clean, I can tell you that, but I kept them something to eat. . . . I guess my greatest accomplishment was working on a job while raising my kids."

—Leona "Dink" Carver (1995)

"Daddy gave me one whipping—one whipping. Mama gave me many whippings—I didn't keep count." —Annie Perry (1975)

"A man likes a woman to take care of him and the home. That's a wife's job anyway. That's what being a wife means. If a woman wants a career, she should never get married.

"Oh, she can get a job long enough to help out, and she should never let a job get in the way of being a wife. She should clean the house, make it a home, and take care of her family, no matter what."

—Letters from Annie Part 2 (1974)

"I wish they hadn't [given women the right to vote] 'cause they gave 'em that privilege, and now they're a-tryin' t' take over. I don't like that— even if I am a woman. I think that's men's work. 'Course, they're makin' a right smart mess out of it. Maybe if th' women had it all, they might do better." —Aunt Celia Wood (1973)

"And like it is by dressin'. Years back, well, if a woman had her dress up and somebody saw her knee, [it was the] awfullest thing there ever was, but now they don't pay no more attention for their knee than they do for their hands." —Maud Shope (1973)

"I reckon he [Buck Carver] wanted me to help him [build stills], so I'd help him. I wouldn't do it again. . . . It was hard work, your arms pushing

PLATE 196 Aunt Arie working in her garden, with Foxfire students helping

against the brads as hard as you can. Why, sometimes my arm would get numb. And it made too much racket. It was hard on me."

—Leona "Dink" Carver (1988)

"I've been made fun of for bein' old-fashioned, but it don't matter t' me a bit in th' world. If anyone tries t' run over me, they'll find they've run up against a stake that won't budge 'cause it's made out a' locust! I've always done the work of a man. God's been good t' me. He's given me strength."

—Anna Howard (1972)

"I think that I am fairly self-sufficient. I can do just about anything. I can do things that a lot of women have never done. As I get older, I may not be able to do them, but right now I figure I can do just about anything to survive." —Dorothy Kilby (1998)

Changes in mountain women

In 1975, Bit Carver, a daughter of the renowned Buck and Leona Carver (featured in numerous Foxfire *books and magazines) started an independent research project on the changing roles of mountain women. Two of the four interviews that she conducted are presented here, one with Lawton Brooks and another with Andrea Burrell Potts.*

Lawton was a cherished Foxfire contact whose wisdom has spanned the decades. Andrea Burrell Potts was a young woman and former

Foxfire student who exemplified the changes in mountain women. She was the granddaughter of Pearl Martin, yet another esteemed contact featured in numerous Foxfire publications. Lawton's knowledge of our mountains and their people and Andrea's ability to compare herself to her grandmother made each of them prime contacts for a study on the evolution of the roles of mountain women. I would like to thank the families of each of these contacts for allowing us to share their stories. They taught us so much, as they will you, too.

Lawton on how he thought the role of women had changed as of 1975:

"Well, it has changed. It has changed a lot. One thing, the way they dress. You used to didn't see women dress like they do nowadays. You never seen women wearing britches back when I was a kid a-comin' up. They didn't do that. They always wore dresses, and they had to be down below the knee. Now, girls your age, their dresses had to be halfway below the knee, or they wouldn't let 'em wear 'em. Now, you take the difference between now and then—what about the difference in the cloth it would take to make your [Bit's] dress and then make what you could wear back then. There's a lot of difference there, you see. It's changed a lot in that length of time. The change really started, I'd say, back in the 1920s. I think it started in the twenties and worked its way on up, but I'd say the biggest part of it started then.

On women working and where they worked:

"No, they didn't go nowhere and work then, the women didn't. Once in a while they'd get [a job] as a maid and go into a house. Now, my mother had to get one. She kept a lady that stayed with us after I was born. I was the baby, and she was sick all the time after I was born. She was never stout anymore, and she died when I was fifteen years old. I stayed in the house with [my mother] the biggest part of the time, and then we got this lady to come and stay at the house, but as working somewhere—they didn't get out and work anywhere.

"They didn't have a chance to go and work then. There weren't any factories a-going then, and if they did go to work, they had to go and work for another lady and help her with her house, but there was mighty little of that done. I never knowed of my mother ever doing any of that."

On women's educational opportunities:

"Well, [women] didn't have too good of a chance to get an education then, honey, and I'll tell you the reason why; then, you had to buy all these books. There wasn't anything free. The teachers didn't make too much. They didn't make over twenty or thirty dollars a month a-teachin' school, and you had to buy all your books."

On girls who would stay home to help their mothers instead of going to school:

"There was a lot of 'em that done that. There was a lot of girls that stayed in and helped their mother out. Now, my sisters went to school, but they had to work in the fields, too. The girls had to work in the field the same as the boys. My sisters went right to the fields—every day they was right in the fields. All of 'em worked in the fields but me, and I had to stay home with my mother. They didn't have a chance to get their education like they do nowadays. I don't see why no child don't go on and get their education. Do you?"

Andrea Burrell Potts on women's role in society as of 1975:

"No, 'cause . . . we don't depend on our husband like we used to. I think that that is one of the main things. Back then, if a woman was by

PLATE 197 Andrea Burrell Potts cooking ramps—a strong wild onion

herself, it was a lot harder on her. I don't think people got married on account of love, but on account of the *need* because there was so much hard work that a woman just almost couldn't do. I don't know if that's true or not, but that's the way it seemed to me. Well, just, like, cutting with a crosscut saw, there's very few women that I've ever seen that could really do it. Most of 'em are like me, they're weak . . . physically, anyway."

On whether women are still obligated to have children:

"No, everybody used to have kids, but I don't think it was that they wanted them so much, but because they had no way of birth control. I like [children], but I don't think everybody should have 'em."

On the role she believes that she plays in her home compared to her grandmother, Pearl Martin:

"Well, she just didn't have time to sit down and take it easy or anything like that, you know. It was just, 'Go! Go! Go!' I think she had to care for either her mother or Grandpa's mother [Pearl's mother-in-law], one [or the other], and they didn't have any modern conveniences, so they didn't have any time of rest, except on Sunday—I don't think they were allowed to work on Sunday. Now, just like softball, it's fun for me to take off and play ball, to get out of the house and not just become a mama and a wife. I'm a ball player, but [the home was] all they had. They didn't have any outside activities unless maybe quilting, but then that all went back into the house—they were doing that for the house. That's all they had, working for the kids and the house."

On the opportunities she had versus those Pearl may have had:

"They had no outlets. They couldn't get off the creek—how could they do anything? If they come off, it'd take 'em a day to get off and a day to get back and in a wagon. Then, later on, I think Billy Long's was the only car on Betty's Creek. I think that on Saturday, everybody met Billy Long and rode out with him. What can you do? If you can't get out, you can't do much. I could pretty well [I have the opportunities to] do what I wanted to if I took a notion, I guess."

In response to "What do you think made it possible for you to have more opportunities than your grandmother did? Was it because you had a better education or because times have changed?":

"Not that I had a better education, because Ma Martin could learn anything. It is easier to go. That's one of the main things that held women back: They couldn't get out, plus what little time they had off. They didn't have much time to go because it took so much longer for them to do what we have to do. They wove clothes and a whole lot of stuff. Now the water and everything else comes to you instead of you having to go get it, but the main thing was transportation, because just think of how hard it would be to ride off the head of Betty's Creek in a covered wagon with a muddy road."

In response to "Do you think that women today are more aware of themselves as a person?":

"Yes, they have more time—that's the thing. Today, they have more time to themselves, more time to themselves because they don't have as much to do. There was just no way back then that they could take time to fix their hair up or take time to go play ball or take time to just get together. And when they did get together, ninety times out of one hundred they were doing something, like quilting, for their homes. They just didn't have the time. They weren't an individual; they were the family. That's the way it goes. They weren't as lucky as we were, I don't guess. If one copped out, that threw the rest of 'em back or behind in the chores.

["When I was expecting Bobby,] I had a baby shower and everything was given to me, and people passed on stuff, but Mama, she made the T-shirts for her babies and the diapers for her children. She only had so many diapers, and she had to wash diapers every day, not in the washing machine always either, but sometimes down by the creek. She didn't have time to be just a woman. She was always a mother.

"Lots of those women would only go to town maybe once a month, and it was a big deal if you got two cents to spend, but we weren't underprivileged that bad. We had a real wonderful childhood. I think that was one of the main reasons Mama is like she is today, is because of the way she had to wash clothes and things; I think that's why she has arthritis. You know, maybe it just broke her down so bad that she got it."

On how her mother's circumstances compare to her grandmother's:

"She [Mama] had electricity, and then they came along with the washing machine, and she used it and a refrigerator. You didn't have to walk to the spring, so she had more time, but they worked. They would have liked to have had time to be individuals the same as we have, but they didn't have the time."

PLATE 198 Pearl Martin making soap

The current-day women of Appalachia have an inner strength, determination, and nurturing nature that is just as strong as their forebears. They come from a generation of modern conveniences, TV dinners, microwaves, vacuum cleaners, that are supposed to make their lives easier. . . . However, there is consistency in women's roles across generations. The modern-day Appalachian woman is still the primary caregiver, cook, housekeeper, and sometimes breadwinner for her family. Although she has many more freedoms, her natural instinct is to put others before herself. She most likely works outside the home and feels the same anxiety as many women about all she has to accomplish in her public role as well as in her family role. She keeps moving along, doing the best she can to continue the family traditions instilled in her by her own mother. In the subsequent section, quotes from more recent Foxfire contacts are presented, along with interviews with Maxine Darnell and Sue Patton on how women of Appalachia have changed.

Changes in Appalachian women according to recent
Foxfire contacts

"[Pants on women]—only acceptable when the temperature drops below zero." —**Mildred Barnard West (2006)**

"If they were home working, then they just had a housedress on. The next generation probably had blue jeans on. There were little morning dresses. A morning dress was what you wore before you got dressed for the day. When you got dressed up, in Mama's case, she always had a hat [and] gloves." —**Janie P. Taylor (2014)**

"The girls, they could do about the same work as the boys did. They could just about do anything they wanted 'cause they knowed how. They had done it enough, and they knowed how to do it all, every bit of it."
—**J. P. Speed (2005)**

"Just lookin' back, you didn't see a lot of Dad because Dad worked all the time, but Mom was the central figure around the house. She cooked and cleaned. Not many women worked [outside the home]. They took care of the kids and disciplined. . . . So, we were pretty much raised by our mothers. When we got out of line, Mother would say, '[If] you don't straighten up, son, I'm gonna tell ya' daddy,' and you didn't want that."
—**Carl Shoupe (2009)**

"How women coped is beyond me. I can remember bitter cold days when Mother would be washin' clothes right below the stream. There'd be a big ol' black pot boilin', and kids would have to 'feed' it . . . I can remember it bein' so cold that as she hung the diapers and clothes, they'd freeze. Mother would be washin' 'em in that boilin' water and then cold water. We used lye soap, and it made her hands raw. That used to get to me even though I was a child." —**Bob Justus (2005)**

"Well, she [Mother] just done for everybody because, back then, people would walk from one place to another. They'd come through Popcorn, and some of 'em lived on Plum Orchard [**Editor's note:** located in the western part of Rabun County], for the most part. She took care of anybody that come through. If it was late in the evenin', they'd spend the night there on Popcorn.

"[She was] more of a quiet person because she had to milk and take care of the hogs and all of the other things. She took care of all things. She never was all that friendly. She was busy doing and had [things] to do."

—Waymond Lunsford (2014)

"Oh, my mother was the most influential person [in my life]. She was a fighter. Let's put it like that. She was a tough one. She saw that—when we moved from North Carolina in the middle of the Depression—we made do with whatever. My father lost his health about that time. And so Mama became the breadwinner for the family. He died when I was about eighteen, and Mother saw to it that we were all educated and raised us. My first memory was Mama doin' washin' at the spring down there with the black wash pot and the scrub board."

—Janie P. Taylor (2014)

After fifty years, Foxfire has connected many students with their elders in the community. Few are more influential than Mrs. Janie P. Taylor. Janie passed away in 2015, shortly after allowing Foxfire to interview her one last time. For years, Janie was an advocate for and a cherished contact to the Foxfire program. She helped in any way possible to accomplish Foxfire's mission of preserving the Appalachian culture and heritage. Janie was a member of the Foxfire Community Board, volunteered in the Museum Gift Shop, and demonstrated quilt making for various Foxfire events. Janie P. taught in the Rabun County School system for many years, influencing the lives of thousands of students. The most outstanding quality of Mrs. Taylor's was her pride in her homeplace and those who came before her. She radiated a sense of satisfaction for her home of Tiger Mountain, her community, and her people. The work that she did with Foxfire, from storytelling to painting, will continue on to remind people of life here in Appalachia. She was a shining example of the modern-day Appalachian woman.

"I think that my inspiration as a child—I have thought a lot about this, especially as I have gotten older—came from three main people. These three main people played a big part in what I became. One was my mother. She was a very strong and independent mountain woman, and she always encouraged me to work hard and do well. She used to say, 'Take what you want, saith the Lord. Take it and pay for it.' I grew up thinking that was in the Bible. I was a grown man before I realized that's not in the Bible. That was just my mother. What she was saying was, 'You can have anything in this world, but you have got to work for it.' So, I learned hard work from her." —**Zell Miller (1996)**

"Me and sis would do the housework all the time. I don't remember Mama ever havin' to do the housework, except cookin'. She didn't do all that. We helped her. Mama and Daddy worked at the school, and we were expected to have things done when Mama got home. We'd start supper for her." —**Sue Patton (2014)**

"Now, getting back to my wife, think about it. She wa'n't any older than you girls sittin' in here, and I was twenty-two or twenty-three. At that time, she had a brand-new car, and she had a checking account. Back then, that was 'big time' for a girl to have."

—**Tommie Lee Shope (2006)**

Changes in mountain women according to new contacts

In the Spring/Summer 2011 edition of The Foxfire Magazine, *Maxine Darnell and her daughter, Jan Lunsford, were featured in an article titled "Generations of Tradition." The following passage is an excerpt where these Appalachian women discuss the changing roles of mountain women and their thoughts on what roles ought to be.*

Maxine: "I guess that I'm still just a little old-fashioned. It's fine for a woman to work. I don't object to that, but I still think that they have a role in the home. Even if she is working, the responsibility is hers to pre-pare a meal. I feel like it was the woman's place to keep a decent house. The role is difficult, but I think that the woman should still maintain that role in the household. The man is the breadwinner, and the more difficult chores are his. As far as kitchen and general household chores, I feel like the woman still has the greater role to play there in being the mother or housewife. I knew no other way.

"You may go off and do many other different things in life, but you will never forget those values that you're taught at home—the way you do your work at home. In a way, it provides memories you have to cher-ish because it was hard work. There was a bond there in the family that you don't see a lot now, and I think it is because families have missed the togetherness because of those kinds of things not having precedence in the home now."

Jan: "I agree with Mom. You can call me old-fashioned, too. It takes me back to when I spent a lot of time around her grandparents, my great-grandparents, Mamaw and Papaw. She was a very Godly woman. She was the perfect example of a keeper at the home, not just a homemaker or housekeeper, but a keeper at the home and of the home; she kept the house up. She prepared the meals. To a great extent, a whole lot of the garden work fell on her. When it came to the hogs, Papaw raised them, but when they were to come in the house, a lot of the work was done by her.

"It is my personal belief, opinion, and conviction that, when possible, if circumstances permit—and I know a lot of women have to work now—I think that a woman should fill those shoes. I feel that they are hers to fill.

"I have worked. I worked for twenty years. When my husband and I married, I spent those early years at a full-time job. We made a change. I stayed home for seven years full-time, and I was a complete and total wife and mother, taking care of the home and having meals cooked. Back in a working position now, I get a lot of help from my husband at home. I'm thankful for that, but there are still a lot of things that I feel personally responsible for. As busy as I am, I try my best to carry the majority of that load.

"You know, *Little House on the Prairie* is not a made-up concept. That's the way life used to be; everybody pitched in when it came to cleaning and cooking and other chores. From the time that Mom grew up in Papaw and Mamaw's household, to the time that I grew up in Mom's, things were different. It is different even with mine. Still, when I look back to those old days, I feel privileged to have witnessed those values day-to-day, firsthand, in my great-grandparents' house."

The following pieces are from two ladies in our community, Sue Patton and Maxine Darnell. Each provides insight on women of Appalachia: their dress, duties, and changes in women's roles over the years.

Ms. Patton, responding to a question about whether there was a general difference in women's personalities in Appalachia between generations:

It wadn't the generation. I can't say it right. The soft-spokenness or the outspokenness just come from different personalities. I wouldn't think [there was a trend in women's personalities], not that I remember. [One of my grandmas] didn't say a whole lot. My other 'n', now, she'd let you know.

Ms. Patton on changes in women's clothing:

"Now, both grandmas wore dresses all the time, with an apron, all the time. They might a' pulled it off when they went to town or somethin'. They probably did make their own way back years ago. Daddy usually took my grandparents to town. I just jumped in the car, too, 'cause I didn't get to go to town that much either. I remember I was with my grandpa and grandma Henslee, and they went into Cannon's Department Store out here and bought her a dress. He was talkin' on, this would a' been in the sixties, early sixties pro'bly. He was sayin', 'I just bought Ma'am—he called her Ma'am—a dress in there, and it cost twenty-three dollars.' It sounds cheap now, but back then it was pretty high. I think that all her dresses was store-bought. I think my grandmaw Wilburn's was, too. Mama might a' made her one. Back in the day, she probably made her own clothes, but I don't remember. I think of

PLATE 199 Sue Patton's Grandma Wilburn

myself as a granny, and I said, 'Well, I ain't got my apron on with big pockets, and I ain't humped over. I ain't got my little granny shoes on.' [Granny shoes] had a little heel; I guess you'd call them the stack heel. They wadn't pointy. They was as wide as the shoe. They weren't too bad high, about like this [an inch or so]. Old Lady Comforts is what the name of 'em was. They laced up, black. They wore the stockings, my grandmas did.

"Well, Mama wore pants. She was born in nineteen and fifteen (1915). She'd be ninety-nine years old this year if she'd a' lived. She wore dungaree pants back in early years. You know what dungarees are? The big-legged ones that you'd roll 'em up to here. She wore dresses when she went out. She might a' wore 'em out some, but that was her basic home stuff, her dungarees. If she went to church or whatever, she'd wear a dress. Mama's was always just a shirtwaist dress.

"There wasn't a whole lot of difference in the dresses in my grand-mas' 'n' my mama's. Theirs [my grandmothers'] might've been a little longer, but as far as style, it was always shirtwaist dresses.

On women's duties:

"Women did the housecleaning, the cooking, and everything—taking care of children. A lot of time the grandparents raised some of the grand-kids, you know, sometimes under different circumstances. My mother didn't, but one of my grandmothers did.

"[Mama worked outside the house] some. My grandma didn't work outside the home. Well, Mama just had a couple of outside jobs, just here and there every once and a while. I know that she worked at the shirt factory for about six months when I was about four years old because Daddy didn't have a job at the time, but when he got a job, she quit. But Daddy did all of the household chores when she was at work. He was like a housewife. He washed and shrunk some stuff in the washing machine. They had ringer types. It just had a tub, and you had to fill it up with a hose or a bucket of water, and you put your clothes in there, and it washed it. It had a ringer with two rollers that you turned on. You would put your clothes through there and put them in a tub and rinse them. Then you put them through that ringer again and hung them on a line. I love the clothesline.

"For the most part, women's duties have remained constant. The menfolk might help out some, but usually it's put on the woman. I think [men help more than they used to]. I think the women wised up."

Maxine Darnell shares memories of her mother's hard work ethic:

"Well, as a small child, I can remember that Mama always, even if they got home late in the evenin', she had to go to the barn. It was her duty, while Papaw was doin' other things, she would milk the cow. She would bring it in and process the milk. She would do that, and she would cook a meal, a full meal. She never asked Daddy to wash dishes. I don't remember that Daddy ever had to go in the kitchen and do those kinds of things. He was a rugged worker outside. She always would partake of helping with those chores outside. She always worked, in my opinion, just as hard as any man would have to work to get the work done.

"We always raised hogs. When late fall came or wintertime came, they would kill hogs, and Mama would get out there and help scrape the hair off the hogs and get them ready to be cut up and process the hogs. She would do that just like a man would. Going into the woods and bringing in a load of wood or whatever, she was equal to Papaw doin' that.

"Anyway, Mama always shared in those type things outside. There may have been a few times that Mama may have put on a pair of men's pants to work outside when it was real cold, but I can't really remember that. My most fond memories were of her in a dress that came well below her knees and most of the time a dress that had sleeves that came down below her elbows. [She dressed] very modestly. Although it may have been work clothes, it was very modest work clothes. That's just the way she was brought up. Of course, those kinds of things were instilled in us, not that she stood over us and said, 'You have to wear this.' It was just a natural thing as you grew up, and she selected the things that you would wear. I don't remember [if she made our clothes]. She may have when we were very small. I don't remember Mama sewing. I remember her patching and mending things, but I don't remember her actually making anything.

"[She kept] the clothes washed, hung out and dried, and ironed. [Mama was instrumental in] the preparation of meats, from feeding the animals until they were ready for the slaughter to helping the slaughter process, dressing and curing the meat . . . We had a meat house out behind the house in the wintertime. You would cure out some of the types of hams and things. You would cure those out and leave them in a dark building. Late in the afternoons—Mama wouldn't wait until the next morning to get meat for breakfast—she would go slice off the amount of meat she would use the next morning. She would bring it in to have ready to cook for the next morning.

"She would take excess eggs from several laying hens, and we always had a cow. She would process the butter, churn it and get it ready and mold it into bowls. She would take the eggs and the butter to a store in town, one of the grocery stores, to exchange for whatever she needed in the grocery store. He would swap with her."

On whether it was normal for a woman at that time to take up a job outside the home:

"Mama was very independent. At one point, Mama was gone and worked. She drove about forty-five miles away to Helen, where there was a hosiery mill. She even rented a small little house because gas got more expensive. She would stay from Monday morning to Friday evening. From work she would drive back home to Clayton and be there for the weekend. While she was away, Papaw took care of my brother and me.

"At that time, she chose to help do that. She didn't work there all that long. Mama came back home and was the homemaker, but she worked outside some, outside of the home in the plants [factories], but she was mostly the homemaker, taking care of things at home and seeing that things were run in a good manner.

"I never worked on a public job until the year I graduated from high school, and I went to work that summer. I worked before I married. I got married less than a year after I graduated from high school. In fact, I graduated at the end of May in '61, and in January of '62, I married.

On the normality of a job before marriage in previous generations:

"Some people worked. My mother was one of five sisters. Being that big a family, when the hosiery mill came into Clayton, each one of them who was old enough to get a job got one. They knew it was an opportunity to make some money and to help out, even as they planned to get married eventually. Normally, you were trained to work around home. Then working on a public job became a little more prevalent.

"I think it was a more common thing for the women to get married at even fifteen. I think Mama was fourteen when she had her oldest child, or maybe she was fourteen when she married and just immediately went ahead and went through her first pregnancy. Women got married much younger, and it wasn't frowned on I guess because, in the country, a lot of 'em did it. I don't know if it was to get away from home or just to have a better life.

On how the perception of women's roles has changed:

"Well, times have changed and the economy became so that you can no longer just work at home and make a living. If you wanted anything, or if you had children and you wanted to further their education or give them some of the nicer things in life, then you left home, took a job, and worked all you could to bring in money. Of course, the more money you could bring in, the better status you had, but it was always thought that a woman was well-respected if she could stay home and take care of her family. As years rolled on, it became more prevalent for women to go out and get a job outside the home and work.

"Well, for one thing, when some industry did start to come into our county—the one I can remember most was the shirt factory that came in around the early fifties—some office jobs were offered. A lot of times when their husbands couldn't find work, the women went out and sought the work so that they could help provide. A lot of the women had gone to work there. Some of them had husbands who had no jobs. Therefore, when the women had no jobs, it left a lot of them in dire circumstance. A joke was made out of it that some of the men were called 'go-getters' because they would go and drop their wives off at work and come pick her up in the afternoon.

On the women of Appalachia versus women elsewhere:

"I don't know so much about other areas, but here, the way we were raised, it was just a natural thing of the woman to be the homemaker. And she was well thought of. People would make the remarks, 'She really takes care of her family. She's a good mom,' you know, or, 'She's a good wife because she sees that her family is taken care of.' The man goes to work to bring in the bread, but she works to keep things goin' in the home.

"Like I said, you learn at an early age, whether you're a male or female, to accept the difficult work because it helps everybody get along better. If you take a part and help with what's going on, the job gets done. When my brother had to get the wood in, he didn't do it by himself. I went out with him, and I helped. I think it was good—even though it was hard sometimes—I think it was good that I was trained that way. You look at some women in life, and you think, 'Boy, they don't know how to do anything.' It's because of the way they were raised.

"I helped by getting in the garden and gathering or harvesting food, or hoeing the corn, or getting the garden to the state that it was ready to produce vegetables. You know, you just learn to take part in that as a girl when you're really small, but the older you got, the more of those things you took on to help. But, yes, I feel proud now to know that that was part of my upbringing.

"Men, now, a lot of them—if their wife goes out on a public job to work—will pick up half of the duties. Some won't. Some are still old-fashioned and let the wife do it all when she comes home. I think that the men do take more of a responsibility, and I guess if they respect their wives, then that's one of the things, having a big respect for their wives that will work on a public job and then come home and do the house up. I think that they have learned that, when they do a little bit of the chores, they begin to see what the woman has to do in order to accomplish what she has to accomplish. A lot of times, they just love her to where it's like, 'Hey, I'm going to help her get this done so she can sit down and rest.' So, yeah, I think men do a bit more of that now.

"I think in a way it brings about a more compassionate feeling in your life. I'm thankful for my upbringing and most of all, as we said in the very beginning, the faith in God and the morals. All of those things bind together to make a person who they are. I couldn't imagine being a person who would be living without those things, because I need them in my life. And if other people could see—really see—what it could do for their lives, I think it would be much different.

"There were some cases that men didn't have the faith that the women had. Papaw always took care of his duties, but Mama was the one who taught us the religious things. He would take Mama to church. He always drove us to church. He would usually just wait out in the truck during the whole service for us. Now, of course, when my brother got older, he would drive us to church, but Daddy was not the religious figure. In his later years, he accepted and was a very changed person, but all through our younger years, he was not the role model as a Christian, so my mother took all of those responsibilities.

"Back then, the woman was in the home more and [had the responsibility of teaching the children] part of what her ideas were. The men came home tired and took a bath and ate, but the woman was there constantly and had all of those things that she felt responsible for and attended to. In a sense, that was why the woman was more dominant in the teaching of the children."

Women these days can often go to town and have more time for personal interests. In that respect, we have transformed; however, the lessons and beliefs passed from mother to daughter live on. The convictions of such a strong body of women will continue to guide our lives.

As for me, I am proud of nothing more than being a woman bred from such strength and dedication. This section is dedicated to the people who are the heart of Appalachia. Through it, I am able to pass on a fundamental piece of my heritage.

WHAT WE HAVE LEARNED

I think the younger generation has become more aware of the older times and the way things were done, and I think that's good.

—*Ruth Cabe*

After fifty years, we can finally reflect on all the invaluable lessons we have learned from being a part of Foxfire. "What We Have Learned" is broken up into different subsections, with comments in each from the students, the parents, the readers, and the community. Throughout these sections, our readers can discover the relationship between Foxfire and the world, and the effect it has had on Foxfire students, on their parents, and on the entire community. Without recording the knowledge and techniques of elders, the wisdom we possess is lost. What we have learned has extended beyond the bindings of the books and magazines; it has profoundly influenced our lives.

Foxfire has taught us the importance of preserving our roots and acknowledging the impact our ancestors made on our lives, and how they paved the road for the generations that will come. Foxfire pushes its students to go above and beyond the requirements that other students, in other classrooms, simply meet. Furthermore, Foxfire encourages students to get out of their self-centered lives and enjoy all of life's blessings—to make memories and friendships across generations—memories that will last forever.

—Jessica Phillips and Ross Lunsford

STUDENT SPOTLIGHT

FROM PENCILS TO PCS

We were probably more experimental because that was back in the earliest days; we had to experiment. —Laurie Brunson Altieri

Former student Laurie Brunson Altieri discusses changes in the magazine

Laurie Brunson Altieri was an early Foxfire student. This piece shows the change that technology has brought as we've entered into the twenty-first century with the introduction of the computers and the exclusion of older methods. It is crucial to show these changes because they are vital to "What We Have Learned."

—*Jessica Phillips and Ross Lunsford*

I graduated forty years ago, in 1971—that was from Rabun Gap-Nacoochee School. I was not originally from Rabun County. You all may or may not know that, back then, there was the high school here in Clayton (the old high school), but the students from the northern end of the county went to Rabun Gap. I came down from Virginia, and I was going to school at Rabun Gap as a dorm student. That was where Foxfire started. I think it proved to be the kind of medium that was good for Foxfire to begin with. That's how I happened to come into Foxfire. I took the journalism class, got very involved, and just really loved it. That was back in the very beginning. Foxfire was only just a few years old.

Back then, Foxfire was very different. We had no computers. Back then, we had to send the magazines to a printer in Atlanta in what they called picture-ready format. We had to literally cut and paste. The layout we had to do was all by hand. The article transcriptions were done by hand because none of us had a typewriter, and we sure didn't have a computer. Things weren't actually typed until they were ready to be typed, cut, and pasted into the layout. We had these great big things of graph paper; a piece of graph paper would do two pages. It had to be exact. In other words, we had to decide how the page is going to be laid out exactly, and then we paste it in. We had to give directions on how to crop the photographs and how they were going to be laid out. It was nothing like Foxfire is now.

"We had subscribers, by that time, in all fifty states and about a dozen foreign countries."

Back in those times, we mailed the magazine ourselves. We got big manila envelopes, and when it was time to mail one, we would get stacks of them and have an assembly line going. Some of us would scribble addresses on them by hand. Some of us would stamp on there, book rate, and we'd stamp our postal thing [permit number] on there. Then some of us would stuff them, and some of us would lick the envelopes. We had to sort them into state and zip code. We had subscribers, by that time, in all fifty states and about a dozen foreign countries. We had to sort them out and put them into bags. We had postal bags for that very purpose. Then we took them to Mrs. Jean Burch, who was at the Rabun Gap Post Office at that time; we had bags and bags and bags. It was quite a bit different from the way you all do now.

The summer, that was more of a fun time, usually; we didn't mail magazines. We didn't have all that to work on. We went out and did interviews. We had a Foxfire vehicle at that time, a green-and-white Ford Bronco. We went out and did interviews, transcribed tapes, started on our articles, and sorted our transcriptions into whatever articles they were going to go into. We worked on our articles. One summer, there were two older Foxfire graduates who had been hired to work for the summer, and they were women. There were actually seven of us: four guys and three girls. That summer, the three of us girls took a camping trip up into the Smoky Mountains. We went up near Bryson City all by ourselves, and we took the Foxfire Bronco. We had one pup tent that would sleep two, so we alternated around. Two of us would sleep in the pup tent in the campground, and one of us would sleep in the Bronco.

We went up there and basically just started checking around and talking to people. We got a wonderful article out of that; it was great. We just did that kind of stuff.

We pulled a lot of late nights. If we had a magazine layout to do, we would all be up in the very tiny Foxfire office. Believe me, this kind of space was like, "Oh my gosh!" We would be in this tiny little Foxfire office working on everything at one time. Each of us would be working on a different article layout, and then we would put it all together. We might be up there till midnight trying to get everything done.

We did have tape recorders. We didn't have anything digital like you all do now. We would use tape recorders to record the interviews, and then we would sit there and punch the buttons, listen to the tape, and write them out by hand. We had a big reel-to-reel tape recorder for if we wanted something with excellent quality, like something musical, something we wanted more quality on. Mostly, it was cassettes.

Back then, we didn't have digital photography. Foxfire had three very old SLR cameras, the kind that had the film that you wind—you pull it out and wind it. When we took pictures, we had to develop them. We had a tiny little darkroom. It did have running water, which was good. It was a little tiny thing with a shelf, and when you went in there, that's where we developed our film first. Then we would print pictures. We had these different trays of developer, and wash, and the stuff that sets it.

We also had an enlarger. It was one of these great big things that you would put the negative in. There would be these tiny little pictures, like thumbnails on a computer, except they were the actual negatives. Everything in the photo that was light was dark on the negative, and everything that was dark, was light. It was opposite of what you were going to print. So, we had this great big enlarger, and you would put the negative in one place, and a light would shine through—this is all in the darkroom. You had to keep your photographic paper covered very carefully because any light would expose it; it was very sensitive. We had to keep that covered. When we put our negative in, it would shine down; it would magnify it on a surface. Then we would have to focus it. We had a focuser that you would use to adjust the lighting. You had to get it just the way you want it. We learned how to dodge stuff—how to alter the light if the picture wasn't perfect. We did all that, and when you were finally ready, you would turn the enlarger off because it had to be black. We had an infrared light in there. You'd pull out the photographic paper, put it where it was supposed to be, and then you'd turn the enlarger on. When the light would shine down on the paper, it would project your picture onto your photographic paper. You had to be careful how long you burned it because if you burned it too long, it wouldn't be good. You had to really watch it. When you had burned it just enough, you had to immediately grab it and throw it in the developer. At that point, you didn't see anything until it started developing. You would develop it, and when it was developed enough, you would wash it. We had a clear water wash to get all the developer off because you didn't want it to develop any more. Once you washed it, you would put it in the stuff that would settle it. Then, after it was set, we hung them up. We used a clothesline with clothespins. That was how we did pictures.

Everything that we did was by hand. Talking to you all, I feel like our old contacts. We learned from them how they did everything by hand back in the day. They made their own soap; they did all that stuff. Talking to you all, I feel like a dinosaur because that's how we did it. We did everything like that by hand; we had no digital cameras, no computers. When we put together an article, we would have our own handwritten copy of the transcripts and things. We would handwrite our introductions, our directions, and our articles. We would basically cut it up into pieces, and we'd staple them onto typing paper. Then we'd kind of leave a space where we wanted our pictures. We'd staple the typing paper together. We might start at the end of the room, and we'd have all the stapled stuff stretched out on the floor across the room. It would be like a trail. When we got done with our article, we would roll it up, the end of the article first, and then we would give it to whoever was going to type it. When Margie Bennett came, she did it; she became our typist. When they typed it, it had to be perfect because, like I said, when we sent it, we sent it to the printer photo-ready. All the printer had to do was take a picture of it, print the signatures, cut it into pages, and bind it into a magazine.

We also had a little circulation department, and my senior year, one of my duties was being one of the circulation managers. I loved it. We got all the letters, and we would read them. When people would send in a new subscription or renew their old one, we would take the checks and stamp the endorsement for the deposit. We would work up all the deposits. We would also answer all the letters. We had index card files that alphabetized every single subscriber. We had on it the date they subscribed, the dates that they renewed, and the date that it was going to run out, all on these little index cards. They were all handwritten. We would use that card to keep up with them. Every time somebody would renew, we would pull out their card and renew it. Periodically,

PLATE 200 Laurie Brunson Altieri explaining the changes Foxfire has experienced

of course, we had to pull out all the ones that had not been renewed, so we wouldn't send them another magazine. We did all that by hand. We handwrote all of the letters to people. We got a lot of letters from people telling us how much they enjoyed the magazine, and we would share those letters, and let people see them, but we would also answer them.

We did four issues of the magazine per year. Subscriptions were originally five dollars per year, and they went up to seven dollars. I'm trying to remember; it's been a long time. It was like sevenish; they would have to keep going up because of the cost of the paper and that kind of stuff. We didn't do a glossy magazine, like the current magazine. Ours didn't look anything like what you all are doing now. The covers were matte style. We had to design the covers and everything photo-ready.

I just recently was looking at the magazine, and you have a beautiful magazine. If we had seen that back in the day, we would've gone, "Wow, that's an uptown magazine!" We were more like the log cabin model. We would've been really impressed by the technical aspects. You guys have a whole lot more technology than we ever had. We had to fly by the seat of our pants sometimes. I think the biggest difference that I see is that, back when we were doing it, we were just kind of trying things all the time because it was so new. You know what I mean? It was like, "Yeah, this works. Yeah, we can actually do a log cabin issue where people can build a log cabin from it." We were trying things a lot. Everything was just an attempt to see what we could do. We were probably more experimental because that was back in the earliest days; we had to experiment.

The magazine started in 1966. Then the first book was actually published in 1972, which is pretty phenomenal. I think all of us were amazed. We knew the magazine was popular. We knew that in no time. The word was out, and we had subscribers in all fifty states. I think it was twelve or thirteen foreign countries that we had subscribers in. We really didn't know that when Doubleday—the company that published the book—wanted to do the book as a collection of the magazine articles, just how big of a change it would bring. We thought that was fine; that was a great idea.

"None of us had any idea what was going to happen because when that book hit, it was like, 'Whoosh!' It just went crazy."

I remember working on the manuscript that we were going to send. I remember the galleys that they sent back that we had to go through and make any corrections and stuff like that. We sent off the final manuscript in 1971. That was the year I graduated and the summer I worked for Foxfire. None of us had any idea what was going to happen because when that book hit, it was like, "*Whoosh!*" It just went crazy. All of a sudden, everybody in the country knew who we were. All of a sudden, there were articles appearing in *Time* magazine, in *The Washington Post*, and not to mention *The Atlanta Journal-Constitution*. All of the sudden, there were people calling and saying, "So, can we come and do an interview?" All of a sudden, there was all of this stuff. We were like, "Wow." None of us ever thought that it would do that. We had no idea that it was going to take off like it did. We wound up having to be very careful. I can tell you that, for a number of years, the whole time I worked for Foxfire, we were very vigilant because we understood the responsibility we had to this area, to the people, and to our contacts that we loved. We understood that all of this outside media had to be regulated. We were not about to let anybody come in and do anything that we did not totally approve of; we turned down a lot of stuff.

The year after I left, the program moved to the Rabun County High

School. I left Rabun County in 1976. I really did not have an active role after I moved to Virginia. I never really did come back here; this is the first time I have been to the new high school. What essentially happened is the old high school here had a fire. It was already old and crowded, and that did it in. Basically, from what I understand, they were able to get grants to rebuild it. They were going to be able to get some matching grants from the federal government, but it had to become consolidated. Back in that time, the people in the northern end of the county had gone to Rabun Gap, their kids had gone to Rabun Gap, and their grandkids were going to Rabun Gap. They had a special referendum in the county where you voted on whether or not you supported consolidating the new school. The people in the northern end of the county were like, "No! It's not that we don't want you all to have a new high school; we think you ought to have a new high school; we just don't want to bus our kids down there. We want to stay where we've got this school that we already have ties with." It was kind of hard. When I think about it, I was gone at the time the transition happened, but I know that in the northern end of the county, everybody voted no. Of course, it passed, as it should've. It had to happen; it was just the circumstances of the times. I'm sure it was a very big transition. You've got to realize that we had this rivalry between the two schools. Both schools had basketball teams. We had this intense basketball rivalry. They played down in what you all call the Civic Center now; that used to be the old gym. I attended many basketball games there when Rabun Gap would play Clayton. It was a big transition, a huge transition. I cannot speak to what it was like after I left.

You have to realize that forty years ago was when I was doing this. The generation we were interviewing back then was the generation that grew up with a horse and wagon. I mean, this county was isolated. When that grandparent generation grew up and came of age, this county was a very isolated county. Betty's Creek did not even have a paved road until 1957 or 1959, sometime in the late fifties. The road going back in there was so bad, so muddy, so rough, that Doc Neville, who was the local doctor that made house calls, literally had to park his car at the end of the road and ride on horseback into Betty's Creek. That's how isolated it was. Most people didn't have electricity; they didn't have cars. It was a whole different lifestyle. This generation we were interviewing was the generation that went from seeing that in their lifetimes to seeing a man on the moon. Now, we just need to think about that for a moment. Can you imagine, in your lifetime, growing up in a culture that was very close-knit, where if you didn't grow it, then most of the time you didn't have it? You saw very little money in a year. There were whole families that if they saw fifty dollars in a year, they were rich. Can you imagine going from that into the era where they've got a man going to the moon? We knew that our mission was to record and preserve what they had lived before all this change exploded across the nation. That was really our mission, to record it and to record it in such a way that they would be respected for what they did. We wanted to preserve it in such a way that, hopefully, generations following would appreciate what that was like.

That generation was a wonderful group of people who were very willing to share their life experiences. That was the part I loved the most because I learned so much. As a matter of fact, they were amazed that we wanted to know. I think, until that point, they just felt like they were sort of the wheels that were spinning off, and nobody really cared how things had been. They were very willing to share, and we were very open to learning. We were amazed because, in that period, we were as technological as you are now, but our lifestyle was totally different from what they had lived. We had a lot to learn, and we realized that.

PLATE 201 Laurie (*left*) and Suzanne Angier (*right*) cooking
while on a Foxfire interview in the 1970s

I think that people were interested in the magazine because high school students did it, and it was done to a standard by which you could take a high school magazine and build a log cabin out of it. That literally did happen. We had people write to us all the time saying, "We literally did this. We took the log cabin issue, and we built our home. We took your article on building a fireplace out of rocks, and it works." We had a lot of how-to articles: how to make baskets, how to do this, and how to do that. I can't tell you how many people came back to us and said, "We actually did this, and it works." I think that people were amazed that could happen.

The magazine is definitely a different size dimensionally. With us, we had a certain variation depending on what we were doing. I don't know if we really thought about that. I'd say it was probably roughly the same. We had four issues per year, but if we had something with a whole lot of information that had to go out, you had to put it into one issue; you couldn't split it up. We would combine seasons; that's the way we did the log cabin issue. Instead of having summer, fall, winter, and spring, we might combine the fall and winter into one issue; it would be a much thicker issue. We did that on occasion.

> *"What I would say to your generation, at this point, is that you are all pioneers."*

Foxfire was an incredible influence on my life because, as a teenager, I learned so much about relating to people. When you're a teenager, you can be pretty self-centered. It wasn't that long ago, and I think one of the most important things it did for me was help me relate to people who were not in my generation. We just really loved these people. I think about Kenny Runion, and I think about Aunt Arie. We were up at Aunt Arie's a lot. We were in constant contact with her. We would go up there and help her in the garden and take her to church. We would go up there and have big meals. She was the one who showed me how to cook on a woodstove. She would direct us, this here and this here. We'd cook a big meal; we would set it on the big dining room table and then just help ourselves. Then we'd go outside into the yard; her house was small, so there's no way our big group could stay in the house. We maintained a lot of contact with Aunt Arie back then. She was a wonderful lady. Everybody loved going out there. We didn't have to pull or twist any arms to get people to go there.

The generation you're talking to now is beginning to hit on my generation, maybe a little bit older. You're talking to a generation who experienced a different kind of change than the generation we interviewed. One of the things I wanted to talk to you all about is that the change that has happened continues to happen and seems to be accelerating at a tremendous rate. We thought it was accelerating back then; it is accelerating even more now. What I would say to your generation, at this point, is that you are all pioneers. Now, let me explain that. Back in the day, the people who settled this mountainous area were pioneers, and they had a lot of challenges. They had a wilderness to settle into. There were no stores around; you couldn't walk up to Walmart and get your milk. You couldn't just go out and buy yourself new clothes every season. It was a whole different thing. The challenges were incredible. In a time in which there was very little medicine, they had to learn to use a lot of natural stuff. A lot of people died; there were children back then that died with things that we knock out without even thinking about it. They didn't have that; there weren't any antibiotics back then. I would say that your generation is a group of pioneers all over again, but your challenges are very different. Right now, the wilderness that you guys are facing is a cultural wilderness. If you had told me when I was young what it would be like now, culturally, there is no way I would have ever believed you. There's no way that any of us would have ever believed what you are all exposed to culturally because we weren't exposed to it; it wasn't there. You all are facing the cultural wilderness, those potentially lethal challenges are things like drug abuse, alcohol abuse, promiscuity, and reducing people to things and using them. You guys are pioneers. How are you going to handle it? Changes are coming left and right. It's a different kind of wilderness, but a wilderness nonetheless.

HIGHLIGHTING A FORMER STUDENT

An interview with Foxfire alumna Allison Adams

Learning to talk about myself and my experiences in front of other people was a great experience; it taught me a lot. Speaking before people now just doesn't bother me. —Allison Adams

Allison Adams is a superb example of someone who has used the success found in Foxfire to become what she dreamed to be in life. As part of the summer leadership program in the days when it lasted all summer, she helped write books, create new articles, and handle the day-to-day business of the magazine. While in the program she began to realize the effectiveness of teamwork. The program also taught her public speaking skills, which aided her a great deal in college. These are only a few examples of the techniques and skills Foxfire taught her.

About fifteen years ago, Allison decided to pursue her dream of becoming a performing songwriter in addition to her two-decade career as a writer, editor, and faculty-development professional at Emory University. She writes songs based on her experiences as a "whipper-snapper" growing up in Rabun County, Georgia. Much of her music is inspired by the remembrance of bluegrass musicians around her. Being a regionally acclaimed artist, she was invited to share her story on Blog Talk Radio. During the interview, she shared her background and how she came to be the person she is today. Below are a few snippets from the conversation with Lisa Capehart and previous interviews we've conducted. Throughout, she displays her appreciation for her Appalachian foundation.

—*Jessica Phillips and Ross Lunsford*

I really became involved with Foxfire in the tenth grade. I first took a music class with George Reynolds, and then after that, I took Foxfire 1, the introductory course. From there on out, I took the magazine class. I had a wonderful time. I worked for Foxfire in the summer each year and then came back to the class each fall.

My parents really loved Foxfire. They encouraged me in everything that I did. Mama would let me stay late after school for Foxfire, and before I learned to drive, she would come pick me up, even though we lived way far away in Rabun Gap. Later, when I could drive, she always understood when I needed to take the car to school so I could stay late and work afterwards. Even though my brother, Brooks, and I have both graduated from high school and are no longer in Foxfire, my family has still maintained a close relationship with the organization. My father is now a member of Foxfire's Community Advisory Board [in the 1990s]. He and George Reynolds, Foxfire's music instructor, often go fishing together.

It was fun working on *Foxfire 9* in the summer because I got along well with the other students. That was probably one of the best groups of people I've ever worked with in my life—I believe it was Kyle Conway, Chet Welch, and two other people. We worked well together.

Learning to talk about myself and my experiences in front of other people was a great experience; it taught me a lot. Speaking before people now just doesn't bother me. I've learned to be very comfortable with it. After I got to college, I realized how fortunate I had been to have had the experience of giving speeches for Foxfire because I found myself giving oral presentations for professors in classrooms full of people.

I chose to go to Agnes Scott College because I wanted a small college. Also, I thought a women's college would be a good place to go to. I wanted an atmosphere in which I could work seriously at learning and not have the distractions I didn't want. I didn't want male competitiveness in the classroom. Also, I wanted to learn how to address myself in front of a group of people and not have to worry "What do the guys want? What do the guys think?" I loved the idea that I could go to class with a sweatshirt, sweatpants, bushy hair, and no makeup. There's a great deal to be said about that kind of atmosphere.

Agnes Scott is quite a selective college, and Foxfire really helped me, not only in getting admitted but also in getting a scholarship. When I was a senior in high school, I submitted my application, and they accepted me. The admissions officer told me, "Well, along with your acceptance to Agnes Scott, you're a semifinalist for the scholarship competition." So I went down for an interview, and they asked me, "Allison, what have you done?"

I replied, "Well, I've got two book chapters with my name on them published with Doubleday and Dutton. I'm a real published author!" Then I told them all about Foxfire. I won the scholarship, and it paid much of my way through college. If it hadn't been for that scholarship, I wouldn't have been able to go to Agnes Scott, because my family wouldn't have been able to pay that expensive private education.

As a factor in college admissions and in getting hired for jobs, I think it was much more important for me to be published in the book than in the magazine. [On one of my first job interviews, for example, I was] asked, "What have you done?" So I opened up my briefcase and pulled out a shiny color photograph of a hardback book with a nice fat price tag. I think that says a little more than the thin little magazine. It's much more visually impressive.

One of the professors at Agnes Scott College had heard about me being in Foxfire, and he recommended that I be in charge of the oral history project. The director of alumni affairs did the official recommendation for the school. One thing led to another, and the recommendation was approved. This project turned into a summer job between my junior and senior years in college. I lived and worked on campus, and I took what I learned from Foxfire and adapted it to a new situation.

I just can't tell you how much I appreciate what Foxfire had to offer me. I realize the books that came out last fall with Longstreet Press reflect the fact that I had experience in high school and in college proof-reading and editing. You know, my years in Foxfire are going to show because I was taught how to appreciate quality. When you learn that kind of thing, it sticks with you for the rest of your life.

Allison spent a few years in publishing, doing an internship with Susan Hunter, publishing while in college and working for Longstreet Press after graduation. Over the years, Allison has continued her editorial work in the world of higher education, but she has also started writing her own songs and music. In 2014, as a featured guest on Lisa Capehart's Blog Talk Radio, Allison recalled:

I grew up in the Northeast Georgia Mountains of Rabun County. My parents, when we were growing up, had a huge garden and an orchard. My mother was a canner and preserver. I have a photograph from some-where in the 1970s that my parents took of this shelf of canned goods that was in our basement. It was literally bowed down in the middle, from top to bottom. It was probably six to six-and-a-half feet tall, just loaded down with stuff that they had canned and preserved from the garden and the orchard. . . . We didn't call it sustainable living back then, but that's what it was. It was being self-sufficient and learning how to do things for yourself. That was definitely part of what formed me and informed me.

There are a number of us in the community who are interested in living self-sufficiently and being closer to the bottom of the food chain. It's knowing where your ingredients come from and how they become ingredients.

I wrote the song "Plenty" in that economic collapse in October of 2008, when it was getting scary. It looked like people's jobs were going away and people's savings were going to go away. Their homes were going away and their retirements were going away. Even though, at the time, I was in a pretty secure position, there was a lot of unknown and a lot of scariness. I wrote that song to remind myself that these were the things that I needed to have a sense of abundance in the world.

Music is extremely healing for me. I remember playing my first open mike in 2000. After the open mike, I went, "Oh, this is what I'm sup-

PLATE 202 Allison Adams

posed to be doing!" It was a way out of a dark place in my soul, and it got me into a mode of writing. Writing was critical to becoming a better musician. I had a lot of really good teachers and friends who helped me along the way, helping me become a better musician. It was an important focus for me. It's been great—still on that journey; it never ends. [**Editors' note:** To listen to Allison's full interview with Lisa Capehart, visit www.blogtalkradio.com/lisacapehart/2013/12/02/songs-from-the-garden -with-allison-adams.]

WORDS
of
WISDOM

from Students, Parents, Community Members, and Readers

Foxfire and its surrounding community go hand in hand. There would be no Foxfire without the people of the community and their many generous contributions. Foxfire has benefited its community by preserving a way of life, long forgotten by many, that built our community. The symbiotic relationship between Foxfire and its community has embodied Foxfire's endeavors these past fifty years.

The impression that Foxfire leaves on its students stays with them as they exit the classroom out into the world. To understand this effect, we talked with our parents to see the kind of influence that they think Foxfire has had on their children. Their take on the program made us aware of the impact that Foxfire students can make both in and out of the classroom. They expressed their appreciation for the program, all it has done for us, and explained the good that it brings to the community and world around us.

What is, to a certain extent, the most astonishing to us is the impression that Foxfire has made on its readers. The readers of *The Foxfire*

Magazine and the *Foxfire* books are just as important as the ones who write them. Without our readers, we would not have an audience outside our own community. Our readers can be found all over the globe. Many different cultures have been enlightened by our words, and many are fascinated by our way of living. Although different readers view the magazine in different ways, they all have the desire to become better acquainted with the ways of Appalachia. Some may be reminded of their childhood, others may want to learn a particular skill, and many more simply appreciate the lifestyle present in Appalachia.

For this reason, we have included a portrait of you, the reader, and how the people we have interviewed throughout the last fifty years affected you. We have chosen to use initials only, in lieu of first name/last name, to protect our reader's identities, though each, when writing us, was aware from our magazine that letters might be published, and they were, in fact, previously shared in the "Readers' Response" pages of *The Foxfire Magazine*.

—*Ross Lunsford and Jessica Phillips*

REMOVING NEGATIVE STEREOTYPES

We could all do with a little of the 'poverty' of the mountain folks.
—GS, Charlotte, North Carolina

"The Foxfire staff intentionally introduced the students to the 'hillbilly' stereotypes—the Li'l Abners, Snuffy Smiths, and Beverly Hillbillies—and they said that together we would destroy those myths! By and large we did!

"We are the only culture that it is still politically correct to demean. If a comedian cracks a *Deliverance* joke, or a cartoonist depicts us as grotesque Picasso caricatures, it is still okay! We don't have "big name" people or organizations to defend us. Because of who we are, and where we come from, we've never been really comfortable confronting people or standing up for ourselves. But, we are getting better at it!"

—**Kaye Carver Collins, former student**

"Foxfire has helped not just our community, but communities abroad. I think it's helped them to understand the past and times of more simple living. Foxfire probably helps other walks of life to appreciate some of the hardships, endeavors, and inventions that Appalachian people

throughout history have been responsible for. It helps them to appreciate that." —Jan Lunsford, parent of Foxfire students

"For a long time I have resented (since I grew up less than one hundred
miles from Rabun Gap, Georgia) the picture most Americans have of
Appalachia. You have done a great deal to improve this. We could all
do with a little of the 'poverty' of the mountain folks. I have given them
[*Foxfire* magazines and books] to friends and intend to pass my copies on
to my children as a most important part of their heritage."

—GS, Charlotte, North Carolina

"Before reading your books and magazines, this household had a mis-
conception about the Appalachian people. We thought anybody living
in the mountains were shoeless hillbillies, as portrayed in the comic
strip *Li'l Abner*. Much to our gladness, that statement is wrong. After
reading many articles about our Appalachian people, we found that
their way of living is better than any city system one can come up with. I
have tried making some of the toys and other things, and, to my amaze-
ment, I love learning about things I have no knowledge in via your
articles.

"Without the avenue of Foxfire, we would lose part of our American
heritage. Foxfire is the vehicle that connects the old way of life with the
new. The information contained in Foxfire is a living history and can
never be replaced. I am so proud that someone took the initiative to put
the living history on paper to be enjoyed by all.

"To all the Aunt Aries, the Pitts, the Ledfords, the Roanes, the Taylors, the Glenns, and all the others who open their private lives so that
the public can view, I thank you! It would be my wish that the future
students continue the work that has preceded them.

"Not only have we learned that the Appalachian people are not Li'l
Abners, but they indeed are a unique type of people."

—GK, Forest Park, Georgia

DOCUMENTING THE CULTURE AND HERITAGE

It's very important to pass traditions down and instill them in your
children because traditions should never die in their entirety. They
may change some, but the old ways don't ever need to die.

—Jan Lunsford, parent of Foxfire students

"To me, Foxfire means a very real way of capturing stories, personalities, and experiences from the past—preserving Appalachian life through a series of publications, interviews, interactions, and demonstrations that are translated into print for the purpose of preserving that Appalachian life for future generations.

"I think, in a sense, the lives of interviewees of Foxfire have forever changed because someone has taken the time to sit down with them and hear a lengthy story about experiences they have gone through. So, I believe that interviewees' lives have been changed, and I know that there are a host of students whose lives have been changed by being in Foxfire.

"I think Foxfire can make a very big impact on interviewees because you have some interviewees who are getting on up in their years, and for some of them, it may be the last time they sit down to tell a long story and to reminisce about things in their life. I know, recently, you all have had a couple of interviewees who have been interviewed and not very long thereafter passed away. To be able to preserve some of those thoughts they might be having or things they might want to reminisce, and in this case, in the last few weeks of their life, I think it's very special. It's special for their families, who are gonna come along and read those stories based on the interviews done by Foxfire students. It's something they can treasure after their loved ones pass away.

"My knowledge of the railroad coming to and through Rabun County has everything to do with what I've learned through reading Foxfire articles. In some cases, everything that we know about those things from the past come from Foxfire books.

"I am very glad that our children carry on the tradition that Foxfire offers. I think through our children's involvement, both Perry and I have been blessed to have Foxfire step into our family members' homes and capture some stories that, unless Foxfire hadn't entered their door, might never have been told in their entirety, or in as much detail, in one sitting. I have a great-aunt who was interviewed, and I rejoiced at reading that story and learning some things about my family history that I didn't even know. To have our own children be the ones to go in and do that made it even more special.

"I think the Foxfire Mountaineer Festival and books allow the audience to step back in time and maybe by the sights, smells, and sounds, help them experience something that they never have before. It gives them an appreciation for Appalachian life and the history therein.

"It's very important to pass traditions down and instill them in your children because the traditions should never die in their entirety. They may change some, but the old ways don't ever need to die."

—Jan Lunsford, parent of Foxfire students

"I had two sisters that were in the magazines. One of them was in the founding magazines. Her name was Melissa Vinson. She has passed away, so by her being in that magazine, her children and grandchildren have a sense of who she was and things that she had accomplished in her life. She is preserved forever—not just the culture, but also a part of her." —Joy Phillips, former student and parent of Foxfire students

"We are all just very thankful that Foxfire is here. We are thankful that you guys are continuing the legacy. It's wonderful that they keep the young students engaged. You might not realize it, maybe y'all do, but what y'all are learning and what y'all are doing with preserving the history is something that you will carry with you and will remember and appreciate when you are old."

—Teka Earnhardt, Rabun County Tourism Development Authority

"We appreciate the *Foxfire* books, which you, your students, and the wonderful, kind people presented therein have made possible.

"It is very easy to be good sheep, reading, memorizing, obtaining degrees, earning your sheepskin—and one day find yourself on the firing line or at a dead end in the human race toward eternal truth—and to for a moment, look back and see all behind you that paid your way and provided that firm foundation, is forever gone and forgotten! Forever gone before you even had time to talk to those good people who were paying the bills. When parents and grandparents are gone, when family farms are forever forgotten, when all heritage is a city of prescribed truths and facts, there will no longer be an America as pictured by the founders.

"We are thankful for the good works you have been able to do and hope your future will be full of firm foundations."

—SP, Murrysville, Pennsylvania

"I think it is important we learn of our past history from those who made it."

—Mrs. J. H., Elliott, Illinois

"You and your students have managed to do what a large number of so-called historians have so dismally failed to accomplish; you have preserved history in an unbiased and forthright manner that will be used many times in the future by people like myself who enjoyed re-creating history with our craftsmanship in metal, wood, and leather and know that, when we look at the finished product, that it is as near being like the original as human hands can make it.

"You have my undying gratitude for the information that you have preserved for me and the many people like me in the world."

—DS, Kerens, Texas

"Just a note of thanks and encouragement for your work: I grew up in Northeast Alabama and the voices and lifestyles that you are preserving are known and dear to me. My maternal grandfather . . . moved to Alabama from Rabun County, so I feel a special affinity for you folks.

"Papa was a Baptist preacher and rode horseback from church to church on rotating Sundays, as no one community was big enough to have a full-time preacher. At his funeral, an elderly man who knew Papa well told me that 'Preacher Charlie was always up for a horse race after the sermon. Now he wouldn't bet, mind you, and wouldn't allow other folks to bet, but he sure did love a good horse race—and oftentimes won.'

"I spent a lot of time with my grandfather when I was a teenager and was fascinated by his stories. To my great regret, I just let him talk and didn't delve into his youth and specific experiences. Nor did I write his stories down. I'm so sad that I didn't think to ask him and my parents more, which makes me doubly thankful for the Foxfire [Fund] and the books and magazines it publishes. Reading your books and interviews is like having a chat with my own family.

"Having turned sixty this year, I'm getting a real kick out of the fact that some of the folks you are interviewing these days are my contemporaries. Guess I am officially an 'elder' now.

"By the way, Foxfire has quite a following here in upstate New York. (Ottawa is the closest city to us—about fifty miles away.) I've been told that some people here have used and continue to use the books as a how-to reference. We are on the north side of the Adirondack Mountains, and some areas are extremely remote and rugged, subject to power outages and such. The natives of this region are hardy and self-sufficient, as were the people who settled and lived in (and still live in) the Southern Appalachians. It's wonderful that the knowledge and skills of a pioneering people from many regions are being combined and passed on to yet another generation—thanks in a very large part to the efforts of Foxfire and its students."

—MG, Potsdam, New York

REMEMBERING THE PAST

Foxfire has helped my kids relive parts of my childhood, and I'm really proud for that; I'm glad.

—Perry Lunsford, parent of Foxfire students

"The objective is that Foxfire would keep alive things that would otherwise be lost in history—things that are important to my family, not so much in the younger generations, and perhaps so, but you know the older members of the family certainly appreciate that recording of the past.

"When I was young, within just a few hundred feet of the main intersection on Main Street in Clayton, Georgia, there were outside toilets, something that my kids know nothing about. People within the city limits raised livestock. Foxfire has helped my kids relive parts of my childhood, and I'm really proud for that; I'm glad. What you see happening in the mountains now is that the old way is going away fast. Generations in the future need to understand how it was in days gone by."

—Perry Lunsford, parent of Foxfire students

"Today I purchased *The Foxfire Book*, and after reading two chapters am suffering from nostalgia for my childhood home. I grew up in southern Indiana. Our cultural patterns were almost identical with those of Rabun Gap, Georgia. Quilting, hog butchering, planting by the signs, even the recipes, sound the same. My grandfather varied from the signs in thinking that a corn crop would not be fully successful unless planted on the first day of May before sunup. Today, not a sign remains of the old culture. World War II brought invasions of Army camps and ammunition depots into our part of the state, along with "furriners," and the old ways are gone forever. I would be the last one to say that today's ways are better. After a couple of college degrees, I still feel vastly inferior to the woman my grandmother was." —MN, Phoenix, Arizona

"Last Christmas when I discovered Foxfire, I felt that I had rediscovered my childhood. Eleven years ago, I left our farm near Royston, Georgia, for better educational opportunities in the big city. I've never forgotten that half of my life, even though I've traveled this country and Europe, too. After reading *Foxfire* and *Foxfire 2*, I began to wonder why I ever left. Now I know why, after eleven years, I'm coming home again. The local graveyard has a few more tombstones than when I left, and the red clay hills of our farm are covered with kudzu and briars. Maybe Thomas Wolfe was right, but I'm going to give it another try anyway. I just wanted to tell you that Foxfire made that decision for me. I'm coming home this summer because I miss seeing the Blue Ridge on the horizon and hearing the lonesome call of the whip-poor-will on a cool autumn evening. My family has lived in the Georgia hills for seven generations, and I see no better place on earth for me to live. Like so many of my generation, I've been searching . . . with the answer looking me right in the face all the while. When I picked up a *Foxfire* [publication], I realized how simple the solution is. As Stevenson said, 'Home is the sailor, home from the sea. And the hunter, home from the hill.' Once again, I say, 'Thank you.'"

—JM, Williamsburg, Virginia

"I read your Spring/Summer 2006 issue of *Foxfire Magazine*. The mention of one-room schoolhouses brought to mind several memories. My grandma Dora . . . was born in April 1891. She attended a one-room schoolhouse, which she had converted for use as her home . . . with a couple of added-on rooms.

"As your article pointed out, one-room schoolhouses were geographically close to family farms. The teachers taught not only the three R's: Readin', 'Ritin', and 'Rithmetic . . . but also a fourth R: Responsibility. It was an age before guidance counselors came into vogue. Teachers garnered automatic respect, and there was no such thing as a time-out—but there was such a thing as a wooden paddle on the teacher's desk. Discipline was also instilled in the home by parents, too.

"I found it interesting when my dad told me that when his mother (that same grandma of mine) was growing up, she and other kids walked through fields picking up dry buffalo chips and cow chips for use as heating fuel when wood wasn't available for use in the stove at home or school. I ask you, how many kids today would do that?

"I am glad that society enjoys creature comforts of electricity and running water, as well as information technology. However, a return of teaching the four R's would be a welcome blessing."

—JM, Longview, Texas

HELPING GENERATIONS RELATE

It appears these people thought of themselves as poor. Not so! There could never be a value placed on the legacy they are leaving behind. We, the youth of today, are the paupers—only because we do not have the wisdom to look beyond the end of our nose and realize that our world today is not the world it has always been.

—LC, San Bernardino, California

"Transcribing the article proved that I needed more information. Having always been interested in the past, I decided to make the article a personality article, as well as one about Appalachian music. I returned to Mrs. Duncan's home alone one day. After an incredibly interesting interview, we sat and talked for nearly two hours. We discussed life back when Mrs. Duncan was my age, the differences in people back then and people nowadays—just everything. I had such a lovely time that I was saddened when I had to leave; I even telephoned my mama to ask if she would pick up my brother from school that afternoon because I was not ready to end my conversation with Mrs. Duncan.

"I have returned to Mrs. Duncan's home once more since then and hope to do so again in the future. I would like to encourage the younger generation to sit down and chat with their grandparents and, if they are lucky enough to have them around, their great-grandparents. Our elders are full of knowledge and wisdom if we would only take time to listen to them."

—Jenna Lauren Davis, former student [See "Lois Duncan:
Her Life and Appalachian Music Heritage,"
The Foxfire Magazine, Spring/Summer 2000.]

"I spent my first hour of the interview learning many lessons about life. I'd heard it all before, but, talking to him, I realized I know only a little bit about the world. It's funny how your parents tell you truths so that you can get along better in this world, but you just don't really listen. Hearing the same thing said by someone else whom you respect makes it sound all new and interesting. I have since come to appreciate my parents and what they have taught me. Mr. Turpin helped me to understand what my parents tried to tell me. Young people can learn so much from elders who have survived experiences that have made them wise."

—Jacob Butler, former student [See "Albert Turpin:
Keeping Up His End of the Barg'in,"
The Foxfire Magazine, Fall/Winter 2002.]

"As a naïve Montanan, now living and attending school in Southern California, I cannot help but express my appreciation for what you have given America in Foxfire.

"In an age of computers, rockets, and television, you have indeed captured the true Spirit of '76. Many young people, myself included, had never known the side of America that you have shown us. 'Back to the roots' now has meaning.

"It appears these people thought of themselves as poor. Not so! There could never be a value placed on the legacy they are leaving behind. We, the youth of today, are the paupers—only because we do not have the wisdom to look beyond the end of our nose and realize that our world today is not the world it has always been. The ancient Aztecs and Incas died off, I believe, because they progressed too far, too fast—and because civilization had no use for their way of life. As crazy as it sounds, I sometimes wish for a transgression in the cycle of time, so we can once again learn to live.

"You have opened my eyes and I thank you."

—LC, San Bernardino, California

"I have decided to forget for a while all of the things I should do at the moment and write you . . . I have read Foxfire, and after beginning, I was unable to put it down, mainly because I hated to stop the feeling of touching something nearly lost, a way of not just life but also of people.

"Foxfire has surely been one of the most pleasurable things to happen to me in a long time. Like you, I had no sense of belonging to my community. I lived in Los Angeles from birth until nineteen and had little regard for affairs of plain living, but then I moved to Seattle and later north to my farm in the Skagit Valley. I now see the remnants of the same people here that Rabun seems to have. Old people fascinate me and, until a few weeks ago, I was becoming very close to the seventy-four-year-old farmer who owned and tilled the soil we live on. He died not long ago and I am so very glad to have turned on to him while he was living. I miss him very much.

"My letter is meant to let you know of the real value Foxfire has in and of its own. Your kids are to be congratulated on their efforts and the very fine work they have done. I wish they would let all their contacts know that they are people to be listened to and loved for they had the right idea and still do.

"There is still a lot I would like to express about Foxfire to you, but I have a very selfish reason for not continuing. I am going to begin *Foxfire 2* next to the fire before my baby daughter awakens.

"Thank you for not giving up on your Foxfire project. I have really appreciated it. You might like to know that Foxfire has prompted me to get together a quilting bee with several of my friends from a town nearby called La Conner. It's a pioneer town that is keeping its homespun qualities and begrudging little to commercialism. I'll bet you would like it. I belong to that community and it belongs to me and that's how I want it."

—**MH, Mount Vernon, Washington**

"In this day and age of mobility, loss of family units, etc., how wonderful that your students are getting to know their heritage and to build on it. The city dwellers are so prone to provide everything for their children that the students develop little of their potential."

—**NB, St. Petersburg, Florida**

UNDERSTANDING WHAT FOXFIRE MEANS

For me, Foxfire was much more than just a class. It was a way of life. It is still a way of life. It's connecting with the elders, not just in your family, but also in the community. It creates a sense of value, a sense of belonging. It is something that brings people together, something that you truly value and will appreciate for the rest of your life.

—Joy Phillips, former student and parent of Foxfire students

"Foxfire influenced me by getting me out of my shell, but it also had a much deeper impact on me because as I started talking to these old people, I realized that they had something valuable to say and to share. I realized that we needed to listen to it and pay attention to it. I also realized that they weren't just old people; they were my friends. We had a

PLATE 203 Kaye Carver Collins (*middle*) and Maybelle Carpenter (*left*)
on an interview with Annie Perry

connection. I would go visit Lawton Brooks up until he died. It was just
a wonderful connection that I felt to him; he was like a second father to
me." —**Kaye Carver Collins, former student**

"To the students, Foxfire is invaluable. There is no question; it's invaluable. Y'all are proof of that. I still hear the stories from Rabun Gap-
Nacoochee School from the students who come back from where it
started, 'cause I live on the Rabun Gap Campus. Just the memories, the
knowledge, and the training are incredible. As far as the community,
they're also invaluable. From the tourism standpoint of it, that's something that nobody else can claim in the Northeast Georgia Mountain
region—that they have something so interesting and so historical, and so
hands-on. So, they are invaluable to us."

—**Teka Earnhardt, Rabun County Tourism
Development Authority**

ENCOURAGING READERS AND STUDENTS TO GO BEYOND

If you ever get discouraged, remember the folks on the other side of
those beautiful mountains love you and believe in all of y'all.

—SB, Knoxville, Tennessee

"I was born in the hills of Tennessee, just on the other side of y'all. When I was six, my family moved to Miami, Florida. My father worked for the space industry. We were transferred to New Orleans, then finally back to Cape Kennedy, Florida. Funny, though, all my summers were spent in the mountains of Tennessee or North Carolina. When I finished high school in Cocoa Beach and had to decide where did I want to go to school, my parents said, 'You decide.' So I did. I came back to the University of Tennessee . . . My goal—to get back where people are real and lives are lived in love. Back to God's country to stay.

"I didn't really write to tell you about me—but to say thank you—not just from me, but from all the people who read your magazines and books and sit back and realize that a high school in Georgia . . . created what they know is real in life. That credit cards and new cars, houses and clothes and status (whatever that is) are so plastic. That Foxfire—your ideas and love for each other in print form is education and learning—real learning from each other. If you ever get discouraged, remember the folks on the other side of those beautiful mountains love you and believe in all of y'all." —**SB, Knoxville, Tennessee**

INSPIRING AND LEARNING

Your book has opened my eyes to a great many truths of life, and it's been a great inspiration for me to hear some of the wisdom the grown folks have for those of us whose ears are ready to hear and wanting and needing such solid advice in this non-feeling world today.

—GP, Hagerstown, Maryland

"I was so very blessed to receive a few scholarships last night, but it goes without saying that Foxfire was the most important to me! Foxfire . . . love our outstanding Appalachia community for who we really are. The Foxfire program has taught me life lessons I will never forget!"

—**Shanda Speed, former student**

"I really am glad that my children carry on the tradition of Foxfire. I have heard it said, 'Life is too short for any story not to be told.' I'm glad that my kids have been privileged to do something that I didn't get to do. And that is to go get the story. I didn't have the opportunity as a child, but I'm really glad that they get to know some of the things that they otherwise never would have known. It teaches character and responsibility, too. If

PLATE 204 Perry and Jan Lunsford

you've got a job, you've got to do it. They didn't necessarily learn it from Foxfire, but it has definitely been bolstered by Foxfire."

—Perry Lunsford, parent of Foxfire student

"I'm very proud of some of the skills that Foxfire has brought to the table for both Ross and Katie. It has taught them several disciplines. I know they've been taught a lot of things at home, but there are some things that Foxfire probably has instilled in them, such as meeting deadlines, and being disciplined. They both have always been very good at grammar, but Foxfire has given them a greater appreciation for grammar, which is a tool, I think, that they will take with them as they further their education. I know it's already working out for Katie at the University of Georgia, and it will for Ross wherever he goes. Some enhanced grammar skills, well beyond their peers who are not in Foxfire, have helped strengthen their already strong skills in English. It has also helped their people skills because even the shiest of individuals will go face-to-face with an interviewee."

—Jan Lunsford, parent of Foxfire students

"Well, you know in the fourth grade, the students here in the county go up to Foxfire for the tour. It's not just our county. It's all surrounding counties that allow them [their students] to come out of their close-knit communities. They give them a hands-on [experience], and they see those things like the cleaning of the clothes and blacksmithing. You know, those kind of things. My son went this year. They are learning about the Indians being taken [out of Georgia]. To see that one wagon, and hear them talk about how that one wagon was used to round up the Indians and take them off, it really puts it into perspective for something they are learning in the books, to see it in person. I do think that's a great time frame for them to have that, to start gleaning those little pieces of history from there. It just makes them appreciate it further on down the line."

—Teka Earnhardt, Rabun County Tourism
Development Authority

"During my years in school, you could take Foxfire and not be contained to a regular classroom. The classes that were available then were very fun. I absolutely loved getting out and taping music. That's probably where my son Ethan gets it from—going out to the shows, listening to it, and playing it back for other people to hear. I could feel it. I could get into it. It was the same with taking pictures. I loved going out and taking pictures. I still do.

"A lot of that came from the original Foxfire classes. I never owned a camera until I was in Foxfire. We couldn't afford one. That gave me a desire. I started saving money and bought my own camera. Since then, I have lots of those cameras. I have worn out many. I still have a darkroom in my basement that is fully operational.

"Foxfire has given Ethan and Jessica phenomenal Language Arts skills. What I could not teach them, or what their teachers could not teach them, they have learned through hands-on experience in the real world, and that's what Foxfire is—a "real-world" application. All you have to do is reach out and take it.

"Foxfire not only impacted me in my high school life, but it also continues to impact me. I have recently (in the past year) become a member of the Foxfire Community Board. Although it was not my total intention, it allowed me to reconnect with some of those values that I cherished from then. Like I said before, not only did I learn about people in my family, I learned about people in my community and became a part of an extended family. Those values that I learned from the contacts, I may not have learned from my family without having known them. They saw what future generations had to offer and how they could help. Sometimes people in your own family are too busy for you. When you reach out to

PLATE 205 Joy Phillips with her daughter, Jessica Phillips

others, you learn different things. You learn customs or even morals that you can take with you forever. It has always been a goal of mine to learn something from everyone I meet, whether good or bad, then use that to make myself a better person. Foxfire has been a great resource for that.

"I think that the very name of Foxfire is the epitome of diversity. You are talking about diverse beliefs. You are reaching out and sharing different beliefs, such as religions. I think the different beliefs give everyone an understanding of who we are. It doesn't mean you agree or disagree, but the respect part is Foxfire. You respect where they're coming from. You respect where they've been. You understand that if they have a certain belief in a religion or God that you respect that. You don't mock it. You celebrate their way of life. Most of the people around here with diverse beliefs really have a Christian background, a religious background that is shared. If not, it's not spoken of. It's just respected. Foxfire helps provide understanding within diverse backgrounds. It's a learning experience.

"Being a part of Foxfire helps develop them. It helps develop their character, makes them more aware of where they came from, which they can incorporate into their future to show who and what they can be. This will help them reach their full potential. They have roots. Foxfire helps show them their roots. The tree will never grow without roots. When the roots are cut off, the tree dies. It's the same thing with my kids. If they don't have roots, they'll never make it. That helps them become better people. Because they are involved with this program, they have more one-on-one instruction. They have more one-on-one guidance and direction. They have a scaffolding process that the teacher will show them what to do, give them as much support as they need, and then pull back and let them fly. I love that. They are developing social skills and are having a new social network that may not just be kids their own age, but also elders. In turn, they can reach out to people that are younger than them, and involve them, as well. I think all of this has really expanded them, and helped develop their characters, as it did for me and my husband.

"Anytime that you have children that take responsibility or take ownership in what they are doing, they learn more. They have a more firm foundation and have a better concept of knowledge. It is concrete, which means they will use it forever. They will remember it forever. If it is something that you are telling them, that is lecture-based type work and many will never remember it. They get bored. They go to sleep. They tune it out. They are just trying to be there, fill the time, and get out. With this, like I said, it's more discovery. It's more hands-on. It's more about learning what you want to know. It becomes a part of you and who you are. I think that's invaluable. You can't put a price on that. That's more than school. That's lifelong learning.

"Even if you are just reading the magazine, you are getting something out of it. It sparks an interest. It involves the things that have an everlasting value. Sometimes, in this world, it's hard to do that. It helps you slow down and reflect. Sometimes that's just what we need."

—Joy Phillips, former student and parent of Foxfire students

"I wouldn't be a teacher today if I hadn't worked with the kids here and saw how much I enjoyed doing that. It was something I wanted to do for the rest of my life. This past year in my class, we read the book *Blizzard!* by Jim Murphy. It's about a blizzard that takes place in upper New York in the early 1880s to early 1890s. We were able to Skype with Mr. Murphy. We made a connection with our community, and I don't think I would have made that connection without a Foxfire influence. I had the kids go out and interview family members about the blizzard that we had here in 1993. The snow was up to here [your waist]. My son couldn't walk in it because it was over his head. We were without electricity for over a week. So, my students went out and interviewed their relatives about what they experienced in the blizzard of 1993. We also had the sheriff, the EMTs, and Georgia Power workmen come talk to us—we had five or six people come in and talk to all my classes, which were 120 kids. They put together their own books about the blizzard here."

—Kaye Carver Collins, former student

"I hope this note finds you, and all the staff, well and enjoying a prosperous year at Foxfire. Life is busy here . . . I am finishing up my Graduate Thesis in Organizational Development . . .

"Thanks to my many projects at Foxfire, I seem to have an advantage over my cohorts in pulling together a lot of research and interviews to create a project. Amazing how often I utilize those skills I learned at sixteen and seventeen years old.

"Started working on a class project yesterday that concerns the Carnegie Foundation for the Advancement of Teaching and for some reason that took me on a trip back down memory lane to rainy days working in the offices on the mountain. Not sure what exactly I was remembering, but it struck a chord. Amazing how often that happens and how truly blessed I am to have been exposed to so many things in the world of education through Foxfire."

—Rosanne Chastain Short, former Foxfire student

"The first time I met Mrs. Eunice Hunter, she shared her wisdom about marriage, children, religion, and cooking. I learned about how she met her husband, how she overcame her fears, and how she loves to cook for her grandchildren. Many of her stories taught me several of life's lessons. Her past and how she grew up has made her a woman who lives her life by embracing her family, her faith, and her heritage.

"In doing this article, I have come to respect the past and its influence on us today. Many of Mrs. Hunter's stories hit home. She says, 'We just can't do anything on our own without Christ.' I am certain that you, too, will be touched by her accomplishments and by her faith."

—Beth Pruitt, former student

"Getting to know the Foxfire Boys was quite an experience. I was inspired by their musical talent, as well as their outlook on life. They were some of the most enjoyable people that I have ever met. I was amazed by their stories of playing at the Olympics, at the Grand Ole Opry, and with John Denver, and my face was sore from laughing at their stories of practical jokes and pranks. For me, it was an adventure, and for them, like everything else, it was 'a lot of fun.'" —**Austin Bauman, former student**

"Your book has opened my eyes to a great many truths of life, and it's been a great inspiration for me to hear some of the wisdom the grown folks have for those of us whose ears are ready to hear and wanting and needing such solid advice in this non-feeling world today."
                              —**GP, Hagerstown, Maryland**

"When older people organize their past experiences and present them through articles in *Foxfire*, they give us their method of making sense out of their lives. It may not be the best method, but it worked for them and they give us another option to choose from. We come away better off than when we started out.

"In a world full of manipulating people spreading abstract, ambiguous images in an effort to delude us, Foxfire is one outpost in the battle to make the world comprehensible. In a world full of senseless and self-destructive competition, it helps us to build a cooperative society."
                              —**LL, Schenectady, New York**

"As a countryman from West Britain, a countryman who spends far too much of his time in study or in the soul-destroying minor activities of an administrative nature, which are almost impossible to escape in a university, I rejoiced to see evidence that there are still people concerned, very actively concerned, with those priorities we seem to have lost. I refer to the sense of humanity, the sense of place, the sense of tradition, the sense for those pre-scientific intuitions, which technology is crowding out of the world . . .

"I would not be right to say that the whole concept of the volumes and the magazine reflects credit on those responsible—such a phrase smacks of condescension. What I think the volumes do illustrate is the essential rightness of people's tastes, be they young or old, in certain environments where values have not yet been completely corroded by the novel and the ephemeral. I don't know if you will achieve all that you hope to do—though I hope that you do; at the very least the volumes represent an important affirmation, at a time when such things are unpopular, of human values, of the importance of the oral tradition and of conventional wisdom. At the least you have kept back the darkness a little; at the most you might light a new path which folk desperately need." —KB, New Zealand

"I have been reading your *Foxfire* books for many years and have all ten of the series of books. I have read and reread these books many times and find them to be an incredible and remarkable treasure to me and my personal library. I just received *Foxfire 10* for my birthday and have almost finished it, but I had to write to you and convey my deep feelings for what you have done with your Foxfire efforts. In my mind, the Foxfire legacy is another equal endeavor to all of the things you have written about over the years. Too bad that other regions haven't done the same for their history, and these old people can teach us so much about life and how to work, endure, and suffer in order to leave worthwhile legacies of their lives." —MB, Long Beach, California

"I'm happy to praise the work you all do at Foxfire, the preservation of our history and the sharing of the exhibits. It just gets better and better!

"Mr. Barry [Foxfire's Museum Curator, Barry Stiles], thanks to you and the Foxfire staff for making our visit the best ever this year! The improvements you have made at the museum are wonderful to see. The tour and activities you provided for our children helped them to better understand what life was like a long time ago. I especially liked them having the opportunity to churn, carry water and do the wash! Thank you all so very much for providing such wonderful learning experiences. I feel that you provide a wonderful, enriching resource for our area. I wish more of our teachers could fit you into their study units . . .

"Again, thank you for the job you do in preserving our rich heritage and making learning opportunities available for our children . . . It just gets better and better!" —CT, Franklin, North Carolina

MAKING COMMUNITY CONNECTIONS

I will take with me the pride of the Appalachian Mountains . . . and
I will always find my way home. —Chelsi Forester, former student

"I learned things about my family that I did not know before someone interviewed them for Foxfire. I had a cousin in Athens. His name was

PLATE 206 Joy Phillips in the Foxfire classroom

Ernest Vinson. He was over a hundred years old. I actually took someone to interview him and he was phenomenal. He was my favorite person who I ever met. He always had the best outlook on life. I always said if I could bottle that up somehow and share it with the world, it would be a better place. Then I thought, why not through Foxfire? I suggested him to my niece, who interviewed him. She went to his home and left inspired. She said he had the best personality. It's very funny. You have a hundred-year-old man connect with a fifteen-year-old girl. Look at the many generations between them. It's how two worlds can connect. It becomes real."

—Joy Phillips, former student and parent of Foxfire students

"I think having a sense of place and belonging is disappearing from the world; we are a quickly moving society. People are constantly moving, moms and dads are divorcing, grandparents live on one side of the country, and kids live on the other. TV brings us instantaneous news of the war in Iraq. It's a very different world. We are a global society. I'm not saying that's bad. I like knowing what's going on in Iraq. I like knowing that I can call across the country to somebody, but I also like knowing that I belong. I like having a deep sense of place, and I think Foxfire can do that for any kid that's willing to open his mind or heart to it."

—Kaye Carver Collins, former student

THE FOXFIRE BOOK OF SIMPLE LIVING

"Working with Foxfire for three years has given me an educational background I could not have received anywhere else. From learning the equipment and programs to interviewing and layout, it has been an experience I will carry with me throughout my life. I believe it will help me time after time in my educational endeavors. Learning of my ancestral heritage with the Appalachian people has helped reshape my identity. Listening to the deep hypnotic storytelling of Robert Murray [Foxfire's beloved former museum curator] or experiencing my first time watching a chainsaw artist, to the excitement of the annual festivals, all have given me a sense of who I am. I may travel far in my future, but I will take with me the pride of the Appalachian Mountains . . . and I will always find my way home." —Chelsi Forester, former student

"*The Foxfire Magazine* is different to me because it reflects who I am and where I've come from. I can look at *The New Yorker*, and I don't see anything in that. It's different in that it tells real stories about real people, without an agenda, and without a political aspect. It's just about who we are. In the days of news as it is, it is refreshing for me to read."
—Perry Lunsford, parent of Foxfire students

"Foxfire improves the community because it is a resource for people to come here who are specifically looking for Foxfire, and then they see what else is so beautiful about our county. So it brings a demographic of people that might not otherwise come, but they come specifically for Foxfire and what it's teaching. A lot of people learn from it. It's across the nation; it's not just a regional thing. I would say, in that respect, they get people's attention, but just the sheer preserving history of this community that so many people forget—it's easy to forget, so they are preserving the heritage and the culture.

"Foxfire has made an everlasting impact on its community. There is no question about that. They are preserving, and every year they are trying to add new things. I mean like the barn that they are adding now—I'm not sure when that will be open, but just to know that they're not stopping because they say, 'Oh, it's nice. It's great.' They are trying to continue the preservation. Yes, it has definitely had an everlasting impact. Even just the preservation of the land that they have done on the mountain has a great impact. Black Rock is just a special mountain anyway."
—Teka Earnhardt, Rabun County Tourism
Development Authority

LOOKING TO THE FUTURE

I think that Foxfire needs to keep going, and we need to do whatever it takes to keep it going. —Wesley Taylor, former student

"I would like for it to remain as it started out in Rabun County, but that's not an accurate depiction of all the experiences and strengths and hopes of the people in our region of the nation. So, it has progressed, and I think that it has done so marvelously.

"I hope that it will last much longer than it has lasted. To bring the past into the present without being doomed to relive it, but to never forget what it was like before the new highway got to Rabun County."

—Perry Lunsford, parent of Foxfire students

"I believe that tourism will continue to increase in the area. We [the Tourism Development Authority] have finally, over several years, figured out that our only number one goal is to market. We let people know what we have, and to pick out our unique qualities that other areas don't have. Everybody has cute shops, everyone has mountains and lakes, but what

PLATE 207 Teka Earnhardt

do we have that makes us special? Foxfire is one of those things that makes us special that other communities cannot claim. They just don't have it. They might have something kind of like it, but they don't have Foxfire. We do, so that's one of the things that we promote."

— Teka Earnhardt, Rabun County Tourism
Development Authority

"Unless some amount of money comes in, there is not going to be a tremendous amount of growth. Without cash infusion of some kind, it's not going to be easy. Thank God the stock market has turned around. The recession is over, so our endowment is picking up. Several years ago, the board of directors decided that if the endowment reached a certain level, everything would shut down, and that the money would go to preserve this land, these buildings, and the artifacts at the Foxfire Museum. It never reached that point. It came close a time or two, but you can only take so much out of your endowment to operate the budget without hurting your endowment. So, Foxfire is limited in what it can do in the next ten to twenty years unless they can get some capital buildup in that endowment. I already volunteered to get the QR codes at the museum going next summer: I know how to do it. [QR codes are bar codes that would be placed on different buildings at the Foxfire Museum, and information about that building and its contents could be obtained by scanning the codes with a smartphone.] If we can get some quotes to throw in, we'll put some QR codes up around the place. We may not have them everywhere, but we'll have them in some places. We're gonna become more technology savvy so that people can interact more.

"I think it will bring more tourists, and it will bring repeat tourists. You know, once you've seen Aunt Arie's rope bed, you've seen it. You could change the quotes out. One time, you could have Aunt Arie talking about her rope bed. There's another neat story about this guy whose straw tick they replaced, and he lays down that night, and he feels a snake in the mattress. If you replace them, and change them out, people will want to come back and hear more stories. We are talking about doing a partnership with the Digital Library of Georgia where they will put some of our interviews on their website. People could actually come on their website and listen to the entire interview. That's still in the working stages, though. I would like to see Foxfire do that for itself, but that's down the road. Personally, I wouldn't want to include the entire interview. I would want portions of the interview. In twenty years, there will be a new leader here at Foxfire, and I just hope that it will be someone who cares about these buildings, this place, these artifacts, the people that we've interviewed through the years, and is willing to stand up and fight for it.

"I wish that the Foxfire program had the finances to hire more people. There are four people that work down there in that office, and they work their fannies off, constantly. And, of course, Lee Carpenter is here part-time on a contract basis. They rarely have the time to pursue new things because they're so busy just trying to stay in survival mode. In my ideal world, we'd hire a couple of people just to take the burden off them and let them be more creative. For example, I would love to see QR codes at every cabin up here at the museum. That's the way of the future. You go up, click your phone, scan the QR code, and you hear my daddy, Buck Carver, talking about his moonshine still, or how to make moonshine. You can click a QR code and you hear somebody talk about how to train mules. To me, sharing those authentic voices and experiences with visitors would give them even more of that sense of connectedness that I hope we have.

"Where would I like to see Foxfire in ten years? We have a site plan for this place, and in the ideal world where we have more money than we know how to deal with, the road will be paved, and it will be a one-way road where everybody can drive through and stop at the different cabins. There will be more tourists that way because climbing that mountain is not fun, especially for the older people. I hope that twenty years from now, the magazine class is still going and preserving the culture that is here. I would like to see Foxfire grow. I would like to see more of Foxfire in the school. Not everybody wants to write an article. It used to be that the students in the music program or the radio program could apply for Foxfire scholarships just like the students that wrote articles, and they are no less worthy than you guys to get that. Because we no longer have those programs, the students that are more interested in music or more interested in video don't have that opportunity.

"Foxfire has had several missions throughout the years. When Foxfire first started, it was called the Southern Highlands Literary Fund. It was some weird thing. It was a literary thing, but it was also a crafty thing. Over the years, Foxfire's mission has changed. Currently, *The Foxfire Magazine* class's mission statement is to document our community. It used to be the Appalachian community, but a couple of years ago, the students changed that because this community is much more than Appalachia now. We have people from all over who come in and make valuable contributions, and just because they're not Appalachian doesn't mean that they don't deserve to be honored and shared with others through the magazine." —**Kaye Carver Collins, former student**

"Now, I have a project that I would love to work on sometime. I think with Foxfire and the way that it's changing, we truly need to become more of a part of this computerized world. I think in order to do that, Foxfire is going to have to step up just a little bit more. I would love to see, and I think you would get a lot more kids involved with Foxfire, if we had some computer programs available at the high school, where they could work on a Web show—Welcome to the World of Foxfire, a virtual museum, and divide the county into different sections, with a historian appointed for each part of that county. Let them tell a little about the history. Show some of the older pictures. People will see that all over the Web, and they will want to come visit the museum on the mountain. The work that the students get out and do will change. You are not only just doing interviews, you are actually out there videoing and creating reality webcasts. Instead of just taping, like you're doing now, you are out videoing. You are making a new part of Foxfire, and taking that on into future centuries for other kids to enjoy. I don't think this is neglecting the mission statement of preserving, because you can still preserve the older ways and record them with the new digitized ways.

"I hope the program continues to grow and that they find really good strong leaders. I know that Ann Moore here does an outstanding job from this aspect. Barry Stiles works very hard. Paulette Carpenter, Jessica Sheriff, and the whole group are just dedicated. The Foxfire Community Board jumps in wherever they can to fill in, and the board of directors provides needed support, but the high school is where it's going to play the biggest part with the students. If you could get those strong leaders in the high school and teachers that have the same interest and the same convictions that we do involved, and if you could get those people to be constant or consistent and bring more kids in, your magazine will grow and continue to get stronger. Sales from publications would also increase. That's what I would love to see—a new Foxfire world.

"If I had a choice as to where I would see Foxfire in ten years, I would see it as strong. I could see it growing, but I think it's going to take a lot of hard work, which I know that the people who are involved are doing. Like I said, they are doing a great job. I just see in ten years it expanding to all new levels, opening new doors and new horizons. I could see that the Foxfire scholarship could fund hundreds of kids going through college from this area if taken in the right direction. The records that are now being digitized to preserve for centuries to come, I could see that all changing to video. I see it very strong—much stronger than it is now.

"Foxfire is a nonprofit organization, and it gets all of its funding through donations, festivals, the magazine sales, and things like that. Every bit of it [the proceeds] is for preserving culture or helping the students. I'm not sure that it reaches out to student interest. I think that when I was in high school, it seemed to appeal to more students. I don't know if it was because of the era or generation, or because there were more programs available to the students to gain their interest. I think now what we have is just *The Foxfire Magazine* class. Think about if you had a radio production class, the kids that you could reach with that. I'm thinking about the kids that would want to be on the radio or who were involved in music. They could go out and interview people that make music and record them. Think about if you had a photography class like we had, where you are actually taught how to take pictures and do nothing but that part of the magazine, and incorporate those worlds together. Think about if you had a computer class for Foxfire that did nothing but research Web-based articles and preserve Appalachia through the Internet. Don't you think that more students would be a part of Foxfire when they normally wouldn't if they just had to write an article? If they could create an online virtual museum like I was talking about, someone would be responsible for keeping that up. You are involving kids with different interests in the same program, for the same purpose, and the same mission. To me, that would be a whole lot more effective than just the articles."

—Joy Phillips, former student and parent of Foxfire students

What we have gathered over the course of fifty years is astonishing. The growth that Foxfire has experienced is overwhelming. Foxfire has shown the world the impact that a single magazine can have. The creation led to many other magazines in different regions of the country with the same purpose, and what we have acquired is so much more than simply words in an article; it is real-life applications of old-timey methods. As students of Foxfire, we have been honored to learn side by side with our elders and hope to continue to do so far into the future. Every day we, as Foxfire students, learn something new. We know that our readers have also discovered a great deal by reading our publications. What we have learned is something that not everyone in the world is blessed to learn, and for that, we are grateful.

EXPERIENCING ARTS
AND CRAFTS

Southeastern Folk Art and Craft Festivals

There are numerous festivals throughout the southeastern United States. The following list is just a sampling of folk art and craft festivals in our region. These listings are based on information available during the production of this book in 2015–2016; dates and/or locations may have changed.

ALABAMA

Spring
Fairhope's Annual Arts and Crafts Festival
327 Fairhope Avenue
Fairhope, Alabama
annualartsandcraftsfestivalfairhope.com

Jerry Brown Arts Festival
3196 County Highway
Hamilton, Alabama
jbaf.org

NEACA Spring Craft Show
Von Braun Community Center
Huntsville, Alabama
neaca.org

Fall
Claybank Jamboree Arts and Crafts Festival
Downtown Ozark
Ozark, Alabama

Kentuck Festival of the Arts
Kentuck Park
Northport, Alabama
kentuck.org/festival

FLORIDA

Spring
Florida Folk Festival
Stephen Foster Folk Culture Center State Park
White Springs, Florida
floridastateparks.org/folkfest

Melbourne Art Festival
New Haven Avenue
Melbourne, Florida
melbournearts.org

Stuart Craft Fair
Osceola Street
Stuart, Florida
artfestival.com/festivals/stuart-craft-fair

Fall
DeLand Fall Festival of the Arts
100 North Woodland Boulevard
DeLand, Florida
delandfallfestival.com

Great Gulfcoast Arts Festival, Inc.
Seville Square and Park
Pensacola, Florida
ggaf.org

Winter
Indie-Folkfest at the Mennello Museum of American Art
Orlando, Florida
orlandofolkfestival.wordpress.com

GEORGIA

Spring
Bear on the Square
Downtown Square
Dahlonega, Georgia
bearonthesquare.org

Finster Fest
Dowdy Park
Summerville, Georgia
finsterfest.com

Inman Park Festival
Inman Park
Atlanta, Georgia
inmanparkfestival.org

Summer
AthFest
Washington Street
Athens, Georgia
athfest.com

Folk Fest
North Atlanta Trade Center
Norcross, Georgia
slotinfolkart.com

Georgia Mountain Fair
Georgia Mountain Fairgrounds
Hiawassee, Georgia
georgiamountainfairgrounds.com

North Georgia Folk Potters Festival
Banks County Middle School
Homer, Georgia
northgafolkpottersfestival.com

Folk on the Mountain
Foxfire Museum and Heritage Center
Mountain City, Georgia
foxfire.org

Yellow Daisy Festival
Stone Mountain Park
Stone Mountain, Georgia
stonemountainpark.com/events/yellow-daisy-festival

Fall
Foxfire Mountaineer Festival
Rabun County Civic Center
Clayton, Georgia
foxfiremountaineer.org

North Georgia Folk Festival
Sandy Creek Park
Athens, Georgia
athensfolk.org

Prater's Mill Country Fair
5845 Georgia Highway 2
Dalton, Georgia
pratersmill.org

NORTH CAROLINA

Spring
North Carolina Azalea Festival
North Front Street
Wilmington, North Carolina
ncazaleafestival.org

Summer
Craft Fair of the Southern Highlands
US Cellular Center
Asheville, North Carolina
southernhighlandguild.org

Mountain Heritage Day
Western Carolina University
Cullowhee, North Carolina
mountainheritageday.com

Mount Mitchell Crafts Fair
Burnsville Town Square
Burnsville, North Carolina
yanceychamber.com/craft-fair

North Carolina Gourd Festival
North Carolina State Fairgrounds
Raleigh, North Carolina
ncgourdsociety.org/festival

Fall
Autumn Leaves Festival
North Main Street
Mount Airy, North Carolina
autumnleavesfestival.com

Winter
Fearrington's Annual Folk Art Show
Fearrington Village
Pittsboro, North Carolina
fearrington.com/folk-art

SOUTH CAROLINA

Spring
South Carolina Strawberry Festival
Walter Elisha Park
Fort Mill, South Carolina
scstrawberryfestival.com

Fall
Gopher Hill Festival
Downtown Ridgeland
Ridgeland, South Carolina
gopherhillfestival.org

Pumpkintown Pumpkin Festival
Oolenoy Community Center
Pickens, South Carolina
pumpkintownfestival.org

TENNESSEE

Spring
Four Bridges Arts Festival
First Tennessee Pavilion
Chattanooga, Tennessee
4bridgesartsfestival.org

Who-Fest Art Folk Festival
Coolidge Park
Chattanooga, Tennessee
whofest.wordpress.com

Summer
Gatlinburg Craftsmen's Fair
234 Historic Nature Trail
Gatlinburg, Tennessee
craftsmenfair.com

Wilson County Fair
James E. Ward Agricultural Center
Lebanon, Tennessee
wilsoncountyfair.net

Fall
Fall Folk Arts Festival
Exchange Place
Kingsport, Tennessee
exchangeplace.info/fallartsfestival

Foothills Fall Festival
325 South Court Street
Maryville, Tennessee
foothillsfallfestival.com

Tennessee Fall Homecoming
Museum of Appalachia
Norris, Tennessee
museumofappalachia.org

CONTRIBUTORS

CONTACTS

Allison Adams
Brooks Adams
Lester Addis
Laurie Brunson Altieri
"Annie" (alias)
Davy Arch
Rev. John Bagwell
Austin Bauman
Curtis Blackwell
Shane Blackwell
Woodrow Blalock
Doug Bleckley
Effie Mae Speed
    Bleckley
Mrs. Grover Bradley
Berry Bray
Lawton Brooks
Harold Brown
Mary Brown
Olive Ann Burns
David Burress
Ruth Cabe
Aunt Arie Carpenter
Buck Carver
Jeff Carver
Leona "Dink" Carver
Annie Chastain
Louise Coldren
Kaye Carver Collins
Claud Connell
Mae Cragg
Maxine Darnell

Randall Deal
Malcolm Dillard
Susie Hembree
    Dockins
Sarah Dowdle
Thad "Happy"
    Dowdle
Lois Duncan
Teka Earnhardt
Harriet Echols
Jesse Edmonds
Jim Edmonds
Jean Eller
Johnnie Eller
Willie Blalock Elliot
Chelsi Forester
Willie Fortson
Aunt Nora Garland
Hillard Green
Deffie Hamilton
Milford Hamilton
Francis Harbin
Jim Heuser
Roberta Hicks
Dale Holland
Anna Howard
Eunice Hunter
John Huron
Amy Jarrard
Coyle Justice
Daisy Justice
Bob Justus

Azzalee Keener
Ken Keener
Mrs. Ken Keener
Ada Kelly
Dorothy Kilby
Fanny Lamb
Eric Legge
Carlene Lovell
Vernice Lovell
Jan Lunsford
Perry Lunsford
Waymond Lunsford
Clarence Martin
Lois Martin
Oscar Martin
Pearl Martin
Myrtle Mason
Dan Maxwell
Bryant McClure
Tracy Speed McCoy
Kim Hamilton McKay
Louise McKinney
Tonia Kelly McRary
Oliver Meyers
Shirley Miller
Zell Miller
Johnny Mize
Laura Monk
Ann Moore
Lindsey Moore
Lillie Nix
Tom Nixon

Algie Norton
Mann Norton
Mrs. Mann Norton
Margaret Norton
Nell Norton
Mrs. Tommy Lee
Norton
Joleen Oh
Edgar Owens
Eula Parker
Faye "Bit" Carver
Partain
Sue Patton
Annie Perry
Beulah Perry
Cleve Phillips
Joy Vinson Phillips
Andrea Burrell Potts
Beth Pruitt
Beanie Ramey
Edward Ramey
Oliver Rice

Frank Rickman
Vaughn Rogers, Jr.
Kermit Rood
John Roper
Kenny Runion
Bonnie Shirley
Maud Shope
Tommie Lee Shope
Rosanne Chastain
Short
Carl Shoupe
Kim Oh Soon
Shropshire
Donna Bradshaw
Speed
J. P. Speed
Jenny Stevens
T. J. Stevens
Carrie Stewart
James Still
Mary Story
William Swimmer

Janie P. Taylor
Melvin Taylor
Wesley Taylor
Bob Thomason
Jason Townsend
Albert Turpin
Ernest Vinson
Jake Waldroop
Les Waldroop
Mrs. Andy Webb
Mrs. Grover Webb
Mildred Barnard West
Danny White
Joe Williams
Priscilla Wilson
Jerry Wolfe
Aunt Celia Wood
James Paul Wooten
Rodney Worley
Chester York
Beth Kelley Zorbanos

STUDENTS

Allison Adams
Brandon Addis
Stacy Ammons
Alicia Argoe
April Argoe
Robin Atkins
Eric Backer
Vance Bagwell
Robbie Bailey
Sherri Barker
Austin Bauman
Amy Beck
Bruce Beck
Scott Beck
Matt Beirmann
Casi Best

Cheryl Binnie
Rhonda Black
Jack Blackstock
Presley Blalock
Jessica Bleckley
Inge Boot
Ashley Brown
Cody Brown
Jan Brown
Tim Brown
Laurie Brunson
Andrea Burrell
Marella Burrell
Vivian Burrell
Tony Burt
Jacob Butler

David Campbell
Scott Cannon
Tom Carlton
Diana Carpenter
Maybelle Carpenter
Rebekah Carson
Faye (Bit) Carver
Kaye Carver
Rosanne Chastain
Joanna Chieves
Brad Clay
Mike Cook
Ann Cross
Jenna Lauren Davis
Brandy Day
Julie Dickens

Amanda Dickerson
Kathy Dickerson
Lorri Dickerson
Roy Dickerson
Melanie Dietz
Becca Dills
Shannon Dunlap
Stephanie Dunlap
Cindy Dye
Eric Dyer
Bridget English
Breanna Finley
Logan Finley
Candi Dahl Forester
Chelsi Forester
Lacy Forester
Ricky Foster
Shay Foster
Samantha Fountain
Stacy Fountain
George Freeman
Louise Freeman
Darryl Garland
Mary Garth
Heather Giovino
Allie Gragg
Keri Gragg
Teresia Gravley
Cynthia Green
Joey Green
Gina Hamby
Erin Harrison
Thia Heater
Kelsey Henry
Kasie Hicks
Frank Hill
Dana Holcomb
Shane Holcomb
Cailey Horn
Brittany Houck

Kari Hughes
Adam Hunter
Lacy Hunter
Daniel Jackson
Jill Jarrard
Stephanie Jobbitt
Stephanie Jones
Katie Justus
Lauren Korte
Morgan Lanier
Tricia Leavens
Angie Ledford
Julia Ledford
Laura Lee
Jenny Lincoln
Kathy Long
Hope Loudermilk
Corey Lovell
Erik Lunsford
Katie Lunsford
Ross Lunsford
Heather Manter
Patrick Marcellino
Phillip Marsengill
Yvette Marsh
Mary Ann Martin
Ray McBride
LouWanda McClain
Randy McFalls
Ashley Menge
Christina Mitcham
Taylor Mumford
Kayla Mullen
Amy Nichols
Chris Nix
Pam Nix
Suzie Nixon
Ashley O'Shields
Alex Owens
Jesse Owens

Becky Payne
Sherita Penland
David Peters
Anna Phillips
Ethan Phillips
Jessica Phillips
Jessica Pooley
Beth Pruitt
Anthony Queen
Christie Rickman
Mary Rhodes
Celena Rogers
Jolynne Sheffield
April Shirley
Taylor Shirley
Rosanne Chastain
  Short
Stephanie Short
Kelly Shropshire
Leigh Ann Smith
Steve Smith
Shannon Snyder
Logan Speed
Shanda Speed
Cheryl Stocky
George Strickland
Barbara Taylor
Wesley Taylor
Mary Thomas
Abby Thompson
Emily Thurmond
Sandra Thurmond
Sheri Thurmond
Dawn Timko
Dedra Trusty
Richard Trusty
John Turner
Tina Turpen
Matt Veal
Sheila Vinson

Darren Volk
David Volk
Tessa Wall
Lacey Watkins
Jared Weber

Deedee Welborn
Connie Wheeler
Maggie Whitmire
Mitch Whitmire
Frenda Wilburn

Fred Willard
Craig Williams
Hobie Wood
Heather Alicia Woods
Amy York

READERS' LETTERS:
NB, St. Petersburg, Florida
MB, Long Beach, California
KB, New Zealand
SB, Knoxville, Tennessee
LC, San Bernardino, California
MG, Potsdam, New York
Mrs. J. H., Elliott, Illinois
MH, Mount Vernon, Washington
GK, Forest Park, Georgia
LL, Schenectady, New York
JM, Longview, Texas
JM, Williamsburg, Virginia
MN, Phoenix, Arizona
GP, Hagerstown, Maryland
SP, Murrysville, Pennsylvania
GS, Charlotte, North Carolina
DS, Kerens, Texas
CT, Franklin, North Carolina

EDITORS AND STAFF

PLATE 208 *The Foxfire Book of Simple Living: Celebrating Fifty Years of Listenin', Laughin', and Learnin'* editors (*top to bottom, left to right*) Jonathan Blackstock, Ethan Phillips, Ross Lunsford, Jesse Owens, Katie Lunsford, Kaye Carver Collins, and Jessica Phillips

Kaye Carver Collins, editor of this book, has been part of the Foxfire program for decades, beginning as a student in the seventies and since her graduation from Rabun Gap-Nacoochee School. She now teaches at Rabun County Middle School. Over her time with Foxfire, Kaye has been instrumental in the publication of many magazines and *Foxfire 4, 10, 11, 12,* and *The Foxfire 45th Anniversary Book.* Kaye's fascination and love for her own culture is inspiring. It is due to Kaye and others of her caliber that we have been able to record so much of Appalachia in fifty years.

Jonathan Blackstock, coeditor for the publication of this book, is a theater and English teacher at Rabun County High School and has been a facilitator for *The Foxfire Magazine* for four years. Jonathan has a master of arts in literature and philosophy. All of his hard work and commitment to the program these past years has enabled Foxfire to continue to make progress in our culture's documentation.

Katie Lunsford is a graduate of the Foxfire program and a member of the Rabun County High School class of 2013. She served as editor of *The Foxfire Magazine* for two of her four years in the program. Her exceptional aptitude for writing was quite valuable to the success of the magazine throughout her high school career. In addition to being a great writer and editor, Katie has a knack for putting people at ease with her genuine friendliness and exuberance. Katie is currently attending the University of Georgia, pursuing a bachelor of science in education in athletic training.

Ross Lunsford was a junior when we began our work on this volume. Currently he is attending the University of Georgia. Younger brother of Katie Lunsford, Ross has discovered a fascination with photography through participation in the Foxfire program. He can be counted on to capture a picture that enables our readers to appreciate and relive our experiences with contacts.

Jesse Owens is a member of the class of 2014 and spent all of his high school years in the Foxfire program. Jesse is currently attending the University of North Georgia, with a dual major in chemistry and engineering. In the course of composing this book, Jesse's constant smiles kept up the morale of the writing staff.

Ethan Phillips is also a 2014 graduate of the Foxfire program. Known to many as the "falconator," Ethan takes great pleasure in hunting with birds and has shared that interest with the world through Foxfire. Ethan is attending Piedmont College in Demorest, Georgia, working on a bachelor of fine arts, majoring in graphic design.

Jessica Phillips is another younger-sibling Foxfire student. Sister of Foxfire alumnus Ethan Phillips, Jessica is in her fourth year of *The Foxfire Magazine* class. She will graduate this year. Thus far in her Foxfire career, Jessica's most outstanding quality is her ability to create comfortable environments for contacts. In an area where many folks are shy and private, personalities such as Jessica's are essential to Foxfire's purpose.

THE FOXFIRE 45TH ANNIVERSARY BOOK

For almost half a century, Foxfire has brought the philosophy of simple living to hundreds of thousands of readers, teaching creative self-sufficiency and preserving the stories, crafts, and customs of Appalachia. Inspiring and practical, this classic series has become an American institution. *The Foxfire 45th Anniversary Book* continues the beloved tradition of celebrating a simpler life, this time with a focus on Appalachian music, folk legends, and a history full of outsized personalities. We hear the encouraging life stories of banjo players, gospel singers, and bluegrass musicians who reminisce about their first time playing at the Grand Ole Opry; we shiver at the spine-tingling collection of tall tales, from ghosts born of long-ago crimes to rumors of giant catfish that lurk at the bottom of lakes and quarries; we recollect the Farm Family Program that sustained and educated Appalachian families for almost fifty years, through the Depression and beyond; and we learn the time-honored skills of those who came before, from building a sled to planting azaleas and braiding a leather bull-whip. Full of spirited narrative accounts and enduring knowledge, *The Foxfire 45th Anniversary Book* is a piece of living history from a fascinating American culture.

Crafts and Hobbies

THE FOXFIRE 40TH ANNIVERSARY BOOK

In 1966, an English teacher and students in Northeast Georgia founded a quarterly magazine, not only as a vehicle to learn the required English curriculum, but also to teach others about the customs, crafts, traditions, and lifestyle of their Appalachian culture. Named *Foxfire*, after a local phosphorescent lichen, the magazine became one of the most beloved publications in American culture. This anniversary edition brings us generations of voices and lessons about the three essential Appalachian values of faith, family, and the land. We listen to elders share their own memories of how things used to be and to the new generations eager to preserve traditional values in a more complicated world. There are descriptions of old church services, of popular Appalachian games and pastimes, and of family recipes. Rich with memories and useful lessons, this is a fitting tribute to this inspiring and practical publication that has become a classic American institution.

Crafts and Hobbies

FOXFIRE 12

Illustrated with photographs and drawings, *Foxfire 12* is a rich trove of information and stories from a fascinating American culture. Here are reminiscences about learning to square dance and tales about traditional craftsmen who created useful items in the old-time ways that have since disappeared in most of the country. Here are lessons on how to make rose beads and wooden coffins and on how to find turtles in your local pond. We hear the voices of descendants of the Cherokees who lived in the region, and we learn about what summer camp was like for generations of youngsters. We meet a rich assortment of Appalachian characters and listen to veterans recount their war experiences. Inspiring and practical, this classic series has become an American institution.

Crafts and Hobbies

FOXFIRE 11

With this volume in the Foxfire series comes a wealth of the kind of folk wisdom and values of simple living that have made these volumes beloved bestsellers for over three decades. In 1966, in the Appalachian Mountains of Northeast Georgia, Eliot Wigginton and his students founded a quarterly magazine that they named *Foxfire*. In 1972, several articles from the magazine were published in book form, and the acclaimed Foxfire series was born. Almost thirty years later, in this age of technology and cyber-living, the books teach a philosophy of simplicity in living that is truly enduring in its appeal. *Foxfire 11* celebrates the rituals and recipes of the Appalachian homeplace, including a one-hundred-page section on herbal remedies, and segments about planting and growing a garden, preserving and pickling, smoking and salting, honey making, beekeeping, and fishing, as well as hundreds of the kind of spritied firsthand narrative accounts from Appalachian community members that exemplify the Foxfire style. Much more than "how-to" books, the Foxfire series is a publishing phenomenon, fascinating to everyone interested in rediscovering the virtues of simple life.

Crafts and Hobbies